Command in Air War

Centralized versus Decentralized Control of Combat Airpower

MICHAEL W. KOMETER
Lieutenant Colonel, USAF

Air University Press
Maxwell Air Force Base, Alabama

June 2007

Disclaimer

Opinions, conclusions, and recommendations expressed or implied within are solely those of the author and do not necessarily represent the views of Air University, the United States Air Force, the Department of Defense, or any other US government agency. Cleared for public release: distribution unlimited.

Published by Books Express Publishing

ISBN 978-1-907521-03-4
To purchase copies at discounted prices please contact info@books-express.com

Contents

Illustrations

Figure *Page*

About the Author

Colonel Kometer with wife Cheryl, daughters Maria and Anna, and son Michael in 2006

Lt Col Michael W. Kometer, a senior navigator with approximately 1,000 flying hours, was born and raised in Kohler, Wisconsin. He was commissioned upon graduation from the US Air Force Academy with a bachelor's degree in Engineering Sciences in June 1988. He completed undergraduate navigator training in May 1989 as an electronic warfare officer (EWO) and was assigned to the 16th Special Operations Squadron (16th SOS) at Hurlburt Field, Florida, where he served as an EWO on the AC-130H Spectre gunship. His tour of duty with 16th SOS included operations during conflicts in Panama, Saudi Arabia, and Somalia. While flying with the 16th SOS, he was assigned to Headquarters Special Missions Operational Test and Evaluation Center to perform operational flight testing of special operations aircraft. In 1994 he was selected to attend the Georgia Institute of Technology for a master's degree in Industrial/Systems Engineering and, subsequently, was chosen as one of the top 10 graduates in the School of Engineering. In 1995 Colonel Kometer was assigned to a classified location as a special projects test director, later serving as the flight commander and operations officer for the unit. He then attended Air Command and Staff College and the School of Advanced Air and Space Studies (SAASS), both based at Maxwell AFB, Alabama. The SAASS selected him to pursue a PhD, which he did successfully at the Massachusetts Institute of Technology. Upon earning the degree in 2005, he became the director of operations for the 605th Test and Evaluation Squadron at Hurlburt Field, where he took command of the same squadron in 2006.

Acknowledgments

I did not understand at first when a professor, after reading my proposal for this dissertation, said, "I commend you on your willingness to tackle this project." The truth is, I did not know what I was getting into. That I have not exhausted the subject is certain; that I have not clearly communicated all I have learned is due entirely to my own shortcomings; but that the work has become more than I thought it could at first is due to the tremendous contributions of many people.

The journey began when the people at the School of Advanced Air and Space Studies believed in me enough to give me their support, both material and moral.

The people at the Massachusetts Institute of Technology proved the value of that institution through the challenge of meeting the often unstated but ever-present standards. David Mindell's writings and classes were the basis for a lot of the ideas in this book. He allowed me freedom with ideas but guided me through the process, giving me reassurance that I was on the right path. Sheila Widnall modeled some of the principles in this book—she let me do the writing but sent me back to the drawing board until it made sense to me. Joe Sussman boosted my morale by being interested enough to offer to help, and Ted Postol challenged me to be honest just by being that way. Michael Schrage set an example for me and spurred me on by reading my drafts, taking the time to give me an honest opinion, and challenging me to get real.

The people at the Air Force Historical Research Agency, especially Joe Caver, made it easy to get access to, but kept me from getting lost in, the incredible quantity of data available from the recent conflicts.

Many military professionals gave generously of their time to explain the inner workings of this system I have labeled the Combat Air Operations System, or CAOS. I can only hope I have done justice to the conscientious way they approach the difficult job of making decisions under uncertainty. Many of their names appear in writing, but I would like to thank them for taking the time to educate me: Calvin, Zam, UB, Stilly, Alien, Zing, Goldie,

Knob, TSgt Frank Lofton, TSgt Bryan Lanning, Col Jeff Hodgdon, Col Gary Crowder, and Lt Gen David Deptula.

There were other professionals, some of them retired military officers and some not, who work tirelessly to develop and implement the technology and procedures. Many of these doors opened through Ed Green, who put me in touch with talented and dedicated Massachusetts Institute of Technology Research (MITRE) people like Carmen Corsetti, Mike Carpenter, Jack Sexton, Roger Dumas, and Ed Enos. TSgt Dave Pacheco made it possible for me to have a home at Hanscom AFB, Massachusetts, to see what goes on in the world of command, control, communications, computers, intelligence, surveillance, and reconnaissance (C4ISR).

Perhaps the most influential were my family. My wife, kids, and I became a much stronger team during the research and writing of this thesis by resolving the tension between work and family. While my wife was homeschooling, I had to learn to get work done when I really wanted to play with my kids. Fortunately, they got me to play sometimes. Their support and love kept me sane.

And to the One who is really in control, my Lord. In my heart I plan my course, but You determine my path.

Chapter 1

Introduction

On 2 April 2003, the United States–led coalition forces had seemingly won the war in Iraq. In just 21 days they had invaded Iraq, pushed past Iraq's regular army and paramilitary fighters, and entered the city of Baghdad. When a group of Iraqis climbed a statue of Saddam in Firdos Square and looped a rope around its neck, US Marines backed an armored vehicle up and pulled it down. The cheering crowds went wild.[1]

About a year later, Arabs found cause for indignation and horror that silenced the cheering. On 28 April 2004, CBS News broadcast the first ugly images of prisoner abuse at Baghdad's Abu Ghraib prison. It was a prison where Saddam Hussein had tortured thousands of prisoners during his reign. Now it appeared the Americans were no better. Copies of the pictures were sold on Arab streets, confirming fears that Americans were the "Great Satan" that its enemies claimed. Groups such as Ansar al-Islam incorporated these pictures into their recruiting literature, and Abu Musab al-Zarqawi's Tawhid and Jihad movement cited abuses of Iraqi women as justification for the kidnapping and beheading of several Western hostages.[2] The actions of these US troops had become the best propaganda for the militant Islamist movements.

Worse still, the abuses at Abu Ghraib were not isolated instances but evidently part of a larger pattern that included similar misconduct in both Afghanistan and Guantanamo Bay, Cuba. In fact, had they been isolated to special cases—directed from the top as exceptions based on clear and present danger—they may have been more palatable. The United States' enemy in this war was one that did not wear uniforms, organize in large military formations, or respect the traditional laws of war; it depended instead on its ability to break laws in horrifying fashion. Finding and defeating this peculiar enemy depended heavily on the ability to collect intelligence from the terrorists themselves—human intelligence—rather than on more technical forms of intelligence gathering. In fact, it required interrogation—and probably methods of interrogation more coercive than allowed by the same laws of war the terrorists regularly flaunted.

To obtain the required intelligence, the George W. Bush administration had to choose whether to keep tight control of the situation and authorize only specific instances of coercion or to allow more discretion to the soldiers down the line. The administration chose the latter. Top lawyers wrote a series of memoranda that declared the Geneva convention nonapplicable, authorized certain interrogation methods, and narrowed the interpretation of "torture."[3] Soldiers were given the leeway they needed to be more proactive than traditional law allowed.

Certainly, what happened at Abu Ghraib went beyond the intentions of those memos. It is probable the administration meant to give soldiers a tool for use in extreme cases, not wanting to handcuff them by making them wait for approval when fleeting opportunities to use this tool arose. The actual result, however, was a deep scar on the honor of the United States and its military, one that could have dire consequences for success not only in the war in Iraq but also in the global war on terrorism.

Though the venues are different, policy makers and air commanders face similar decisions about the control of combat airpower. During the first 21 days of Operation Iraqi Freedom (OIF), the air component had formed a joint "Time-Sensitive Targeting" (TST) Cell that launched over 50 rapid-reaction raids in the war, some as quickly as 15 minutes from intelligence tip to bomb drop.[4] Many aircraft were sent to orbit Iraq where they awaited tasking from the air and space operations center (AOC) in Saudi Arabia, which would get intelligence and then send the target coordinates to the aircraft as quickly as possible. At times, though, more aircraft and targets were involved than those validated by the AOC (further detailed later). Some pilots began asking ground troops on other frequencies whether they required any of the bombs that would otherwise be transported back to the pilots' station when their time ran out. Although the pilots called back to clear these impromptu attacks through the AOC, most of the time those in the AOC had no way to determine what the target was, not to mention whether it was valid. They had to either refuse to clear the attacks or rely on the pilots and ground controllers to ensure the attacks were safe and in line with the strategy.

The following chapters examine the military's decision-making process by reviewing actual scenarios, focusing on something called *control*. They scrutinize not the *way* people make decisions as much as the *interaction* of the many such decisions determined in different parts of the system that employs airpower in combat, how policy is turned into military actions that achieve desirable political goals, and whether these factors have changed during the information age. The ultimate question is, what has been the impact of the information age on the US Air Force's doctrinal tenet of "centralized control and decentralized execution"?

It is no secret that control of military action is elusive at best. The most rational grand strategy developed by policy makers can appear irrational because of military actions that are counterproductive. As policy gets translated into actionable plans, it must pass through many different layers. Consequently, results may not be the ones originally intended. Furthermore, policy makers cannot foresee all of the situations that may face the troops. Those who are applying the force must be able to react, but they may not react in ways that policy makers would choose. This dilemma is why political scientists have such difficulty analyzing strategy—that is, differences in individual perceptions, organizational routines and interests, and power may impinge on any desired strategy, altering its execution in ways that may seem incomprehensible at times.[5]

This quandary prompts decision makers to remain continually apprised of military actions. In this they are in luck, since the same technology that now allows military forces to respond more rapidly to changing information also allows the decision makers to remain in the loop, should they so desire. This seems to pose a dilemma: there is an apparent tension between the desire to control the actions of the military forces and the desire to allow them to make the most of their information capabilities to respond rapidly. This tension has a long history behind it, as we will see later. But the prominence of this issue in all facets of society in recent years has led many scholars to propose that we are in the midst of a technological revolution that demands an appropriate response from those who wish to remain competitive.

The business world illustrates this dynamic between controlling versus relinquishing control as well. For a century and a half, the trend in American business was toward centrally controlling massive corporations. From single-unit, owner-managed enterprises with independent merchant distributors in the early nineteenth century, the American firm developed into a colossal, centrally-managed behemoth in the late twentieth century. Technology enabled this evolution by allowing professional managers to more efficiently control and coordinate production and distribution despite tremendous cultural opposition and governmental regulation.[6]

The shift of societal institutions in such a completely different direction over the last three decades is noteworthy. Strategy formerly aimed at controlling the actions of businesses now, instead, targets constructing relationships among them, coordinating the use of resources so operations can be flexible yet focused. With today's information technology (IT), workers can retrieve all of the information they need at the right time and place to make decisions on the spot, where they are most crucial.[7] The marketplace is transforming as companies allow competitors, according to their core expertise, to perform parts of their operations for them. "Interlinking" the "value chains" of suppliers, firms, and customers enhances the efficacy of the entire marketplace.[8]

Some analysts point to this change in society and business as a sign that the military must also change, and, indeed, the character of warfare also seems to be changing. They propose that the military must prepare to fight *netwar*, "an emerging mode of conflict (and crime) at societal levels, short of traditional military warfare, in which the protagonists use network forms of organization and related doctrines, strategies, and technologies attuned to the information age."[9] Technology has enabled these new modes because communication is faster, cheaper, and of higher quality. But netwar is not only about technology. Networks are plastic organizations, emphasizing the linkages among actors—ties that are constantly being formed, strengthened, or cut.[10] Most importantly, these analysts claim that "it takes networks to fight networks."[11]

The US military must capitalize on the current information revolution to transform its organization, doctrine, and strategy. It must retain its command and control (C2) capability while becoming flatter—attaining faster response by eliminating some hierarchical levels in favor of pushing information out to all players at the lower levels. Doctrine should be built around *battle swarming*, a process of bringing combat power to bear at nearly any time and place based on real-time information.[12] The term *network-centric warfare* (NCW) refers to a concept that "translates information superiority into combat power by effectively linking knowledgeable entities in the battlespace."[13] Its proponents argue that C2 should not be envisioned as a sequential process as it has been in the past—gathering data, analyzing, making a decision, and then implementing it. Instead, sensors, actors, and decision makers should be networked so that they have a shared awareness of the battlespace. Commanders at the lowest levels will have enough information to take initiative and speed up the response to changing battlefield conditions.[14]

Opponents of NCW argue that linking all actors will further centralize decision making, eliminating a middle layer called the *operational level of war* that is now the link between strategy and tactics. The lowest level will possess the facts necessary to make decisions, but it will be paralyzed by political limitations and will not really have any initiative.[15] On the other hand, it may be that this centralization of control is desirable. Perhaps the reason it has always been desirable to maintain the independence of troops on the battlefield is that the commanders in the rear (and certainly the heads of state) did not know what was happening there. If these remote decision makers have information equal to or greater than the troops, maybe they should make the decisions. Perhaps the only limitation on centralized control should be the ability to move the information around to the appropriate place.[16]

The US Air Force's answer to this tension is the tenet of centralized control and decentralized execution.[17] The phrase, now captured in a joint publication (JP) as well as Air Force doctrine, incorporates the concept of striking a delicate balance.[18] But the language is confusing. Are control and execution separate phases or functions? If they are separate phases, this tenet declares that central authorities should develop a plan, allocate the resources, and then at a certain point in time pass it off to the executors. In fact, another JP calls for "unity of effort, centralized planning and direction, and decentralized execution."[19] However, often there is not enough information about the enemy to develop a complete plan before the designated handoff. With today's sensors and communication technology, the central decision makers can develop only the shell of a plan and then fill in details in real time, so the two phases may overlap. Perhaps, then, the two terms represent two separate functions, implying that the central decision makers decide what to do and what resources to allocate—regardless of whether it is during or prior to execution—and those on the scene execute the plan with the resources given them. But what does it mean to *execute*? Weapons technology increasingly facilitates launching weapons from remote locations. If this is the case, certainly the best people to push the button are those with the greatest knowledge of the entire situation—in many cases the central decision makers.

On the surface, these arguments seem to point to a choice. Should policy makers use sensor, weapons, communications, and IT to increase their own ability or, instead, to make decisions or to empower lower-level decision makers? If there is a "revolution in military affairs" under way, we had better figure out which way is right and head in that direction or risk major defeat in the future.

But, first, we must understand what we are talking about and what is really happening in this revolution. The issues surrounding centralized versus decentralized control are clouded by the fact that they cover a range of categories that are seldom delineated in the discussions. There are civil-military arguments, as when the military claimed Pres. Lyndon B. Johnson and Secretary of Defense (SecDef) Robert S. McNamara should not have been personally picking targets during the Rolling Thunder campaign in Vietnam. The military was similarly frustrated by the North Atlantic Council's (NAC) monopoly on target-approval authority in Kosovo. There are arguments within the military between theater commanders and their subordinates about how far the superior should get into the planning details. Such was the case in Kosovo between Lt Gen Michael Short, combined force air component commander (CFACC), and Gen Wesley Clark, NATO supreme allied commander, Europe. In the 2001 war in Afghanistan, Airmen again claimed that Gen Tommy R. Franks, combined force commander (CFC), and his staff improperly intervened in matters that should have been handled by his air component. Then there is controversy between the commanders on the battlefield and those in the rear over the direction of actions in progress. In almost every conflict, pilots claim that the planning staff intervenes in the execution of missions, which should be the domain of those closest to the action. Over all this lurk the constant battles among the services, such as the battle between the Army and the Air Force over who should control the aircraft that are supporting ground troops. The Army claims the centralized process used by the Air Force is too cumbersome to respond to the needs of the ground troops. It seems that each level thinks another is too involved in the details.

This study looks at these arguments as separate but related issues concerning the control of combat airpower, as opposed to land or sea power, since airpower's speed and range make it especially affected by the debate between centralized and decentralized control. While focusing on developments in the US Air Force, the service that has been most active in defining the doctrinal architecture for C2 of combat airpower, this study also captures differences in the way other services prefer to function. Finally, it will determine how technology and control have affected each other in this, the age of information.

Little research exists on the control of combat air operations in the scholarly literature. Although many writers have evaluated the effectiveness of various airpower strategies, most were concerned with the success of air operations in decisively contributing to victory.[20] Numerous works document the conduct and results of air operations in specific wars,[21] and still others analyze the development of airpower, including the forces that shaped strategy, tactics, doctrine, and technology development.[22] None of these, however, look at the process of turning policy into actions that achieve policy goals.

Classics dealing with C2 of military forces frequently have the limitation of being completed before the advent of military airpower, and their applicability, therefore, is confined to general principles.[23] Marshal Tukhachevsky, one of the first of these classic military writers, discusses the need to combine the effects of land, air, and sea power throughout the depth of the battlefield. His solution, very similar to the Air Force's contemporary doctrinal language, is a delicate balance of top-down directive control and freedom for the frontline forces to take the initiative when the fog and friction of battle demand it.[24]

Many well-known works on C2 focus on the civil-military dimension. Samuel Huntington proposes that *objective control* is the correct method of civilian control because it nurtures the professionalism of the officer corps, thereby harnessing the strengths of the military and ensuring the state's security. He claims that the incorrect method is *subjective control*, which maximizes the power of the civilians over the military by making the military conform to the ideals of the group in power.[25] Objective control supposedly allows civilians to accept the military for what it is—indeed cultivate it—while maintaining effective control over it. Huntington's argument has been oversimplified by critics and fans alike to mean that, for maximum security, civilians and the military should remain clear of each other's turf. This diluted version holds that a state needs a chain of command with civilians in charge and a professional military—but civilians should not delve into the details of military affairs, and the military should not be allowed to delve into political affairs.

Eliot Cohen set out to correct this oversimplification by proposing that, in war, the civil-military relationship must be anything but laissez-faire. Claiming that the United States had fallen prey to a misrepresentation of Huntington's work, Cohen laments the practice of what he calls the "normal" theory of civil-military relations. This theory demands that civilians make the war and then let the military run it. "Taken to extremes, it would free civilians of responsibility for the gravest challenges a country can face, and remove oversight and control from those whose job most requires it."[26] On the contrary, he shows that Abraham Lincoln, Georges Clemenceau, Winston Churchill, and David Ben-Gurion were successful because they got deeply involved in military matters during their respective wars.

Cohen's assessment of wartime civil-military relations is tough on those who think there should be a distinct line between civilians and the military. He claims that the trouble with this relationship during the Vietnam War was not too much civilian control, but not enough. When the Joint Chiefs of Staff (JCS) presented only an all-out solution, the Johnson administration made them largely irrelevant. The military made no effort to conform to the constraints within which civilians thought they had to live. There was no detailed discussion or argument about the ends, ways, and means of the war.[27] Cohen's evaluation of the Pres. George H. W. Bush administration also runs against the grain of popular mythology, proposing that the Gulf War of 1991 was a story of "abdication of authority" by the civilian leadership.[28] The Clinton administration fares no better in that "far from abusing the military by micro-managing it, . . . [it] abused it by failing to take the [1993 Somalia] war seriously and inquire into means, methods, and techniques."[29] Cohen's overall prescription is that civilians must "demand and expect from their military subordinates a candor as bruising as it is necessary; that both groups must expect a running conversation in which, although civilian opinion will not usually dictate, it must dominate; and that that conversation will cover not only ends and policies, but ways and means."[30]

If Huntington's and Cohen's works are viewed as complementary, then together they propose a formula for C2 that advocates empowering subordinates to develop plans, but then grilling them on the details and holding them accountable. Their precept, though, applies to only the policy makers, covering just one part of our spectrum. Another caveat is that both analyses were based almost completely on land warfare, although Cohen applied his to situations that included airpower.

Martin van Creveld dealt with the next level down from policy makers, military commanders, proposing a framework within which they should think about controlling their organizations in battle. He pointed out that throughout history organizations have dealt with the fog of war in basically two ways. First, they try to get more information and second, they attempt to organize by training the lowest levels to work in the absence of clear direction. Those who have chosen the latter route have either made their forces robots or trained the lower divisions to work semiautonomously on specific tasks.[31] To van Creveld, the essence of genius in this respect was to use technology to its limitations and then make those limitations work for you by turning them into advantages, claiming that this was the brilliance of Napoléon's corps system.[32] His advice to all commanders would be to (1) use a *directed telescope*, that is, a method the commander can direct at will to collect less structured—but more customized—

information than that collected by normal channels, and (2) develop organizations that can operate in uncertain conditions when the battle outpaces the command decisions.[33]

However, this advice may fall short when it comes to today's air war. The full impact of the information revolution was not felt until after the release of van Creveld's book in 1985. Since then, it appears the Air Force has undergone a transformation in its control of combat operations. Although much of the technology for this transformation was developed before 1985, the organizational and operational implementation of the transformation evolved through the wars, experiments, and doctrinal development in the 1990s, as well as in response to a change in the security environment (facilitated by the collapse of the Soviet Union).

Furthermore, van Creveld gives almost no attention to air war—his case studies examine nothing but land warfare. Command in air war, especially today, is different. Modern air war involves smaller numbers of units under a single command, and units act over much longer ranges with much greater speed and precision, with less regard for enemy military actions.[34] Battle in air war looks much different from battle on the ground. In air war, units that do not know each other converge from geographically separated bases to fly relatively short duration engagements against an often unseen enemy that is not necessarily the target, but more of an obstacle, and then disperse. Consequently, while the motivational part of command is much more difficult to consolidate, the control part is more routine. Pilots are accustomed to relying on others to coordinate with everyone in the air to ensure their safety and efficiency, depending on communications to perform even the ordinary parts of their missions, such as takeoff and landing. Over the long distances involved, whoever has the information about what lies ahead may be in the best position to control the mission. In today's air war, with today's technology, this advantage goes to the people in the rear. If van Creveld's instruction is to be followed, it must first be shown to withstand the translation to air war in the information age.[35]

The few works that have examined the specific question of whether the control of combat airpower should be centralized or decentralized generally focus on the issue of differences among the military services. RAND analysts James Winnefeld and Dana Johnson suggest that the joint force air component commander (JFACC) was a solution to a longtime problem with airpower—lack of unity of control. Since the dawn of military airpower, the United States has struggled to coordinate disparate air forces from the separate services to serve the larger military strategy. This problem was highlighted in Vietnam, where the use of route packages rendered airpower ineffective.[36] In another work specifically aimed at the argument of centralized versus "organic" control, Lt Col Stephen McNamara reviewed the history of airpower to discover lessons applicable to today. He found that the centralized control of air at the operational level was nonnegotiable in the Air Force—it had learned too many hard lessons about breaking airpower up into "penny packets" to turn back. However, he noted that ground commanders thought the JFACC concept was too slow to adapt to their needs. The solution lay in the ability of the JFACC to keep control while relinquishing the details of the daily flights to decentralized authorities.[37]

Because the subject of the control of airpower in the information age has not been treated often in scholarly literature, the prevailing view of combat air operations is stunted. When people think of air war, they may think of arguments over whether a given strategy was decisive in war, or perhaps of a service that has forever struggled to prove its worthiness to be independent and that leans on the technology of the aircraft and the doctrine of strategic bombardment. They may view the air tasking order as a tool for micromanagement—an overreaction to failures to achieve unity among diverse air forces from different services. What does not tend to come to mind, though, are either the two thousand people in the AOC attempting to control air operations and produce the results, or that they are part of a system of interrelated parts where, try as they might, are controlled even as they attempt to control.[38] Until we can perceive this complexity, we will not be able to engineer the system to produce our desired results while avoiding harmful side effects.

This work will develop a more complete picture of the various ways airpower is controlled in combat, and their subsequent consequences, by presenting airpower as a system, placing the above theories in their proper context within that system, and accounting for the interaction among them. While using primarily historical concepts to illustrate types of control, this study attempts to add to the body of knowledge on human-technology systems and about the airpower system in particular. The questions it will answer along the way are:

1. *How has the information age affected C2 of combat airpower?* While it's true that technological developments have been momentous, the international security environment, organization of the US military, and the types of wars it has fought have evolved as well. The interaction among these factors must be addressed to see whether there have been any fundamental changes in C2 or if new modes have arisen for specific circumstances.

2. *Have technological changes impacted the military's adherence to the doctrinal tenet of centralized control and decentralized execution?* Whether changes have been fundamental or have arisen because of specific circumstances, some have alleged that commanders and policy makers have not adhered to this tenet. As discussed above, the arguments span different parts of the spectrum and often talk past each other. This study will discover what happened in each case, what part of the system was affected, and the overall effect on the system.

3. *Is there a general formula that better characterizes the system's C2?* This approach will lead to factors commanders should consider when determining how to delegate authority, as well as recommend a general formula for C2 of combat airpower, filtering theories through the evidence from the study. This will be a sort of repairing, or synthesis, of these theories and should be a more precise way to describe C2.

4. *Where are these changes heading?* Many elements within the airpower system may have affected and been affected by technology, but human influence likely limits this interaction in the system. In order to discern the future of warfare, we have to recognize these limits. This study will recommend factors to consider during development of new technology and practices. Two basic methodological problems present themselves in answering these questions. We want to analyze the relevant issues using only the applicable facts for each one (so as not to confuse apples with oranges) and also determine whether there are interactions among them. To discover the facts pertinent to each topic, we

will study the same historical period several times, using a different viewpoint each time. We will concentrate on four wars: Operation Desert Storm in 1991, Operation Allied Force (OAF) in 1999, Operation Enduring Freedom (OEF) in Afghanistan from October 2001 through March 2002, and OIF in March and April of 2003. These wars are revisited five times, but each time we will use a different lens to see the salient characteristics.

These lenses are the frameworks that guide the analysis of each particular issue. History is not a completely objective process of laying out facts in chronological order; instead, historians are guided by an agenda formed by their particular expertise, affecting source selection and prioritization of material. Later, a more mature agenda, often explicitly informed by other thinkers, helps the historian "weave [a central] theme into a historical narrative."[39] Each time we traverse a period of our study, we marshall evidence from participants' interviews, briefings they used to convey their ideas, notes and logs they compiled at the time, and their official reports on lessons learned. Because these sources come from different parts of the system, new stories emerge that compel us to repeatedly consider new angles on the central question.

Constructing interactions among these different viewpoints is a problem tailor-made for "systems thinking." We will analyze the issues as if all the players involved were part of a system, which we will refer to as the Combat Air Operations System (CAOS), a "system" that is not explicitly recognized as such in any literature. In showing the interactions among the above issues, we will be in effect constructing a system by linking diverse players in feedback loops. The word *system* is overused in everyday language. A good definition would probably have to include interacting components having a well-defined (although not necessarily well-understood) behavior or purpose.[40] Humans in the system organize themselves in some type of hierarchy, which means some decision makers coordinate the actions of larger groups than others.[41] Decision makers at higher levels impose constraints on lower levels to make the actions of lower levels adhere to some desirable emergent characteristics—this is the essence of control in systems thinking.[42] But the decisions they make often do not account for the existence of feedback loops. The delays from cause to result and the confounding effect of multiple feedback loops cause people to misjudge the effect of their actions and often take action that makes a problem worse.[43] This study will show many cases where the type of control used at one level affected operations at many other levels, well beyond the predictable, because of similar delays and feedback loops.

We will therefore portray these interactions by treating the CAOS as a complex, large-scale, integrated, open system (CLIOS). Using the information gleaned from our five stories, we graphically represent the issues as components of subsystems. The five issues cross multiple subsystems, so they share certain components—this is what produces the interactions. The graphical technique is a way to impose rigor on the analysis. Indeed, this entire process cannot be presented to the reader without it becoming too confusing.[44] The results presented here are the product of several iterations of research involved in developing a model, examining hypotheses emerging from model building, and then refining the model. Thus, the graphical depiction and the research each impacted the other. Obviously, only the final results are presented here, but this rigor helps to keep us from proposing interactions from pure speculation. This, then, is the story of the impact of the information age on the tenet of centralized control and decentralized execution.

Throughout the 1990s, during wars for less than vital interests and in the absence of a peer superpower, US policy makers often used specific constraints that gave them direct influence over ongoing air operations. This occurred because of a feedback loop between technology and national security strategy. With the Soviet Union removed as a major threat to the United States, American politicians were free to intervene with military force in many situations that were less than vital. But they used military force with the caveat that it could not entail high costs, especially in terms of civilian and US military lives. Consequently, airpower was the tool of choice, and it needed to be a surgical instrument at that. In fact, policy makers were so keenly aware of this need that they often chose strategies that depended on their ability to control military action by rules of engagement (ROE) and target approval instead of becoming intimately involved in discussing and tracking military plans. The Air Force found airpower somewhat wanting for effectiveness within the imposed constraints. The solution was to develop impressive loops of sensors and communications technology—“sensor-communication loops”—that allowed better real-time decision making in the AOC.

These constraints affected the way the joint force commanders (JFC) defined command relationships. The tighter the constraints from the strategic level, the less the JFC empowered component commanders under him. The less these components were empowered, the less likely they were to overcome cultural barriers and coordinate with each other, regardless of their technological capability to communicate. Yet at the same time, the need for integration of these components increased because airpower became more tightly integrated with the attack sequences of other components—whether it was through using special operations troops as sensors or through providing information to these ground troops from sensors on the aircraft.

The JFACCs in charge of the air operations in this study initially tried to stay out of ongoing missions, but two parallel trends brought the air component into the time-sensitive targeting business. First, sensor-communication loops that the Air Force developed to help accomplish the complete control cycle also made it possible to direct the missions. In fact, the air component gained much more success at intervening in these missions than at assessing the aggregate results of operations. At the same time, because of policy constraints, airpower was called on to accomplish missions that required rapid, but very precise, response. To accomplish this, someone had to pull information together quickly and feed it to the strike aircraft. The two trends came together to pull not only those from the AOC, but also analysts from all over the globe, into the business of aiding ongoing air strikes.

In some cases, this has led to a redistribution of tasks that used to be performed in the cockpit and a corresponding change in the aircrew's role. The proportion of missions for which the aircrew can preplan their route and attack sequence has shrunk. The ability of the AOC to contribute useful information in real time, as well as the ease with which this information can be passed to the weapons, have increased. For instance, a global positioning system (GPS)-guided munition only requires accurate coordinates. Therefore, the aircrew's job can become one of delivering munitions based on information provided by someone else. But the training and capability of the aircrew has not decreased. In fact, with new sensors on the aircraft, they are capable of even more autonomous work. The result is an increase in the number and complexity of ways that an attack can occur.

This can be either dangerous or helpful. In some situations, commanders want their troops to be able to show initiative and exploit opportunities. In other cases, the risk that these adaptive exploitations may be harmful to the overall strategy outweighs the potential military benefit. But even where strict adherence to orders is required, people often drift away from established procedures if not observed and corrected, a phenomenon Scott Snook refers to as *practical drift*.[45] Then, in an emergency, they are often unable to revert to established procedures, and human initiative can go astray. This is what happened in the shootdown of two Black Hawk helicopters over northern Iraq in 1994.[46]

In the end, the theories we considered can be synthesized to form a better overall description of the control of combat airpower. Centralized control and decentralized execution is a good concept at any level, but it suffers from lack of precision. Cohen and Huntington's combined theory that civilians should empower the officer corps, but engage them in a bruising debate and then hold them accountable, is also appropriate for military commanders and their subordinates. Likewise, van Creveld's directed telescope is a way for policy makers to get a feel for military actions, stay involved in ongoing discussions with its leaders, and make them answerable. At all levels, commanders should set the goals and strategic vision for organizations under their command, as well as organize command relationships and empower subordinates to establish their own plans to accomplish goals. They should also maintain a running dialog to challenge the details of those plans and then use a directed telescope to track their accomplishment and make adjustments to the strategy.

The aim of this method of C2 is to produce something we will call "depth" of command relationships. This depth is a measure of the extent to which diverse players at the scene of battle can be coordinated, prioritized, and redirected when the situation calls for it. It is not simply pushing information and authority down, but extending the spiral of empowerment and accountability so that decisions made on the scene are consistent with the larger strategy. With sufficient depth, commanders can make deliberate decisions about when to allow subordinates to exploit opportunities; without it, they must either prescribe their subordinates' actions or allow them complete independence.

It is possible to look at the solution as a trade-off. With knowledge of the trade-offs, policy makers and commanders can make their own judgments about the amount of authority to delegate. The basic trade-off at each level is between specific results and empowerment. The factors that should influence the trade-off are the certainty of the effects needed for success and the requirement for interactions among different organizations to achieve these effects. A commander at any level can specify, constrain, and even in some cases direct specific results in great detail with today's technology. But the more a commander relies on these specific constraints and direction, the less empowered subordinates will be, decreasing their ability to integrate with others and innovate to adapt to new challenges. So in limited cases where the policy maker or commander knows exactly what needs to happen and the actions do not require complex interaction among the players, it is appropriate to use specific direction of the details. The more uncertain the actions needed and the more complex the interactions required, the greater the need for adherence to the general formula for C2.

The next eight chapters will tell this story. Chapter 2 lays a historical foundation and outlines the issues involved. It recounts the control of combat airpower from World War II (WWII) through Vietnam, showing how the control of airpower has varied among different types of wars and even among different missions within the same war. In the process it exposes confusion about the terminology of the arguments and attempts to lay them out in plain language.

Chapter 3 develops the approach for the rest of the book. It defines the necessary terms, explains the CLIOS framework, and clarifies the CAOS concept—what will be included, who the important stakeholders are, and what the subsystems are. By fitting the historical foundations into a systems framework, it also shows what areas will be explored in the rest of the book.

Chapters 4 through 8 perform this exploration. Chapter 4 discusses the relationships between policy makers and military commanders throughout the 1990s, analyzing the methods of control at this level. Chapter 5 shows the effect of these different methods on the ability of the various military organizations to work together. Chapter 6 shows how the AOC has become what Bruno Latour calls a *centre of calculation*, using sensor-communication loops to plan, direct, and assess airpower missions.[47] However, the "centre" was far more successful at using these loops to intervene in ongoing missions than to assess the aggregate results. Chapter 7 demonstrates that this intervention was necessary in many cases to perform some of the politically-constrained missions airpower was given, and yet commanders still learned to delegate in order to shorten the observe, orient, decide, act (OODA) loop. Chapter 8 portrays these new modes of controlling airpower as a move toward what Edwin Hutchins terms "distributed cognition." Technological development has brought more people into the attack sequence or "kill chain," reducing the portion of that chain that any single member—including the pilot—performs. This occurs in all types of time-sensitive targeting, including close air support (CAS) and armed reconnaissance types of missions.

Chapter 9 analyzes the potential for accidents in the CAOS, proposing that the distribution of the tasks involved in air strikes makes the CAOS more complex and more susceptible to practical drift. It is left to chapter 10 to extrapolate some of the potential implications for the future of the control of combat airpower.

The venerable Carl von Clausewitz advised that all wars must be judged by the peculiarities of the times, in addition to general laws of war.[48] Yet his eighteenth century work on the nature of war is treated as wisdom in military classrooms to this day. This work does not debate whether there has been an information revolution. It is enough to recognize that there has been a significant amount of technological development in the last two decades, much of which has changed the way airpower is commanded and controlled. The true challenge is to recognize how deeply those changes reach. Have the fundamental truths been altered, or just their implementation?

Notes

(All notes appear in shortened form. For full details, see the appropriate entry in the bibliography.)

1. "U.S. Troops Topple Saddam Statue."
2. Carter, "Road to Abu Ghraib."

3. Ibid.

4. Cappacio, "U.S. Launched More."

5. Jervis, *Perception and Misperception*, 28; and Allison, *Essence of Decision*. The writings of Robert Jervis and Graham Allison illustrate some of the ways analysis of strategy will fall short if it looks only at what a "rational" actor would do in a given situation. Although the two differ slightly in their levels of analysis, they both point out that it is difficult to anticipate the exact result of international strategy in any given situation. Jervis proposes that it is essential to analyze a decision maker's beliefs about the world and his images of others in order to understand crucial decisions. He also acknowledges that other "levels of analysis," such as bureaucratic politics, the nature of the state and domestic politics, and international politics also play roles. In fact, analysis at all these levels may be necessary to explain a single decision. Jervis explains the four levels and proposes that "domestic politics may dictate that a given event be made the occasion for a change in policy; bargaining within the bureaucracy may explain what options are presented to the national leaders; the decision-maker's predisposition could account for the choice that was made; and the interests and routines of the bureaucracies could explain the way the decision was implemented" (15, 17). Allison concentrates on three levels of analysis, the Rational Actor Model (model one), the Organizational Process Model (model two), and the Governmental (bureaucratic) Politics Model (model three). He shows that analysis of policies and actions becomes significantly richer when analysts considers not only what they would have done in the policy maker's shoes, but also what organizational routines may have influenced the information and options available and what power struggles may have dictated the choices. He suggests that "Model I fixes the broader context, the larger national patterns, and the shared images. Within this context, Model II illuminates the organizational routines that produce the information, the alternatives, and action. Within the Model II context, Model III focuses in greater detail on the individual leaders of a government and the politics among them that determine major governmental choices" (258). I think his evidence equally supports the conclusion that model one may in some circumstances furnish the proposed solution, and models two and three modify the execution of that solution, similar to Jervis's proposal.

6. Chandler, *Visible Hand*, 497.

7. Castells, *Rise of the Network Society*, 177–78. Although Castells says this change has occurred with the information revolution, he also says the impetus for organizational change may have preceded, and in fact driven, the technology (185).

8. Porter and Millar in "How Information Gives" explain the concepts of *value chain* and *interlinkage* (149–60). Venkatraman discusses transforming businesses and marketplaces in "IT-Enabled Business Transformation," 73–87.

9. Arquilla and Ronfeldt, "Advent of Netwar," 6.

10. Williams, "Transnational Criminal Networks," 67.

11. Arquilla and Ronfeldt, "Advent of Netwar," 15.

12. Arquilla and Ronfeldt, "Looking Ahead," 439–40. They propose that the information revolution should be the basis for a "revolution in military

affairs." These are rare, but when they occur they bring major paradigm changes to warfare, and those who are quick to capitalize on them reap great rewards. The United States—the only nation able to construct a truly global information network—is currently well positioned to capitalize on this revolution and is already in the lead in developing military C2 based on information systems.

13. Alberts, Garstka, and Stein, *Network Centric Warfare*, 2.

14. Ibid., 74, 91, 118–19.

15. Vego, "Network-Centric Is Not Decisive."

16. Leonhard, *Principles of War*, 180.

17. Air Force Doctrine Document (AFDD) 1, *Air Force Basic Doctrine*, 23.

18. JP 3-30, *Command and Control*, I-3.

19. JP 3-0, *Doctrine for Joint Operations*, x.

20. Pape, *Bombing to Win*; and Byman, Waxman, and Larson, *Air Power as a Coercive Instrument*, are two good places to start. Pape does an in-depth study of denial versus punishment strategies, concluding that strategic bombing of populations has never been as effective as bombing military targets to convince an enemy he cannot win. Byman et al. present a less detailed but more balanced look at the factors that make airpower effective as a coercive instrument.

21. The list is too long to document here. Determining whether airpower was decisive in a particular conflict has probably been the focus of most airpower history. The following are some references of interest: Mierzejewski in *Collapse of the German War Economy* gives an excellent account of the success of tactical airpower in doing what strategic bombardment could not: topple the German war machine. The most comprehensive work on the Korean War is probably Futrell's *United States Air Force in Korea*. Clodfelter's *Limits of Air Power* is a must for anyone who wants to understand why airpower at first did not, and then did, work in Vietnam. Keaney and Cohen's *Revolution in Warfare?* is the *Gulf War Air Power Survey* in published format.

22. In *First Air War*, Kennett looks at the development of airpower in World War I (WWI). Sherry's *Rise of American Air Power* is what I would consider a broad view of the emergence of strategic bombing in the United States. However, he is a bit polemic in places and never puts the broad views into a systems framework that can be used to develop policy. Lambeth's *Transformation of American Air Power* is also a comprehensive look at the many factors that have influenced the development of airpower in the last three decades.

23. Sun-Tzu, Clausewitz, Jomini, Moltke, Mahan, and Corbett are some of the authors of classics in the use of military force before the development of airpower.

24. Simpkin in association with Erickson, *Deep Battle*, 165.

25. Huntington, *Soldier and the State*, 80–85.

26. Cohen, *Supreme Command*, 13.

27. Ibid., 180.

28. Ibid., 198.

29. Ibid., 201.

30. Ibid., 206.

31. van Creveld, *Command in War*, 269.
32. Ibid., 59.
33. Ibid., 75, 272–74.
34. Allard, *Command, Control*, 155–57.
35. There are unpublished works that attempt this task. Maj David K. Gerber attacked the subject of centralized versus decentralized control by studying complexity theory in his Air University (AU) master's thesis, "Adaptive Command and Control of Theater Airpower." When applying lessons about complex adaptive systems to the Air Force's current system for planning and directing air operations, he found the current system too centralized. Gerber claims the Air Force tries to manage the microlevel details in order to develop a macrolevel strategy—a task for which there really is no good theory right now. He proposes the Air Force should use more general, mission-type orders and then use IT to monitor the implementation of the details and adjust as necessary. Another AU master's thesis from Maj Mustafa R. Koprucu, "Limits of Decentralization: The Effects of Technology on a Central Airpower Tenet," points out that, despite the elevated importance of "decentralized execution," the air component has always striven for centralized execution. It was mainly held back by the lack of technological capability. This capability is coming of age today, leading to the need for a reexamination of what constitutes overcentralization. Any attempt to decentralize execution must at least acknowledge this trend and its roots.
36. Winnefeld and Johnson, *Joint Air Operations*, 63–82.
37. MacNamara, *Airpower's Gordian Knot*, 151–54.
38. There is, of course, at least one exception. Anyone who has ventured to read the colossal *Gulf War Air Power Survey*, in all ten parts of five volumes, cannot long hold onto the above misperceptions. Hone's "Command and Control" is an exceptional treatment of the very type this author can only hope to approach. I hope to add a temporal dimension to this analysis to distill the effects of time, technology, and human innovation.
39. Mindell, *Between Human and Machine*, 16. The previous thoughts on bias in the selection of sources and narrative also come from Mindell.
40. Bertalanffy, *General System Theory*, and Leveson, *Safeware*, expound on the shortcomings of the classical analytical approach. Magee and de Weck, "Attempt at Complex System Classification," give probably the best overall definition of a system, if one is dealing with systems that are made of substantial human and technological components.
41. Thompson, *Organizations in Action*, 59.
42. Leveson, *Safeware*, 138.
43. Sterman, *Business Dynamics*, 26–28.
44. Dodder, Sussman, and McConnell, "Concept of the 'CLIOS Process,'" 2, 4.
45. Snook, *Friendly Fire*, 194.
46. Ibid., 200.
47. Latour, *Science in Action*, 223–27.
48. Clausewitz, *On War*, 593–94.

Chapter 2

Historical Foundations of Airpower Control Issues

Because of the Air Force position that employment of airpower requires centralized control and decentralized execution, it may seem that there is little left for debate in this area. It is true that Air Force basic doctrine presents a well-thought-out way to think about the trade-offs between centralization and decentralization of control. The 1997 version remarks that this position provides a clear way for commanders to "focus on those priorities that lead to victory" while achieving effective span of control and fostering "initiative, situational responsiveness, and tactical flexibility."[1] However, the concept of centralized control and decentralized execution is confusing, and it means something different to everyone involved. Further, the language is ambiguous—what "control" is to one person may be "execution" to another. In fact, is control not a part of execution? The writers of the 1971 Air Force Manual (AFM) 1-1, *United States Air Force Basic Doctrine*, seemed to think so.

It wasn't until 1992 that Air Force doctrine provided the rationale behind this rather recent and evolving philosophy. AFM 1-1 explains that this principle evolved to correct the ineffective division of airpower in WWII as well as its micromanagement at too high a level in Vietnam. First identified as an Air Force principle in 1971,[2] the original wording was "centralized allocation and direction and decentralized control and execution."[3] It was the 1975 version that first called for "centralized control, decentralized execution, and coordinated effort."[4] Then in 1979, the document attempted to lay out the division of labor between higher-echelon and lower-echelon commanders. It said the former should "define the missions and tasks, and then direct lower echelons to conduct the operations," while the latter should be responsible for "details for mission planning."[5] In fact, this edition claimed, the principle of "decentralized execution" reflected an "aspect of our national character," which was to trust and enable individuals to perform to the best of their abilities.[6]

There is widespread doubt about whether the Air Force always follows this doctrine. For example, research papers coming out of Air University (AU), the Air Force's school of professional military education, often characterize the system used by the Air Force to employ airpower as overly hierarchical or centralized. Some propose that the Air Force should strive for a more decentralized organizational structure, which would strengthen command and encourage networked forces to innovate and adapt to unforeseen situations.[7] This is in line with the network-centric warfare recommendations in chapter 1. Conversely, others suggest that as central decision makers gain the ability to collect and process information about the battles that their headquarters may instead be the best place to make many of the decisions that are currently delegated.[8]

This chapter delineates various arguments about control, presenting those commonly used to validate the need for either centralized or decentralized control of combat airpower, and then further differentiates them by how far each hierarchical level gets into the details. At the politico-military strategic level, policy makers in different wars have shown disparate propensities to get involved in putting constraints on tactical actions. Generally, the more limited the aims of the war, the more detailed this intervention has been. At the operational level, officers in the Army Air Forces (AAF) and Air Force have always strived for centralized control of air forces by an Airman with the authority to command unity of effort. The different services, though, have always had different ideas about the best way to control airpower.

At the tactical level, the amount of control that commanders have exercised over missions has varied with the type of mission. Since the Air Force has historically preferred to perform deep-strike missions to hit key enemy vulnerabilities, it has always tried to preplan as many of the details as possible. It has had to learn and relearn how to relinquish the direction of mission details to ground troops on the battlefield when Airmen fly supportive missions such as CAS. Lurking over all of these issues is an affinity for technological advances that allow decision makers at each level to get more information (and make more decisions) about the actions of the levels illustrated below. In fact, the military is constantly striving for technological development that changes the character of some of the arguments.

The Levels of War

The "levels" of war, as just noted, are abstractions that prescribe different functions in conflict based on different hierarchical levels. In his classic, *On War*, Clausewitz spends considerable effort separating war into three levels—policy, strategy, and tactics. He describes policy as the domain of the government, strategy as the purview of the general, and tactics as the actions on the battlefield.[9] Today, we recognize these three levels as the strategic, operational, and tactical levels of war. At the strategic level of war, the overall aims of the conflict are determined. Here governments try to figure out how to incorporate military action into their overall grand strategy. Many times writers will also include another, *politico-military strategic* level, dealing with military strategy as opposed to grand strategy. This differentiates the SecDef and the JCS, who could be expected to delve more deeply into military details, from the National Security Council (NSC) as a whole. For our purposes, the two will be considered the same—we will call them *policy makers* or *strategic-level decision makers*. At the operational level of war, plans are made to maneuver military resources to bring them into action at the right time and place in the *battlespace* (a term that includes the surface, the air, the space, and even the information). This is the link between these battle actions and the strategic-level aims. The actions themselves happen at the tactical level of war, where military units actually do things that kill people and break things—or whatever it takes to put the right pressure on the enemy.[10]

Strategic Level and the Nature of the War

At the strategic levels, state governments have always attempted to improve their control over the instruments of their power. In the sixteenth and seventeenth centuries, for instance, Maurice of Nassau taught European states how to tame their armies by establishing drill procedures. Soldiers whose every move was governed by procedure had to practice daily to perfect their skills, keeping them out of trouble during peacetime and making them much more effective and controllable during war—double the benefit. The stability provided by these improved armies allowed the states to concentrate on overseas trade and, later, conquering and controlling the overseas lands with the same armies.[11] Leaders during this period were often both governor and general, with Napoléon being one of the last of this breed in the western world.[12] Napoléon, realizing that he could not control his huge army at all times, developed the corps system, splitting his army into corps that marched and sustained themselves separately. He then developed the ability to gather and process information on their operations and make them conform to an overall design—to exert control (although this was operational-level control).[13]

It appears that the level of details the policy makers try to manage depends on something we will call the *nature of the war*. Clausewitz claimed that the strategist's most fundamental job is to figure out what the nature of the war is.[14] He was also the first to explicitly establish the virtual axiom that war is an instrument of policy that is, simultaneously, limited by policy. However, in the same breath, he related that policy does not extend to the operational details.[15]

Depending on the portion of the *spectrum of coercion* they are trying to use, policy makers may allow more or less independence. Coercion implies that a coercer is trying to influence a target in order to obtain an end state that would not otherwise occur. The influence may be an attempt to maintain the status quo (deterrence) or to change the status quo (compellance) to force the target to either stop what it is doing or take some new action. The spectrum of coercion, therefore, has deterrence on one end, progresses through diplomatic measures to compel, then to forceful measures to compel, and ends with pure brute force on the other end. The nature of every conflict will fall somewhere on that spectrum.

Whether or not the target is coerced is the target's decision, to be made based on its calculation of the costs and benefits involved. However, this is anything but a sanitized calculation. Motivation, culture, perceptions, bureaucratic politics, and organizational processes combine to make it difficult to tell what decision a target will make and when.[16] This calculation becomes even more muddled when the coercer uses force. Compellance can involve direct use of force and/or actions that will result in the use of force if they are not halted—if the target modifies its behavior, the use of force is halted; if not, force is used.[17] The more directly force is responsible for modifying the target's behavior, the closer compellance comes to resembling pure brute force. Brute force takes; compellance commands: "Give it to me!" Brute force pushes; compellance commands: "Move!" Brute force halts the target by incapacitating it; compellance tells the target to stop. Of course, in each case, compellance either threatens force or applies some measure of it to convince the target it is serious and promises (1) more pain if the target does not comply and (2) an end to the pain if the target complies. So the tricky part is that it's often hard to tell compellance from brute force—it can often become brute force if the target does not comply.[18]

WWII was a case where compellance became almost complete brute force. The Allies' demands of unconditional surrender ensured a high level of motivation on the parts of both Germany and Japan. The United States knew it would have to fight to the end. In fact, Japan surrendered before the United States had to invade; Germany did not. Japan was compelled; Germany was defeated by brute force.[19] However, in both cases, the United States and the Allies used all of the effort they could muster, with the intent to eventually defeat the enemy through brute force.[20] This is because interests were high enough to warrant the massive destruction that accompanies the use of brute force. So we can say WWII took place at the brute force end of the spectrum. It is instructive to see how control of airpower was handled in this, the age of total war.

For the most part, Pres. Franklin Roosevelt and Gen George Marshall stayed out of the business of telling Airmen what to do. When Airmen offered the air plan for the war in Europe, Air War Plans Division, Plan 1, "Munitions Requirements of the Army Air Forces," it was passed without comment by these policy makers. At Casablanca, when the Royal Air Force (RAF) and the Army developed plans for the Combined Bomber Offensive, it was Gen Ira Eaker who spoke for the United States. Eaker was an Airman, and not even the senior one at that (although he was arguably the most qualified to talk about the bombing campaign).[21] The distinguishing characteristic of airpower control in this war was the absence of involvement by policy makers, with the exception of the dropping of the atomic bombs on Hiroshima and Nagasaki. Because the interaction among governments in WWII occurred toward the brute force end of the coercion spectrum, strategic decision makers were able to give the military significant freedom to operate. The interests at stake were so vital that decision makers were able to give the military clear goals and accept a great deal of collateral damage.

It is noteworthy, though, that a critical feedback loop was not yet established during this war. The media was unable to obtain accurate information about the bombings of Europe and Japan, and their reporting was generally sympathetic to the war effort. With the overwhelming support of the American public, undiminished by contrary press feedback, the US government was not forced to confront the harshness of its military's actions at the time.[22] The subsequent analyses of area bombing in Germany, and especially in Japan, have no doubt contributed to the US military pressing toward greater precision. The time it took to cycle through this feedback loop decreased dramatically by the time the United States fought in Vietnam.

In Vietnam, the US government was determined to be more aggressive in its control over the military forces. This reaction was probably due to events more recent than WWII. In Korea, Pres. Harry S. Truman's failure to subjugate Gen Douglas MacArthur's battlefield strategy to a prudent grand strategy had goaded China into the war.[23] Then, in the Cuban Missile Crisis, Pres. John F. Kennedy had been repeatedly frustrated at his inability to control the actions of his forces. The military's failure to remove missiles from Turkey as he had directed left open the possibility that the United States would have to respond to a Soviet counterstrike against nuclear weapons if the United States chose to attack the Cuban sites. An errant U-2 flight over the Soviet Union at the height of tension came dangerously close to provoking military action. Then the Air Force failed to disperse its fighter aircraft after the president ordered it do so.[24] In fact, it was in the immediate wake of these events that SecDef McNamara ordered the development of the Worldwide Military Command and Control System (WWMCCS) to tie together all military and civilian communications and establish a centralized C2 system.[25] With this capability, McNamara (who had seen the value of quantitative managerial methods in industry) hoped to be able to precisely control the application of military force and respond "flexibly" to any conflict. This was the policy that led to the source of the greatest argument over centralized and decentralized control in US military history.

The conflict in Vietnam took place on a very different part of the coercion spectrum than WWII had occupied—at least for the United States. In WWII, the United States had thrown everything at its enemies ("everything but the kitchen sink" may apply in Japan's case, but the kitchen sink—invasion—was on its way when Japan surrendered). In Vietnam, the United States tried to influence the North Vietnamese with a strategy described as *calibration*. The trick was to pick the level of force that would not only convince Hanoi to stop supporting the Vietcong because it could not defeat the United States, but also to avoid solidifying the North Vietnamese, provoking the Chinese, arousing world opinion, or precluding eventual negotiations.[26] The aim was not so much to defeat the target (North Vietnam) as to communicate to it that it was better to acquiesce than to face a determined United States.[27]

The difference was the interests involved—Vietnam was not the true focus of the Vietnam War for US presidents Kennedy and Johnson. They had accepted the logic of containment laid out as far back as the 1950 NSC Report 68, "United States Objectives and Programs for National Security." This meant that containment of the Soviet Union required confronting communism wherever it surfaced, and the two therefore felt compelled to honor all treaty obligations, including the Southeast Asia Treaty Organization (SEATO). But this set up a vicious cycle. To convince the Europeans, Japanese, and Taiwanese that US commitments were credible, US leaders thought they had to do whatever it took to honor the SEATO treaty. So while Kennedy initially avoided sending any combat troops, the level of involvement got ratcheted up gradually until Johnson eventually had over 500,000 soldiers in Vietnam to protect this credibility. The detailed attention McNamara and Johnson gave to the means involved in Vietnam blinded them to the fact that the means were gradually outstretching the ends.[28]

Nowhere was this detailed attention more visible than in the 1965–68 air campaign known as Rolling Thunder. It was a campaign where the intensity of the bombing and the location of targets were gradually calibrated to put increasing pressure on Hanoi until it acquiesced. Accordingly, policy makers chose all of the targets and many of the tactics. Adm Ulysses S. Grant

Sharp, Jr., commander, US Pacific Command, chose targets in cooperation with his subordinate commanders and sent them to the JCS, who forwarded them to Secretary McNamara for consideration at the weekly Tuesday luncheon. Although no military members attended these luncheons until late in 1967, policy makers nevertheless imposed specific constraints on the bombing campaign. Some of these constraints seem appropriate, especially given their strategy. For example, the imposition of restricted areas around Hanoi and Haiphong was consistent with the desire to communicate with the leadership in Hanoi (although these restricted areas precluded implementation of the military's desired strategy of sudden, intense, sustained pressure—this was a difference of opinion in strategy). Other constraints, however, specified tactical details that affected the pilots. Aircraft were not allowed to hit surface-to-air missiles (SAM) until photographs had been analyzed, by which time the SAMs had usually been moved. In September 1965, they were for the first time allowed to strike bridges—but only two specific bridges, simultaneously, and only once.[29] These restrictions affected the way the Airmen had to fly their missions—and denied them the ability to apply force in what they thought was the most effective way.

Policy makers, however, learned that military actions can drastically affect their strategies. They learned that television has the ability to create a feedback loop from the battlefield to the home front and give strategic consequences to tactical events. In late 1967 the Vietcong and North Vietnamese launched a coordinated campaign to draw US and South Vietnamese troops out of the cities of South Vietnam so they could attack the cities. Their intent seems to have been to attack civil authorities to undermine the confidence of the people and stoke the coals of revolution in the south. They succeeded in drawing troops out of the cities, but US and South Vietnamese forces were still able to repulse the attacks, which began on 30 January 1968—the lunar new year, or Tet. The fighting was so bloody and brutal, however, that it shook the Americans' confidence in leaders who had told them the United States was winning the war. Gen William Westmoreland, the commander of all US troops in the war theater, tried to seize the opportunity to ask for a large number of reinforcements, sufficient to mobilize the reserves. But President Johnson perceived he had run out of the political capital required for this kind of escalation and consequently decided to withdraw from the race for reelection. In 1968 the United States was marked by violent protests and political turmoil, and its leaders had no choice but to back out of a war that simply appeared too costly. Tet was a tactical victory for the United States in many respects because it broke the back of the Vietcong and left the North Vietnamese regulars as the only force capable of uniting Vietnam—it turned the guerilla struggle into a conventional war. There were, nonetheless, strategic consequences that not even the North Vietnamese had anticipated.[30]

The military took a different lesson from the war—the comparison of the ineffectiveness of airpower during the restricted Rolling Thunder campaign and the effectiveness of the all-out Linebacker campaigns. In 1972 the North Vietnamese Army invaded South Vietnam in an attempt to unite the country by conventional force. The United States and South Vietnamese defeated the attempt with ground forces and a heavy conventional air attack. But the South Vietnamese government, excluded from peace talks between the United States and the North Vietnamese, refused to accept the ensuing peace agreement, and talks broke off. So in December of that year, the United States launched an all-out bombing campaign, including B-52 strikes on Hanoi, after which the three parties (North and South Vietnam and the United States) did in fact negotiate a peace agreement. Many in the military, especially Airmen, saw the war as a lesson that airpower should only be employed with full power and without political constraints. They saw Linebacker as a vindication of the potency of airpower when used effectively, and Rolling Thunder as a warning of what happens when it is used ineffectively.[31] In 1978 Sharp wrote that "the aims or objectives of an international political strategy may . . . be limited, as were ours in Vietnam, but the actual application of military force required to achieve those aims cannot and *must not* be tactically limited" (emphasis in original).[32]

This contrast between Rolling Thunder and Linebacker is not the only interpretation of the events of the Vietnam War. The two operations occurred in totally different wars. Linebacker was attempting to get the United States out of the war; Rolling

Thunder was trying to win it. By the time Linebacker took place, Pres. Richard M. Nixon had politically isolated North Vietnam from the Soviet Union and China and did not have the same worries about intervention that Johnson did during Rolling Thunder. In addition, while this conflict was a guerilla war during Rolling Thunder, it became a conventional war after the Tet Offensive—especially when the Linebacker operations took place. Bombing had relatively little effect on the ability of the Vietcong to operate in South Vietnam, but it had a large effect on the conventional North Vietnamese regulars.[33] Certainly, the relaxing of restrictions allowed airpower to perform more effectively, and, just as certain, the restrictions were an important part of Johnson's strategy.

Awareness of these differences between WWII and Vietnam is key to comprehending the strategic-level issues involved in centralized control and decentralized execution. WWII occurred in an age of total war, where all the resources of the combatants were involved in the war effort and, therefore, were considered fair game for attack. The Allies were asking for unconditional surrender, using every bit of brute force at their disposal. Furthermore, the press was unable to relate the horrors of war as efficiently as they do today. Strategic-level decision makers were able to give military commanders significant latitude to prosecute the war in the most militarily effective way. By contrast, Vietnam was a war of limited aims for the United States. Whether or not the grand strategy of coercion and communication could have been successful with better implementation in Vietnam is outside the scope of this study. But given this strategy, it was natural that the political decision makers wanted a high level of control over the actions of the military, and especially airpower—the military forces in closest contact with the North Vietnamese government and civilians. Politicians also learned that tactical actions have strategic consequences. It is interesting to note, however, that the types of controls Johnson and McNamara attempted to exert became counterproductive because, while they limited the destructiveness of US airpower, they did not preclude military force from hardening the resolve of the North Vietnamese or turning Americans against the war. In fact, these controls had quite the opposite effect of creating severe friction between the military and civilians, rather than the close cooperation necessary in war.

Command Relationships at the Operational Level

At the operational level, the biggest issue throughout the history of US military airpower has been the struggle to gain unity of effort from all air forces. In this matter, officers from air and ground forces have differing opinions. Airmen, of course, are the ones who have always claimed airpower should be unified under a single commander. Because aircraft can move much faster and farther during a battle than ground troops, Airmen have always seen less need to constrain aircraft supporting a geographical area in the way ground troops are constrained. Commanders of air forces can be given responsibility for areas that are an order of magnitude larger than their ground peers. In fact, Airmen claim, if aircraft are constrained by a ground commander's geographical view, they will be wasted. Aircraft may be waiting on the ground to support a ground commander who is not engaged with the enemy, while another ground commander is in desperate need of more aircraft but cannot obtain them. As Brig Gen William "Billy" Mitchell put it in 1925, "The system of command of military air power should consist in having the greatest centralization practicable. An air force now can move from one to two thousand miles within twenty-four hours. Military elements on the land or water can move only a fraction of this. . . . To assign air force units to any one of these ground organizations would result in the piece-meal application of air power and the inability to develop the maximum force at the critical point."[34] Air Force officers credit the Goldwater-Nichols Defense Reorganization Act, over six decades later, for finally setting the conditions to allow a single Airman to command all air forces in the 1991 Gulf War.[35]

On the other hand, ground officers have always put priority on synchronizing ground and air operations. Probably the first to document this need was the Soviet marshal Mikhail Tukhachevsky. Writing between the two world wars, he realized that airplanes and tanks had opened up the opportunity for a new type of combat maneuver after World War I (WWI). He predicted that future wars would be won by the side that was able to coordinate the many heterogeneous actions of the different types of forces throughout the depth of the battlefield. To do this, commanders would have to concentrate these forces on clear objectives but avoid "firm" control or a "tight rein."[36] Later, this was to be the idea behind AirLand Battle doctrine that the US Army would develop to defeat the numerically superior Warsaw Pact—namely, combined arms doctrine, which holds that the most important effect of a weapon system is not its killing potential, but the enemy reactions it causes. Ground officers see the benefit of having complementary capabilities in that one weapon causes the enemy to react in a way that leads him right into another weapon.[37]

The issue, then, was over command relationships. Airmen wanted to have an Airman in command of all air forces, with the authority to task the aircraft on a theaterwide basis. Those on the ground wanted the aircraft to be organic to the ground units so the actions would be synchronized for the greatest effect. Different experiences in WWI had sparked this argument. Then during the years of peace between the world wars, the US Army was plagued by short budgets and fights for scarce resources as well as the sheer boredom that peacetime brings for militaries. These factors elevated the argument to a bitter fight for independence of the air arm that went way beyond the question of who would command air forces during wartime.

During WWII the issue came to a head in the Army, specifically during the campaign in North Africa where AAF units had been split up into what was later called penny packets under the control of ground commanders. The ground commanders used aircraft to support their individual ground units, which were largely confined to defined geographical areas. At one point, Gen Lloyd Fredendall, II Corps commander, told Lt Gen Carl Spaatz, Northwest African Air Forces commander, that he wanted aircraft constantly flying over his troops and concentrating only on the enemy troops immediately in front of them during an attack.[38] This made it difficult for the Allied air forces to coordinate an attack on the German army as a whole, not to mention defeating the Luftwaffe to gain air superiority. British and American chiefs of staff were in the midst of trying to solve these disputes when Field Marshal Erwin Rommel attacked the

US 1st Armored Division and destroyed half of its tanks. Although the Allies stopped the attack by throwing in reserves, it was nonetheless a fiasco. Despite air having played only a small part in the effort, the battle of Kasserine Pass became the force that drove ground and air commanders to work out their coordination problems. As a result, in 1943 the doctrine document Field Manual (FM) 100-20, *Command and Employment of Air Power*, specified that there would be an air commander equivalent to the ground commander.[39]

The doctrinal solution did not end problems in the battlefield with unity of airpower effort. In Korea and Vietnam, air resources were not parceled out to ground commanders, but they certainly did not achieve unified, coherent effort. Air Force, Navy, and Marine air efforts were now three separate campaigns, and the best coordination they could muster was to attempt to deconflict missions so one service did not interfere with another. In both conflicts theater commanders recognized that the situation was undesirable and attempted to rectify it near the end of the war. In Korea, Navy and Air Force aircraft finally worked together on a single target during the raids on the hydroelectric plants on 23 June 1952.[40] This marked the beginning of continued cooperation between the two services, where each would at least inform the other of its plans and sometimes even request support for a particular operation.[41] Then in 1953, Gen Mark W. Clark, supreme commander of the United Nations (UN) forces in Korea, directed the Navy to participate with the Air Force in a joint operations center to facilitate cooperative planning between the two services.[42] Although this was done late in the war and probably had little impact, the desirability of unified effort was at least acknowledged.

Despite coming to a solution near the end of the Korean War, the services encountered the same problem in Vietnam. Neither the Air Force nor the Navy would relinquish control of its resources to the other, so there could be no overall commander. Instead, Admiral Sharp designated Maj Gen Joseph Moore, commander of the 2d Air Division of the Pacific Air Forces, the "coordinating authority" for Operation Rolling Thunder attacks. He could not communicate well enough with the Navy to exchange information on a mission-by-mission basis, so he worked with the Navy's Task Force 77 to come up with an arrangement that would allow the two services to stay out of each other's way. The answer was to divide the country into seven geographical areas called *route packages* (there were only six numerical designations, but route package VI was divided into VIA and VIB). Moore gave the Navy four and the Air Force three (although the Air Force had the largest area), consequently allowing the Navy to plan its own missions without coordinating with the Air Force and vice versa.[43] This arrangement, however, precluded any sort of coherent timing of effects that would have been necessary for McNamara's synchronization. It also hampered cooperation between the two services for the use of resources, intelligence, or even lessons learned.

If the lack of unity hampered the attacks in Operation Rolling Thunder, it was worse for the ground war in the south where aircraft were required to coordinate closely with ground troops. Here the support was primarily provided by USAF, US Marine, and Vietnamese air force aircraft. But the US Air Force and Marines practiced different doctrine and coordinating procedures, so there were overlapping systems with no manager to deconflict the separate air forces. General Westmoreland suggested to Admiral Sharp that the large number of ground troops and resources in South Vietnam warranted a single air manager—Sharp disagreed.[44] In 1968, when the Tet Offensive began, President Johnson issued a special directive ordering the defense of the Marine base at Khe Sanh because of the historical analogy a loss there would have made with the French disaster at Dien Bien Phu.[45] With this heightened importance, both the Air Force and the Marines scrambled to send all the air sorties they could muster to the rescue. The result was near chaos because the only coordination between the two was essentially through ad hoc arrangements. The flow of aircraft was uneven, causing shortages during some critical times and bottlenecks of too many aircraft during some quieter times. Westmoreland forcefully insisted that all air operations be controlled by a single air manager from the Air Force, namely Seventh Air Force commander, Gen William W. Momyer. This move caused such controversy the decision was eventually appealed all the way to President Johnson. The Marines, in particular, claimed that having a single point of control for all US airpower was not as effective as its own system. In any case, this shift of control was not implemented until after the battle for Khe Sanh (Operation Niagra) was over.[46]

Throughout the conflicts during this period, officers in the AAF and Air Force pushed for the authority to manage all air resources. They believed only a single manager could properly direct resources to the highest priority missions, whereas local commanders—by virtue of not having a theater-level view—might waste these resources. Hampering the drive toward a single manager, though, were the different services' fears about relinquishing their assets to a commander of another service. Each thought this arrangement would mean they would lose total control.

Different Levels of Control for Different Tactical Missions

There is another level to the arguments. The Airmen who strived for this central authority learned over and over that the type of control that was appropriate varied according to the type of mission. The type of control that was appropriate for strategic bombing missions differed from that necessary for successful CAS. When aircrews flew CAS missions, they developed ways to work closely with the soldiers on the ground to find targets. In Europe during WWII, the centralized control of these missions—requiring a full day for scheduling a target—was ineffective at supporting the D-day invasion and even proved dangerous to friendly troops. Americans developed a method of scheduling a steady stream of aircraft over an armored column, with a VHF radio in the lead vehicle to assign targets as the aircraft arrived. Later, a forward air controller (airborne) (FAC[A]) took over this function. Thus, although the aircraft were still scheduled and routed by a centralized "combined operations center," they were often given targets on the scene.[47] In the Southwest Pacific, the same sequence occurred. At first, air strikes had to be scheduled a day in advance. Target acquisition was difficult, especially in the jungles, so ground troops tried to mark the targets with smoke. It was 1944 before the ad hoc forward air observer team brought aircrews into contact with the ground forces. By the end of the year, communications with the ground were an accepted part of close support. There was never any operational control of aircraft by ground commanders—they could only request strikes. The ground controllers were air personnel who accompanied the ground forces.[48] Still, the Airmen learned that the best people to pick targets for CAS aircraft were those on the scene.

Strategic bombing was a different matter. Washington basically directed targets for bombing raids on Japan conducted by the 20th and 21st Bomber Commands. The Japanese targets were picked and put into mission folders by Gen Henry "Hap" Arnold, chief, USAAF, and his committee of operations analysts.[49] Arnold and Gen Lauris Norstad, Twentieth Air Force chief of staff (also located in the United States), were decidedly hands-on in their direction of the 21st Bomber Command operations, as well. When Gen Haywood Hansell did not live up to their expectations as commander of the 21st Bomber Command, they replaced him with Gen Curtis E. LeMay. They pressed both commanders for incendiary attacks on Japan, at one point even specifying the tactics the B-29 crews should use (although LeMay is given credit for the final low-level tactics that produced most of the destruction).[50]

This involvement by high-level officials is understandable, given their complexity and the interests the AAF had in strategic bombing. In the interlude between WWI and WWII, the Army Air Corps had developed a strategic bombing doctrine. During the war, the AAF staked its bid for independence on the efficacy of strategic bombing. After the war, the new Air Force was convinced the strategic bombing of Japan, including fire bombing and the atomic bombs, had been the decisive factors in the victory.[51] Added to this, the missions deep into enemy territory were dangerous and involved the cooperation of bombers and pursuit fighters, which were not stationed together. High-level AAF officials took great interest in the details of these missions because of both their political significance and complexity.

Because of the interest in strategic bombing, the new Air Force did not pay as much attention to CAS as did the Marines following WWII. The lessons were not lost—the AAF had collated the lessons learned from close support in WWII into the 1942 FM 31-35, *Aviation in Support of Ground Forces*. But these were a mix of lessons from two theaters, each of which used significantly different procedures. They were developed to work primarily with the Army, which placed heavy reliance on organic artillery and preferred aircraft for the deeper strikes except in critical situations. By contrast, the Marines had learned all their lessons on the beaches of the South and Central Pacific. After WWII, Marine air and ground troops organized around the amphibious assault mission. Consequently, the Marine air wings were finely tuned to working with forward air observers to provide close support, while the Air Force placed more emphasis on deep strike operations.[52]

Because of this difference in concentration, the Marines were ready for Korea; the Air Force was not. The early battles to defend the Pusan Perimeter consisted of many desperate situations requiring close support of troops who were in contact with the enemy. The Air Force had to relearn the value of coordination with ground troops. Fifth Air Force had to improvise to get air controllers out with the ground troops and set up a communications net. They also flew slow, unarmed T-6 Mosquito trainer aircraft that could loiter over the front lines to help locate targets and direct attacks against them.[53] But the ground troops, not the FAC(A), were the ones who needed to pick the targets—the FAC was only an airborne extension of the soldiers' eyes.[54]

After Korea, the Air Force did not incorporate the lessons into doctrine and initially ran into some of the same problems in Vietnam. In the beginning, cumbersome C2 procedures kept CAS from being responsive to the ground commanders' requests. By the end of the war, Army veterans of WWII and Korea considered CAS in South Vietnam the best they had ever experienced. The Air Force had to relearn to decentralize the target-picking and traffic-control functions of CAS. The single air manager did not have a lot of say in CAS. During the defense of Khe Sanh, while the argument over a single air manager was taking place, the management of aircraft was chaotic, with an uneven flow of aircraft and congestion over target areas. Still, with the help of a modified C-130 called the airborne battlefield command and control center (ABCCC), FACs, and close communications, aircraft and ground troops worked well together, and air support is credited with saving Marines at Khe Sanh from the fate of the French.[55] This seemed to show that with CAS, control at the scene during the missions is more important than centralized control—the job of the operational level is to get the planes there.

By contrast, the intense, 11-day bombing campaign in 1972 that brought all three sides back to the bargaining table was a decidedly centralized affair. Known as Linebacker II, this was a massive B-52 effort to strike Hanoi and coerce the North Vietnamese into accepting US and South Vietnamese terms for ending the war. President Nixon gave the military almost carte blanche, telling them, "This is your chance to use military power effectively to win this war and if you don't I'll consider you personally responsible."[56] Gen John C. Meyer, commander of Strategic Air Command (SAC), decided the operation would be planned in Omaha, Nebraska, at SAC headquarters, on the other side of the world from the theater where the strikes would take place. Trying to overcome time zone differences, communications problems, and a general culture that placed predictability over innovation, SAC put out a plan that the Eighth Air Force staff in Guam considered tactically unsound. They flew it anyway, and the first nights of flying led to near-disastrous losses of B-52s.[57]

Of course, the fact that the initial missions were a disaster suggests that this centralization was a mistake. Indeed, one of the fixes was for SAC to relinquish many of the details to the Eighth Air Force staff at Anderson AFB, Guam. This actually had the effect of aiding centralized control, not decentralizing it. On the first four nights, although the bomber operations were planned in Nebraska, the support from fighters was arranged by Seventh Air Force in Saigon. The communications difficulties and time-zone difference meant Seventh Air Force had been getting the orders so late that they were unable to arrange the best support. Starting on 26 December, the two staffs in-theater were able to coordinate better tactics and better support for the massive bomber raids.[58] The complexity of the missions demanded centralized control, and moving the planning to the theater helped consolidate control of all airpower. Sometimes, holding authority at too high a level dilutes centralized control.

Through these conflicts, the air commanders had to learn that there was a difference in the amount of details they could manage centrally for different missions. Because strategic bombing went after fixed targets, required the coordination of many different types of airpower, and held high political visibility, the details for these missions were determined by high-level officials. But in each war, the Air Force had to relearn that the success of CAS missions depends on the ability of those on the scene to determine the details on the spur of the moment.

Technology's Role

Technological development was an integral part of all three of the preceding categories, so it remains a central part of the arguments. States (and their policy makers and commanding generals) have always grasped at technology that allowed them to better influence the actions of their militaries. Railroads and telegraphs went hand in hand because, whereas the one allowed more rapid flows of goods and people, the other was necessary to communicate when and how much was flowing and to synchronize supply with demand.[59] In the same period, the range and accuracy of rifles increased, making the American Civil War such a deadly affair that the Europeans refused to learn any lessons from it. Using railroads and telegraph, Helmuth von Moltke, chief of the Prussian general staff, could precisely plan and direct the strategic deployment of his armies, but his field generals could not ensure their men would fire with discipline in battle. The Prussian solution was to retrain the entire army to use new, standardized tactics. In the Franco-Prussian War in 1870–71, to the amazement of all the world, a citizen-soldier Prussian army quickly defeated Europe's best professional army. The Prussians allowed their troops to spread out and make better use of cover, while the French still massed in columns for their attacks.[60] Furthermore, while the Prussians had taken advantage of the new technology and found new ways to influence the troops using it, the French had stayed with their old tactics to maintain control—at the expense of the new capability that technology afforded.

At first, aircraft were seen as a way to ameliorate these control problems. In WWI, the airplane was initially a favorite method of directing artillery fire. The pilot, with his 10,000-foot vantage point, could see much more of this expanded battlefield than any commander on the ground. But getting the information to the ground was difficult. At first, the pilot had to land or drop notes to communicate. Then, the aircraft were equipped with wireless telegraphy so they could tap Morse code. Aircrews directed the artillery to fire, watch for the muzzle flash and the ensuing explosion, and relay the accuracy of the shot. It was a tedious method, but better than any alternative.[61] The aircraft could also bring other useful information to the ground troops. Since it was difficult to remember and accurately relay all the information, the aircrew began using aerial photography, which was at the time over a half-century old. Now the aircrew could bring back high-fidelity representations of the battlefield—ideal for situations of low urgency. When time was of the essence, however, the aircrew still had to try and take what they saw and translate it into digital beeps over wireless, with all of the loss of information that entailed.[62]

The aircraft, then, was a sort of directed telescope, in van Creveld's parlance. In WWI armies realized it could also be used to strike the enemy; consequently, commanders needed a directed telescope to keep track of the aircraft as well. The speed and range of aircraft took the problems posed by the rifle another order of merit—the battlefield was now more appropriately a battlespace that went as far as an aircraft could fly. Wireless communication was not much help because the receivers were large and heavy, and the aircraft were noisy. By the end of the war, radio sets in the aircraft allowed commanders on the ground to influence the actions of the aircraft out to a limited distance of about three miles.[63] In WWII radio was the standard method of communication, although it still could not reach as far as the aircraft could fly. There was also another problem. Even if a commander could communicate with the aircrews, he still had to piece together many bits of information to understand what was happening in the huge geographical area (or, more appropriately, volume) that could be encompassed by the battlespace.

The first systematic attempt to deal with this problem was the air defense system that helped the RAF defeat the Luftwaffe in the Battle of Britain during WWII. The RAF had constructed radars called Chain Home on the coastline of the island to warn them of approaching enemy aircraft. They had also established a Royal Observer Corps which could watch for and help identify enemy aircraft. Radar contacts were sent from the Chain Home radars to the Fighter Command Center at Bentley Priory, near Stanmore, Middlesex. Here a filter center cross-checked all the contacts to try to eliminate redundancy. Then the operations room next door sent all the information to the group headquarters. Observers also sent their data by radio to the headquarters, which disseminated it up the chain to Stanmore and down the chain to the sector headquarters. Inside the command center, as well as in the group and sector headquarters, workers executed a well-choreographed dance to take the information from the phone lines and radios and transfer it to a tabletop map. This map was a similar, standardized representation at all levels, except as the scope of the headquarters increased from sector through command, it represented a correspondingly larger portion of the total area. The groups made the decisions about which squadrons would attack which enemy formations. They passed orders to the sectors, which took over to control the fighters by radio. The sectors directed the fighters to contact with the enemy until the fighters were within sight, at which time the fighters took over. After the battle, the sector again took over to direct the fighters back to base.[64]

This system assembled a picture of the entire air situation using bits of information from many sources. The bits of information were simple enough—position, altitude, heading, type, number, friendly/foe—that they could be passed from person to person over telephone or radio without losing much information. The headquarters took these pieces of information and ascribed to them a relationship that gave them meaning beyond what any of the individual reporters, radar, or observer could have ascertained. The headquarters was then in a better position to make the decisions about who should attack where. But, since the fighters had a better view of what was happening in the narrower confines of the actual engagement, they took over command at contact.

By the time the United States fought in Vietnam, much of the equipment was better, but the concept of operating was about the same. The United States had an organized system for developing a representation of the air battlespace by combining input mostly from ground radar systems, called control and reporting posts or centers; various models of airborne radar aircraft designated EC-121; and a signals intelligence aircraft designated the RC-135 Rivet Joint. Although these sensors far surpassed the RAF's capabilities, they still communicated with each other primarily by voice.[65] Operators from these posts or centers had to call the Seventh Air

Force's tactical air control center (TACC) by landline or radio to give them information. At the TACC, operators transferred the information to a plexiglass display to create an integrated representation of the air picture. If aircrew on the EC-121 aircraft wanted to direct a friendly aircraft to an intercept with the enemy, they called the pilot on the radio and relayed the instructions. By the late 1960s, Air Force officials saw the need to automate the exchange of information. The capability seemed to be there as well: both the Navy and the Marines had rudimentary data links to link some of their radars, and the Air Force began a project called Seek Dawn to accept this information, as well as its own radar and Rivet Joint information. In fact, the program made headway and developed the ability to perform this integration at one of the subordinate TACCs in Vietnam. However, the Air Force cancelled the program in 1970 when it was deemed too costly and complex for a war that the Air Force thought was almost over. Although the USAF had significantly better sensors in Vietnam than the RAF had in the Battle of Britain, it was still unable to create an automated, integrated representation of the battlespace.

It is important to note, however, the significant difference between the ability to assemble details about the battlespace in the air and on the ground. The previous two discussions from the Battle of Britain and Vietnam dealt with air-to-air missions. Air forces had successfully developed the ability to use radar as a sensor to get information on airborne targets back to command headquarters and act on it quickly. No such success had been made with ground targets. The United States did use RF-4s, RF-101s, and unmanned vehicles to take aerial photographs in Vietnam, but since these had to be processed after the aircraft landed they were only useful for planning future missions. During the course of planned missions, the enemy would of course react, providing targets on the ground that often had to be attacked within a specific time period.

Because of the difficulty of assembling a picture of the ground, there were two ways to attack these targets. One of them, as previously mentioned, was CAS. When the enemy targets were close to friendly ground troops, the friendly troops could act as the "sensors," detecting the targets and requesting strikes. Then they would even direct the aircraft to the target. By Vietnam, the United States had an elaborate system of liaisons and controllers set up to perform this function. The Air Force also had the ABCCC to talk to the strike aircraft, act as traffic manager, and even make some decisions about the priority of the strikes. The gap here was that if there were no friendly ground troops, there were no sensors to help the aircrew find dynamic ground targets. The only way to find and attack these targets was to fly around and look for them with the sensors on the aircraft—usually the aircrew's eyes. In WWII the Allies were highly effective using this method (called *armed reconnaissance*) to interdict the German transportation system. However, it required a high degree of air superiority and a lot of aircraft relative to the area to be searched.[66]

Essentially, on this type of mission, the pilot performs almost the whole command loop: he is the sensor, the targeteer, the decision maker, and the pilot.[67] The only way for someone else to become involved in the loop is for the pilot to relay his knowledge of the target and its surroundings over the radio. But the pilot cannot transfer his knowledge—only try to describe it over the relatively low-bandwidth channel that is voice communication. This would give that person a significantly lower-fidelity picture of the target area than the pilot, so it was usually better to constrain the pilot using the ROEs that dictate what type of target he could and could not attack and when. As we will see later, this would change as the military developed the technology to allow commanders to insert themselves into these loops.

Technology, then, affected the arguments about control of airpower in two major ways. First, commanders constantly tried to gain the ability to monitor and track airpower—to use a directed telescope to assemble a picture of where the aircraft were in relation to each other and the enemy. Second, to specify details about the missions, commanders needed to find the targets. Radar helped solve this for air-to-air missions, but no comparable technology emerged for air-to-ground missions. Therefore, the details of missions to attack emerging ground targets had to be released to those on the scene.

Conclusions

These comparisons make it clear that there are several different arguments hidden underneath the umbrella of the centralized control and decentralized execution issue. At the strategic level, there is controversy over what level of details the policy makers should be concerned with. This is partly an issue of civil-military relations and partly a question of how to use preplanned constraints like ROEs and target approval to influence military action. Admiral Sharp's view of this issue was that the civilian policy makers should determine the aims of the war and then let the warriors run the war. Perhaps he and other officers who disagreed with the way the Vietnam War was run were conditioned by the fact that WWII and Korea were handled in much different manners. The civilians had been much more hands-off, leaving the military to develop and direct the war plans. In fact, these officers probably saw a trend—there were political limitations placed on airpower in Korea that had not been there in WWII, and now Vietnam had multiplied these limitations. They perceived that the effectiveness of airpower decreased accordingly and did not wish to see the trend continue.

The question remains whether this was a trend or an indication of the different strategies employed in different situations. It appears the amount of control the strategic-level decision makers wanted varied with the portion of the coercion spectrum on which they were working in a given conflict. Policy makers were gauging the amount and type of violence that would achieve their positive aims without negatively affecting the political situation. The Johnson administration's strategy for keeping this balance required a high degree of control.

Below the level of civil-military relations, there are other control arguments. The Air Force continuously struggled to gain the authority and then the ability to control all air resources so they could be integrated into a coherent effort. This struggle probably began in WWI and was nurtured by the desire of the Airmen for an independent service. However, in the Airmen's mind the need for this centralized control was proved in Africa during WWII. The AAF was unable to mount sufficient resistance to the Axis air forces to gain air superiority while they were broken up into penny packets under the command of ground forces or subject to the strategy of defending ground forces like an umbrella. There had to be an Airman with the experience and knowledge of how to best use airpower's flexibility and offensive capability and, simultaneously, the authority to command all air forces. However, even though this principle was recognized and written in Army doctrine during WWII, it still was not realized. In both the Korean and Vietnam wars, the air effort was divided among the services in the beginning. In both wars, commanders called for a single manager or commander near the end. The first war with a joint air commander was still to come.

Yet another level down from this part of the argument, a new factor emerges: not all missions are created equal when it comes to the level of control they receive. Much of the planning for the B-29 missions into Japan was done by analysts and commanders in Washington. Ground support missions, though, had to be planned closer to real time. It was in WWII that the concept of FAC was born. Later, in Vietnam, the same split emerged. Bombing missions into North Vietnam were subject to approval by President Johnson and Secretary McNamara at the Tuesday luncheons. B-52 missions during Linebacker II were planned in Nebraska at first—even when SAC was convinced to relinquish the detailed planning to the theater, the aircraft still took off with the mission planned in detail. But fighters, FACs, and the ABCCC again learned how to coordinate in real time with the troops on the ground and to find and interdict enemy targets in South Vietnam.

At each of these levels, the organizations involved were trying to make the military actions conform to some plan. Each tried to figure out what was happening in the battlespace and adjust it. This involved getting information and then assembling it into some kind of representation that allowed them to see how to make these adjustments. In some situations, though, speed and range of aircraft made this difficult. When targets were in the air, radar helped get the information. But to attack emerging targets on the ground, there was no parallel technology, so the principal sensors remained the aircrew and ground troops.[68]

The history we have used to understand the concepts of centralized and decentralized control does not adequately describe the "system" we must study. Throughout the period from WWII through Vietnam, the Air Force learned repeatedly that airpower was more than just strategic bombing. In every conflict, Air Force pilots had to relearn the principles of decentralized control vital to CAS. Yet, although pilots and ground observers learned how to work within both types of control, the Air Force did not place as much effort on the missions that required this sort of decentralized control as it did on the strategic bombing mission. After WWII, officers in the new Air Force were convinced that strategic bombing had won the war. The strategic bombing mission required the highest technology and, therefore, the most funding. In terms of the detailed planning required, it was the most complex: the combination of known targets and high threats lent themselves to a high-level effort to plan and coordinate multiple resources with great precision. From the inception of the Air Force until 1982, every single Air Force chief of staff was a bomber pilot, formed in the culture that valued such detailed, centralized planning. The Air Force could not change equipment and tactics while its top generals saw "limited" wars such as Korea and Vietnam as flukes compared to the important mission of deterring the Soviet Union.[69] We need to see how this system developed from the Vietnam era to its present state.

We can already form a picture of the main issues to address in the study. The control of airpower varies with the type of war, the command relationships, the type of mission, and the technology. An answer to the question about centralized versus decentralized control must at least address these issues, but a complete answer must also determine whether there is any interaction among them. For this, we need a systems approach.

Notes

1. AFDD 1, *Air Force Basic Doctrine*, 23.
2. AFM 1-1, *Basic Aerospace Doctrine*, vol. 2, 113–15.
3. AFM 1-1, *United States Air Force Basic Doctrine*, 28 Sept. 1971, 2-1.
4. Ibid., 15 Jan. 1975, 3-1.
5. AFM 1-1, *Functions and Basic Doctrine*, 5-2.
6. Ibid., 5-3. This explanation of the evolution of Air Force doctrine is actually a summary of a more complete discussion given in Koprucu's "Limits of Decentralized Execution," 1–5.
7. Gerber, "Adaptive Command and Control," 173–74.
8. Koprucu, "Limits of Decentralized Execution," 77–78.
9. Clausewitz, *On War*, 128.
10. JP 3-0, *Doctrine for Joint Operations*, II-2–II-3.
11. McNeill, *Pursuit of Power*, talks about the Chinese and overseas ventures (45–46); explains the logic behind establishing drill (126–32); and con-

cludes with the feedback loop whereby armies allowed more overseas ventures, providing more taxable income, allowing bigger armies, and resulting in European nations eventually outpacing the others and setting the foundation for imperialism (143).

12. Chiang Kai-shek and Mao Tse-tung were both governors and generals, so this model survived elsewhere.

13. Van Creveld, *Command in War*, 97.

14. "The first, the supreme, the most far-reaching act of judgment that the statesman and commander have to make is to establish by [the nature of their motives and of the situations which give rise to them] the kind of war on which they are embarking; neither mistaking it for, nor trying to turn it into, something that is alien to its nature. This is the first of all strategic questions and the most comprehensive." Clausewitz, *On War*, 88–89.

15. "Policy converts the overwhelmingly destructive element of war into a mere instrument. It changes the terrible battle-sword . . . into a light, handy rapier—sometimes just a foil for the exchange of thrusts, feints and parries." Ibid., 606.

16. The concept of asymmetry of motivation was a major contribution made by George and Simons in *Limits of Coercive Diplomacy*, 281–82. They contend that in some cases this asymmetry is fixed by the nature of the conflict, but in others the coercer can create an asymmetry in its favor by sticking to its own vital interests while avoiding those of the target and by offering carrots to the target. In *When Governments Collide*, Thies proposes that it is extremely difficult to control escalation because, first of all, it is difficult to ensure that the coercer's actions and intentions will match and, second, it is difficult to predict what message will actually be received by the target even if this match is achieved (376–89).

17. Schelling, *Arms and Influence*, 10. Schelling initiated the use of the term "compellance" in the context described here.

18. Pape, *Bombing to Win*, 38. There are different strategies for using force for compellance, two of which are punishment and denial. Denial is essentially the same as brute force, only with the hope that the enemy will acquiesce before it is necessary to bludgeon him to death.

19. It is, of course, debatable whether Germany was completely defeated—there were portions of the army that were still capable of fighting when the cease-fire was signed. The distinction is made between Germany and Japan to show that, although the outcomes differed by a significant degree, the Allies had the same intentions in both cases.

20. It is true that, on the surface, it is hard to justify firebombing and atomic bombs other than as instruments of coercion—removed from that era of total war, it is hard to imagine viewing an entire country as the enemy. But here Michael Sherry's point is convincing: Airmen were merely doing all they could to create more destruction without coherent thoughts as to how they would end the war. If asked how bombing would end the war, they usually answered that it would destroy the economy. Marshall and Roosevelt did not think bombing would end the war, but that it was preparation for an Allied invasion of Japan. Sherry, *Rise of American Airpower*, 236–37.

21. Ibid., 148–49.

22. Ibid., 132.

23. The entry of the Chinese into the Korean War is a more complex issue than this implies. See Stueck, *Korean War*, 85–126 for a good explanation. He says it was the "will and influence of a commander in the field" combined with the "almost pathological concern of US officials to avoid any hint of weakness to the enemy" that together "produced the reckless UN offensive of late November and forced the Chinese hand" (125).

24. These are some of the incidents used as evidence of the effect of organizational processes on strategy in Allison, *Essence of Decision*, 139–42.

25. Pearson, *World Wide Military Command*, 51–54.

26. Gaddis, *Strategies of Containment*, 246–47.

27. I agree with this interpretation by McMaster in *Dereliction of Duty*, 62. It is an operationalization of Schelling's description of conflict as a process of communication with the enemy (*Arms and Influence*, 234–45). But Schelling was being more descriptive than prescriptive. Thies points out that although war definitely is communication, it is a type of communication where the message received by the enemy cannot be easily controlled. *When Governments Collide*, 376–89.

28. Gaddis, *Strategies of Containment*, 240–44.

29. Sharp, *Strategy for Defeat*, 86–87. These are all Admiral Sharp's personal recollections, but given his position, should be valid. McMaster, in *Dereliction of Duty*, obtained the same information from the archives and gives specific examples of where the strategic level held authority to cancel for weather (233) and to pick specific targets (250, 255, 286).

30. Herring, *America's Longest War*, 186–220.

31. Clodfelter, *Limits of Air Power*, 206–10.

32. Sharp, *Strategy for Defeat*, 270.

33. Clodfelter, *Limits of Air Power*, 203–6.

34. Mitchell, *Winged Defense*, 217. Giulio Douhet, the Italian who was probably the first and most outspoken air advocate, also came down clearly on this point, saying, "It is only when we arrive at the term 'Independent Air Force' that we perceive an entity capable of fighting on the new battlefield, where neither army nor navy can take any part. Planes operating under command of the army or navy can be considered as no more than auxiliary weapons." *Command of the Air*, 33.

35. Deptula, "Air Force Transformation."

36. Simpkin in association with Erickson, *Deep Battle*, 150–51.

37. Leonhard, *Principles of War*, 69–71.

38. Syrett, "Northwest Africa," 241–42.

39. Syrett, "Tunisian Campaign," 170–74. It also stated that the priorities for airpower would be air superiority, interdiction, and then CAS. This is the genesis of the continuing controversy between the Air Force and the Army over CAS.

40. Futrell, *United States Air Force in Korea*, 489.

41. Ibid., 492.

42. Ibid., 676.

43. Momyer, *Air Power in Three Wars*, 90–91.
44. Sbrega, "Southeast Asia," 456.
45. Harmer, "Enhancing the Operational Art," 42–43.
46. Sbrega, "Southeast Asia," 457–63.
47. Jacobs, "Battle for France, 1944," 251–75.
48. Taylor, "American Experience in the Southwest Pacific," 332–33.
49. Sherry, *Rise of American Air Power*, 219–25. See also Werrell, *Blankets of Fire*, 52–53, 102, 128.
50. Werrell, *Blankets of Fire*, 138, 151–57.
51. The *United States Strategic Bombing Surveys* may have contributed to this interpretation. This document actually covered the many facets of the war fairly well. As such, it may have given many different interests fuel for their fires. At times it extolled the virtues of strategic bombing, claiming "no nation can long survive the free exploitation of air weapons over its homeland," 110. In others, it acknowledges the importance of "air control" or railway attacks. Mierzejewski's *Collapse of the German War Economy* makes a good case that it was in fact the bombing of the German transportation system that had the greatest effect on Germany's ability to prosecute the war. Certainly, gaining air superiority was also an important factor in both the European and Pacific theaters.
52. Futrell, *United States Air Force in Korea*, 704–5.
53. Ibid., 705–6.
54. Ibid., 43–44.
55. Sbrega, "Southeast Asia," 423, 456–63, 470.
56. President Nixon, quoted in Michel, *Eleven Days of Christmas*, 55.
57. Ibid., 59–69.
58. Ibid., 185–89.
59. Chandler, *Visible Hand*, 195. "The railroad and the telegraph marched across the continent in unison" (ibid.). On the use of these instruments in the military, the consummate work is Showalter, *Railroads and Rifles*.
60. McNeill, *Pursuit of Power*, 250–53.
61. Kennett, *First Air War*, 33–34.
62. Ibid., 36–38.
63. Crawley, "How Did the Evolution of Communications," 11.
64. Wood and Dempster, *Narrow Margin*, 118–19.
65. Koprucu, "Limits of Decentralized Execution," 35–37.
66. Mark, *Aerial Interdiction*, 408. Mark contends that it was because of the lack of air superiority and the lower number of aircraft that the effectiveness of armed reconnaissance fell off sharply after WWII.
67. Werrell, *Chasing the Silver Bullet*, 19–23. There are exceptions. When the AC-130 fixed-wing gunships were developed during Vietnam, they had infrared, low-light-level television, and radio frequency sensors to aid the aircrew in detecting targets, even at night. However, these were still on-board sensors (ibid.).
68. There was an EC-121 variant called Igloo White that attempted to locate moving targets electronically, using a primitive phenomenology to monitor the Ho Chi Minh Trail for movement of people and trucks. This was probably a fore-

runner of the E-8 Joint Surveillance Target Attack Radar System (JSTARS) that will be discussed later. Lambeth, *Transformation of American Air Power*, 44.

69. Worden, *Rise of the Fighter Generals*, 236–37. See also Ehrhard, "Armed Services and Innovation," for a list of the service chiefs (24). Ehrhard calls this a *monarchic* type of organization and discusses its implications for innovation in the Air Force.

Chapter 3

The Combat Air Operations System

In reality, what has happened is that a new air-ground system has come into existence where you no longer talk in terms of one being supported and the other supporting. That would be like asking if the lungs are in support of the heart or if the heart is in support of the lungs. It's a single system.

—Vice Adm (ret.) Arthur Cebrowski
Quoted in *Army Times*, 25 Nov. 2002

Whenever a problem is too complicated to completely comprehend on the surface, you can bet it will be described as a system. Similarly, when someone says a "systems approach" or "systems thinking" is being used, that usually means the solution will include a broad spectrum of factors that would not be obvious to the casual observer.

It certainly seems that the problem at hand—the best way to manage airpower—calls for a systems approach. The argument over centralization is comparable to an onion—each time you peel away a layer, there's a fresh, new way of looking at it (illustrated in chap. 2). What looks like delegation at one level appears to be micromanagement at another. It may even be that different levels of centralization are appropriate for different situations—different wars, different missions, and different levels of technology. However, because of the interactions among such factors, an answer cannot be determined by looking at any one of them in isolation. Instead, what is required is a method that accounts for these interrelations.

A systems approach is developed in this chapter and used as a framework for providing alternatives for airpower management. Key terms are defined, and concepts—used later to help classify the historical evidence and clarify the differences between centralization and decentralization—are described. To accomplish the feedback loop that is C2, commanders have a great deal of leverage in the way they handle command relationships.

On one end of the spectrum, they can organize relationships among their subordinates and empower them to work within guidance to accomplish the mission; on the other end, they can give specific directions and constraints. Different methods affect the Combat Air Operations System in complicated ways. These impacts are frequently not anticipated because the system is often understood at only a cursory level. The four subsystems that comprise CAOS—strategic, planning, adjustment, and force application—are all influenced by the actions of key players in a policy sphere. To apply this system with a greater measure of insight requires awareness of not only the *processes*, but of also the *places* where one part affects another. Analysis of these subsystems will help establish those areas key to determining what types of authority are delegated or held, and why.

Combat Air Operations

The scope of combat air operations is too broad a category to adequately cover in this venue. Therefore, the term *combat* is used here mainly in a conventional sense. A spectrum of coercion, with deterrence on one end and brute force on the other, was previously described. The type of combat analyzed in the following cases can take place in any part of this continuum as long as the potential for purposeful violence—violence with a political end in mind—exists. These situations mainly describe the fight of one conventional, uniformed military against another to gain an advantage in a political struggle. However, at times examples of unconventional warfare, where nonuniformed insurgents struggle to change an existing political order, are also included. This analysis does not venture into the realm of the use of nuclear weapons.

In the ensuing discussion of the control of airpower, the term *airpower* includes everything that uses the air as a medium to escape the friction and geographical barriers of the earth's terrain and rapidly project influence. This encompasses weapons from the Army, Navy, Air Force, and Marines, as well as many nonlethal capabilities. In fact, airpower could be used to refer to everything that enables those air vehicles to perform, including logistics, maintenance, and ground crews. It certainly includes functions that project influence by delivering troops, supplies, information, or humanitarian aid rather than bombs.

The cases refer almost exclusively to the type of airpower that delivers destructive influence. This is not because it is more important, but because lethal force has the potential to create a bigger immediate impact in terms of its effects on the humans. That is why the issue of who should control it is so divisive. A misplaced bomb can kill the wrong people, raising questions about the competency or even intentions of those who are employing force for political ends. Principles that pertain to this most explosive form of airpower will be easier to apply to nonlethal forms of airpower than the inverse.

Effects-Based Operations

Another word for influence is *effects*. The term is used here to signify that the phenomenon in question applies to more than just destruction—it could be any type of result airpower is capable of creating. *Effects-based operations* is an expression used in the military today to describe the use of military force to produce a predictable result or impact rather than mere destruction. As will be seen later, air planners in Desert Storm were probably the first to explicitly use this type of planning. Its definition has since been clarified and expanded so that the purpose of effects-based operations is now to create a physical stimulus that starts a chain of events that, if properly planned, will eventually cross into the cognitive domain and affect the decision maker.[1]

Emphasizing effects enables leaders to specify *what* they want to happen instead of *how* it should happen. An example of the former is a commander asking subordinates to ensure that the enemy army will be unable to use external power sources for the next seven days. An instance of the latter is directing the air commander to destroy all electric power plants. Shifting the focus to results frees the air commander to determine the best way to accomplish a tasking. Because this strategy puts the onus on commanders to determine what they want to happen instead of how, some may find it difficult to adjust to this, especially if they are experts at the "how."

Command and Control

Part of the challenge of C2 is knowing when to direct and when to delegate. The US military's joint doctrine considers command "the art of motivating and directing people and organizations into action to accomplish missions."[2] It also says that control is a regulation function inherent to command, allowing a commander to delegate authority, standardize requirements, allocate resources, measure performance, and correct deviations.[3] In this light, command is the impetus, while control is the means for getting people to accomplish a given mission. Command is perceiving and deciding, whereas control is communicating the decisions, organizing to carry them out, and then monitoring and measuring performance to feed back to command. Commanders are then able to decide whether the performance is on track and adjust accordingly.[4] The entire cycle will be termed the *command and control loop.*

This C2 loop explains the essence of the doctrine of centralized control and decentralized execution. A commander (and staff) initiate this loop by specifying the *what* to subordinates. They, in turn, determine the *how*, and the commander measures and adjusts the *what* based on the results. This leads to what the military refers to as *strategy-to-task* methodology, or the art of breaking a complex strategy into progressively simpler bits until it is replaced by executable tasks. Theoretically, policy makers develop an overall strategy for a war that includes military force contributing to the overall goals of foreign policy. A military strategy specifying the military objectives and types of forces that will achieve these goals is then accomplished. Theater commanders translate strategy into plans to achieve these military objectives, including specific tasks for each type of force (land, air, sea, special operations [SO]). Finally, they delegate these tasks to lower-echelon commanders who plan and execute missions to complete the tasks. The amount of centralization is therefore related to the level of detail included in the plans at each level.

For airpower, the level of detail at a given level varies according to circumstances (as chap. 2 describes). For strategic bombing missions, the C2 loop at AAF headquarters included a great deal of information in its specification of the target and even tactics, whereas for CAS only those on scene knew target locations. In situations where subordinates need to work with others to get the information they need to accomplish a mission, there must be something else involved as part of the C2 loop.

Command Relationships

The missing piece in such circumstances is command relationships. Joint doctrine specifies several types of command relationships that can be used to define who is in charge. The commander with combatant command authority (COCOM) has complete authority over the troops, to include disciplinary actions, logistics, budgetary responsibility, and mission accomplishment. Parts of this authority may be delegated. For instance, operational control (OPCON) may be given to another commander who then has the power to organize supporting forces and accomplish the mission (without the disciplinary, budgetary, or logistics authority). A commander who has COCOM or OPCON authority may delegate tactical control (TACON) to another commander, allowing him or her to give "local direction and control of movements or maneuvers to accomplish [a] mission."[5] While these relationships involve transferring control of units, they do not relieve the delegating commander of the ultimate responsibility of accomplishing the mission.

The most common way to develop these relationships is to designate component commanders. The commander of all US forces in a theater of war is called either the joint task force (JTF) commander or JFC, or—when other nations are present—the CFC. Vested with command authority of all the forces, the JFC is authorized to organize forces as appropriate. There will, however, be service components to provide forces from each service. Usually there will also be functional components, such as air, land, maritime, or SO. The JFC then appoints a commander of each of these components, such as the JFACC, joint force land component commander (JFLCC), and so forth.[6] While the service components provide the forces, the JFC normally gives OPCON to the functional component commanders who determine the missions those forces will accomplish. (Fig. 1 shows these relationships as well as how the JFC may organize other subordinate JTFs for special purposes.)

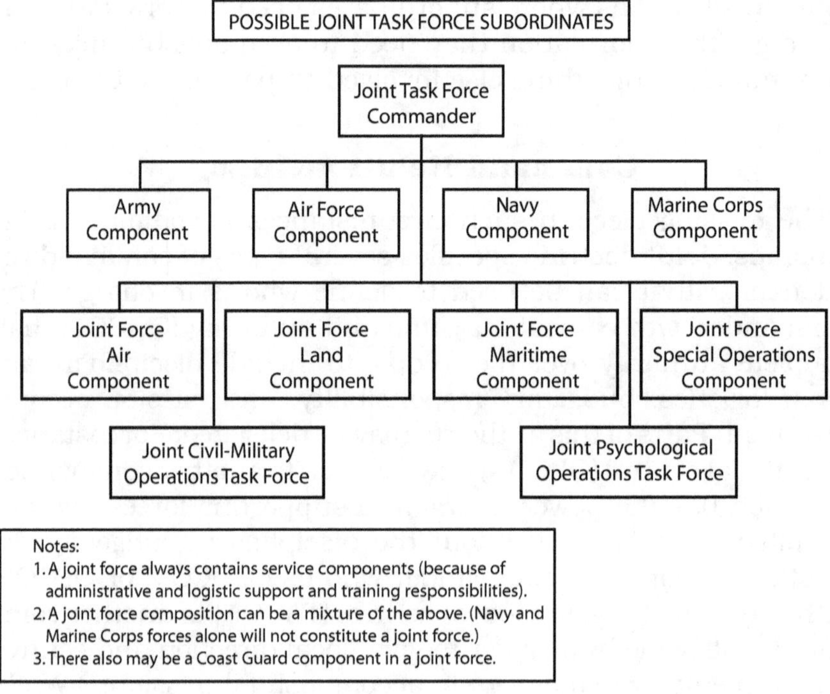

Fig. 1. Typical subordinate commanders under the JFC. (Reprinted from JP 5-00.2, *Joint Task Force Planning Guidance and Procedures*, 13 Jan. 1999.)

The relationship not shown in figure 1 is that of the JFC's staff to the component commanders. Typically, the JFC will have a staff consisting of six different areas along with some special advisors. The six primary areas are called J-1 through J-6, and each has the responsibility to support the JFC in one particular area (e.g., intelligence for J-2, operations for J-3, and plans for J-5). Thus, the authority of these staff organizations can sometimes become confused with the authority of the subordinate component commanders.

The COCOM, OPCON, and TACON labels most often deal with a superior-subordinate relationship. To varying extents, these relationships give a commander the ability to directly specify how the subordinates are to act. The JFACC does this through an air tasking order (ATO)—it is an "order" that tells the aircrews where and when to fly, what weapons to employ, and how to communicate. Since the job of making sure the aircraft can communicate, can get refueled, and do not run into each other is so important and complicated for large operations, JFACCs have tried to include everything that flies in a single ATO to ensure everything is coordinated. The other services, however, do not relish the prospect of allowing the JFACC (who is usually an Air Force officer) to command their forces. They have therefore been reluctant to give the JFACC command authority (OPCON or TACON) over specific forces. Everything that flies must be in the ATO; but although this is an order, not everything in the ATO is technically under the command of the JFACC.

This points out an important difference between the types of commanders who can maintain C2 of land versus air forces. In land combat the forces under a commander generally fight together, and the commander is responsible for maintaining C2. The commander integrates the subordinate units, each of which carries out a portion of the mission under the C2 of their respective commanders. Thus, the JFLCC develops the land component plan and gives each corps a part of it. The corps commanders develop a plan to accomplish their part of the overall plan and give each division a part in it, and so forth. But in air war, the commanders under the JFACC do not exercise C2 of a portion of the mission. For one thing, aircraft from different organizations will find themselves working together. One mission may demand a mix of fighters, tankers, and electronic jammers, while the next mission may demand a mix of fighters and bombers. There are not enough resources to ensure each wing has enough of everything to do every job imaginable.

The main reason lower-echelon air commanders cannot command and control airpower is that they lack the capability to do so. Tracking and directing aircraft with today's range and speed requires sophisticated technology. The Air Force maintains the theater air control system (TACS) for this purpose. The AOC is the "senior element" of the TACS, responsible for ensuring that the aircraft follow the constraints developed by the plans subsystem. The TACS also includes organizations in close contact with ground units to request and coordinate air support for ground forces' activities: the air support operations center (ASOC) and tactical air control parties (TACP). Ground-based radars (the control and reporting centers or elements) that work with other air defense assets to protect friendly airspace from air attack also comprise the TACS. Additionally, there are airborne elements of the TACS to provide information—intelligence, surveillance, and reconnaissance (ISR)—and on-scene airspace control. These include the Airborne Warning and Control System (AWACS),

Joint Surveillance Target Attack Radar System (JSTARS), ABCCC (now decommissioned), and FAC(A)s.[7] The TACS is the Air Force's portion of the theater air ground system that includes similar pieces from the Army, Navy, and Marines. While ground commanders can delegate authority to increasingly lower-echelon commanders, when the same authority is to be passed for air combat, it must be passed down from the JFACC to elements of the TACS. However, none of these elements command the assets they control, which is why Air Force doctrine talks about control and not command.

Another command relationship is that of *support.* A commander can designate one subordinate commander the *supported* and another as the *supporting* commander whenever one type of force should aid, complement, protect, or sustain another. In this relationship, the supported commander determines what type of assistance is necessary, but the supporting commander determines how to provide this assistance with the forces under his or her command. The supported commander provides general direction of the effort, whereas the supporting commander determines procedures, tactics, forces, and communications to carry it out.[8] For example, CAS is a type of support relationship in which air forces are supporting ground forces. Ground commanders determine how much support they need and where, and the JFACC provides the aircraft and the C2 of those aircraft through the ground portion of the TACS.[9]

Leveraging and Depth of Command Relationships

Through these command relationships, the JFC can adapt the hierarchical organization of the forces and arrange them to work together to do whatever the situation requires.[10] This "leveraging" of command relationships to make them more useful and effective is one way the JFC can strike the balance between allowing subordinates the freedom to innovate and maintaining a coherent strategy. But leveraging, or organizing, command relationships to effect specific actions takes significant attention to these relationships. The JFC must create a sufficient "depth" of command relationships so that there is clear unity of effort at all times.

This depth is needed because the military is a human organization. People create organizations to accomplish complex tasks by dividing them into smaller, more specialized tasks. They then develop a subdivision for each specialized task, and the subdivisions routinize these specialized tasks as much as possible. In this way, organizations attempt to replace uncertainty with stable relationships and standard operating procedures (SOP).[11] The military services were created to deal with the different environments in which wars would be fought. They then created further subdivisions to develop equipment and train people to accomplish the tasks in those environments. Thus, an A-10 pilot and a tank commander are trained and equipped to accomplish different tasks. If only all these subdivisions could "stay in their lanes" and remain isolated and pure, the control problem would be more tractable. However, the tasks are often put together to accomplish a single mission.

Not all missions require the parts to work together to the same degree. Theorist Karl Weick used educational systems to demonstrate that organizations are, to a greater or lesser extent, loosely coupled. If an organization were a machine, where each moving part directly affects another and predictably causes some action, the results would be relatively easy to design. But in loosely coupled organizations, although events are responsive to some degree, they also maintain their own identity. That is, although actions by one part of the organization may have some effect on another part, the parts also act somewhat independently.[12] According to Weick, there are actually many advantages to this loose coupling, including localized sensing, adaptation, and the ability to "seal off" a breakdown.[13]

Charles Perrow picked up on this concept and uses it to describe the degree of centralization that is appropriate for each system. He proposes that linear, tightly coupled systems are best centralized—operators must adhere to strict standards, or their output will affect the other parts of the system.[14] Complex, loosely coupled systems are best decentralized—any attempt to control them centrally may result in missed opportunity for operators to innovate and adapt when unexpected or unintended interactions occur. Since the systems are loosely coupled, this local innovation does not significantly affect other parts of the system. However, complex, tightly coupled systems are a problem. Their complexity begs for decentralization to make adjustments when unintended interactions occur. At the same time, because they are tightly coupled, the local innovation allowed by this decentralization greatly affects the other parts of the system—the only cure for this is centralized control. Perrow notes that a system cannot be both centralized and decentralized at the same time, although many have some type of hybrid arrangement that asks operators to perform with autonomy but be responsive to overriding.[15]

Only with sufficient depth of command relationships can the system exhibit the type of flexibility Perrow describes. Adequate depth of command relationships means that when these different parts come together to accomplish a mission, there will be a control node capable of coordinating their actions so they will be working toward the same goals. This node must have the situational awareness to know what is happening with the parts and the authority to direct them—or to allow them autonomy, as required. Achieving this depth therefore helps to leverage command relationships to achieve both capability and adaptability.

Constraints on Specific Actions and Time-Sensitive Targets

Leveraging command relationships is not the only way to control military actions. There are other more direct methods—commanders can put constraints on specific actions, telling the military what actions it can or cannot take. The ROEs are one way that commanders can do this, as these rules specify when and in what conditions troops can use force. The president, SecDef, and commanders use ROEs to impose not only legal but also practical and political limitations on the use of force, as well.[16] When airpower is involved, another way the JFC or policy makers can put constraints on specific actions is by withholding the authority to approve targets.

Newer technology gives commanders another option: giving direction during ongoing operations. Instead of letting forces perform their missions in accordance with the preplanned constraints, they can make decisions during the performance of the missions. The TACS routinely performs a certain amount of this real-time direction because air traffic control is a normal part of airpower. But during the period of this study, air commanders have gotten increasingly involved in directing ongoing missions by specifying the targets while the aircraft are airborne. These targets are referred to by several names. Because they emerge in response to battle actions or timely intelligence, they are at first called *emerging targets*. Then, upon identification, if the JFC makes the determination that a target must be attacked during a certain window of vulnerability (not necessarily immediately), it becomes a TST.[17] General Franks, the JFC in Operation Iraqi Freedom, specified what types of targets would be considered TSTs. Other emerging targets that were considered urgent to the air component, even though they did not fall into any of the TST categories, were known as *dynamic targets*.[18]

The CAOS as a System

Technology that allows hierarchical levels to interact, then, has been added to organizations that cannot "stay in their lanes." The result, as Admiral Cebrowski is quoted in the beginning epigraph, is a system.

The word *system* has to qualify as one of the most overused terms in the English language. It is often used to refer to a bunch of things that seem to work together, especially if the way they work together is not completely understood. Therefore, it is deemed appropriate to talk of an economic, political, or distribution "system," even though the speaker would usually be hard-pressed to define what is included in such systems, much less how they work. Still, systems thinking and the systems approach are becoming accepted as valid academic pursuits as they are shown applicable to a greater variety of problems.

Systems thinkers generally agree that there are valid reasons to group things together when they may not otherwise be seen as a single unit. The classical reductionist analytical approach is to break single units apart into components, analyze their functions, and then piece these functions together to ascertain the performance of the whole. The approach has worked well for many of the physical sciences when there are parts that have a mechanistic performance that obey rules. It even works for some complex systems—as long as it is the "unorganized complexity" of many somewhat randomly acting parts and can therefore be analyzed using probabilistic principles. But when the parts interact it is usually futile to use such linear methods, which assume that the behavior of the whole is the sum of the behaviors of the parts.

These are cases of "organized complexity," commonly found in systems where humans interact.[19] The type of system we are interested in is "a set of interacting components having well-defined (although possibly not well-understood) behavior or purpose; the concept is subjective in that what a system is to one person may not appear to be a system to another."[20]

Typical depictions of the CAOS and its processes tend to downplay the interactions of these components. For example, figure 2 represents the system as a hierarchically structured one, where guidance from one level is broken down into more detailed plans and tasks at the next—the strategy-to-task methodology referred to earlier. The CAOS is driven by the strategy-to-task methodology, but there are many places where the players deviate from this hierarchical process. CAOS can be better understood when the occurrences of these interactions are depicted.

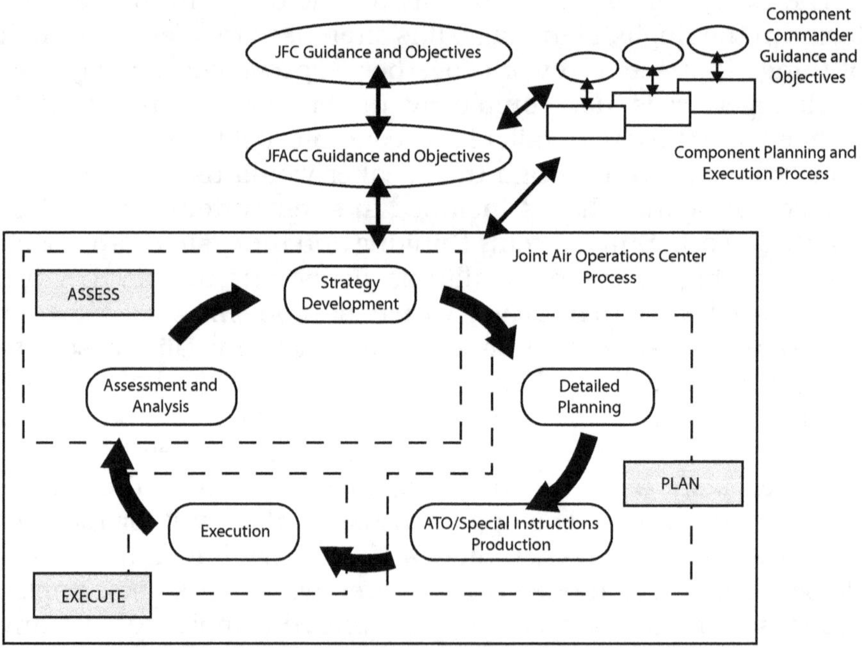

Fig. 2. The aerospace assessment, planning, and execution process—non-CLIOS representation. (Reprinted from Air Force Doctrine Document 2, *Organization and Employment of Aerospace Power*, 17 Feb. 2000, 74.)

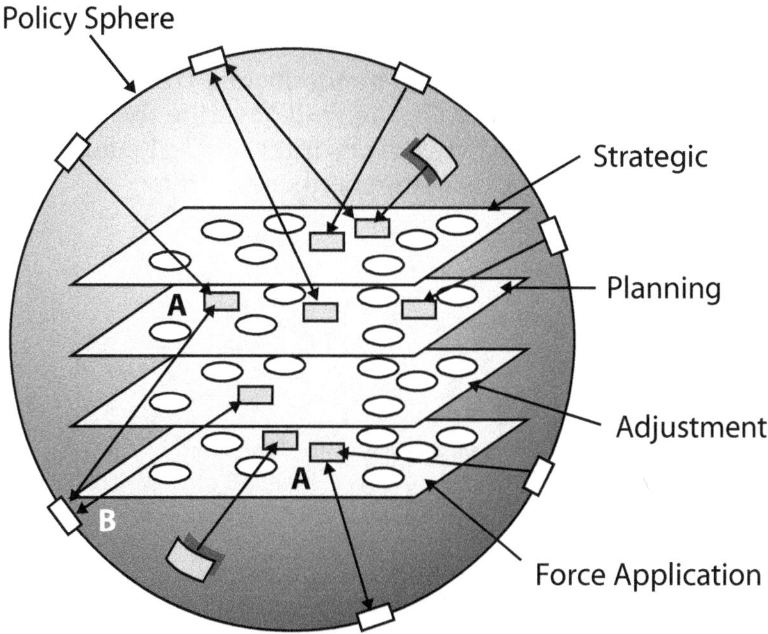

Fig. 3. CLIOS diagram of subsystems in policy sphere. (Reprinted from Rebecca S. Dodder, Joseph M. Sussman, and Joshua B. McConnell, "Concept of the 'CLIOS Process': Integrating the Study of Physical and Policy Systems Using Mexico City as an Example." Paper presented to the Massachusetts Institute of Technology [MIT] Engineering Systems Symposium, Cambridge, MA, 31 Mar. 2004.)

In its simplest form, the CAOS looks like the diagram in figure 3—four subsystems in a policy sphere. The historical look at airpower in chapter 2 shows that the system that employs and controls airpower includes a politico-military strategic layer that is affected by public opinion, the media, and other governments. It encompasses a theater-level military layer where the different services and components have different ideas about how to manage and use airpower. The CAOS also includes a layer, built around the TACS, that actively regulates, tracks, directs, and otherwise exchanges information with airpower during operations. And of course, it also contains the actual application of operational effects. Since all of these factors influence the control of airpower, they must be considered in the system analysis. These factors are referred to here as the strategic, planning, adjustment, and force-application subsystems.

The concept of representing systems this way is from the complex, large-scale, integrated, open system framework developed by Joseph Sussman, a specialist in intelligent transportation systems at MIT. The rest of the chapter will describe the makeup of the subsystems and show where they interact.[21] The following symbology is used to describe components and links:

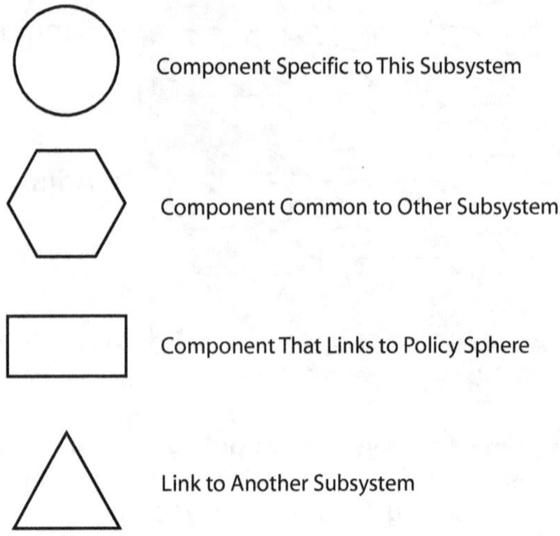

Fig. 4. Symbology for subsystem CLIOS diagrams

The CAOS Policy Sphere

Many of the players who can influence the system by setting policy—the "policy sphere"—have been previously identified. Obviously, the president of the United States, his SecDef, and the JCS are important players, and there will be other offices such as the secretary of state, some cabinet members, and the national security advisor also involved. Congress not only has a definite, constitutional role but also has an indirect role. Pursuant to the Goldwater-Nichols Act of 1986, it was clear there would be an overall JFC who would direct functional component commanders for the land, sea, air, and others. The JFC may also have charge of service component commanders as well as smaller task forces under the joint force for accomplishing specialized parts of the mission, depending on the type of conflict.[22] There will probably be other countries in a coalition with the United States, so their forces and governments are important players, and, of course, there will be an enemy organization (which could be any type of political entity, such as a government or terrorist organization) and its military forces. This study has also illuminated several other indirect players, to include the media, the people of the United States, and coalition countries. Based on the concern given to avoidance of collateral damage, those who could potentially support the enemy organization and the noncombatants in the combat zone are important players as well.

The results of this analysis should have several significant consequences. First, they should show these policy-sphere players the trade-offs involved with the policies they set. Second, they should identify the areas where these players have the option to intervene in the control of combat airpower. Finally, the findings here should illustrate to policy makers the consequences of intervening in specific ways.

The Subsystems

Thus far, this study has not demonstrated the means to graphically represent the structure of the subsystems that make up the CAOS. The following presents such a depiction for each of the subsystems in order to help clarify the function of and interplay within these systems. The ultimate goal is to bring these concepts from an abstract to a practicable level.

The Strategic Subsystem. The organizations that operate in the system are subject to control by the strategic level, either directly or through feedback loops that indirectly influence their actions. (Fig. 5 shows a diagram of the strategic subsystem.) Policy makers use military force as part of a grand strategy for achieving strategic objectives. Normally, the overall military strategy is developed by the NSC—composed of at least the president, the SecDef, the secretary of state, the Central Intelligence Agency (CIA), the national security advisor, and the Chairman of the Joint Chiefs of Staff (CJCS).[23] To achieve their goals they also use other instruments of power, such as diplomatic and economic tools, which are not dealt with here. The JCS and the JFC then develop

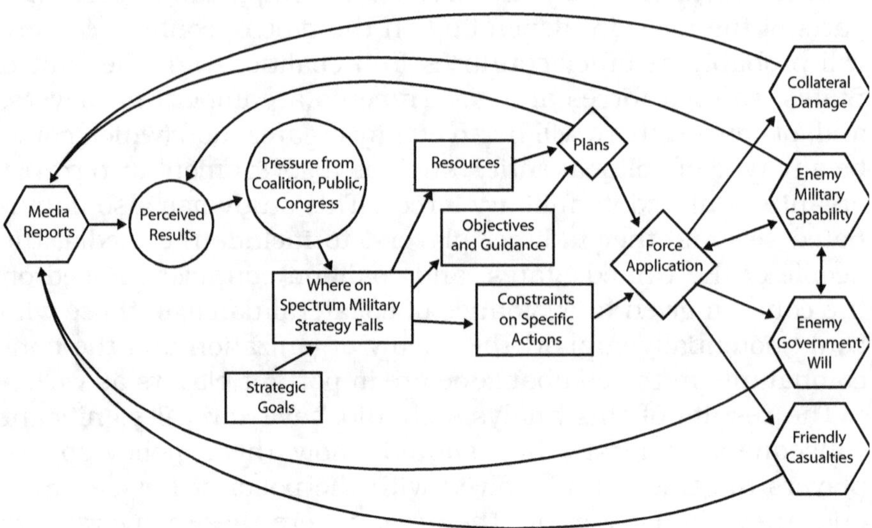

Fig. 5. Strategic subsystem

a plan to use available resources to achieve the strategic objectives within that military strategy.[24] It would be far simpler for the military if it were told to destroy the opposing army, no matter the cost. But the coercive bargaining process brings up restrictions on the military's actions. This is because—in addition to the actual objective for which it is using military force—the government may have to worry about pressures of coalition support, the support of its own people, and even internal solidarity among its branches and political parties.[25]

The degree to which the government has worried about these pressures relative to its strategic goals has played a big part in where, along the spectrum of coercion, military strategy has fallen in the past. In WWII, when the United States had been attacked and Allied partners were fighting for their survival, the strategy was near the brute force end of the spectrum. In Vietnam, where the American public arguably lost track of why we were fighting and the United States was worried about potential involvement from China and the USSR, the strategy was much more calibrated.

As discussed above, policy makers can use varying degrees of two basic methods of control. They can either give the military objectives and guidance and allocate resources, letting the theater commanders determine the best way to use them, or they can put constraints on specific actions when these actions might intensify pressures internal or external to the government. As is seen from figure 4, the difference is in the directness with which these two routes affect military actions. When policy makers simply give objectives and guidance, they are allowing the military's plans subsystem considerable leeway to define how military actions will interpret the guidance and achieve the objectives. This study demonstrates that this leaves room for SOPs and internal agendas to produce results that may be harmful to the strategy.

Furthermore, policy makers may find themselves under time pressures that disqualify normal military channels. Military force produces effects on the enemy's military and government; but it also inevitably leads to friendly casualties and collateral damage—innocent people sometimes get killed. The plans subsystem has provisions for assessing results so that policy makers can determine how well the strategy is working. The news media, however, with the ability to produce an almost immediate feedback of some of the more spectacular results, often shapes the perceptions that drive the pressures described above, and so is a forceful intervening factor. The information is generally reflective of facts—or at least official debate about facts—so the problem is not necessarily that the media changes the debate. The problem for decision makers is that the media essentially becomes an amplifier that can shorten decision cycles by raising the gain in one particular feedback loop over another.[26] Thus, we will see that policy makers often feel pressure to increase the amount of specific constraints to show they are trying to reverse any adverse results.

Plans Subsystem. In the plans subsystem, the military translates the strategy developed from the strategic subsystem into plans for military action. For airpower, this means apportioning the available aircraft to the different tasks, developing target lists, scheduling the missions, and developing the procedures and constraints that allow the TACS to control the flow of aircraft.

The diagram in figure 2 is not a CLIOS diagram but does depict the process that forms a foundation for the way the CAOS performs. The bulk of this process takes place in the air and space operations center, which is organized in divisions that focus on the different parts of the cycle.[27] The AOC usually resides in a single building, although the Air Force is moving toward being able to perform these tasks in a distributed manner as well.[28] The diagram is based on the strategy-to-task methodology. The JFC gives guidance and objectives to the component commanders who break this down into guidance and objectives for their components.[29] The JFACC's strategy division develops a daily air operations directive that spells out the JFC's guidance, breaking it down into objectives, tasks, and, ultimately, targets to accomplish those tasks.[30] Each component gives input on the targets they would like attacked, and the JFC convenes a joint targeting coordination board (JTCB) to prioritize these and come up with a final list of targets. The JFC can determine who runs this JTCB and the extent of its authority.[31]

The air component takes the list of targets, called a joint integrated prioritized target list (JIPTL), and does some detailed planning to attack the targets. During this process, it also tries to determine what other tasks airpower will be called on to perform besides attacking these targets. Some examples could be mobility missions for supply, movement of troops, or humanitarian aid. Planners also try to anticipate the need to react to the enemy as the battle unfolds. The AOC is organized to include liaisons to the Army, Navy, Marines, and SO, respectively, the battlefield coordination detachment (BCD), the naval and amphibious liaison element, the Marine liaison office, and the SO liaison element.[32] Together with these liaisons, the air component planners try to earmark enough missions to support the other components, including CAS. Recent wars demonstrate that they have also started allocating missions to attack time-sensitive or dynamic targets. They also plan to send ISR sensors to look for the emerging targets.[33]

An ATO that gives the details of the missions that the aircraft will fly is the end result of planning. Missions can be extremely detailed, with target locations, times, and munitions. But when the aircraft are tasked to support dynamic targeting, the mission will be less detailed. The ATO also contains constraints for the missions, such as ROEs, airspace control instructions, and other special instructions. The air component convenes an ROEs board to develop air-operations rules to supplement the ones from higher levels, refining them for each new phase of combat.[34] An airspace control order (ACO) gives the procedures for maintaining the flow of aircraft safely.[35]

The AOC subsequently monitors the execution of the ATO and makes any changes that occur based on the operations. The sensors from the ISR sorties and any ground troops (including SO) alert them to emerging opportunities and return pictures or reports of battle damage to the AOC. The AOC performs *combat assessment* to see how the attacks affected the enemy's forces and plans and whether there are any exploitable opportunities. It also performs *operational assessment* to determine how successful the overall campaign has been and whether the strategy should be adjusted.[36]

Figure 6 shows a CLIOS representation of the plans subsystem. The next five chapters show what happens when strategic decision makers and the JFC use varying levels of constraints. Constraints from the strategic subsystem raise the level of accountability for specific results at the JFC's level, resulting in the retention of authority for targeting and C2 with the JFC's staff. The air component is not empowered—and often not fully exercised to the extent of its capabilities—and does not integrate as well with the other components. The reduced empowerment and the centralized C2 lead to a lack of depth in the command relationships. Furthermore, constraints on specific actions hamper the use of effects-based operations and strategy-to-task that the air component prefers, often leading it to focus on ongoing missions rather than longer-term strategy. Certainly, this focus is also a result of the need and increasing capability to pull information together to react to the enemy as the battle progresses. Since the increase in dynamic missions has made it more difficult to assess the results, this, in turn, makes it more likely the strategic subsystem will want to use constraints on specific actions.

Adjustment Subsystem. Planning and coordinating occur simultaneously with operations. But there is also a need to adjust during the operations. When the aircraft execute the sorties designated in the ATO, many real-time adjustments have to be made. With thousands of sorties happening at the same time, it takes a sophisticated system to perform this function; this is the TACS that we discussed earlier. Because sensor-communication loops are such an important part of the issue, the ISR sensors will be considered a part of this same subsystem. Thus, the ad-

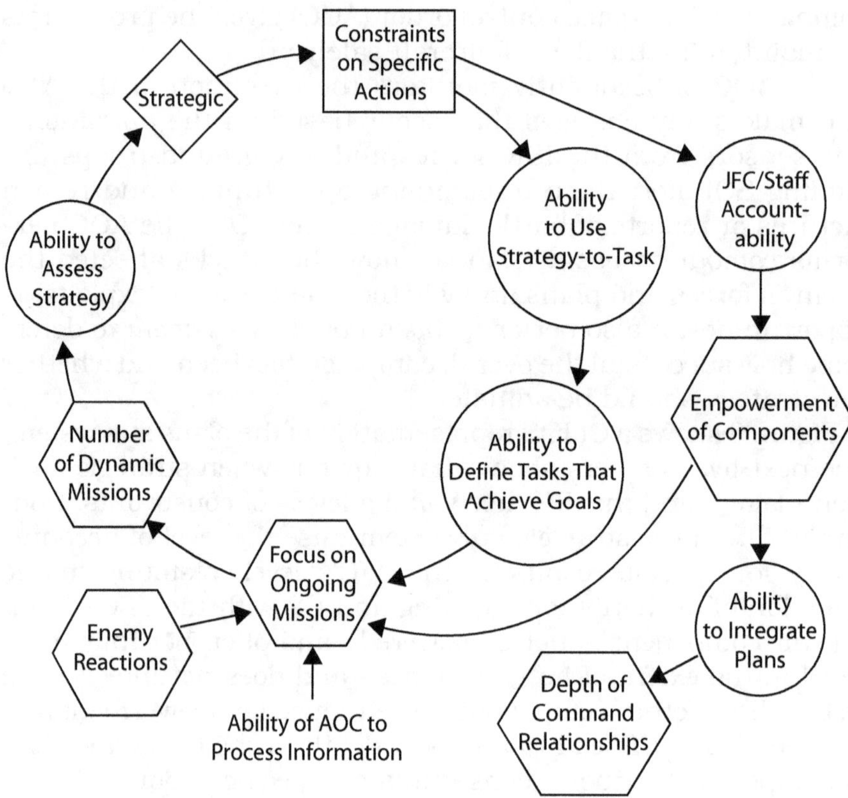

Fig. 6. Plans subsystem

justment subsystem helps to ensure that the aircraft perform the missions as ordered in the ATO and to guide the aircraft through the procedural airspace controls. It also gathers information to help react to the battle and assess the results. Figure 7 depicts the CLIOS diagram for the adjustment subsystem.

The next five chapters demonstrate that the performance of the adjustment subsystem is dependent on the depth of the command relationships developed in the plans subsystem. Adjustment aims at achieving the balance between quickly getting weapons to targets—including emerging targets—while ensuring these targets contribute to strategy and do not derail it. In this subsystem, rapid weapons delivery deals with the ability to shorten the

OODA loop—a C2 paradigm covered later. To support strategy alignment, the adjustment subsystem coordinates with decision makers as rapidly as possible and tries to engage the targets as precisely as possible. Consequently, the two concrete factors those in this subsystem end up balancing are speed (the OODA loop) and precision—the two hexagons at the bottom of figure 7.

To balance these two elements, the people in this subsystem need to find targets, get the weapons to the targets, and get approval to engage them. Finding the targets and getting approval to engage have been aided tremendously by technology. The JFC and component commanders do have to make sure the right sensors are available, including humans in contact with the enemy when appropriate. This depends on the environment and the enemy. But sensor and communications technology has increased the ability of sensor-communication loops to find these targets and get the information into the hands of the AOC. Collaboration technology has increased the ability of the people in the AOC to get approval. Of course, it is still much quicker to get consent when the approval level is close to the AOC than when the JFC or even SecDef are involved.

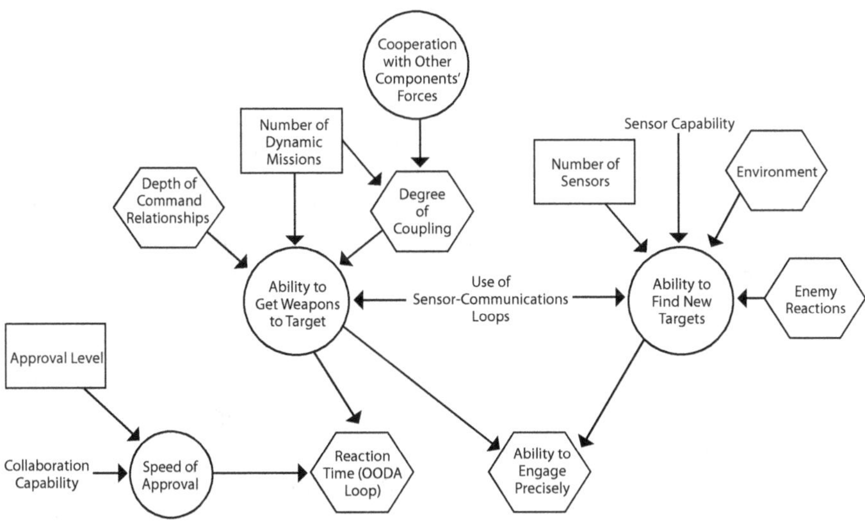

Fig. 7. Adjustment subsystem

Getting the weapons to the target is often complicated. It will be seen that in some cases, where the situation is loosely coupled, the depth of command relationships does not matter. All that is necessary is to get information on the target and feed it to a GPS-guided weapon. The trouble is that the ease with which this occurs can cause component commanders to think it is not necessary to provide the same depth of command relationships they normally would. They may not set up certain command nodes, like the ASOC, because the ground controllers and aircrew can coordinate directly. Then, when the situation becomes more tightly coupled, the people near the action need the resources to be allocated smoothly and automatically. If every request for support triggers an ad hoc solution and an approval chain, this will not happen. It only happens if the command relationships are so deep that there are command nodes at low levels with the situational awareness and the authority to make these decisions quickly and in accordance with preplanned procedures. It takes more than information sharing to perform this kind of resource allocation among disparate entities—it takes authority and information together with the ability to communicate.

The degree of coupling can be a function of environmental factors or the enemy's reactions, but it can also be influenced by the interaction among dynamic players. When there is much coordination among different components and many dynamic missions looking for new targets, there will be tight coupling. The actions of any one player could drastically affect those of the others because the airspace is crowded, and the actions of the aircrews must be coordinated with those of the ground troops. The fewer dynamic players and the less coordination, the less the players' actions depend on each other and the looser the coupling. On one hand, having many dynamic missions helps get the weapons to the target; on the other hand, it also increases the degree to which people's actions depend on each other (coupling) and makes the adjustment more complex.

Force-Application Subsystem. Air Force doctrine cites centralized control and decentralized execution as fundamental to the proper employment of air and space power, as shown in chapter 2. No one sitting hundreds or thousands of miles from the battlespace is supposed to tell the person in the cockpit how to fly his or her airplane. Supposedly, doing so could hamper the accomplishment of the current mission and stifle any initiative on the pilot's part for future missions. Yet many tactical actions are now the result of information passed from remote decision makers, and this will become increasingly automatic in the future. Consequently, it is important to examine the force-application subsystem to see what effects control has on the tactical level.

Planners at the AOC send the ATO to air bases all over the theater. Here Airmen in a wing operations center (WOC) review the individual missions and do the detailed planning aircrews will need to fly the missions. They extract all the applicable target data, procedures, frequencies, and other instructions for each mission assigned to aircraft from the wing. Mission planners also get intelligence about the threats in the area to help plan the routes to and from the target; coordinate with tankers, electronic warfare aircraft, or other support; and get the weather reports for the mission time. The aircrews who will fly the missions come in a couple of hours before the takeoff time, get briefed on the mission, study the data provided for them, and do last-minute preparations.[37] Finally, the aircrews take off to fly the missions. If they are flying a mission to a preplanned target, they can fly the mission as planned, guided by the TACS to ensure proper flow through the airspace. But on dynamic missions, aircrews are often dependent on the TACS for information on new targets as well.

The next five chapters show that the evolution of these sensor-communication loops to perform dynamic missions has in some cases reduced the role of the aircrew in the attack sequence. With GPS-guided munitions like the Joint Direct Attack Munition (JDAM), it is often possible for an aircrew to drop a weapon at night or through bad weather based only on coordinates they receive over the radio or data link. Instead of having to find the target visually and then aim the weapon at the target by maneuvering the aircraft or pointing a laser beam, the aircrew just needs to fly to an area within the weapon's envelope and "pickle" (press the switch to release the weapon). This dynamic mission puts demands on the aircrew to adjust routes, frequencies, and threats without the ability to preplan.[38] But much of the job of finding, fixing, targeting, tracking, engaging, and assessing (the kill chain) is done by people in remote places.

The force-application CLIOS diagram (fig. 8) shows a resulting tension between the ability to engage targets precisely and the potential for accidents in the CAOS. What this really means is that the types of controls leaders use to ensure precision engagement of targets can also contribute to the potential to cause friendly fire or collateral damage. The very things that increase precision—the use of sensor-communication loops and weapons like JDAMs that take information in digital form—also distribute the tasks performed in the attack sequence or kill chain. The role of the strike aircrews is reduced (except in the attack sequence where their workload increases in some respects) and makes the interactions more complex, involving distributed teams. The ability of the aircrews to perform information gathering has also increased this complexity—now many aircraft are sensor platforms as well as strike platforms. At the same time, the increase in the number of dynamic missions means there is more adjustment during the missions. More complex interactions made in real time increases the tendency to drift from global procedures because of the inconvenience these inevitably bring. When the CAOS is loosely coupled, there are often no consequences for this drift; in fact, the convenience of the locally adapted procedures gives people incentives to ignore the global procedures. Then, when the CAOS becomes tightly coupled, there is significant potential for accidents. This is based on Scott Snook's theory of practical drift—deviating from rules and procedures due to inconvenience and impracticality when performing day-to-day activities—evidence of which is illustrated later.

For example, pilots who had flown in Vietnam and then worked in the TACC during Desert Storm took pains to allow as much freedom at the tactical level as possible. They had grown disillusioned as planners in Saigon levied what the pilots thought were unreasonable constraints on them, until pretty soon they had lost confidence in their leadership and refused in many cases to follow some of the direction they received.[39] Another problem that occurs with a high level of constraints is that pilots may feel the need to get permission before taking any action, whether it is allowed by the constraints or not. When this occurs, as it did in

Kosovo, pilots lose their ability to innovate and react rapidly to new developments.[40]

The cure for this balance is again found in the depth of command relationships. If the command relationships are sufficiently deep, command nodes exist at a low enough level to affect the actions of the aircrew more directly. This does not mean the aircrews are always under the direction of the command nodes. With such depth, the aircrew can be intentionally given discretion to act on their own when there is low risk of collateral damage or friendly fire. Where this discretion is not appropriate, the command node is in proximity to the force applicators with the authority to direct the action. This intentional delegation is only possible when there is a commander with the situational awareness to do it. We will see examples where the different actors at the force-application level were able to innovate in loosely coupled times but lacked a commander who could step in to direct them when the action got intense.

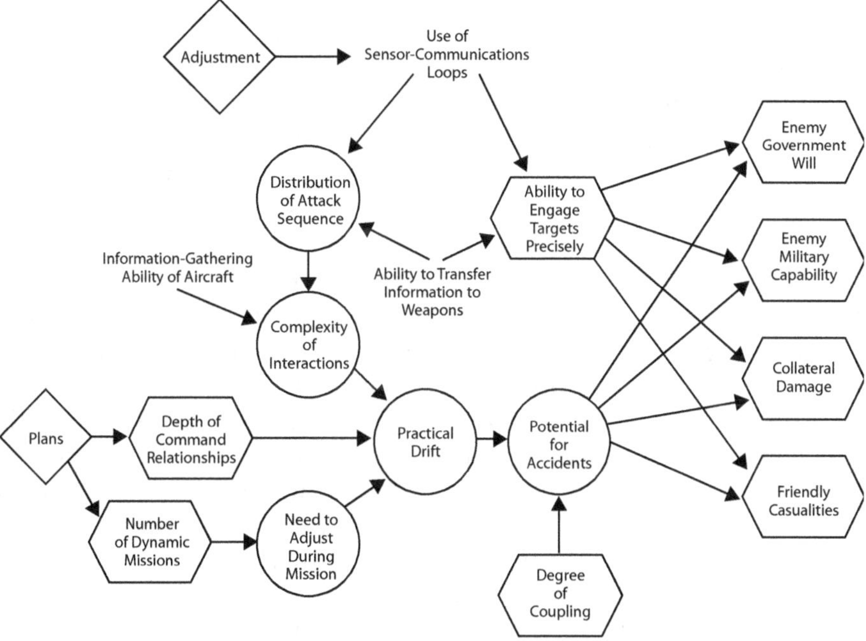

Fig. 8. Force-application subsystem

Conclusions

The CLIOS analysis suggests several significant issues, which the following chapters examine in detail, using historical evidence. At the strategic level, the dominant issue is the extent to which policy makers should levy constraints on specific actions. The quest to understand the trade-offs involved in centralized and decentralized control starts here, by analyzing what causes policy makers to opt for either more or less specific constraints. These choices have short- and long-term consequences for the CAOS. Clearly, the short-term consequences are that, by using specific constraints like ROEs and approval of targets, policy makers gain the ability to more directly affect military actions. Some of the long-term consequences need to be assessed as well.

One long-term result of putting specific constraints on the theater level is that the CAOS may have evolved in response to the technology and policy choices made at this level. It appears policy makers may start a chain of events in the other subsystems affecting the degree to which the JFC can empower component commanders. Their choices affect the way the JFC develops command relationships. In particular, it appears the more the strategic level uses constraints on specific actions, the less authority the JFC delegates to the air component. In turn, the amount of authority the JFC delegates to the air component in developing the airpower targeting strategy affects how well it is able to integrate with the other components.

Another consequence of a commander levying more constraints at this point is that it becomes harder to assess plans and strategy. Developments in technology have made it easier to get and process information from the battlespace in command centers. However, the CAOS diagrams suggest that this has not made it easier to assess and adjust strategy. Specific constraints lead to a focus on specific (ongoing) actions, and the air component has consequently developed the ability to intervene in these actions more so than the ability to assess their results in the aggregate.

The capability to intervene in these actions has also become more important to achieving the overall mission. The politically sensitive missions the air component has been asked to perform require a combination of speed and precision. The air component has attempted to achieve this balance by increasing the use of sensor-communication loops to find the targets and get the information to the weapons. In the meantime, they have had to develop collaboration to get approval to attack the targets they find emerging on the battlefield.

Finally, the development of sensor-communication loops and weapons that use digital information has distributed the tasks involved in the attack sequence, or kill chain. The resulting complexity of interactions leaves the door open to practical drift, which can potentially lead to accidents.

Two dominant threads emerge throughout this analysis. The first is that the extent to which the players in the CAOS need to and are able to conform to centralized direction depends heavily on the degree of coupling in their area at the time. This explains chapter 2's conclusion that there have often been different degrees of centralization at the same time in different places or in the same place at different times. The second is that the extent to which military commanders can establish depth in their command relationships determines their ability to leverage these relationships and strike the balance between precision and flexibility. Defining relationships, instead of specific actions, at all levels gives commanders the ability to delegate authority and still hold people accountable. As the interactions among participants become increasingly complex so that, as Admiral Cebrowsky puts it, you can "no longer talk about one being supported and the other supporting," achieving this depth will mean ensuring there is always someone who has sufficient authority as well as superior situational awareness to be able to integrate these forces.

Notes

(For interviews by the author for which there is no formal documentation, the full citations are given in the endnotes and are not included in the bibliography. For interviews by the author with transcripts or recordings, the shortened note form is given in the endnotes, and the full citation is included in the bibliography.)

1. Smith, *Effects Based Operations*, 304.
2. JP 3-0, *Doctrine for Joint Operations*, II-17.
3. Ibid., II-18–II-19.

4. Holley, "Command, Control, and Technology," 268–69.

5. JP 0-2, *Unified Action Armed Forces*, III-2.

6. JP 3-0, *Doctrine for Joint Operations*, II-15–II-17.

7. Air Force Policy Directive 13-1, *Theater Air Control System*, 1-2.

8. Ibid., III-9.

9. Certainly, the Army and Marines each have their own aircraft to support some of their CAS requirements. The Marines, in particular, maintain a robust CAS capability because they consider aircraft to be an integral part of their combined arms doctrine. Marine commanders are therefore reluctant to give the JFACC control of Marine sorties and will only give control of those sorties in excess of what the commander thinks he will need. As will be seen, JFACCs have responded by allowing them this leeway and shifting most of the other CAS to Army areas.

10. JP 3-0, *Doctrine for Joint Operations*, II-6.

11. Wilson, *Bureaucracy*, 221. This is obviously a very rational view of organizations; many are much more loosely coupled, where goals are not necessarily top-down directed but negotiated. Weick, *Sensemaking in Organizations*, 70.

12. Weick, "Educational Organizations," 1–3.

13. Ibid., 6–7.

14. Perrow, *Normal Accidents*, 78. We are not concentrating on defining complex versus linear interactions, as Perrow did. He notes that these terms are not opposites, although his usage seems to denote such a relationship. His purpose is to describe the degree to which a sequence of events can be understood and predicted, based on the perceived interactions in the system. Nonlinear and simple did not seem to apply to these characteristics.

15. Ibid., 332–34.

16. Air Force Operational Tactics, Techniques, and Procedures (AFOTTP) 2-3.2, *Air and Space Operations Center*, 219. The ROEs have been called "the tether between the SECDEF and the soldier (ibid.)."

17. Joint Forces Command, *Commander's Handbook*, I-1–I-3.

18. Moseley, *Operation Iraqi Freedom*, 9.

19. Bertalanffy, *General System Theory*, 18–19, 34–35.

20. Magee and de Weck, "Attempt at Complex System Classification," 4.

21. Dodder, Sussman, and McConnell, "Concept of the 'CLIOS Process,'" 2–5.

22. JP 3-0, *Doctrine for Joint Operations*, II-6.

23. JP 5-0, *Doctrine for Planning Joint Operations*, I-1, II-1.

24. Ibid., I-1–I-2. There may be an existing plan formed by a "deliberate planning process" that includes many more players during peacetime. This is then transformed into a more specific plan during the crisis. Alternately, the plan may be formed entirely by "crisis action planning" (ibid., I-9–I-10). The process mentioned above deals only with the actions in the crisis.

25. Byman, Waxman, and Larson, *Air Power as a Coercive Instrument*, 59–67, also comment on a previous draft by Dr. Sheila Widnall, Institute Professor, MIT, and former secretary of the Air Force.

26. Ibid., 68–69.

27. The AOC is nominally organized into five divisions: strategy; plans; combat operations; intelligence, surveillance, and reconnaissance; and mobility. These five divisions and several supporting/specialty teams are supervised by an AOC director who works for the JFACC. See Air Force Instruction (AFI) 13-1AOC, *Operational Procedures*, 15–16.

28. Ibid., 11.

29. A campaign is a series of operations that together accomplish the strategic and operational objectives for a theater. It is the responsibility of the JFC to develop the campaign plan and objectives using all the joint forces available to him and considering the strategic political environment and guidance from the policy makers. See JP 3-0, *Doctrine for Joint Operations*, III-4–III-7.

30. AFOTTP 2-3.2, *Air and Space Operations Center*, 17–18.

31. Ibid., 45–46. The guidance, apportionment, and targeting process produces a prioritized list of targets and ISR collection priorities that are then approved by the JTCB (ibid.).

32. Ibid., 5.

33. Headquarters Air Combat Command, "Combat Air Forces Concept of Operations," 11–12. In a process called *predictive battlespace awareness*, planners determine where targets are most likely to emerge due to the terrain and location of enemy forces. They then try to arrange sensor coverage (ISR) of these areas, with on-call sorties nearby to respond. However, this could loosely cover instances where the ground troops or airborne FACs will be present to designate targets. These concepts are described later.

34. AFOTTP 2-3.2, *Air and Space Operations Center*, 36–37. The board, headed by someone in the strategy division, includes a Judge Advocate General representative and representatives from other services and countries. The new ROEs have to be approved by the JFACC, JFC, SecDef, and the president.

35. Actually, the ACO is a daily order that implements an overall airspace control plan (ACP). Both the ACO and ACP specify restricted areas and procedures for control and avoiding conflicts. The ACP also has to provide ways to transition from peace to conflict and back, as well. See JP 3-52, *Doctrine for Joint Airspace Control*.

36. AFOTTP 2-3.2, *Air and Space Operations Center*, 32–33.

37. There is very little written about aircrew actions at the wing level. Gen Charles "Chuck" A. Horner relates his experience working in a WOC during Vietnam in Clancy with Horner, *Every Man a Tiger*, 75–81. Pilots who flew A-10s in Kosovo relate their experience in Haave and Haun, *A-10s over Kosovo*. I have filled in some of these general actions from my own experience during Desert Shield in 1990.

38. Pilots have to wade through a staggering amount of procedures and publications to make changes on the fly. In OIF, F-16 pilots reduced this information to a four-inch thick "smart pack" containing frequencies and procedures for refueling and other vital activities. There were 10–12 pages of frequencies alone. When told to switch to another frequency, the call would be to switch to a color, for the sake of brevity and security. They would then look up the frequency that corresponded with this color in the smart pack. This is just one example of the hassle involved in performing even seemingly

simple tasks "on the fly." Stolley, interview. Lt Michael Stolley, USAF, 77th Fighter Squadron (FS) at the time of this writing, was an F-16 wingman during OIF.

39. Feinstein, interview. Lt Col Jeffrey Feinstein, 77th FS at the time of this writing, was an F-16 wingman during OIF. See also Clancy with Horner, *Every Man a Tiger*, 85–87.

40. For instances where pilots probably did not have to ask permission but did, see Haave and Haun, *A-10s over Kosovo*, 148, 207. Lt Col Phil Haun confirms that pilots felt the need to check because the combined air operations center (CAOC) had started retaining the authority to give permission to strike. Haun to the author, e-mail, 11 Mar. 2004. Lt Col Phil Haun, 355th Fighter Squadron/CC at the time of this writing, was an A-10 pilot during OAF and OIF, as well as an A-10 FAC(A) in Kosovo.

Chapter 4

The Strategic Level and Control in the Information Age

The creation of strategy resembles Penelope's web—beautiful loom work by day unraveling at night.

—Eliot A. Cohen
Supreme Command: Soldiers, Statesmen, and Leadership in Wartime

The mind of man plans his way, but the Lord directs his steps.

—Proverbs 16:9
New American Standard Bible

Air Force aircraft were not involved in the battle in Mogadishu, Somalia, on 3 October 1993—Army helicopters were the only air-power available to the Rangers. Although the military commanders involved would have liked more support, including AC-130 gunships and armor, they did not think it was needed to succeed in picking up two of Mohammed Farah Aidid's lieutenants. The military did not disagree with the overall mission to find and capture Aidid, either—the primary advocate was Adm Jonathan Howe, the leader of the UN mission that had been unable to bring relief from famine to the area because of the actions of Aidid's thugs. After 18 Rangers were killed, and television news showed pictures of Somalis dragging the dead through the streets, military members disagreed with the Clinton administration's decision to abandon the mission. The Rangers had accomplished their mission—although at a huge cost—and wanted to continue. Because they wanted to believe their mission had always been important enough to justify the loss of their comrades, this setback would not stop them. However, they felt abandoned by their civilian leadership.[1]

Policy makers learned a different lesson from Somalia: the consequences of tactical military actions can affect overall foreign policy. Pres. William J. Clinton's military advisors had convinced him that this was a mission they could handle, and now there were embarrassing and disturbing pictures all over the news.[2] This experience arguably shaped the administration's foreign policy, from the decision not to intervene in Rwanda to the decisions not to get involved in ground wars in Bosnia and Kosovo.[3] It was also a big factor in the early departure of SecDef Les Aspin.[4]

Airpower became the favorite tool for foreign relations. The United States found that, in the absence of another superpower and with stealth, precision, and IT, it could use airpower to make bold statements in areas of less than vital interests without too much risk. Airpower offered policy makers the potential to avoid the pitfalls of traditional military strategy. Because of the limited aims in these small wars, policy makers were better able to identify what was undesirable than what was desirable from their exercise of military airpower. US airpower seemed to offer them the ability to tweak military action within the bounds of a broad policy, rather than letting the military perform according to its SOPs.

The relationship between policy makers and military commanders did not always fit our preferred C2 paradigm of guidance, empowerment, debate, and accountability. In Desert Storm and Iraqi Freedom, the relationship came closest to this archetype. But in Kosovo, there was no relationship—only constraints on actions that could have negative consequences. For military commanders, avoiding these negative consequences comprised a large portion of their responsibility to "implement strategy"—a frustrating exercise, but nevertheless a fact of life.

Although some strove to change this relationship, overall the response was introspective. Policy makers were giving airpower the chance to prove its worth and Air Force leaders fuel for their interservice budgetary arguments. Airpower did not work as well as its proponents had hoped in all cases, and Air Force leaders found themselves chasing the ability to strike rapidly emerging targets with minimal risk to civilians or Americans. To embrace these technological and political changes, the Air Force went through some adjustments of its own. Its leaders welcomed the power of IT and used it to develop the ability to exercise control of airpower at the operational level, in an AOC.

They crafted new visions from the top that drove research and doctrinal development.

This chapter tells this dual story. It reveals the pressures that drove policy makers to use constraints on specific military actions instead of turning military strategy over to military commanders. In the process, it shows the complicated interaction of national security policy, organizational processes, and technological development that produced an evolution of airpower C2—from its inability to achieve unity of effort in Vietnam to a system that many say is managed at too high a level today.

From Vietnam to Desert Storm

The concept of airpower in the previous chapter connotes an integrated whole. This is in stark contrast to its depiction in chapter 2, where there was no single manager of air resources. Airpower was not a tool that was responsive to policy makers' strategies. Furthermore, there was very little cooperation among the different services to produce a coherent effort using all of their assets.

The 1970s and 1980s saw the rise of the fighter generals, with their experience in fighting limited wars in Korea and Vietnam and their need to innovate tactically and materially.[5] Throughout this period, the Air Force, Navy, and Marines refined the precision munitions, sensors, communications and IT, stealth technology, training, and operational doctrine that would eventually lead to a major victory in the Persian Gulf in 1991. In 1975 the Air Force developed Red Flag, a large-scale exercise that put fighter pilots through their first 10 combat missions in as realistic an environment as possible. Along with the Navy's Top Gun program, this training helped US aircrews develop tactics and proficiency to deal with the heightened air defenses demonstrated in the Vietnam and Yom Kippur wars. The Air Force added the F-15, F-16, and A-10 to its inventory, while the Navy added the F-14 and F-18, and the Marines gained the AV-8 and F-18.

Meanwhile, the services were also working to upgrade their weapons capabilities. In the late 1970s, the Air Force started the Armaments Division at Eglin AFB, Florida, to develop non-nuclear munitions. Through the mid-1980s, the Air Force introduced 10 new ground-attack weapons, plus plans for six more. When these new precision weapons were added to another airframe, the revolutionary F-117 stealth fighter, it would prove to be a devastating combination in the 1990s.[6]

These developments were aimed at making pilots better at accomplishing their missions. The truth is, throughout the 1980s, there was little progress in the control of airpower at the operational level, even though the Air Force began an exercise called Blue Flag in 1977 to practice C2 of large air operations. The Army and Air Force began to collaborate on doctrinal development, but that effort actually crystallized into part of the problem. Both saw that it would take teamwork from the air and land components to defeat the huge threat from the Warsaw Pact. Air Force and Army generals agreed to work out details of AirLand Battle doctrine, which foresaw extensive use of tactical airpower and sensors to fight the close battle and the deep battle simultaneously. However, another doctrine developed simultaneously in NATO, called follow-on forces attack (FOFA), proposed to use airpower to strike even deeper, at theater-level targets that would isolate the enemy frontline troops from support and reinforcements. AirLand Battle subjected airpower to the corps commanders' plans, while FOFA called for controlling airpower at a theater level for the best use of the assets.[7] The argument between the two could have come straight out of WWII, where Airmen complained that airpower was being split into penny packets under ground commanders.

Although the equipment and tactics were well developed by Operation Desert Storm, the C2 arrangements were not. In 1982 the JCS had begun a joint doctrine pilot program. Through the program, they had sanctioned the concept of the JFACC, which seemed to be the "single air manager" the Air Force had been seeking. However, the Marines and the Air Force significantly disagreed over the authority of the JFACC. The Marines interpreted the position as a coordinating office, insisting on the 1986 Omnibus Agreement that ensured they could maintain OPCON over sorties they needed for direct support of Marines. They would make excess sorties available to the JFC, the JFACC's boss, and the JFACC would then be a *coordinator*. The Air Force thought the JFACC needed to be a *commander*, with the authority to direct joint air forces to accomplish missions.

Lessons from Desert Storm

This difference was never reconciled before Desert Storm. In fact, because the Navy and Marines were not committed to the JFACC concept, they had neither trained for it nor purchased equipment necessary to implement it. Even the Central Command (CENTCOM) plan for hostilities in Iraq, OPLAN 1002-90 (published one month before Operation Desert Shield began), contained the seeds of ambiguity over the issue.[8]

The 1986 Goldwater-Nichols Amendment helped set the stage for unity of effort in Desert Storm by giving tremendous power to joint commanders. When Desert Shield kicked off in 1990, Gen H. Norman Schwarzkopf set up his staff with one air commander to control the use of airpower from all services. The Navy and Marines resisted to some extent, and the Army refused to allow its helicopters to be controlled in this fashion, but the result was still a very well coordinated effort compared with Vietnam. This unity allowed air planners to coordinate the effects of airpower attacks to take advantage of the advances made in the 1970s and 1980s.

Desert Storm brought together technology and lessons from the preceding two decades in a startling way. For the first time, the concepts of stealth and precision became part of a single, integrated effort—an operational level strategy versus independent tactical actions. By integrating them for the first time, the Airmen that ran the air forces in Desert Storm showed the United States that it (1) could be done and (2) needed to be done better. Though most agreed airpower had been largely responsible for a great victory, the US Air Force still took lessons from it and spent the 1990s developing its ability to obtain and use information to prosecute war more smoothly at the operational level.

First, Desert Storm taught a lesson about the new security environment. Even before the war, the Air Force had begun sketching a vision for its role in the post–Cold War era. Donald Rice, secretary of the Air Force (SAF), and Gen Larry Welch, chief of staff, US Air Force (CSAF), put together a white paper entitled *Global Reach, Global Power*, laying out how the Air Force could continue to provide security as the country demobilized its overseas presence.[9] Desert Storm showed that, in the absence of the great power of deterrence that characterized the Cold War, the United States would be able to engage in warfare on a large scale in protection of its interests. The Air Force had been called on to lead an airpower effort of thousands of sorties per day against a well-equipped enemy in open conventional combat—unheard of in the Cold War.[10]

In this new environment, without the worries about intervention by other superpowers, policy makers could give military commanders freedom to accomplish a mission. That is, strategic-level decision makers not only gave military commanders clear, achievable objectives but also the power to attain them. Pres. George H. W. Bush, himself, set forth the national objectives within a week of the Iraqi invasion of Kuwait. He called for (1) securing the immediate, unconditional, and complete withdrawal of Iraqi forces from Kuwait; (2) restoring the legitimate government of Kuwait; (3) assuring the security and stability of the Persian Gulf region; and (4) protecting American lives. Military planners embraced these objectives wholeheartedly, citing them in all key briefings of their efforts. The first two obviously called for the dislodgement of the Iraqis from Kuwait. The third was not quite as clear but was interpreted as a call to reduce the capability of the Iraqi military. The fourth became a moot point when US hostages were released in December 1990.[11] In these objectives the US military found the basis of a clear military strategy.

But that did not give the military commanders carte blanche to do as they pleased. Desert Storm also taught that in this security environment, there would be coalitions of the willing—willing, at least, for the moment. The Desert Storm coalition consisted of countries like Syria that would otherwise never have considered themselves on the same side as the United States. To hold this coalition together, the civilian leadership had to manage some details of the war. Despite having clear objectives, the military was called on to do some things it considered militarily insignificant. Namely, it was called on to hunt the surface-to-surface missile systems commonly referred to as Scuds.

The "Great Scud Hunt" was the source of considerable friction between policy makers and military commanders in the battle theater. US forces in-theater did not consider the Iraqi Scuds to be a viable threat to the coalition, but they were thinking militarily only. Back in Washington, policy makers were taking extreme measures to keep the Israelis out of the war. When the Iraqis launched the first Scuds into Israel on 18 January 1991, Israel requested the United States release its identify-friend-or-foe (IFF) codes so the Israelis could launch a retaliatory strike. The United States refused but had to show that it was doing everything it could to defeat the threat. This included sending Patriot missile batteries to Israel, allowing the Israelis to nominate targets, and launching an all-out effort to find and destroy the mobile launchers in Iraq. But on 19 January, SecDef Richard Cheney scrubbed the daily flight schedule and discovered the air planners in Riyadh had not stepped up the Scud-hunting efforts.[12] He exploded, and CJCS Gen Colin Powell got the word to the Airmen in Saudi Arabia: get serious about Scuds. The resulting Scud hunt (which included efforts by special operations forces [SOF] on the ground) was ultimately unsuccessful at finding and destroying mobile Scud launchers, but it was successful at suppressing the launches and, more importantly, keeping the Israelis out of the war.[13]

Other incidents reinforced the relationship between tactical actions and political impact. On 13 February 1991, F-117s struck a C2 bunker in the Al Firdos district in the suburbs of Baghdad. Military targeteers had ignored the bunker at first but later indications were that the Iraqis had begun using it. However, planners did not know the Iraqis were also using the bunker to shelter families of some of their elite. When television news stations ran pictures of Iraqi civilians killed in the attack, military leaders saw that all the precision in the world could not overcome a lack of intimate knowledge of the target. More importantly, if this lack of knowledge led to mistakes, the political stakes were high as leaders would have to take swift and decisive action to win a public relations battle. In this case, that meant severely limiting strikes on Baghdad.[14]

The Air Force also learned that space was a valuable medium. Gen Merrill "Tony" McPeak, CSAF, called Desert Storm "the first space war." In Desert Storm, space assets provided warning of missile launches, showed where cloud cover would inhibit air operations, carried long-range communications, supplied imagery to update maps and aid strike packages, and provided GPS navigation.[15] Nonetheless, Gen Charles "Chuck" A. Horner (USAF, retired), the JFACC in Desert Storm, had found space capabilities difficult to deal with due to security concerns. He found his ability to incorporate space information into C2 processes was hampered by space operators' fears of making mistakes with the highly classified information.[16]

After the war, General Horner became the commander of the unified US Space Command, and his primary concern was changing the culture to a more operationally-oriented one. In fact, the next five commanders (including Horner) were all fighter pilots. The Air Force also conducted a Blue Ribbon Panel on Space in 1992 as part of the initial analysis of Desert Storm. Under Horner's watch, Space Command established a Space Warfare Center (SWC) at Falcon AFB, Colorado, modeled after the USAF Weapons School at Nellis AFB, Nevada. The SWC began developing tools to enable air component commanders to apply the information from space capabilities to the fight. In 1994 Project Strike II led to the ability to retarget an F-15E to hit a mobile Scud launcher using coordinates derived from space imagery.[17]

The Air Force made even more sweeping organizational changes in the wake of Desert Storm. Recognizing that all aircraft would have to play a role in the new conventional warfighting and deterrence roles, the Air Force restructured the traditional Military Airlift Command, Tactical Air Command, and Strategic Air Command. It realigned its bombers and fighters into one Air Combat Command and put the assets that get them to the fight—tankers and airlift—into one Air Mobility Command.[18] Bombers and the fighters would both be ready to work together in conventional strike packages, and tankers would be positioned to support airlift and fighters in the event of a conventional contingency rather than sitting alert for the nuclear bombers. The Air Force aligned itself more toward the ability to project conventional power worldwide rather than the ability to support a nuclear strike at a moment's notice.

Integrating with the Clinton Administration

When President Clinton took over as commander in chief (CINC), relations between the new administration and the military were tense. In a 2002 article, a retired colonel and former

Air Force historian called this a period of "the most open manifestation of defiance and resistance by the American military since the publication of the Newburgh addresses over two centuries earlier, at the close of the American war for independence."[19] Yet in the next eight years, the administration was to grapple with the use of force more than any since Vietnam. In the process, it was to shape the US military and its vision for the future.

In 1995 Dr. Sheila Widnall, SAF, and Gen Ronald Fogleman, CSAF, realized that the Air Force's vision did not make enough of the information revolution. They began a strategic planning effort by inviting Alvin Toeffler, Carl Sagan, and other scientists and visionaries to tell them what the future held for the Air Force. This led to the Air Force's first vision document, *Global Engagement: A Vision for the 21st Century Air Force.*[20]

Global Engagement attempted to keep the Air Force in step with the Clinton administration and the Joint Staff while also increasing the Air Force's capabilities. The president's national security strategy demanded the military be prepared to participate with diplomatic efforts to enhance the stability of critical regions throughout the world.[21] Accordingly, in 1996 CJCS Gen John Shalikashvili had published *Joint Vision 2010*, a document that described how the US military forces would accomplish this security strategy. The joint forces would have to develop new operational concepts and something called *information superiority* to perform all the missions that would be required of them in war and peace. This would allow forces to work together so they could accomplish their objectives without huge numbers.[22]

The Air Force completely agreed. *Air Force Vision 2010* pointed out that these new operational concepts required speed, global range, stealth, flexibility, precision, lethality, global/theater situational awareness, and strategic perspective—exactly the things that airpower could deliver better than any other type of force. In order to really become global, the Air Force would have to become the *Air and Space Force* and, eventually, the *Space and Air Force*. In the meantime, it would have to develop the ability to get its people and machines to the conflict fast. The space and air components would be packaged in air expeditionary forces and would be ready to deploy together (in fact, would practice deploying together) at the drop of a hat. The Air

Force would also have to develop the ability to "locate the objective or target, provide responsive C2, generate the desired effect, assess our level of success, and retain the flexibility to re-engage with precision when required." The document even called for a cultural change: in the future, anyone who was experienced in the employment and doctrine of air and space power would be called an operator (a big step in a service dominated by fighter pilots).[23]

Air Force Vision 2010 was an ambitious and controversial document. The single line about moving to an Air and Space Force and then a Space and Air Force generated heated debate among senior officers.[24] The move to expand the definition of *operator* required a huge cultural change and has still not matured. Nevertheless, this document gave Air Force leaders the impetus to move toward information age warfare, enabling the Air Force to fight for its right to maintain control of space.[25] It justified further work on unmanned aerial vehicles (UAV) and other sensors for gathering information and getting it back to decision makers and pushed for further work on precision munitions. Finally, it pressed for innovation that was in-line with civilian and joint force policies, but in a way that expanded Air Force capabilities.

Intervention with Caution—Somalia and Bosnia

A slight detour is in order here. Bosnia is not one of the conflicts that will inform our study of the CAOS. However, it is instructive to see how it bridged the gap between the disaster in Somalia and the 1999 war in Kosovo. When Dr. Widnall arrived in Washington, DC, in 1993 to take over as SAF, she spent her first weekend glued to the television. Mixed with the anguish that the rest of Americans felt as they watched the bodies of dead soldiers being dragged through the streets of Mogadishu, Widnall had another observation: "Now we won't go into Bosnia."[26] She correctly predicted that the debacle in Somalia would make the Clinton administration think twice about getting involved elsewhere.

In the end, the United States did enter the Bosnian conflict, but warily. The UN Protection Force had been established in

Croatia in January 1992. When the Bosnians declared independence from Yugoslavia in March of that year, the Serb military advanced and quickly carved out most of the new state for its own. The United States and several European states recognized Bosnia in April, and by June the UN's mission was extended to include protection of humanitarian relief supplies into Sarajevo Airport.[27] Yet, in 1995 the Clinton administration was still deeply divided over what to do about the conflict. President Clinton wanted to provide American leadership to allow the use of force, but at the same time wanted to avoid putting 20,000 Americans on the ground. By 9 August 1995, he decided to intervene.[28]

Airpower under close supervision was the answer. The UN was already using caution in employing NATO airpower to enforce a no-fly zone (NFZ). The UN and NATO had developed a C2 arrangement they called "dual key," meaning both had to agree if any action was taken. If UN peacekeepers on the ground needed CAS, the director in the combined air operations center (CAOC) could authorize it. Offensive strikes required the overall NATO air commander approval. On the UN side, Boutros Boutros-Ghali, secretary-general, was the approval authority for offensive strikes, while Amb. Yasushi Akashi's approval was required for CAS. This is despite the fact that the two sides had already negotiated the ROEs for military action. Repeated requests for CAS were denied, and the first offensive strike in November 1994 was so watered down it had no effect.[29]

By the time the Clinton administration made its diplomatic move to intervene with force, the precedent for tight constraints on airpower had been set. The NATO air commander, Lt Gen Michael Ryan, was in charge of planning the air strikes for a campaign called Deliberate Force. Officially, the purpose of the strikes was to protect UN peacekeepers on the ground. In fact, the United States took great care to keep Ryan separated from Amb. Richard Holbrooke, the de facto leader of the diplomatic contact team that was negotiating with Slobodan Milosevic. It would have been inappropriate for the two to cooperate because that would have made the air strikes a tool for coercion of the Serbs, as opposed to a neutral protection force.[30]

Yet even without intervention from political leaders, Ryan chose to be sensitive to political considerations. He maintained tight control of the strikes, personally choosing every aimpoint and making every decision regarding the weapons to use on a given target.[31] In fact, Ryan was probably more conservative about the political consequences of the air strikes than Holbrooke and his team. Ryan was concerned that the political support for the air strikes would not withstand a significant collateral damage incident; Holbrooke had no such fear.[32] But the close coordination between bombing, actions on the ground, and diplomacy was one key to the success of the effort.

Institutionalizing Command and Control

Bosnia was a small war, but it contributed to the Air Force's understanding of the way airpower fit into the current political environment. It was another example that airpower had to be ready to fit into a carefully choreographed political strategy. Accordingly, the Air Force began to put more effort into the ability to control airpower at the operational level of war. A 1996 Air Force Scientific Advisory Board study illuminated the need for improvements in C2 processes and technology.[33]

In response, Air Force leaders started an organization called the Air and Space Command and Control Agency (ASC2A) to integrate air and space, eliminate duplication of effort, and modernize C2. Before this, any organization that needed C2 equipment submitted a budget for it; as a result, there were 67 different C2 systems in the 1997 budget. The agency's job was to drive toward a common operational architecture while also developing a baseline for the AOC.[34]

Air Force officials were only beginning to get a handle on the scope of the problem. The 67 systems were those that communicated information from place to place or processed it when it got to its destination. Looking only at those systems, one could imagine a decidedly closed-loop C2 system that automatically processed and disseminated information. But the sensors that pick up data from the battle area were an important part of the real, open-loop system.

These ISR sensors were also evolving. In Desert Storm, the JSTARS made its debut even before it was a fielded system. The JSTARS program was still in developmental testing when Lt Gen Frederick Franks, commander of the US Army VII Corps, observed a demonstration in Europe in the fall of 1990. He was so impressed, he had General Schwarzkopf briefed, and Schwarzkopf got the system deployed to the desert.[35] JSTARS was instrumental in detecting troop movements in the Battle of Khafji and would later be used extensively in Kosovo, Afghanistan, and Iraq. In fact, it was in Kosovo that JSTARS first teamed up with another development in airborne ISR—the UAV.

UAVs had been used for reconnaissance as far back as Vietnam but had always suffered from the slow delivery of data and inaccurate navigation. The Predator was the first vehicle to incorporate GPS-enhanced navigation and commercial satellite data links for control and imagery transmission, so it was released from the bonds of line-of-sight operations.[36] Developed by General Atomics in response to a request for proposals in 1993, it saw combat in the Balkans 17 months after the contract was awarded in January 1994. It was built using off-the-shelf components and acquired using a quick-reaction strategy called the Advanced Concept Technology Demonstration.[37] When General Fogleman saw how important the Predator had become by virtue of its service in Bosnia, he went all-out to make it an Air Force asset, mobilizing support and creating an operational squadron even before the USAF was designated as the lead service.[38] Besides this, Air Force generals were becoming more aware of space capabilities.

The Air Force realized it had to incorporate ISR into its C2 paradigm. Every year Air Force generals hold a series of meetings known as Corona. At the 1997 Corona Fall Meeting, the generals pointed out that no one was in charge of ISR sensors, which were becoming integral parts of the C2 process. Instead of creating a new center, the Air Force included this additional responsibility into the Aerospace Command and Control Agency (AC2A), making it the Air Force Command and Control, Intelligence, Surveillance, and Reconnaissance Center (AFC2ISRC).[39]

If ever there was an organization dedicated to developing the capability to employ van Creveld's directed telescope, this was it. This agency was responsible for developing the tools and training to create formal feedback loops from sensors, to decision makers, and then to action takers. With separate, "stove-piped" systems, this was impossible, but if the systems could be made common, or at least interoperable, then these sensor-communication loops could become formal processes. The AFC2ISRC gathered input from the war-fighting commanders and then worked with Electronic Systems Command and the Massachusetts Institute of Technology Research (MITRE) Corporation to develop the technology into usable capabilities as quickly as possible.[40]

One key to this rapid development occurred in 1998 with an annual experiment called the Expeditionary Force Experiment (EFX). Its purpose was to exploit the revolution in military affairs and demonstrate "emerging Air Force capabilities to deploy and employ decisive aerospace power for the joint force commander through an Aerospace Expeditionary Force."[41] Recognizing that the technology used to command and control airpower was changing faster than the acquisition system could develop new systems and techniques, this yearly event began trying a more flexible method called *spiral development*. The first experiment focused on collaborative tools that allowed people to perform distributed operations from multiple locations and also tried to develop a process for targeting dynamic, "time-critical targets."[42]

Kosovo

The changes did not keep up with the pace of world events, however. Within six months of the conclusion of the first EFX, the United States found itself fighting a war in Kosovo. The 1999 Kosovo conflict was similar to Bosnia in that political controls were again a huge consideration in airpower employment.

The war in Kosovo was unprecedented in that it was fought for solely humanitarian reasons without a mandate from the UN. Although both Prime Minister Tony Blair and President Clinton also referred to the destabilizing effect of refugee flows, the primary reason for the intervention seems to have been the plight of the Kosovar Albanians.[43] The Kosovo Liberation Army (KLA) and the Serbs had been fighting since 1991, and up until 1999 NATO had been merely trying to get the two sides to stop fighting. But in January 1999, 45 Kosovar civilians were massacred at Racak. Then the Serbian delegation to the Rambouillet peace conference refused to agree to NATO peace conditions. At the same time, Milosevic switched to a strategy of trying to drain Kosovo of ethnic Albanian supporters of the KLA.[44] This gave NATO a clear choice of sides in the war.

It did not, however, make for a clear choice of military strategy. US political objectives were to demonstrate NATO's opposition to aggression, deter Milosevic from further attacks, and damage Serbia's capacity to wage war. NATO's political objectives were to stop the killing in Kosovo, end the refugee crisis, and create conditions for political solutions based on the Rambouillet Accords.[45] These are far more nebulous objectives than the Desert Storm coalition had received. They are also best achieved with ground troops. Regardless, with less than vital interests at stake, there was little stomach among the NATO nations for risking the lives of their soldiers.

Furthermore, they did not think they had to. Throughout the 1990s, airpower was involved in applying force in a number of different situations that were short of a full war. Examples include the Bosnian conflict, the containment of Saddam Hussein with NFZs, and the effort to coerce Saddam into complying with UN inspections in 1998. These cases are characterized by short, quick applications of airpower to effect a short-term change in the behavior of the opponent versus long-term strategies to accomplish strategic objectives. Correspondingly, the system that employed airpower in each of these incursions was only a fragment of the one that had fought Desert Storm. In Operation Southern Watch, for example, the day-to-day operations to enforce the NFZ were coordinated by a crew of about 500 people in the AOC in Riyadh, Saudi Arabia. Whenever a coordinated attack occurred, as when President Clinton ordered retaliation against Saddam in January 1993 for the attempt on (then) President Bush's life, a larger group would take over. They would plan the actions and get the targets approved while still in the United States (at Shaw AFB, SC). The commander of Ninth Air Force would subsequently deploy to Riyadh with his handpicked staff to run the operations during the brief period of increased intensity.[46]

This mentality carried over into the Kosovo war at first. The recollection of Gen Wesley Clark, supreme allied commander, Europe, is that he was mentally prepared to step up from limited attacks to more major attacks and then to a ground invasion of Kosovo, and even Serbia, if necessary. This contrasted with the mind-set in the political arena where there was a desire for a couple of days of strikes and then a bombing pause, just as in

Bosnia.[47] A shallow reading of the 1995 Bosnia intervention suggested Milosevic was vulnerable to combined bombing and diplomacy. A deeper reading would have reminded everyone that the Dayton Accords had followed a series of sharp reversals on the ground and that the bombing had not been against Serbia proper.[48] Yet in August 1998, when military planners presented the NAC countries with military options for a potential crisis, any involving ground troops were shelved. President Clinton and Madeleine Albright, secretary of state, made public statements that told Milosevic there would be no ground invasion—only bombing from the air.[49]

There was no coherent strategy, no mechanism to link the allowable means to the required ends. It will be seen later that even the air commander, General Short, knew he could not stop ground troops from performing ethnic cleansing without troops on the ground. He did think airpower could convince Milosevic to capitulate, but only by going to downtown Belgrade to attack the bases of Milosevic's power. This approach was precluded by the policy makers as well.

In the absence of a clear mechanism, policy makers used a target-approval process to implement strategy. This was really the only strategy guidance between the strategic-level decision makers and the military. General Clark was not involved in any discussions with his CINC or SecDef William Cohen.[50] Target approval was done by a committee of NATO governments, any one of which could veto individual targets. The process was slow and sporadic, and the bombing did not produce nearly the effects the Airmen thought it could have.[51]

Mistakes in the bombing had the potential to destroy NATO's moral high ground. Strategic-level decision makers found more evidence in Kosovo that tactical actions can have strategic effects. Intelligence officials targeting a Yugoslav arms agency selected the wrong building from overhead imagery. They were unaware that the building they were mistakenly targeting was the Chinese Embassy because the map they were using did not show the correct location of the embassy, which had moved in 1996. These two mistakes combined to produce a diplomatic nightmare when a B-2 precisely bombed its target (which turned out to be the Chinese Embassy). This triggered a crisis between Beijing and Washington, caused an international uproar that threatened the coalition's solidarity, disrupted moves to negotiate an end to the conflict, and halted bombing in Belgrade for two weeks.[52]

In retrospect, the approach taken by policy makers implies they were more concerned about the NATO alliance than about the ethnic cleansing. They ruled out ground troops and discounted the only other strategy that may have forced quicker capitulation, both in the name of maintaining the NATO alliance. Actually, this only shows that political pressures at times outweigh "military effectiveness" in policy makers' decision processes.

In the end, the Air Force learned some hard lessons from the conflict. In Kosovo, airpower had been the United States' only military instrument, and it had been found wanting in several respects. Although the strikes on Belgrade seem to have had an effect on Milosevic, the valiant efforts against his army in Kosovo were unable to stop the ethnic cleansing or even destroy the Serb air defenses because the Serbs were able to disperse and hide. Airpower needed an improved ability to engage fleeting targets in a politically sensitive environment. In Kosovo this had been done through a process called *flex targeting*, which made up an unusually large proportion of the total strikes. This brought remote decision makers in on the execution to a greater degree than ever before. Often, Short's CAOC staff tried to direct aircraft based on real-time intelligence from ISR sensors. Essentially, he was taking extra care to ensure targets met the ROEs protecting civilians before approving the strikes.[53] However, this process illuminated the need to enable the tactical level's ability to respond more quickly based on the same information. Although there are cases where this slowed the tactical actions down, there are also instances where aircraft were not able to respond quickly enough to strike a target that the CAOC had approved.[54] The official lessons learned are that the military needed to improve precision engagement and procure common tactical data links to tie sensors to shooters, producing a "common tactical picture."[55]

In fact, these were the things that the Air Force had been working on. The lessons of Kosovo reinforced the lessons from Bosnia and the other small conflicts in the '90s. Whether Air Force leaders agreed with it or not, this type of warfare was probably here to stay. Airpower would have to use information to conduct precision attacks with low collateral damage in a way that was tailored to political circumstances.

Ascendance of the AOC

Five years after he was the JFACC in Deliberate Force, General Ryan wrote the next Air Force vision document as CSAF. Like its predecessor, this document followed directly from the *National Security Strategy* and *Joint Vision 2020* but went into more detail about how the Air Force would use its information. In it, Ryan and SAF F. Whitten Peters stressed the necessity of getting information to the air commander: "We will strengthen the ability of our commanders to command and control aerospace forces. Their AOCs will be able to gather and fuse the full range of information—from national to tactical—in real time and to rapidly convert that information into knowledge and understanding—to assure decision dominance over adversaries."[56] Ryan and Peters expanded the targeting process that Fogleman and Widnall had laid out in their document—now the process was to "find, fix, target, track, engage, and assess." This kill chain was to be executed (eventually in minutes instead of hours) by an integrated "system of systems." Only now, instead of an Air and Space Force, it was an Aerospace Force.[57] Put in perspective, this was not a downplay of the significance of space. It was an effort to reinforce the fact that everything worked together, in a system of systems, with the AOC as the control hub of the system. Ryan's experience had taught him the AOC was the right place to control airpower. The thing to do was to make it more effective by feeding all the information to it.

Certainly the technology was now available to pull data into the AOC and process it. Numbered air forces, those organizations responsible for controlling Air Force resources in case of a war in a particular area of the world, had already begun constructing AOCs. The Ninth Air Force, which had fought Desert Storm under Horner, finished one at Prince Sultan Air Base (PSAB) in Saudi Arabia in 2001. This was a brand new facility, built from the ground up for the purpose of running an air war in Southwest Asia.[58] But manning the AOCs in time of war took a lot of manpower, and the drive from the Defense Department was to cut down on this overseas presence. Each numbered air force also wanted another facility at its home station to execute what was called *reachback*. Because of the incredible leaps in bandwidth available over fiber and satellite technology, much of the analysis work could be done here, leaving the analysts and their equipment at home during a war. The Air Force built a single reachback facility, the Rear Operations Support Center, at Langley AFB, Virginia.

This centralization put tremendous pressure on the AOC as a hub. If all of the decision making was to be accomplished there, it had to be done well. Training the people had long been a concern. The Air Force traditionally had not put emphasis on learning to do the job of controlling airpower—flying the planes was its business. When (then Maj) Jack Sexton left the Philippines because of the eruption of Mount Pinatubo in 1992, he was sent to the Ninth Air Force at Shaw. There he became the training officer for the people who had run the air campaign in Desert Storm. One of the first questions he was asked was "what do you do?" Certainly, Sexton must have some hobbies or something that would keep him occupied because the people there were only used in case of war, which left a lot of spare time.[59] They spent almost no time training or refining their trade. It was seen as a dead-end job for those who would soon retire: "civilian below the zone."

The Air Force attempted to change that, too. In 2000 Ryan announced that the AOC would now be treated as a weapons system. This unprecedented step took a formerly ad hoc arrangement of technology and people and transformed it into a real entity. Now, someone had to figure out how to operate it, standardize the operating procedures, and train people to set it up and maintain it. The EFX (later called Joint Expeditionary Force Experiment [JEFX] to enhance the *joint* aspect of airpower) would provide the medium for experimentation. Also in 2000, Ryan started a senior mentor program. Based on a similar program in the Army, this program took four retired three-star generals (including Short) and gave them the responsibility for passing on their lessons of how to employ airpower at the operational level of war. They now help mold exercises by planning them and playing key parts, assessing the performance of senior officers in those exercises, and lecturing to more junior officers about the operational level of war.[60] They have also helped form training courses to teach officers how to run an AOC. More importantly, these generals have been firm advocates of assigning officers from the Air Force's elite training and education schools—like the USAF Weapons School and the School of Advanced Air and Space Studies (Maxwell AFB, AL)—to positions where they will work in an AOC.[61]

The senior mentors worked in concert with a former part of the AC2A. Soon after AC2A was organized, it took on a subordinate organization at Hurlburt Field, Florida. The organization that had been responsible for the Blue Flag exercises was renamed the Air Force Command and Control Training and Innovation Center. In the next six years, this center would undergo two more reorganizations, finally achieving the status of a wing with three groups under its control. In 2004, the 505th Command and Control Wing became responsible for training people, developing formal processes, and testing systems to perform air and space C2. The wing established a formal training unit, mission qualification classes, and continuation training for those who will work in AOCs. It also ran exercises using a mixture of modeling and simulation with live aircraft, and the senior mentors provided experienced critiques of the results. The 505th developed the doctrine documents that describe how C2 is exercised in the CAOC and was responsible for testing the equipment and procedures during JEFX and other experiments and operational tests.[62] On paper at least, the Air Force had achieved a formal recognition that C2 at the operational level of war required a cadre of professionals in the field who were competent with formal processes and up-to-date equipment.

A New Administration and the War on Terror

It was during this period that the new George W. Bush administration came to the White House. President Bush won an election by an electoral technicality, receiving more electoral votes but fewer popular votes than Vice Pres. Al Gore in the 2000 election. Nonetheless, in the eyes of the military he was the CINC. His administration included such heavyweights as Donald Rumsfeld, in his second term as SecDef; Vice President Cheney, the former SecDef who had served during Desert Storm; and Secretary of State Powell, the former CJCS during Desert Storm. This was a group that was anything but intimidated by the Department of Defense (DOD), and it immediately went to battle with the military. The 2001 Quadrennial Defense Review demanded transformation, including a reduction in traditional procurement programs like the F-22 and Crusader. Secretary Rumsfeld proved to be a hard-nosed boss who saw it as his personal duty to guarantee civilian control of the military.

When terrorists attacked the World Trade Center and the Pentagon on 11 September 2001, the resulting war presented a much different civil-military case than the previous Kosovo war. That it would be a war, in the conventional sense, was not at all guaranteed by the terrorists' attacks. Bush made the response to the 11 September attacks the central issue of his presidency. At daily NSC meetings for the next month, the strategic-level decision makers wrestled with how to wage war on an entity as nebulous as the enemy in this war. Throughout, they were very conscious of the image the world had of an America that simply lobbed cruise missiles in response to any attack.[63] Bush stressed that he knew the war would be long and entail loss of American lives.[64] There would be American "boots on the ground," not just aircraft and missiles in the air. Nevertheless, the cost would be justified.[65]

Translating this strategic vision into a military strategy was difficult, to say the least. The principals had a hard enough time trying to decide who the enemy was; they could not immediately tackle how to attack that enemy. This was left to the military, and Rumsfeld was not initially happy with the way it handled the challenge. He wanted the military to come up with innovative ways to fight this war that would also spur the transformation he was trying to encourage: "If you're fighting a different kind of war, the war transforms the military."[66] Rumsfeld and the other principals set the conditions for military strategy by sending in CIA and military SO teams on the ground to work with the native opposition forces in Afghanistan. They expected the military to figure out the details.

Still, there were some specific actions the Bush administration felt it needed to constrain. To avoid any perception that the war was against the people of Afghanistan or Islam, the military actions had to remain clean and not cause much damage to the area. The NSC made a decision that all potentially "sensitive" targets were to be cleared by Secretary Rumsfeld himself. This seemingly inane constraint had the effect of severely narrowing the allowable targets by including all infrastructures such as electrical power, roads, and industry. The military also had to get approval to strike any target which could be expected to cause moderate to high collateral damage. The authority for these decisions was eventually delegated to Gen Tommy Franks, the CENTCOM commander and JFC, and then later to his staff.[67] This was not like Kosovo, where the strategic level had to approve all targets. However, it was not Desert Storm—the air component was not the one making the plans.

The Bush administration also had a difficult time getting the military and the CIA to work together smoothly. The NSC principals knew that the CIA and military SO teams needed to work together hand-in-hand to accomplish the mission. In Bob Woodward's published account of his interviews, CIA director George Tenet thought he made it clear that the CIA paramilitary teams would work for Franks. Yet, it appears Rumsfeld was not comfortable with the arrangement. He did not command the CIA troops and wanted his own military troops on the ground.[68] In Franks' memoirs, he also recalls having been given control of CIA assets, including Predator.[69] But workers at CENTCOM knew that, given the unusual nature of this interagency arrangement, command authority stopped at the JFC. At the beginning of the war, only Franks could direct the CIA Predator.[70]

Consequently, the US military deployed hastily to an unfamiliar area halfway around the world. The air component set up in its brand new facility in Saudi Arabia and prepared to direct Navy and Air Force aircraft and work with the CIA and SOF on the ground. Franks, however, spent most of his time in Tampa Bay, Florida. He was able to communicate with his component commanders by video teleconference (VTC) and collaborative tools, so he only spent about 25 percent of the first three months in or around Afghanistan. Franks proposed that communications leaps "permitted us to provide intent and guidance without doing the tactical work of subordinate commanders."[71]

We will see later that the air component officers saw things differently. Commanded by Lt Gen Charles Wald, combined force air component commander, the air component planners felt they got very little strategic guidance but a great deal of detailed direction. The CENTCOM staff held the authority to approve targets in planning and during operations. It appears the initial decision by Rumsfeld to hold this authority created a precedent; even when he released that authority, the next in line assumed someone had to hold the authority for sensitive targets. This still meant that a staff officer, thousands of miles and several time zones away, held authority that air officers thought should have been delegated to the air component in-theater.[72] This was symptomatic of the fact that policy makers and military commanders had a difficult time defining a military strategy.

In the absence of an operational level strategy, those at the tactical level continued to work on the problems at hand. By the end of October, the ineffectiveness of the bombing campaign led the media to declare the United States and the coalition were in trouble. Then the CAOC workers, pilots, and "boots on the ground" learned how to work together to achieve a devastating effect on the Taliban forces. In fact, the effects were so devastating that they transformed the overall military strategy and even the strategic objectives for the war. Gradually, the object became to support the Northern Alliance in a regime change, where originally the idea had been to coerce the Taliban into giving up its support of al-Qaeda. Had there been more time to develop a diplomatic strategy, the rifts in the Taliban could have been exploited to achieve this effect without creating a power vacuum. As it was, teaming up with the Northern Alliance proved the only viable means to extricate the coalition from its strategic problems.[73] While higher-level decision makers were focused on tactical actions, these actions were redefining strategy—not in a way that was incongruent with the overall vision of policy makers, but in a logical evolution that nevertheless narrowed the options. Unlike the Kosovo case, the problem in Afghanistan was not the failure of policy makers and military commanders to work together. It was instead the inability to predict what the war would look like.

This was not the case in OIF. The objectives were clear from the beginning. Back in November of 2001, before Franks was even involved, Bush had told Rumsfeld they would "protect America by removing Saddam Hussein if we have to." Then in December, Rumsfeld sent Franks a two-page order to prepare a plan to remove Saddam, eliminate the threat of weapons of mass destruction (WMD), and choke off Saddam's support of terrorism.[74] Moreover, the United States and its coalition had clear, conventional means at hand to accomplish these goals. The loss of the use of Turkish soil notwithstanding, the coalition had ample bases within reach of Iraq where it could station its aircraft, position a large invasion force, and set up supply lines and lines of communication. The policy goal of regime change was suited to a large conventional force operation. According to Franks, during December 2001, he and the NSC prodded each other on the details of the overall plan so that the military strategy seemed to grow from and complement the grand strategy.[75]

This was a process that would continue throughout the next year and a half. Franks began developing the military strategy and grand strategy concurrently. He and Rumsfeld talked frequently in Rumsfeld's office and over dinners—"grinding back-and-forth planning sessions" that both men called "an iterative process."[76] Rumsfeld tried to convey to Franks the subtleties of his concerns by constantly picking at Franks' plans. In his interview-based book on the planning for the Iraq war, Bob Woodward describes Rumsfeld as "a dentist's drill that never ceased."[77] Franks started with a sketch of what he called the "'lines and slices' working matrix." Slices were the pillars that supported Saddam and his Baathist regime—the "foundations of Iraqi power"—and the essential elements of the Iraqi nation and its people. Lines were the operational tasks that the coalition could perform in the conflict, like "operational fires," "SOF operations," "information ops," and even "civil-military operations."[78] The matrix was a way of breaking down the complex job of strategy into the much simpler job of determining which slices were affected by which lines.

From this, Franks developed the military strategy. Again, it would have the familiar four phases: (1) preparing, (2) shaping the battlespace, (3) conducting decisive operations, and (4) implementing post-hostility operations. By February 2002, he envisioned five fronts in the operation: two simultaneous conventional assaults from Kuwait and Turkey, SOF occupying the "Scud baskets" of the western desert, information (including psychological) to erode the resolve of the Iraqi military, and an "operational fires" front focusing on Baghdad and the Republican Guard.[79]

In both the Afghanistan and Iraq wars, military strategy became more dependent on hitting fleeting or emerging targets.

Just as OIF was about to begin, the CIA established surveillance on Saddam Hussein in a hiding place in southern Baghdad. Meeting in the Oval Office, the president, SecDef, secretary of state, national security advisor, and CJCS ordered a last-second change in the war strategy in order to make assets available for this opening strike.[80] TSTs like this were only a small fraction of the overall number of strikes, although they drew a large amount of attention when they occurred.[81] But during OIF, Franks got no second-guessing from Washington.[82] He and Rumsfeld had worked through the plans, and evidently Rumsfeld was satisfied.

Conclusions

Clausewitz proposes that "the first, the supreme, the most far-reaching act of judgment that the statesman and commander have to make is to establish [by the nature of their motives and of the situations which give rise to them] the kind of war on which they are embarking; neither mistaking it for, nor trying to turn it into, something that is alien to its nature."[83] This is quite a demanding task, and one that its author claims should be done in cooperation between the military commander and statesman. The balance to this statement is the recognition, attributed most famously to Helmuth von Moltke, that strategy is altered by tactical realities.[84] More recently, Eliot Cohen put it this way: "The act of waging war leads—in fact, forces—statesmen to alter their objectives and purposes, thereby frustrating those who hope to reduce strategic aims to checklists."[85]

That is why it is important to see Cohen's and Huntington's advice about civil-military relations as complementary and not conflicting. It is vital for policy to reign supreme in the development of military strategy and for military strategy to adapt itself to the situation. Only a continuing dialogue between policy makers and commanders will ensure this balance exists, as supported by evidence from this chapter.

In Desert Storm, the policy makers set the objectives and let the military determine the strategy, but still overruled the military at points. There were times, such as the Scud Hunt, where they had to step in to ensure important political considerations were addressed. The fact that Cheney stepped in here was in agreement with our preferred C2 theory; in making strategy, there should be a conflict between the political and military considerations and that conflict should be resolved by policy makers after careful review of the expert advice from the military. In fact, the absence of such conflict could be dangerous. Both Cohen and Huntington warn against forcing the military to insert political views on their own, a foul that Cohen says occurred in several cases in Desert Storm.[86] It may have occurred again in Bosnia, where Ryan appeared to take it upon himself to inject political sensitivities into the planning process. In that case the result was success, so it is difficult to argue.

Instead of taking on this conflict in Operation Allied Force, policy makers used constraints on specific actions to keep the strategy in check. Absent was the back-and-forth discussion of strategy; in its place was a system for target approval that was supposed to ensure the military actions remained coherent with policy. This did not empower the military to adapt to the changing situations—the ethnic cleansing continued unchecked. When combined with the conflicts in Bosnia and the NFZ in Iraq, it may also have shaped the way the military thought about controlling airpower in the long term. It did, however, allow policy makers to control the nature of the war. The war was slow and ineffectual militarily, but the NATO alliance outlasted Milosevic, who capitulated (to some extent) in the end.

The second Bush administration appears to have come down in the middle of the two previous methods. In Enduring Freedom–Afghanistan, policy makers held substantive discussions about military strategy with the commander. Instead of precisely defining the eventual strategy, this only reinforced the difficulty of the task. Policy makers also sought to impose a few seemingly inane constraints on the types of targets that could be attacked. This actually forced the two levels to communicate during the ongoing operations—a practice that was soon ended when Rumsfeld delegated authority for these attacks to Franks. As a way to set a precedent for the amount of care to be taken, this was probably effective. But as will be seen, it had far-reaching effects on the ability of the military to leverage command relationships. This scenario does not fit our preferred method of combining a bruising discussion with empowerment and accountability. By the time OIF started, the Bush administration and Franks had worked through these issues. While the planning stage was still characterized by an intense debate between Rumsfeld and Franks, this time there were no constraints that forced the theater commanders to check with Washington about an ongoing operation.

The degree to which policy makers used constraints on specific actions or empowerment to control the military affected the way airpower was employed in both the long term and the short term. In the long term, it taught Air Force leaders lessons that they used to shape innovations in C2. The small wars in the 1990s reinforced the fact that, now that airpower's stealth and precision made it a low-risk instrument, political leaders would be more willing to use it in situations where US interests were less than vital.[87] After suffering unexpected casualties in Somalia, the United States used airpower as a coercive tool rather than risk ground troops in both Bosnia and Kosovo. In both cases, the employment of airpower was restricted—in one case by the Airman in charge and in the other by the political leaders and allied commander. Led by the new generation of fighter pilots who thrived on innovation, the Air Force took similar lessons from Bosnia and Kosovo and kept the pressure on to develop the capability to engage targets anywhere with high precision and low risk of collateral damage—exactly what the policy makers were asking of it.

Air Force leaders did this by developing the ability to get and process information from the field as quickly as possible—in the AOC. Desert Storm introduced the need to expand the TACC and formalize some of the ad hoc processes that had developed under Horner in the Gulf War. The Air Force developed this capability to the point where it constructed buildings from the ground up for the express purpose of acting as an AOC. It also built a special facility at Langley AFB to act as a reachback center. The Air Force reorganized to put emphasis on integrating C2 and ISR and on training its people to work in C2 positions. There has clearly been a trend toward increasing the ability of the AOC to use sensor-communication loops to make real-time decisions that would otherwise be preplanned, left to the discretion of the pilots, or prohibited by the ROEs.

In the short term, the relative mixture of constraints and empowerment affected the extent to which the military was able to develop depth in its command relationships. The next chapter demonstrates how constraints used by policy makers affected strategy development and command relationships.

Notes

1. Bowden, *Black Hawk Down*, 337–41, 354–56.
2. Ibid., 334.
3. Crocker, "Lessons of Somalia," 7.
4. Dr. Widnall, a member of the author's doctoral committee at MIT, added this insight in her review of this chapter when it was in dissertation form.
5. Worden, *Rise of the Fighter Generals*, 237.
6. Lambeth, *Transformation of American Airpower*, 59–80.
7. Ibid., 85–87.
8. Cohen and Keaney, *Gulf War Air Power Survey*, vol. 1, pt. 2, *Command and Control*, 358–68.
9. Fogleman, "Air Power and National Security."
10. It is true that the effort in Vietnam was huge by the end of the war. However, it began slowly and built up to that level. In fact, that's the whole point: in Vietnam, President Johnson thought he had to calibrate the level of violence so it would convince the North Vietnamese that the United States was serious without causing the Soviets or Chinese to enter the war. In Desert Storm airpower was calibrated at its maximum effort from the very beginning.
11. Cohen and Keaney, *Gulf War Air Power Survey*, vol. 1, pt. 1, *Planning*, 83–84.
12. This is referring to the air tasking order.
13. Gordon and Trainor, *Generals' War*, 227–47.
14. Keaney and Cohen, *Gulf War Air Power Survey*, 68–69; and Thompson, "After Al Firdos," 355.
15. Moorman, "Space, A New Strategic Frontier," 19–20.
16. Horner, interview by the author. Gen Charles A. Horner, USAF, retired, was a wing planner and pilot in Vietnam and the JFACC in Desert Storm.
17. Lambeth, *Transformation of American Air Power*, 238–41.
18. Fogleman, "Air Power and National Security."
19. Kohn, "Erosion of Civilian Control," 10–13.
20. Fogleman, "Air Power and National Security."
21. White House, *National Strategy of Engagement*.
22. *Joint Vision 2010*, 16–26. According to this document, joint forces would have to develop new operational concepts called *dominant maneuver*, *precision engagement*, *focused logistics*, and *full-spectrum force protection* in order to perform all the missions that would be required of them in war and peace. These concepts would rely on *information superiority*, which would allow decision makers to decide whom, where, how, and with what to engage to accomplish security objectives. Instead of massing forces, the military would mass effects by applying the right force in the right place at the right time.
23. United States Air Force, *Global Engagement*.

24. Sheila Widnall, former SAF, interview by the author, Cambridge, MA, 2 Dec. 2003. (Author's notes in personal collection.)

25. Ibid. Professor Widnall stated that one of her priorities while she was in office was "maintaining Air Force equities," by which she meant holding onto and perhaps expanding the boundaries of the Air Force's responsibilities and, by extension, capabilities.

26. Ibid.

27. Owen, "Balkans Air Campaign Study: Part 1," 8.

28. Daalder, *Getting to Dayton*, 80. See the next chapter for a good discussion of the interagency process that led to the decision.

29. Owen, "Balkans Air Campaign Study: Part 2," 15–18.

30. Ibid., 17.

31. Ibid., Part 1, 9. The aimpoints were referred to as *desired mean points of impact* but are now called *joint desired mean points of impact* (JDPI).

32. Ibid., Part 2, 18.

33. History, Aerospace Command and Control Agency, vol. 1, 30.

34. Ibid., 1. The agency's name was changed in Sept. 1998 to the Aerospace Command and Control Agency, versus the Air and Space Command and Control Agency. This is why, although the acronym was originally ASC2A, I use AC2A, since that was the eventual name. The DOD identifies systems by categories called program elements, and in response to the 1996 Scientific Advisory Board report, the Air Staff had counted 67 of them just for C2 (ibid., 30).

35. Cohen and Keaney, *Gulf War Air Power Survey*, vol. 1, pt. 2, *Command and Control*, 101–3.

36. Ehrhard, "Armed Services and Innovation," 227.

37. Palmeri, "Predator That Preys on Hawks."

38. Ehrhard, "Armed Services and Innovation," 230–32.

39. History, Aerospace Command and Control Agency, vol. 1, 19–22. At this time, the AC2A was actually called the ASC2A (see n. 34).

40. Ibid., 9.

41. "EFX 98 Assessment Report," executive 1-2. The report is unclassified, but in order to view it you must get permission from the Air Force Experimentation Office.

42. Ibid.

43. Although there was no resolution directly authorizing force, there were, in fact, UN resolutions that gave some legitimacy to NATO's side of the issues. Resolution 1199 of 23 Sept. 1998 demanded a halt to all actions by security forces that affected the civilian population. Resolution 1203 of 24 Oct. 1998 demanded Serb compliance with accords of Belgrade earlier that month. The NATO states probably did not ask for a vote because Russia and China had vowed to veto any such resolution, and this would probably have robbed the movement of the impressive legitimacy that it had despite the lack of explicit direction. Roberts, "NATO's 'Humanitarian War,'" 105–7.

44. Headquarters, U.S. Air Force, *Initial Report, the Air War over Serbia*, 2–4.

45. Ibid., 9.

46. Pritchard to the author, e-mail.

47. Ellis, "View from the Top." Adm James Ellis was commander, Joint Task Force Noble Anvil, during OAF. See also Clark, *Waging Modern War.*

48. Roberts, "NATO's 'Humanitarian War,'" 110–11.

49. Stigler, "Clear Victory for Air Power," 127–28.

50. Clark, *Waging Modern War*, 201–2, describes the US target-approval process, and 218–20 describes Clark's quest for political guidance, which he got from NATO secretary-general Javier Solana but not from either President Clinton or SecDef Cohen. He later wonders: "Wouldn't they have been able to make better decisions, and have them better implemented, . . . if they brought the commander into the high-level discussions occasionally?" Ibid., 341.

51. *Kosovo Air Operations*, 8–9.

52. Lambeth, *NATO's Air War for Kosovo*, 206–7.

53. Grant, "Reach-Forward," 45–46.

54. Harmer, "Enhancing the Operational Art," 87. In one particular case, Short and Clark were watching live Predator video, imploring a pilot to find three tanks they saw moving along a road. The pilot, clearly agitated by the high-level attention, was unable to find the tanks. This pilot was actually General Short's son. After the third prodding: "Gen. Short really wants those tanks killed!" the FAC answered back, "[expletives deleted] it Dad, I can't see the [expletive deleted] tanks!" Ibid.

55. Department of Defense, *Kosovo/Operation Allied Force*, 50.

56. Department of the Air Force, *Global Vigilance*, 3.

57. Ibid., 6.

58. Col Jack Sexton, USAF, retired (9th AF training officer after Desert Storm), interview by the author, Bedford, MA, 3 June 2003 (author's notes in personal collection); and Bradshaw, interview. Lt Col Jim Bradshaw was in Ninth Air Force from 1992–96 and is now a contractor working on the technology in the AOC. He was part of a three-man team that went to Saudi Arabia to help stand up the CAOC at Prince Sultan Air Base and then helped get it ready for OIF.

59. Sexton, interview.

60. Message, R 230952Z AUG 00, HQ USAF, Washington, DC/CVA to MAJCOMs.

61. The School of Advanced Air and Space Studies is a master's degree program that takes graduates of one of the Air Force's professional military education institutions, Air Command and Staff College, and teaches them the art and science of airpower strategy. In 2002 the school began sending its students through an advanced course in command and control taught at Hurlburt Field.

62. Jones, "505th Command and Control Wing."

63. Woodward, *Bush at War,* amounts to a series of published interviews with the principal players in the Bush administration, as well as some special forces. See also 48–49, 61–62, and 81–82 for descriptions of wrestling with the scope of the war, and 37, 144–45, and 175–76 for Bush's view of leading but delegating to the experts.

64. Bush, "Address to a Joint Session of Congress."

65. Woodward, *Bush at War*, 44, 51–52.

66. Ibid., 135. The quote is Woodward's formulation of Rumsfeld's thoughts about transforming the military while fighting a war. For a description of Bush and Rumsfeld trying to push the military to come up with innovative solutions, see 43–44, 62–63, and 99.

67. Arkin, "Rules of Engagement." The exception was if the CIA had bin Laden or al-Qaeda leadership "in its crosshairs," according to Woodward. See also Crowder to the author, e-mail; and Woodward, *Bush at War*, 166. Col Gary Crowder, 505 CCW/CV at the time of this writing, was the deputy C-3, OAF, and the senior offensive duty officer, OEF, 7 Oct.–28 Nov. 2001.

68. Woodward, *Bush at War*, 166, 193–94, and 247.

69. Franks, *American Soldier*, 290.

70. Knaub to the author, e-mail, 5 Nov. 2004. Lt Col Brett Knaub worked in CENTCOM/J3 during OEF–Afghanistan.

71. General Franks, quoted in Ricks, "War That's Commanded," A16.

72. Deptula, interview by the author, 22 Apr. 2004. Lt Gen David Deptula, USAF, was chief of the Iraq Cell in TACC during Desert Storm and CAOC director during OEF.

73. Conetta, "Strange Victory." See also Woodward, *Bush at War*, 149, 154, 174–75, 215, and 234.

74. Woodward, *Plan of Attack*, 30, 38.

75. Franks, *American Soldier*, 290. Franks' recollection of the 28 Dec. 2001 meeting on 347–56 is a good example. Franks proposed diplomatic options to the NSC members, who also probed him with questions about what he would do about the "fortress Baghdad" problem and WMDs, each wanting to line up with the other's strategy.

76. Thomas and Brant, "Education of Tommy Franks."

77. Woodward, *Plan of Attack*, 98.

78. Franks, *American Soldier*, 335–40.

79. Ibid., 376–77. See also sketch, 396.

80. Gellman and Priest, "CIA Had Fix on Hussein."

81. The air component executed 156 TSTs that General Franks had specifically designated as such, to include terrorists, leadership, and WMDs. Additionally, there were 686 strikes on other targets, called *dynamic targets*, using the same procedures but attacking targets that General Franks had not specifically designated TSTs. Moseley, "OIF by the Numbers," 9.

82. Thomas and Brant, "Education of Tommy Franks," A-1.

83. Clausewitz, *On War*, 88.

84. Moltke said that "the demands of strategy grow silent in the face of a tactical victory and adapt themselves to the newly created situation. Strategy is a system of expedients." Hughes and Bell, eds., *Moltke on the Art of War*, 47.

85. Cohen, *Supreme Command*, 196.

86. Ibid., 195.

87. O'Mara in "Stealth, Precision" gives an in-depth analysis of this point and presents his conclusions (100–106).

THIS PAGE INTENTIONALLY LEFT BLANK

Chapter 5

Command Relationships in the CAOS

On 27 July 2004, JEFX 04 was conducting simulations to give CAOC operators practice prior to the deployment of aircraft. However, those in the "Time-Critical Targeting" (TCT) Cell were frustrated. Several simulated Scud launches had been conducted that morning, and the team had been unable to get permission in time to attack any of them before they moved. The TCT Cell team chief went to talk to the senior officer on the operations floor of the CAOC, who sent a message (via "instant messaging") to the CFACC. In this (e-mail) chat session, he told the CFACC that the air component had been unable to target Scud missiles even when ground troops had spotted the launchers and strike aircraft were in the area because coordination with other components and with the combined forces commander had taken too long. He suggested that the CFC make the CFACC the "supported commander" for these attacks.[1]

The next day, the CFACC informed the TCT team members that they had received permission to execute the requested change. From then on, launcher sightings were handled using a much abbreviated process since the CFACC was the supported commander for this objective. Interestingly (as shown later), this mirrors a change in procedures that occurred between OEF in Afghanistan and OIF. Between the two operations, General Franks, the CFC, worked out many kinks in procedures mainly by realigning command relationships.

The impact of technology on the principles of centralized versus decentralized control cannot be determined without also considering the influence of other factors: organizational issues are some of the most prominent. The organizations that make up the US military are a disparate bunch, as has been illustrated. Their various cultures and constraints shape the way they view the world, especially in terms of C2.

Part of the definition of control was influencing others to act on command decisions. The CFC does this partly through organizing components in a way that empowers them to accomplish the right missions. Previously, it was proposed that command relationships have always been one of the factors that determined whether the control of airpower was centralized (see chap. 2). The issue for the Air Force (and, earlier, the AAF) was that there should be a single manager of airpower. Thus, to the Air Force the important thing is not *how* centralized the control of airpower is but *where* it is centralized.

These issues are examined here by exploring how command relationships were handled in the four major conflicts in the period of this study—Desert Storm, Allied Force, Enduring Freedom–Afghanistan (including Operation Anaconda), and Iraqi Freedom. This chapter demonstrates that there is a definite link between the way the components performed and the way they were empowered by the combined or joint force commander. During this time, the air component was most proactive about developing strategy when given the freedom to develop it—to include targeting—at the air component. When the CFC set up organizational processes that took air strategy development out of the air component's hands, it became less proactive, and coordination among all of the components suffered. The components kept innovating at the tactical level, but operational strategy suffered. Increased communications technology was no silver bullet for this problem—it took hard work on organizational relationships to solve it.

Command relationships went beyond the ability to plan operations. Ground and air forces from multiple components became integrated to an extent not seen before and needed to find a way to use the strong points of each. In some cases, it was beneficial to ignore global procedures and give as much discretion to those on the scene as possible. In others, this discretion meant no one was able to prioritize and allocate resources. The tighter the coupling, the more imperative it was to provide depth—to extend authority to the lowest level so someone on the scene had the ability to allocate resources based on good situational awareness.

Organizations and Command Relationships

In his book, *Bureaucracy*, James Wilson proposes that it is nearly impossible for governmental bureaucracies to resolve the tension between trustful delegation and maintaining accountability.[2] Bureaucracies have inherent barriers that are purposefully manipulated in order to help the organization perform its functions. This leads to the development of organizational cultures—distinctive ways of seeing and responding to the environment. Often, as in the military, these cultures are formed by the actions of founders or heroes, whose stories are retold to keep their ethos alive. The culture becomes a mission, helping drive the members to action when they normally would not be inclined to act. It also helps reduce the amount of direction the leaders need to give and provides a shared framework for analyzing information, reducing distortion of transmitted information.[3]

Many have attempted to account for the differences among the US military services in terms of origin, function, structure, or culture—most seem to fall short. In one of the more well-known efforts on the subject, Carl Builder tried to put labels on the service cultures.[4] In doing so, he failed to analyze perhaps the most distinctive of the military services, the Marine Corps. He also suffered from unfortunate timing as his analysis was completed before the effects of the Goldwater-Nichols Defense Reorganization Act and the transition to the "fighter generals" could be assessed.[5] Even if one disagrees with the applicability of the particular labels Builder chose, or even with his ability to choose labels, it is nevertheless evident that the services see the world differently. While claiming to do what they do in the interest of national security, in reality, they all respond in ways that seem to protect their own assets. The concept of command probably produces the greatest disputes among the organizations in the US military. It was seen previously that all but the Air Force resisted the concept of the JFACC—especially the Marines, which insisted on an Omnibus Agreement giving them OPCON of their air assets. The reason for this is simple. It is one thing for a subordinate unit to submit to the direction of its superior commander; it is quite another to develop a lateral command relationship. Although Air Force wings may desire a bit more autonomy in the planning of their missions, they generally agree with the concept of centralized control *by an Airman*. After all, it is usually an *Air Force* Airman. Consequently, to gain control of Navy, Marine, and Army aviation, the JFACC will have to overcome extreme resistance.

The principle is similar when talking about components, as opposed to services. Air commanders see WWII as the proof that air forces should not be parceled out to ground commanders. The two mediums have spawned vastly different cultures that influence the way their members see C2. Many scholars have linked this difference to the formative influence of theorists.[6] However, it is likely these theorists' writings were symptomatic as well as formative. The physical constraints of the mediums within which the forces do their work have much to do with the way they view war. Aircraft are relatively unhindered by terrestrial barriers and have the range (with refueling) and speed to go almost anywhere in a theater of war. The main concern of Airmen is, then, ensuring resources are prioritized based on the most important objectives. Tying scarce resources such as electronic warfare aircraft or ISR assets to an area risks not having them where they are needed. Only a theater-level view can overcome this. Ground forces, on the other hand, are subject to terrestrial barriers. Because of these constraints, ground commanders must try to gain advantage by maneuvering in conjunction with firepower—the two are inseparable. They need to be assured that they can place firepower and the other effects of airpower where and when they are needed.

Differing viewpoints of the services and components make it difficult to take full advantage of the technology that is available today. The same thing happened in the business world. In the 1980s, the infusion of IT enabled bureaucratic rigidity, not decentralized decision making. It was not until organizations started crossing oceans and cultures that the full potential of networking began to be realized. Corporations had to learn to depend on a complex web of strategic alliances, subcontracting, and decentralized decision making enabled by computer networks.[7] They are learning to outsource parts of their operations to others who are more capable of performing a certain task.[8] In the same way, the ground, air, and SOF components—and even the CIA—have come to depend on one another in recent wars. In some cases, it is acceptable, even necessary, for these organizations to do whatever it takes to accomplish a mission. In others, it is essential for them to adhere to global procedures. Command relationships have to be deep enough so that there is always some type of command presence with the situational awareness and communications capability to strike this balance.

Thus, the integration of ground and air forces presents challenges. The first of these is allocating resources so that the broader theater objectives—one of which is working with ground forces—are all supported in priority order. The second is determining how to leverage command relationships so interacting components can take full advantage of the capabilities when they need it most. These are both issues of command relationships.

Desert Storm

Chapter 4 proposes that developing a policy that leads clearly and simply to a military strategy that, in turn, plainly elicits tactical actions that achieve the policy is not an easy task. In actuality, it is not a serial task—policy and military action often interact to change each other as a conflict goes on. This becomes most obvious in a conflict where strategic objectives are nebulous. But even where those objectives seem clearer, strategy development is rarely straightforward. While the previous chapter claims that the objectives in Desert Storm were clear and easily adaptable to military strategy, in the beginning it was not obvious how to translate these into actions.

This is why, when General Schwarzkopf received a briefing from Col John Warden (USAF) on 10 August 1990, he was pleased. Much had transpired—Saddam had taken Kuwait in three days, deployed the world's fourth largest army immediately across the border from Saudi Arabia, and held American hostages in Baghdad. Schwarzkopf had been meeting with Pres. George H. W. Bush and saw his concern that the United States would have no viable options to back up the strong national objectives he had set (listed in chap. 4). Now Warden was in Schwarzkopf's office laying out in detail, in a plan called "Instant Thunder," how airpower could defeat the Iraqi dictator in six days without sending in American ground troops. One of Warden's officers recounted Schwarzkopf proclaiming, "You've renewed my confidence in the US Air Force."[9] Indeed, Warden's Checkmate office, normally focused on developing strategy against the Soviet Union, had shown remarkable initiative in coming up with a plan. It did so by piecing together strategic objectives from speeches by President Bush and other officials at a time when everyone was in motion reacting to the surprise invasion of Kuwait.[10]

The fact that the strategy had been developed by a single office in a single service and was briefed to the key players one by one created a conflict of its own. On 11 August, Warden briefed CJCS Powell, who questioned the premise that airpower by itself would yield a satisfactory outcome. Although on the whole Powell was pleased with the effort, Lt Col Ben Harvey (USAF) remembers him saying, "Your strategic air campaign cuts out the guts and heart, but what about his hands. . . . I want to leave smoking tanks as kilometer posts all the way to Baghdad!"[11]

The reaction Warden's Checkmate team got from General Powell paled, however, in comparison to the reception they got from General Horner in Riyadh, Saudi Arabia, nine days later. On 6 August, Schwarzkopf had put Horner in charge of the forces in Saudi Arabia, while Schwarzkopf went back to the United States to do the high-level coordination. From that moment until the briefing on 20 August, Horner had been consumed with getting forces in-theater and establishing a working relationship with the Saudis.[12] An advance copy of Warden's briefing only served to make Horner more wary of the efforts going on in Washington.[13] The briefing by Warden and three others flopped. Horner accepted the plan as a starting point but had serious questions about many of the targets and, especially, the overall concept of winning with air alone. He asked three of Warden's deputies to stay and help him plan but extended no such invitation to Warden.[14]

Five days later, their proposal was part of a larger CENTCOM plan. On 25 August, Schwarzkopf briefed Powell on a four-phase plan to eject Iraqi forces from Kuwait. The first phase was remarkably similar to the Instant Thunder plan, only without the intent to win the entire war through the strategic air attacks. The second phase was to gain air superiority over Kuwait, the third phase would prepare the battlefield by reducing Iraqi ground forces, and the final phase was a ground offensive into Kuwait.[15]

With this unprecedented opportunity for the air component, Horner built his organization around the adapted Instant Thunder plan. He established a top secret division, later called the "Black Hole," under (then) Brig Gen Buster Glosson, and set the group to work developing the targeting strategy from Instant Thunder into an operations plan for war. There was no doctrinal basis for this organizational design—doctrine at the time specified only a TACC with four divisions: the Combat Operations and Enemy Situation Correlation Divisions for today's war, and the Combat Plans and Combat Intelligence Divisions for tomorrow's war.[16] There was also no provision for developing strategy. Yet Horner set up this ad hoc organization and gave it tremendous authority within the overall air component. Later, on 5 December of that year, he formally reorganized Central Command Air Forces (CENTAF) around the new division. The Black Hole became the Iraq Cell in the new Campaign Plans Division, while the Combat Operations Planning Division, which had built a plan for the defense of Saudi Arabia, became the Kuwaiti Theater of Operations Cell. At the same time, Horner expanded Glosson's role by giving him command of the provisional air wing that included all Air Force fighters in-theater.[17]

During most of Desert Storm, the Black Hole planners, who were now the Iraq Cell planners, had broad authority and minimal direction. Lt Col (now Lt Gen) David Deptula, one of the three officers who had come with Warden back in August, became the principal planner. He described it as a "planner's dream" in that there were very few externally imposed limitations. "The [principal] guiding element was mission effectiveness . . . and accomplishing the objectives—which, in fact, we developed!"[18] Working in a top secret area where only a small group of people could enter, Deptula developed a master attack plan (MAP), a document that conveyed the air strategy as a list of attacks by specific weapons systems against specific targets at designated times. Glosson attended a meeting with Schwarzkopf each evening to explain the MAP and get Schwarzkopf's guidance. He would then bring the guidance back informally and give it to Deptula verbally. Using this data, Deptula made any changes to the next day's missions or the following day's MAP. He also wrote an air guidance letter (officially from Horner) to convey direction to the other divisions about details that were not in the MAP.[19]

To determine what targets best accomplished the objectives, Black Hole planners reached out to establish contacts with other agencies. Warden continued to support them with Checkmate's extensive contacts at the NSC, the CIA, the Air Force intelligence shop, and the Defense Intelligence Agency in Washington.[20] SAF Rice helped get information from US and foreign contractors to analyze the target systems in Iraq.[21] Although Glosson had close ties with Adm Joseph McConnell, the intelligence director on the joint staff, this was really an instance where those in-theater were calling back to use the expertise and contacts of those in Washington—reachback.[22] The Black Hole reached out to pull all the information in and assemble it into a "big picture," the entirety of which was only visible in their top secret working area.

With this amount of ownership over the information, Deptula was able to create an extremely intricate plan. As he put it, the MAP was the "operational level 'blueprint' which tied the strategic-level objectives to tactical level execution."[23] Normally, targeteers would apply weapons to a prioritized list of targets, destroying as many targets as possible with the available weapons. Inevitably, this meant that some lower-priority targets would not be attacked. Deptula and Warden saw the enemy as a system and thought the best way to disable it was to create effects across all target categories simultaneously. In Deptula's mind, it was better to achieve effects short of destruction on all the targets than to destroy some and not touch others. Failing to attack some of the lower-priority targets could nullify the impacts of completely destroying the higher-priority targets. Consequently, he spread scarce resources such as F-117 stealth fighters across many targets, using only one or two per target instead of enough to guarantee destruction in the conventional sense. Still, the stealth and accuracy of these planes and their precision munitions made them very effective when used in this manner.[24] It was the first explicit use of effects-based operations.

During the initial phase of the war, this detailed planning method seems to have been acceptable to most of the participants. Ground commanders were not concerned with the areas deep in Iraq. Attacks on Baghdad, while potentially helpful by disconnecting the Iraqi troops from their C2, were out of their purview. Even the Scud Hunt, while politically sensitive, had little bearing on when the ground invasion could be undertaken.

Conflict gradually brewed. The JFACC was a new and untested concept of command. Now, not only had Schwarzkopf named a JFACC, but he had given that JFACC a large part in determining the war strategy. For the first three phases of the war, the air component was the only one fighting in enemy territory, and the view of the enemy as a system worked just fine. Ground commanders did not see the enemy this way.

As is normally the case in a conventional conflict, the ground commanders had been given separate areas of responsibility. During the planning for the land offensives, Schwarzkopf's staff tried unsuccessfully to buck this trend and integrate the services in a single attack. Graduates of the US Army's School of Advanced Military Studies, nicknamed "Jedi Knights," initially tried to use the Marines as a breaching force in advance of the Army attack. Schwarzkopf backed Marine lieutenant general Walter Boomer in shooting the idea down. He also rejected the next idea, to use the Marines in a "fixing attack" to give the Army a cover for its "left hook." The Marines were to be given their own area of operations and left to come up with their own plan of attack.[25]

Marine air forces were therefore destined to be focused on a geographical area instead of the enemy as a whole. The Marines already disagreed with the concept of the JFACC; now they had justification to demand control of their aircraft. Since they do not have much heavy artillery, they rely on—and are considered very good at—the cooperation of ground and air power. They deploy troops in a Marine air-ground task force, complete with C2 systems, and consider their air forces inseparable from their ground forces. Schwarzkopf's assignment of an area of operations made the Marines responsible for "shaping" this area so the eventual attack would be successful. Combined with the Omnibus Agreement, this was enough for Maj Gen Royal Moore, Boomer's air commander, to try and justify holding Marine air forces back from the JFACC.

Now Horner had to make a decision. As the plan was written, it was the JFACC's job to prepare the entire battlefield, and the air component wanted to use airpower in an integrated effort to do this. The Marines' viewpoint was focused on the upcoming ground battles, not the air battles. Handing sorties over to the JFACC made the Marines nervous that they would not be able to use them for CAS in the ground battles, and they began withholding more and more sorties from the targeting process.[26] In the end, the air component planners realized the smart thing to do was to let the Marines perform any of the shaping that had to be done in their area of operations.[27] Air Force and Navy aircraft could fly the remaining sorties elsewhere. This was possible because there was no shortage of non-Marine aircraft.

The Army had some of the same concerns. As the air campaign progressed, Army commanders also became impatient for the air component to focus on the Iraqi units immediately across from them. On 9 February 1991, SecDef Cheney and CJCS Powell met with Schwarzkopf and the component commanders to discuss when to begin the ground war. Deptula attended and wrote in a memo afterward that he found it frustrating to hear Army colonels asking, "When will we get 'our' air?"[28] With the ground war approaching, ground commanders were requesting that the air component help them shape the battlefields for which they would be responsible. When they perceived that the air component was not filling all the requests, they got upset.

But Horner was following orders from Schwarzkopf. Schwarzkopf had not designated a land component commander; he basically fulfilled that role himself so that he had final say on where the air resources would be used to support ground forces. Schwarzkopf chose to use the preplanned sorties mainly on the Republican Guard units, even though this was not the way his ground commanders wanted it. The trouble was that the Army commanders were not privy to the meetings between Schwarzkopf, Horner, and Glosson on these matters. Horner remembers Schwarzkopf settling the matter one evening by telling air and ground commanders alike, "Guys, it's all mine, and I will put it where it needs to be put!"[29]

The JFC finally decided to lend some formal organization as the solution to this problem. He put his deputy, Gen Calvin Waller, in charge of the target-nomination process. Waller took all the target nominations from the corps commanders and prioritized them, and this was the list toward which the air component planned. Put in perspective, Horner claimed he was comfortable with the arrangement because now, instead of five or six lists, he got one—and it had a certain legitimacy about it.[30]

Horner thought the point was moot—he believed the best way to support the ground commanders was to create the ability to adjust the missions in real time. His planners were not concerned about the targets the ground commanders were nominating because they had made provisions to attack those targets, in addition to the preplanned targets. They sent interdiction missions to 30-nautical-mile-square *killboxes* to attack the fielded forces there.[31] Essentially, as with armed reconnaissance missions, the pilots became the sensors, decision makers, and executors—a cockpit fusion cell. Later, when pilots had trouble finding the targets in the high threat environment, the aircrews came up with a concept called the *Killer Scout*, placing a single pilot in charge of directing other pilots to targets in the killboxes (addressed in greater detail in chap. 8).

When the ground war started, the planners also made provisions to have aircraft available for the real-time CAS requests that they knew would emerge. Horner had crafted a concept he called "push CAS," whereby a steady stream of aircraft would fly to the battle areas. If the ground troops needed them, they performed CAS. If not, when replacements came, they went to a preassigned target. The difference between interdiction and CAS was whether the mission occurred within a designated area close to the ground troops. The boundary to this zone was the fire support coordination line (FSCL). Aircrew flying short of the FSCL had to be under the control of the ground troops; those long of the FSCL were sent to killboxes.[32] In this situation, there was sufficient depth in the command relationships to handle this allocation. It was the ABCCC's job to route aircraft to the appropriate place and make decisions to redirect the aircraft as necessary. An ASOC filtered the requests from ground troops to prioritize them.

Notice the difference between the solutions in relation to the degree of coupling of the situations. When strikes were long of the FSCL, air and ground forces did not have to coordinate. The friendly troops were well clear, and the targets were not of urgent importance—they would affect the friendly troops later rather than sooner. These are loosely coupled situations, and Horner did not care whether the targets were preplanned and provided by the ground troops or found by the Killer Scouts (although he thought the latter more effective, if not efficient). For the tightly coupled operations in the vicinity of friendly ground troops, however, the disparate forces needed a way to reallocate resources. The ABCCC and ASOC were decision makers in constant communications with those on the scene. Obviously, they could only mediate conflicts based on priorities and information received over the radio. They did not have access to a good picture of the battlefield, so their situational awareness was limited.[33]

Schwarzkopf and Horner were at liberty to establish these relationships because the policy makers had imposed relatively few specific constraints. Schwarzkopf was free to give Horner significant authority to develop strategy, and Horner was, in turn, free to release authority to his TACS. Horner also coordinated well with the land component. It is true ground commanders were not happy with their inability to influence the targeting, but their dispute was with their land component commander—Schwarzkopf. The air component set up killbox interdiction (KI) and push CAS to support the ground commanders' immediate needs.

Allied Force

As discussed in chapter 3, in the 1990s the US government had developed a pattern of using airpower to deliver short, hard knocks, which had been relatively successful in containing, deterring, or even compelling adversaries in Bosnia and Iraq. Consequently, when the United States detected intransigence from the Serbs in 1999, it sought to deliver the same type of treatment that had been successful before.

Thus, on 24 March 1999 when the war started, there were no plans for a sustained effort to accomplish strategic objectives. Instead, there was a target development and approval process. Whereas in Desert Storm Schwarzkopf had initially let the Black Hole develop the targets—supported by informal contacts in Washington—now General Clark's staff directed the process, and the intelligence network was formalized. Clark gave guidance to set the intelligence community in motion to obtain information on appropriate targets. Then the Joint Analysis Center (JAC), RAF Molesworth, England, validated the targets and posted the materials (messages, imagery, etc.) on its servers. The Navy (for Tomahawk missiles) and Air Force planners took the information and created target folders that were then visible on a secure network worldwide. They also created special presidential slides (known as POTUS for President of the United States) for President Clinton, outlining the target and the options for attacking it along with projected collateral damage estimates.[34]

This process was possible because of the development of Web technology. On 3 March 1994, the DOD had brought online a separate backbone router system to handle transmission of classified data. This system, the SECRET Internet Protocol Router Network (SIPRNET), used the same protocols as the unclassified Internet and quickly became the preferred method of transmitting classified data among US organizations.[35] Target folders could now be shared among all the participants in this process—all the US participants, that is.

Yet as formal as this process seems, it was the informal part that caused the most headaches in the air component. Each day, Clark would convene VTCs to disseminate guidance and discuss issues. Because President Clinton wanted to have the ultimate approval authority for each target, Clark was held to a high level of accountability for the specific targets being attacked. As a result, he used these VTCs to discuss the status of individual targets whenever necessary. That sometimes meant adding or deleting targets that were on the ATO for the next day.[36] This was a problem for the air component because each change affected many other missions due to tanker and other support required. Also, these changes were never documented in writing—the memories of the VTC participants were the only record. Air planners came to refer to these VTCs as the "1,000 kilometer screwdriver."[37] As airpower analysts have pointed out, the end result was that the focus of the air component became the prosecution of targets versus the creation of effects to accomplish goals and objectives.[38]

This strategy debate soon devolved into an argument between Clark and his CFACC, General Short. In the absence of ground troops, Short thought the way to get Milosevic to stop the ethnic cleansing and remove his 3rd Army from Kosovo was to hit him at home in Belgrade. He realized that without putting troops on the ground, NATO would not be able to cause enough damage to the Serb forces to cause them to go home.[39] When Milosevic intensified his ethnic cleansing efforts after 31 March, expelling over 400,000 people in a week, Clark saw the chance to step up attacks in Kosovo.[40] However, he did not yet have permission to increase the attacks in Serbia. Short knew that the USAF had neither the equipment nor the techniques for hunting down the Serb forces that were free to disperse and hide because they were not subject to an opposing ground force. US Air Force A-10s, in-theater for rescue efforts, tried to innovate but were extremely limited until the last two weeks of the war when a KLA attack forced the Serbs to mass in defense.[41] Short knew he could not "win" by attacking Serb forces in southern Kosovo with airpower alone. Clark knew he could not "win" without these attacks.[42] Milosevic's strategy of ethnic cleansing gave NATO the opportunity to stay on high ground as long as NATO was seen to be trying to do something about it.

It added up to an odd situation for the air component. Just as in Desert Storm, it was the only one of the components fighting in enemy territory. The difference this time was that it was not allowed to develop the strategy by first constructing a systemic view of the enemy and then dismantling that system in order to achieve strategic objectives. Because of this difference, the air component had to look for ways to do a job for which it had not prepared. The long campaign against the Serb army was unexpected, as was the difficulty finding and destroying mobile SAMs that the Serbs would not use in order to keep hidden. The Air Force found itself in a 78-day conflict, with the Serbs refusing to radiate with their mobile threat radars. As the Serb army was the most wanted—and least restricted—target set, the air component had to take action. The quest to hit moving targets was, in the beginning, an attempt to take the fight to the Serb army in the daytime.[43]

In April, Short established a "Flex-Targeting Cell" that was really two cells in one. The Integrated Air Defense System (IADS) Targeting Cell, under the C-2 (deputy for intelligence) attempted to fuse intelligence to find and destroy the elusive threat of SAMs. The Fielded Forces Attack Cell, under the C-3 (deputy for operations) attempted to find and destroy the Serb forces that were carrying out the ethnic cleansing campaign. On 14 April, the planners finally established a "Kosovo Engagement Zone" (KEZ) to allow the attacking aircraft to engage targets of opportunity. The KEZ was similar to killboxes that had been used in the past (including Desert Storm) to destroy armies in the field. Only now the army was not in the field but hiding amongst the civilians and under camouflage. Suddenly, A-10s that had been brought to the war for the sole purpose of conducting search and rescue had a new mission—they were the FAC(A)s.[44]

In this way, constraints from the strategic level determined the amount of authority the air component could exercise in developing strategy. The constraints from the strategic level were that (1) there would be no ground troops, and (2) the policy makers would control the target approval process. This led Clark to put the emphasis on attacking Serb ground troops with airpower and to take a personal interest in the fixed target selection. The result was that the air missions were overwhelmingly geared toward fleeting targets (due to their ability to hide and not mass for the defense)—IADS and fielded forces. A total of 23,300 strike missions were conducted in OAF, directed at 7,600 aimpoints associated with fixed targets and 3,400 flex targets.[45]

With little empowerment and its focus narrowed to ongoing operations, the air component did not develop very deep command relationships. It will be seen that the CAOC became the de facto approval authority for the emerging targets that the FAC(A)s found in Kosovo. The pilots had to call back through AWACS or ABCCC, which in most cases functioned as radio relays for the CAOC.

By using such constraints, policy makers had also transformed the war into a loosely coupled situation. There was no need to integrate air and ground forces. Air attacks were not allowed unless approved at a high level. Only when aircrews tried to attack Serbs in the vicinity of civilians did conditions become tightly coupled, and the CAOC had developed restrictions to avoid this type of scenario. Of course, these were the very times when coordination of forces was most needed to stop ethnic cleansing. If outlasting Milosevic was more important than stopping the ethnic cleansing, then the transformation to a loosely coupled situation was appropriate. If not, the constraints on ground forces and targets were mistakes.

Enduring Freedom

The Bush administration was determined to give the military more say in the way it fought. As noted in chapter 3, the NSC staff had numerous discussions with General Franks, CENTCOM commander, to come up with the strategy in the war. It was a difficult task. SecDef Rumsfeld kept pushing Franks to develop innovative options but was frequently disappointed.[46] In fairness to Franks, no one really knew exactly what to do or how to do it. In the beginning, the NSC staff thought only about exploiting cracks in the Taliban to cause them to break up. There was no formal call for actually helping the Northern Alliance overthrow the Taliban—there was too much risk in that.[47] It was not until later that this shift occurred.

It is no surprise that the overall military strategy was the subject of controversy. In Franks' memoirs, he recalls crafting a four-phase plan: (1) set conditions and build forces to provide the national command authority credible military options; (2) conduct initial combat operations and continue to set conditions for follow-on operations; (3) implement decisive combat operations in Afghanistan, continue to build coalition, and accomplish operations AOR-wide; and (4) establish capability of coalition partners to prevent the reemergence of terrorism and provide support for humanitarian assistance efforts.[48] He and his staff discussed the options to accomplish these phases, and decided on: (1) a massive Tomahawk land-attack missile (TLAM) strike, (2) an air campaign consisting of a TLAM strike followed by B-2 strikes, (3) the same air campaign followed by SOF support to the Northern Alliance, and (4) option three followed by a large deployment of conventional American ground forces. As Franks recalls, his position was, "First we see what the Northern Alliance, with our help, can do. Then we use larger formations if we have to."[49] Combining the phases with the options, in retrospect it seems clear that the CENTCOM commander meant to use the air campaign and SOF/Northern Alliance options for Phase 2 and American forces for Phase 3.

The air component differed with this viewpoint—it was trying to be decisive from the beginning, 7 October 2001. When CENTCOM sent out an order for Phase 2 on 1 November, officers in the air component responded vigorously that the plan was flawed. They claimed the order misrepresented what was going on and did not include a method to achieve any objectives in Phase 2. They also pointed out that the coalition JFACC had the preponderance of assets carrying out the strikes and was the only one with the C2 systems to control them. Their position was that Franks should make the coalition JFACC the supported commander for the phase and concentrate on fighting what was turning out to be a decisive, conventional war for control of Afghanistan. The failure to do so had resulted in disjointed operations, such as some SOF teams going in "without the training and equipment to effectively orchestrate the air support that they required."[50] In fact, as seen later, the marrying of airpower with the Afghanistan opposition fighters through US special operations liaisons on the ground turned the tide, allowing the coalition to completely wrest control of the country from the Taliban. Yet this was only Phase 2B in the CENTCOM order.[51] Of course, the war was not over when the Taliban was overthrown. However, less than two years later in Iraq, Franks would recommend that President Bush call an end to "decisive combat" after the Ba'ath Regime was removed from power, even though the same tasks remained there.[52]

The point is that the strategy was anything but clear in the beginning, and Franks did not want to delegate the task of writing that strategy to his air component. The winning strategy evolved as the SOF began linking airpower with Afghanistan's opposition forces. The situation sounds similar to the one in OAF, except that in OEF, the air component was ready to fight a sustained war. The complete organization was ready to work.

It was therefore a source of frustration to the officers in the air component that they were given little authority to develop strategy. Now General Deptula, the planner from Desert Storm who was given the freedom to develop the MAP using effects-based planning, became the CAOC director in Afghanistan. He was appalled that CENTCOM essentially issued targets to its air component, taking much of the planning out of its hands.[53] F-16 pilot Maj David Hathaway was in a similar position to the one Deptula had filled in Desert Storm, but found that his job as deputy chief of strategy involved little strategy development. He felt the CENTCOM J-2 (deputy for intelligence) was trying to force the air component to follow its strategy by releasing only a select few targets at a time.[54]

In fact, CENTCOM workers were struggling with target development as well. Lt Col Brett Knaub, an Air Force officer working for Maj Gen Gene Renuart (USAF), Franks' chief of operations (J-3), crafted guidance each day that Franks would sign and brief to the component commanders during a daily VTC. The purpose of the guidance was to prioritize objectives for the next four days, but it also delved into specific targets. CENTCOM maintained the entire target list (JIPTL) and decided which of the targets would be hit when. The air component still put together a MAP (now called MAAP for master air attack plan), but it was based on explicit direction from Tampa Bay.[55]

That CENTCOM was the one collecting all target nominations, determining the priority of each, and deciding what effort was to be apportioned to each was not lost on Deptula. He remembers the point in Desert Storm where this had occurred in response to ground commanders' perceptions that they were not getting "their" air. It seemed a misguided attempt to satisfy all players—one that, in his opinion, had failed in Kosovo and seemed to promise only the "suboptimization" of airpower.[56] To others, including such specific targeting details in what should have been broad direction made CENTCOM's daily guidance too "complex."[57]

While there are several possible reasons this situation occurred, it appears to be partly due to the ROEs. As mentioned in chapter 3, the NSC staff had developed a category of "sensitive" targets for which the military had to seek approval. The military also had to get permission to hit any targets that could be expected to cause moderate to high collateral damage. In Afghanistan, unlike in Kosovo, these strategic-level decision makers did not hold the entire target-approval process at their level. The restrictions were probably designed to ensure that proper diligence was used in avoiding excessive damage. Although the authority for target approval was delegated to Franks soon after the war started, the precedent had been set that targeting was to be watched carefully by the highest levels.[58] It was predictable that Franks' staff would be heavily involved in the targeting.

An unusual command structure also contributed to the consolidation of decision authority at CENTCOM. As previously indicated, Franks thought "decisive operations" would not occur until later. However, the war became decisive early, and the United States–led coalition had no land component in this largely conventional war. Albeit that much has been made of the unprecedented cooperation between SO troops and airpower facilitated by sensors and precision weapons, the fact remains that the airpower was still largely in support of conventional troops on the ground. One analyst called it a "surprisingly orthodox air-ground theater campaign in which heavy fire support decided a contest between two land forces."[59] When the air effort assists the ground effort, normally the air component is made the supporting component, and the ground component is the supported component. This was not possible because the ground had no representation. The troops were the anti-Taliban forces, who had little firepower and thus relied on the United States–led coalition's airpower. They were not, however, under Franks' command—he could only coordinate with them. The SOF troops were his means to do that.

The SOF also contributed to the unfamiliarity of the command structure. There were two joint SO task forces—one in the northern part of the country and one in the southern part.[60] Although these forces eventually all had tactical controllers, they did not have the C2 capability that conventional forces bring with them. For example, they did not have an ASOC with the ability to see the ATO and determine which sorties were available so they could prioritize. Also, the SOF could not allocate resources, only call for and provide terminal control for them. Thus, the air component was the one providing the bulk of the force and the ability to command and control that force, but it was not in contact with the ground forces except through the SOF troops.

The CIA was another wrinkle in the command structure. As discussed previously, although the CIA had agreed to work for Franks, the authority to command and control the CIA's (UAV) Predators stopped here. The unusual nature of this arrangement and the discomfort it caused at the top led CENTCOM to hold authority to coordinate with the CIA at the staff level in Tampa Bay.

Another possible reason that CENTCOM kept decision authority at its headquarters is that the war was small and Franks did, in fact, have substantial technology to keep track of events. The first night's strikes were aimed at only 31 targets, using 50 Tomahawk missiles, 15 heavy bombers, and 25 attack fighters along with support aircraft.[61] During the first three months, rarely more than a dozen aircraft were over Afghanistan at any given time, making it possible to watch the action on a map-like display projected on a wall in the CAOC. The Global Command and Control System (GCCS) had an application called the *com-*

mon operating picture that showed a digital map of all aircraft (among other things) fused together from different sensors.[62]

The available sensors were also much improved. The combination of Air Force and CIA Predators, the Global Hawk UAV, the JSTARS, U-2 and RC-135 aircraft, and satellites meant that the force had multispectral sensors with some pretty good endurance. The fact that the Defense Department had purchased all the commercial satellite bandwidth in the region on 12 September meant they could pass the information back immediately.[63] What made the real difference, though, was the addition of ground troops. The CAOC and CENTCOM got unprecedented volumes of human intelligence because of the SOF troops operating with the Afghanistan opposition.[64]

The result of all this was that a great deal of the responsibility for the plans in the first months of the Afghanistan war fell to the CENTCOM planners. Strict ROEs led to a high level of accountability for targeting. Franks thought that the initial stages would just be a period of setting conditions for US troops to come in and win the war. When the Northern Alliance became surprisingly successful, Franks had no way to control the planning of this ground war from CENTCOM. He had an air component, but they were technically in support of this ground force, so he probably saw it as inappropriate to let them take over strategy. The special forces were divided and did not have the C2 capability to perform the role. The CIA forces were joined with the military only at Franks' level. So all lines led back to CENTCOM in Tampa Bay. Franks felt he had the ability to handle this situation, given the technology and the size of the war.

Despite the increased communications capability, interaction between the different components of Franks' force appears to have been poor. Interestingly, troops from different services serving at the same location seemed to develop a team attitude that sometimes overshadowed ties to fellow service members at other locations. Even as an Air Force officer, Knaub relates that he found it difficult to defend some of the air component's actions to his CENTCOM coworkers at times.[65] Planners at CENTCOM thought the planners at the air component were following their own priorities, not those of CENTCOM. When Franks learned three leadership targets had not been attacked in the first round, he sent a message to Wald: "In the future pay attention to my priorities—

priorities based on the needs of the joint team, not the desire of a single service."[66] CENTAF planners, on the other hand, insist that no sorties or targets issued by CENTCOM were ignored or changed, except for weather or maintenance.[67] Similarly, Deptula briefed that cooperation among the different services within the CAOC was "seamless" and "unprecedented."[68] This painted a somewhat rosier picture than existed, as air planners not only thought that CENTCOM was trying to do their job for them, but also that it had little insight into what was happening on the ground in Afghanistan. Officers in the CAOC overwhelmingly agreed that they were unable to receive information about either the SOF's locations or plans in time to develop strategy to help them—despite the fact that there was a SOF liaison in the CAOC.[69]

A few days before the battle of Mazar-i-Sharif, Knaub found out there had been no planning for CAS in support of the anticipated Northern Alliance offensive. Although this is normally the duty of planners at the CAOC, Knaub and other officers at CENTCOM took up the task and developed some phase lines to aid the controllers in calling for CAS.[70] Though it was not a charge that Knaub wanted to take on, he felt that it was an important job that was being ignored because of a lack of coordination among the component planners. Yet when the facts are reviewed, it seems almost inevitable that this type of coordination would have been done at his level, given that CENTCOM was the only authority that could coordinate with all the different players. This turned out to be a foreboding incident.

Operation Anaconda presents a graphic illustration of the potential problems that can result from the lack of integration among the components. The 17-day operation, initiated on 2 March 2002, was an attempt to surround and destroy remnants of al-Qaeda that had escaped to the Shah-i-Kot region over the previous months. At this point, a combined forces land component (CFLC), commanded by Lt Gen Paul Mikolashek (CFLCC) had been established. On 12 December 2001, Mikolashek had created a forward command post at Karshi-Khanabad Air Base, Uzbekistan, under the command of Maj Gen Franklin Hagenbeck. Hagenbeck's 10th Mountain Division was supposed to provide force protection for some special forces there. Instead, when al-Qaeda leaders escaped after the battle for Tora Bora, Mikolashek put Hagenbeck in charge of planning and leading

Operation Anaconda, designating him commander, Combined Joint Task Force (CJTF)-Mountain several days before the fight began.[71] This meant a drastic change of responsibilities for Hagenbeck and his staff.

The CAOS during this period did not have the depth in its command relationships to handle the switch from a loosely coupled to a tightly coupled situation. Hagenbeck had not deployed with either an ASOC or a TACP. Up to this point, the air support had been low volumes of TST directed by the special forces. It was loosely coupled, so the lack of on-scene command presence was not fatal. In Anaconda, there would be a requirement for classic support of troops in contact with the enemy. The control system and the ROEs were not set up to handle this.[72] Hagenbeck also did not have control over many of the SOF troops under CJTF-Mountain, admitting later that the designation of CJTF was "more in name than reality."[73]

Hagenbeck did not reach out for support from other components in the planning because he did not know he had a problem. Neither he nor Mikolashek's staff was familiar with the way the ROEs in this war shaped its character. Instead of linear control measures like the FSCL and phase lines with which the conventional Army was familiar, the battlespace control measures in Anaconda were a veritable "jigsaw puzzle" of areas of varying restrictions.[74] The ROEs stated that bombs could be dropped in one of three ways: with CENTCOM's approval, in a joint special operations area, or through the defensive reactions of ground controllers. In Anaconda the forces would have to rely almost entirely on the third type, so only those requests from ground controllers who were under fire could be filled.[75] Even though Hagenbeck knew he would get plenty of air support, he did not realize that it would all clash in a small area under desperate circumstances.

Worse, the air component was not advised of the plan for Anaconda until late in the game. Working-level coordination between the air and land components did not start until 20 February, and it was 22 February before any flag officers in the air component learned of it. The 28-page operations order published on 20 February had six lines of guidance for the CFACC.[76] If there was to be any coordination, it would have to be done on the fly.

The air component was not ready to coordinate with the newly established task force. Inside the CAOC, the Army liaison—the BCD—had not been involved in the largely SO-oriented fight to this point (recall that when they should have been, Knaub had stepped in to do the CAS coordination). It has already been seen that the air component was not involved in development of the plans from the beginning, instead reacting to detailed guidance from CENTCOM. It was in a following mode, not a leadership mode. Shortly before the operation started, Air Force controllers at Hagenbeck's headquarters attempted to put together an ad hoc group of 15 controllers as a stand-in for the ASOC.

It was too little, too late. There were more enemy forces than expected in the Shah-i-Kot Valley, and they did not retreat as expected. Hagenbeck was forced to issue an emergency appeal for air and naval fire, as well as logistical assistance.[77] As is illustrated later, the ground troops were heroic, the Airmen who responded were heroic, and the effort was successful. It will also be seen that many of the actions were unnecessarily hazardous. Proper CAS coordination was lacking: there were no preplanned aids to get aircraft in and out of the area efficiently and help them find targets. The ground commander had not coordinated through his liaisons at the air component to create initial points that complemented the ground scheme of maneuver until it was too late.[78]

OEF was another example of the trade-offs involved with control by constraints. That the NSC, especially Rumsfeld, tried to empower military commanders to develop a strategy for the war is supported by evidence. But there were several key constraints: it was clear that targeting was to be given careful consideration and that the strategy was to include cooperation among the conventional military, SOF, and the CIA. High-level attention was focused on these issues, resulting in a meeting of all lines of authority at CENTCOM headquarters in Tampa Bay. The air component was not empowered, and there was little depth to the command relationships. This was fine in the beginning, when the players were loosely coupled, but dangerous during Anaconda, when participants were more tightly coupled. The hazards of not having depth in times of tight coupling are revisited later. If command relationships are truly deep, there will be a command presence with the authority to allow exploitation of opportunities during loosely coupled times, but with the ability to strictly control procedures during tightly coupled times.

Iraqi Freedom

Between Operation Anaconda and the beginning of Operation Iraqi Freedom, the various players in CENTCOM put forth some hard work on the relationships among them. Analysts called Anaconda a "wake-up call" to establish common procedures for air operations.[79] Planners in OIF all commented that a major factor in their success was that many of them had worked together in Afghanistan, and most had practiced together for almost a year before combat began in March of 2003.[80] Lt Gen T. Michael Moseley (USAF), the CFACC during Operation Anaconda and future CFACC in OIF, worked with General Franks to iron out the C2 relationships for developing air strategy and for executing air operations, especially time-sensitive targets.

Developing a military strategy for the Iraq war became an intensively joint process. Franks had worked with the NSC to define clear objectives and a strategy that included a much more obvious mechanism for victory—at least for the overthrow of the regime. He was prodded and debated by Secretary Rumsfeld, but in the end the plan was his. His five-front plan integrated land, sea, air, and SOF, defining the part that each would play in relation to the others. This was a "strategy-to-task" effort. Each component got its part to plan, and then all components sat down together to plan the integration. Now "strategy" for the components became a job of working with one another and CENTCOM to ensure the objectives fit the capabilities and then to break the objectives down into a list of tasks. Ultimately, components would be called on to coordinate the accomplishment of these tasks, together comprising the air campaign plan. Lt Col (David) Hathaway, Moseley's chief of air campaign strategy, remembers this effort as a tedious, time-consuming, but inherently joint process—not glamorous but definitely effective.[81]

One of the most joint of these tasks was to work with SOF to suppress Scud attacks from the western desert. Although the Great Scud Hunt in Desert Storm had sufficed to satisfy the strategic level at the time, the word was out that it had been unable to find and destroy the mobile Scuds. This time, the coalition would have to be militarily, as well as politically, effective. When President Bush asked General Franks what the forces were going to do about the Scud threat, the Air Force was tagged to develop a plan. Brig Gen Dan Leaf, who had been a wing commander during OAF, headed a "kill chain task force" designed to figure out how to find and engage the mobile Scuds before they could threaten the coalition. Leaf held live-fly rehearsals at Nellis AFB in October and December of 2002 and January of 2003 to smooth the working relationships that had begun in Afghanistan.

By the time OIF started, the air component had a well-oiled machine to accomplish TST, as well as a plan to find the Scuds.[82] Its approach was to study launch patterns in Desert Storm and lay out possible maximum and minimum ranges for the various missiles. The air component also observed the transportation system in western Iraq to identify "launch baskets" (the most likely places from which the Iraqis would fire the Scuds), hide sites, and storage and maintenance locations where the SOF and other ISR assets could focus. With this information, it developed a plan to keep these areas under scrutiny using dedicated ISR assets and any fighter aircraft that had ISR capabilities.[83] Despite this planning, the targets were obviously not known until the operation began, so most of these missions were targeted in real time.

Certainly, none of this could have been done immediately without air superiority. But in parallel with the planning effort, Saddam made it possible to gain air superiority in advance. Coalition aircraft patrolling southern Iraq in support of the UN resolutions from Desert Storm came under increased attacks starting in June 2002. Their response, designated Operation Southern Focus, was to increase the scope of attacks on Iraqi air defense and C2 capabilities. Although, as General Moseley put it, these responses were made within existing ROEs and "never expanded attacks beyond what [were] necessary, proportional and authorized by the [commander in chief] in self-defense," they nevertheless dismantled a good portion of the Iraqis' air defense.[84] This made it possible for Moseley to concentrate on his other tasks.

During this same period, the components and CENTCOM worked hard on the air-to-ground targeting process. It was one of the things Moseley and Franks concentrated on before OIF. The resulting process called for the air component to run the joint guidance, apportionment, and targeting (JGAT) process that assembled all target requests and made recommendations to Franks about the guidance for the next couple of days. CENTCOM still held a targeting VTC (called a combined targeting coordination board) but, unlike in Afghanistan, it was an approval authority now—not a target development authority. Knaub, who still worked at CENTCOM, described it as a "more traditional [read USAF doctrinal] approach to the C2 relationship between CENTCOM and CENTAF."[85] In fact, during OEF the CENTCOM intelligence shop had developed a way to feed CENTAF only the targets CENTCOM thought would satisfy the objectives. In September of 2002, at a conference at Camp Doha, Kuwait, the two camps met to hash out the differences, and the air component strategists were given the authority to develop enough targets so they could pick and choose those that best fit the air and space power strategy, including the ability to change targets during execution. It was a huge shift in Hathaway's eyes.[86]

The shift was evidence of a change of influence on Franks. Whereas during OEF's opening months Franks had relied mostly on the joint(J)-staff that worked with him in Tampa Bay, he now started deferring more to his component commanders.[87] On this J-staff, Knaub perceived a shift from Franks' reliance on intelligence (J-2) to more confidence in operations (J-3). The move to put Moseley in charge of the JGAT process ran counter to the way things had been done in Afghanistan. In Afghanistan, Franks' intelligence staff, led by Brig Gen (now Lt Gen) John (Jeff) Kimmons (USA), had been able to introduce targets almost at will. Now CENTCOM had to submit targets to its air component to be prioritized against the inputs of the components. The operations staff, led by General Renuart, had pushed for the move. When Kimmons' intelligence people tried to introduce targets directly anyway, Renuart came up with a special category of target called the joint critical target—something that was not a TST but was vital and had to be interjected too late for the normal targeting cycle. Renuart kept the number of these targets down by requiring that the intelligence staff clear them through him personally.[88]

Another sign that Franks was shifting more of the authority to his component commanders was his naming Moseley the space coordination authority for OIF. Franks could have kept this authority himself. Instead, two days before the war began, he gave the job to Moseley, allowing an unprecedented amount of cooperation between space and aircraft operators in Moseley's CAOC.[89]

The shift carried over into ongoing operations as well. CENTCOM's TST Cell had been in the intelligence area, although run by Renuart, during OEF. Between the two wars, Renuart pushed to get it moved out onto the operations floor and to make it more of a monitoring function. After Anaconda, intelligence pushed for a joint fires cell to coordinate air and artillery fires right there on Franks' staff. Operations fought against the idea but lost. However, again Renuart made sure it was established out on the operations floor where he could oversee it.[90]

These changes led to a greater buy-in from the air component than in Afghanistan. The opinions of the officers who had worked in the air component were that CENTCOM had been too involved in the details during OEF, but that the relationship had been fixed by OIF.[91] In Afghanistan, officers high up in the air component claimed that CENTCOM had not given any guidance, even though CENTCOM staff claimed they had given it daily; in Iraq, the air component leadership had a direct hand in crafting this guidance.[92] The difference was in the ranks of the officers involved in coordinating the guidance, which probably indicates the guidance in OIF was less detail-oriented than that in Afghanistan.

The changes also seem to have empowered the component commanders and improved their relationships. This was the first war where the CFC established clear components (other than himself) for each medium of the fight: land, air, maritime, and special operations. Both the air and land components realized they had not done a great job of coordinating during Operation Anaconda in Afghanistan. This poor showing seems to have been the impetus for establishing a new liaison between the two: the air component coordination element.[93] Teams of six to 10 Airmen were set up with ground elements at seven places throughout the theater. Although under Moseley's command, the Airmen were to work face-to-face with surface commanders in order to enhance their communication with the CFACC.[94] The most prominent of these was headed by General Leaf, who worked in the headquarters of the CFLCC—Moseley's ground counterpart, Lt Gen David McKiernan. This increased the collaboration between the two components early in the planning and helped make adjustments, such as moving the FSCL, during the fighting as well.[95]

As Horner had done in Desert Storm, Moseley conceded that the Marines would use their aircraft primarily to shape the battlefield in their area. In fall of 2002, he had prepared for this by convening a conference with top Marine generals to work out the C2 of Marine airpower. Without any formal written agreements, the generals worked out an arrangement that allowed the Marine air commander to tell the air component how many sorties the 1st Marine Expeditionary Force (MEF) needed. The planners in the CAOC then allocated these sorties, arranged all the support for them, and sent that information back out in the ATO. To make this plan work, Moseley insisted the Marines provide some of their best officers to serve as liaison officers, one of whom became the CAS planner for the entire theater.[96] It was another example of working out relationships prior to the conflict to make the electronic collaboration run more smoothly during the conflict.

The relationships made it much easier to handle any changes. For instance, when Franks called Moseley to tell him the ground invasion had to be moved up to 20 March, Moseley responded that the air component could support it with CAS, rather than moving its big effort, which was not scheduled to start until 21 March.[97] This meant the mischaracterized shock and awe air strikes would not be the opening act of the war.[98] Moseley and General McKiernan, the land component commander, also had personal contact, resulting in great trust between them that the air component would be there to support the land component's rapid push to Baghdad.[99]

Support for the land component in its invasion from the south was, in fact, the largest of the tasks for the air component. Through the first 21 days of OIF, over 15,000 of the 20,000 total sorties were dedicated to supporting the land component. This was actually two separate attacks. The US Army's V Corps, under Lt Gen (now Gen) William Wallace (USA), moved up the middle of Iraq west of the Euphrates while the US Marines' 1st MEF, under Lt Gen James Conway (USMC), moved up the coast toward Basra to secure the oil fields before heading to Baghdad. The Marines' direct air support center (DASC) and DASC (airborne) handled the flow of air support into the 1st MEF sector while the V Corps ASOC handled the flow of air support into the Army's sector.

In a lessons-learned conference after Iraqi Freedom, the air component pointed out that there had been a difference in the way the Army and the Marines directed air support. Because of the speed of the attack, the FSCL was often pushed far out ahead of the ground troops. The Army handled all missions short of this FSCL as CAS and required them to be controlled by the ASOC or a TACP designated by the ASOC. The Marines, on the other hand, chose to create another line called the battlefield coordination line (BCL), which was closer to the ground troops than the FSCL. The Marine DASC opened up killboxes further out than this BCL—so as a result, air support going into the Marines' sector had a greater chance of being sent to an open killbox than that going to the Army sector. To the aircrew, the difference in flexibility was so stark that pilots regularly requested to be sent to work with the DASC rather than the ASOC.[100]

The difference should have been predictable. The Marines were operating under their doctrine of centralized command and decentralized control. Since they had de facto command of most of the air in their sector (due to the arrangement with Moseley), they were able to delegate the decisions on the details of the missions by letting the pilots operate freely in killboxes as opposed to directing them through TACPs.[101] The Army, on the other hand, was trying to integrate air support with its artillery, which is longer-ranged than that of the Marines. Wallace called the effort to create detailed effects in his area and then synchronize the corps' maneuvers with its fires *corps shaping*. To accomplish this, Wallace had to be able to carefully choose the targets to attack and the weapons with which to attack them.[102]

The difference is in the degree of coupling the two services saw in these operations. To the Marines, beyond the BCL, the efforts of the ground and air forces were not tightly coupled and did not need to be closely managed. They preferred to decentralize the authority to find targets there and get as many aircraft through as possible. To the Army, the efforts of the ground and air forces were tightly coupled all the way out to the FSCL because the corps' ability to maneuver depended on the fire support. Aircrews were more closely managed, so Wallace had more visibility into the targeting, but aircrews related it took longer to perform a mission in the Army's sector than in the Marines' sector.[103]

In OIF, it has been seen that all the players benefited from the "practices" of OEF. Constraints from the strategic level had been eased. Franks shifted authority from his staff to the component commanders, such as giving the air component more authority in the targeting process. Component commanders had more clearly defined command relationships. They, in turn, were able to create depth in the command relationships by delegating authority downward. Although the ways in which the services controlled airpower differed, they were suited to the situation. Authority was given at a low enough level that the aircrews were able to adjust to each situation, despite their having preferences for one over the other. In fact, the variances in the way airpower was handled from one sector to the other showed the flexibility that comes from having depth in command relationships.

Conclusions

This chapter has demonstrated the effect of the different ways policy makers control airpower as an instrument of policy. In Desert Storm and OIF, where military strategy was the result of debate between the strategic and operational levels, the CFC was able to empower the component commanders to take responsibility for planning their portion of the strategy. In OEF, this same debate took place but resulted in constraints that affected the ability of the CFC to pass authority downward. In OAF, there was no debate about strategy, and the constraints from the strategic level created paralysis at the operational level.

In cases where the component commanders were empowered, they created command relationships that allowed them to pass authority even lower. Elements of the TACS were able to make decisions about allocating resources on the scene, so that in tightly coupled situations there were strict global procedures, and in loosely coupled situations there was more discretion. As Wallace remarks,

> In fact, it is completely conceivable that we might put some of our artillery and attack aviation under the control of the [coalition forces air component commander] for a specific task and purpose. For example,

> we might want to execute a surgical strike that requires the synergy of simultaneous attacks by, say, [the Army Tactical Missile System (ATACMS)], Army attack aviation and Air Force F-16s. We would put them under one commander for the attack and on the ATO. It doesn't matter who actually owns the munitions or aircraft as long as we whack the bad guys.[104]

The thing the component commanders were not able to do is to give these lower levels the situational awareness to truly interlink the value chains of the components. Forces at the scene of battle were still following procedures based on supported and supporting relationships.

Notwithstanding, throughout the period of this study, airpower's roles showed a subtle change. The shift to hitting emerging targets rapidly and with great precision was accompanied by a concurrent shift toward acknowledging that airpower had the potential to affect the situation on the ground in areas that are remote from friendly forces. The Scud Hunt, the hunt for Serb forces in Kosovo, and TST in Enduring Freedon and Iraqi Freedom all called on the air component to find ways to deliver precision firepower against enemy forces that did not necessarily fit typical mission molds, such as CAS or interdiction. In fact, the attempt to rapidly hit emerging targets became a process that could span the spectrum of missions from CAS to strategic attack.[105] It is often hard to put a name on a particular mission. This problem only grows more severe as the war becomes less conventional, and airpower is increasingly called on to do whatever fits the current situation—ISR, supply, humanitarian aid, or show of force. The end result is a blurring of the lines that determine what type of control is appropriate in a given situation. Traditionally, joint doctrine has used geographical area to stipulate the difference between CAS and interdiction. It becomes harder to determine who is supported and who is supporting.

In reality, this could change during the battle. It was almost a year later that the United States decided to launch an offensive on Fallujah for the first time since the war began. Insurgents had basically taken control of the city, and two weeks earlier they had burned American contractors alive in their automobile. On the first night, 4 April 2004, an AC-130U gunship crew was tasked to escort some Marines into the city. The Marines were moving slowly, so the gunship crew did some reconnaissance ahead of them. When it returned, crew members saw shots being fired at a small group of four or five Marines that was trying to set up a defensive position. They also observed about 60 people moving into positions behind houses about 150 meters away from the group. The crew asked the Marines for clearance to fire, but the Marines were not confident they knew enough to give that clearance. Consequently, the Marine acting as controller, call sign "Woody," started calling up his chain to get clearance. While waiting for clearance, Woody started going through the nine-line brief to ensure they were ready to engage when the call came. But about halfway through the brief, the enemy started firing rocket-propelled grenades at the Marines, and immediately Woody called, "cleared to fire, cleared to fire!"[106]

When the gunship started firing, the enemy split into two groups. The gunship crew fired at one group with the infrared sensor directing the 25-millimeter (mm) gun and fired at the other group with the television directing the 40-mm Bofors cannon. Woody was able to see only one of the enemy groups, but both streams of fire, so he attempted to direct both guns toward the enemy he could see. The gunship, nonetheless, kept firing at both groups. When the gunship's fire forced both groups to converge and then retreat, the Marines were very appreciative. After that night, Marines gave AC-130 gunships immediate clearance to fire at their own discretion.[107]

In any such scenario, recognizing the need to shift discretion from the ground troops to the aircrew calls for a command presence with total situational awareness. However, while this is optimum, it may not always be entirely feasible due to existing capabilities to compile information from both the air and the ground to form the bigger picture. The next chapter looks at the efforts of the CAOS to do this.

Notes

1. Author's personal notes, JEFX 04, 27 July 2004.
2. Wilson, *Bureaucracy*, 370.
3. Ibid., 109.
4. Builder, *Masks of War*, 18–20.
5. Although many would point to the F-22 as another sign that the Air Force is continuing its marriage to the technology of the airplane, that would

ignore the devotion to command, control, communications, computers, intelligence, surveillance, and reconnaissance (C4ISR) that Gen John Jumper, USAF, retired (former CSAF), has shown.

6. Kenneth Allard says the US Army was influenced mostly by Jomini and Clausewitz, who emphasized the dominance of the decisive battle; the Air Force was influenced by the writings of Douhet and Mitchell, both of whom emphasized the ability of air weapons to bypass ground combat and directly win wars. Allard, *Command, Control*, 11.

7. Castells, *Rise of the Network Society*, 177–78.

8. Based on Michael Porter's concept of the value chain. A *value chain* is described as "divid[ing] a company's activities into the technologically and economically distinct activities it performs to do business." Porter and Millar, "How Information Gives You Competitive Advantage," 151. Prof. Stuart Madnick of MIT calls this "interlinking value chains" (from a class the author took with Dr. Madnick).

9. Harvey, memorandum, 10 Aug. 1990.

10. Reynolds, *Heart of the Storm*, 53.

11. Harvey, memorandum, 11 Aug. 1990.

12. Clancy with Horner, *Every Man a Tiger*, 185, 190–233.

13. Deptula, interview, 22–23 May 1991, 33.

14. Ibid., 47.

15. "Offensive Campaign: Desert Storm."

16. Cohen and Keaney, *Gulf War Air Power Survey*, vol. 1, pt. 2, *Command and Control*, 131–33.

17. Ibid., 185–89.

18. Deptula, interview by the author.

19. Deptula, interview, 10 Dec. 1991, 53–58.

20. Deptula, interview by the author.

21. Rice, interview, 11 Dec. 1991, 5–6.

22. Deptula, "Reflections on Desert Storm," slide 25; and Deptula, interview by the author.

23. Deptula, "Reflections on Desert Storm," slide 25. This is actually an updated version of the graphics that (then) Colonel Deptula used for his 1991 briefing. Deptula, transcript of briefing to Richard Davis.

24. Deptula, transcript of briefing, 11, 14–16.

25. Gordon and Trainor, *Generals' War*, 159–63.

26. Cronin, "C3I during the Air War," 34. After the war, one Marine major described why. Horner had always planned on executing the different phases of the air war as simultaneously as possible—the different phases were merely a way to convey them to a ground-centric JFC. The Marines took the phases literally. When it appeared the air campaign was entering phase three—preparing the battlefield—but some Marine air was still being used to strike Iraq, the Marines grew wary that they would not get the use of their air even in the impending attack (ibid.).

27. Corder, interview, 24–29. Schwarzkopf, himself, weighed in to assure the JFACC would still be valid but the Marines would retain maximum flexi-

bility for shaping the battlefield in their sector. Message, 011330Z FEB 91, Schwarzkopf to Boomer.

28. Deptula, memorandum for record, CHP-5A.

29. Horner, interview, 26, 55; and Clancy with Horner, *Every Man a Tiger*, 451, 471–74.

30. Horner, interview, 56–57.

31. "Concept of Operations," atch. 2, i–v.

32. Ibid., 4, 7.

33. The Army used this arrangement to its advantage. The Army liaison officers on board the ABCCC had access to the Army target list, which was usually different from the list the TACC had put out containing Schwarzkopf's guidance. They also received "pop-up" targets from Army commanders. The ABCCC crew made many decisions about which targets to strike, so the Army priorities often got two chances to influence the operations. 8th Air Support Operations Group, *Operations Desert Shield/Storm*, 9. This caused problems for the people in the TACC, who did not know what targets had been hit. Battle damage from these attacks was supposed to be relayed by the strike aircraft and Killer Scouts to the ABCCC, which would then pass it to the TACC. But poor communications and a heavy workload meant the TACC often did not get information on the targets or the results of these strikes. Hone, Mandeles, and Terry, "Command and Control," vol. 1, pt. 2, 318. The end result was that the Army battle damage assessment (BDA) analysts could not verify that targets had been hit, despite the fact that they had the opportunity to influence the targets in real time.

34. Schneider, Hura, and McLeod, "Command and Control," 12.

35. Federation of American Scientists, "Secret Internet Protocol Router Network."

36. Schneider, Hura, and McLeod, "Command and Control," 18. See also Clark, *Waging Modern War*, 201–2.

37. "Analysis of the Effectiveness," vol. 2, sec. 2, Focus Area 4, 16–17.

38. Schneider, Hura, and McLeod, "Command and Control," 19. Lambeth calls it a "continuously evolving coercive operation featuring piecemeal attacks against unsystematically approved targets, not an integrated effort aimed from the outset at achieving predetermined and identifiable operational effects." *NATO's Air War for Kosovo*, 21.

39. Tirpak, "Short's View."

40. For refugee numbers, see the slides "Daily Refugee Flow" and "Total Refugee Flow" from the 13 May 1999 NATO briefings.

41. Priest and Finn, "NATO Gives Air Support," A1. See also Crowder, interview by the author, Nellis AFB, NV, 28 July 2004 (also refer to chap. 4, n. 67). (Notes in author's personal collection.)

42. Crowder, interview.

43. Ibid.

44. Schneider, Hura, and McLeod, "Command and Control," 36, 30; and Crowder, interview.

45. Department of Defense, *Kosovo/Operation Allied Force*, 87.

46. Woodward, *Bush at War*, 99, 129, and 135.

47. Conetta, *Strange Victory*. Woodward's interviews show the progression of these events. *Bush at War*, 149, 154, 174–75, 215, 234, and 264–67.

48. Franks, *American Soldier*, 270–72.

49. Ibid., 259–61.

50. Message, 011241Z NOV 01, USCINCCENT to COMUSARCENT et al.; and CENTAF reply to "CFC ORDER 002," 11.

51. Ibid. Opinion on the victory comes from Davis, "How the Afghan War Was Won," 6–7.

52. Franks, *American Soldier*, 523–24.

53. Deptula, interview by the author.

54. Lt Col David Hathaway, USAF (20th Fighter Wing Chief of Safety at the time of this writing; Chief of Air Campaign Strategy for USCENTAF, June 2001–Sept. 2003; and Deputy Chief of Strategy, OIF), interview by the author, Shaw AFB, SC, 24 Mar. 2004. (Notes in author's personal collection.)

55. Knaub to the author, e-mail, 22 Sept. 2004.

56. Deptula, interview by the author.

57. Crowder to the author, e-mail. As we will see later, (then) Lt Col Crowder played a big part in development of CAOC tools and operations during OEF.

58. Knaub lent credibility to this line of reasoning with his assertion that the strict ROEs were the major cause of the extremely centralized process. Knaub to the author, e-mails, 22 Sept. and 5 Nov. 2004.

59. Biddle, *Afghanistan and the Future*, 6.

60. Benoit, Miller, and Gregg, interview. During OEF, Benoit was an electronic warfare officer (EWO) on AC-130H gunships, Miller was a pilot on AC-130H gunships; and Gregg was a pilot on MH-53J Pave Low helicopters. Miller and Gregg were also planners during OIF.

61. Leibstone, "War against Terrorism," 19.

62. Throughout the 1990s, the Defense Information Systems Agency had been working toward a GCCS, using resources from the agency's Defense Information Systems Network. Like the WWMCCS before it, GCCS was supposed to be a White House-to-foxhole system incorporating off-the-shelf technologies as they became available. Pearson, *World Wide Military Command*, 339–40.

63. Ackerman, "Operation Enduring Freedom," 3–4.

64. Deptula, "Operation Enduring Freedom."

65. Knaub to the author, e-mail, 22 Sept. 2004.

66. Franks with McConnell, *American Soldier*, 288.

67. Comments on an earlier draft of this book by Deptula to the author, e-mail.

68. Deptula, "Operation Enduring Freedom."

69. Lt Col Mark Cline, USAF (MAAP chief in OEF and OIF), telephone interview with the author, 11 Nov. 2003. (Notes in author's personal collection.) See also Crowder, interview.

70. Knaub to the author, e-mail, 22 Sept. 2004.

71. Grossman, "Army Analyst Blames Afghan," 1.

72. Neuenswander, "JCAS in Afghanistan."

73. Grossman, "Army Analyst Blames Afghan," 1.

74. Headquarters United States Air Force, "Task Force Enduring Look," 38–39.

75. Ibid., 32–33.

76. Ibid., 29.

77. Grossman, "Army Analyst Blames Afghan," 1.

78. Jansen, "JCAS in Afghanistan," 24–29.

79. Erwin, "Air Wars Demand More," 22.

80. Lt Col Karl Wingenbach, USA, US Army Training and Doctrine Command, Futures Center (at the time of this writing), and Lt Col John P. Andreasen, USA, retired, telephone interview with the author, 21 May 2004. Both worked in the CAOC battlefield coordination detachment in OEF and OIF. (Notes in author's personal collection.) See also Cline, interview.

81. Hathaway to the author, e-mail, 29 Sept. 2004.

82. Backes, interview. Lt Col Gary Backes, USAF, retired, was a TCT Cell trainer during OIF.

83. "CTBM CONOPS." This briefing was received from Lt Col Kevin Glenn, USAF, 30th Intelligence Squadron/CC at the time of this writing and chief, Combat Operations ISR Cell, OIF.

84. Moseley, quoted in Haag, "OIF Veterans."

85. Knaub to the author, e-mail, 5 Nov. 2004.

86. Hathaway to the author, e-mail, 21 Mar. 2005. Hathaway related that CENTCOM got the idea the air component just wanted to blow everything up during OEF, when the air strategists continuously pled for more targets. The air components' strategists thought there would be a master target list that included some restricted and some prohibited targets. On the contrary, CENTCOM created separate restricted and prohibited lists, then gave the air component a smaller master target list that was CENTCOM's estimate of the best targets for the objective. At the September 2002 conference, the air planners pointed out they could theoretically destroy the entire planned master target list for Iraq on the first day. By the time OIF started, Hathaway had the leeway to develop a viable air and space power strategy with the available targets.

87. Ibid.

88. Knaub to the author, e-mails, 22 Sept. and 5 Nov. 2004; and "OIF Targeting CONOPS Update."

89. Rees, "Naming CFACC," 1.

90. Knaub to the author, e-mail, 5 Nov. 2004.

91. In Horner's personal interview, the general expressed a very strong opinion that Desert Storm and OIF had been done well from the standpoint of JFC-JFACC interaction, whereas Kosovo and OEF had been done very badly. Crowder's and Deptula's personal interviews also revealed that during OEF they had seen no guidance from CENTCOM until late November; instead, CENTCOM had intervened in tactical events. In Hathaway's personal interview, he stressed that, as discussed above, CENTCOM had been trying to specify the targets during OEF and was surprised to find during OIF that the air component had an effects-based methodology for targeting.

92. Knaub to the author, e-mail, 22 Sept. 2004.

93. Butler, "As A-10 Shines in Iraq," 1.
94. "Air Component Coordination Element."
95. Ripley, "Close Air Support."
96. Moseley, interview.
97. Franks, *American Soldier*, 439.
98. The term *shock and awe* came from the book, *Shock and Awe: Achieving Rapid Dominance*, published in 1996. Its focus was the potential of capitalizing on the techniques behind the planning and execution of Desert Storm, particularly the effects-based aspects of the Desert Storm air campaign. Authors Harlan Ullman and Jim Wade were both confidants of the SecDef, and it's likely this is where the Office of the SecDef picked up the term. When the press got a hold of the term it became a sound bite—however, it is important to recognize that shock and awe, as described in the book, was NOT executed during the opening of OIF. In deciding how to accomplish the job of attacking Baghdad and the Republican Guard, the air component had come up with an aggressive but deliberate plan. But Hathaway recalls guidance came from Secretary Rumsfeld and President Bush that they were to do it more aggressively and with fewer ground forces—the idea was to allow the ground forces to move rapidly to Baghdad to preclude undesirable events like oil fires. Thus, the phrase shock and awe seemed appropriate to describe the act of knocking the regime off guard and never letting it catch up. Hathaway to the author, e-mail. 29 Sept. 2004.
99. Moseley, interview.
100. "Task Force Enduring Look Lessons Learned," slide 48.
101. Credit for this insight goes to Lt Col Dave Wilkinson, a Marine S-3 pilot who was a fellow at MIT while I was earning my PhD. Wilkinson to the author, e-mail.
102. Wallace, "Joint Fires in OIF." General Wallace was the commander, V Corps, in OIF. According to his briefing (slide 12), the Iraqi 11th Division was at 84 percent strength before OIF, 81 percent after knowledge-integration shaping, and 63 percent after corps shaping. The Medina Republican Guard Division, 96 percent before the war, was reduced to only 92 percent by killbox interdiction, but to 29 percent by corps shaping. The Hammurabi Division went from 97 percent before KI to 73 percent after, and to 23 percent after corps shaping.
103. Ibid. Coe, interview, also provided other lessons learned. Maj Richard Coe, AF/XORC at the time of this writing, was the F-15E weapon systems officer during OEF and OIF. It is difficult to tell which method was more "effective" because the data on the rate of destruction does not exist.
104. Hollis, "Trained, Adaptable, Flexible Forces."
105. Deptula and Dahl, "Transforming Joint Air-Ground," 23–25. Deptula called for a new mission area, battlefield air operations.
106. Goldberg, Valentino, and Frazee, interview. They served in OIF as AC-130U copilot, EWO, and sensor operator, respectively.
107. Ibid.

THIS PAGE INTENTIONALLY LEFT BLANK

Chapter 6

The Center of the CAOS

The history of command can thus be understood in terms of a race between the demand for information and the ability of command systems to meet it. That race is eternal; it takes place within every military (and, indeed, nonmilitary) organization, at all levels and at all times.

—Martin van Creveld
Command in War

Wisdom is better than strength. Nevertheless the poor man's wisdom is despised, and his words are not heard.

—Ecclesiastes 9:18
New King James Version

The ability to put together information from various places to form a bigger picture of the world—this is what we said commanders need to make their decisions. Some analysts say centralized control is the way of the future because commanders will then be able to obtain more complete information. Let us look at the efforts to do this in the CAOC.

During a distinguished visitor tour at JEFX 04, guests got a briefing from every division in the Nellis CAOC. Each time, the major or lieutenant colonel giving the brief tried to show how the new initiatives were being incorporated. Each briefer included a short explanation of how machine-to-machine interfaces were changing the way they did their jobs. To the Strategy Division, this meant no rekeying of information was needed from one plan to another. Information from the CFC or CFACC guidance was passed directly into the applicable areas of the subplans. To the Plans Division, machine-to-machine meant the information from the Joint Targeting Toolkit (JTT) was automatically transformed into the master air attack plan via the MAAP Toolkit. In the Combat Operations Division, machine-to-machine meant its databases would automatically be updated with the status of some of the aircraft via Link 16.

To determine the effect of technology on the CAOS, the ability of the AOC (and elsewhere) to assemble information and make decisions must be assessed. Air Force officials have emphasized the development of this capability, to the point of calling the AOC a "weapon system." The AOC has become similar to Latour's center of calculation (see chap. 1). In his book *Science in Action*, Latour describes the way scientists do "science": by bringing data into the laboratory to manipulate it they are able to make sense of the world. The scientist takes samples from the field and tries to make them mobile, stable, and combinable enough to transport to a place where they can be integrated with other types of samples to create a meaningful representation of the world. In this way, scientists are able to "act at a distance, that is to do things in the centers that sometimes make it possible to dominate spatially as well as chronologically the periphery."[1] In other words, by building their own models based on samples of the real world, scientists are more knowledgeable and better able to solve problems than those who are out on the "front lines." However, Latour insists that to understand science it is not the thought process of the scientist, isolated in his or her office, that needs to be studied. Instead, it is what he calls the "logistics of immutable mobiles," or the way the scientist gathers those samples and assembles them into a representation of the world to solve a problem.[2]

This chapter examines the way those in the AOC did this. They acted on the "periphery" by turning plans into actions. Then they brought information about the battlespace back and attempted to assess what was happening so they could revise the plans. This is the purpose of van Creveld's directed telescope. The actions in this feedback loop became more automated as the information they dealt with became more digital. Still, assessing the aggregate results has been a weakness of the CAOS—just determining what happened was difficult, not to mention measuring results and comparing them to somewhat subjective goals.

Along the way, the AOC found this directed telescope was also useful for making command decisions about ongoing missions. This did not entail assessing the results before changing plans—

merely reacting to the enemy whenever the opportunity arose. It required a simpler physical representation of the world—"where am I, where are my buddies, where is the enemy?"[3] Gains in ISR, information, and telecommunications technology along with new organizational procedures led to the shrinking of the time-sensitive targeting cycle. Nevertheless, other constraints still exist. For example, because information comes in from many sensor-communication loops and cannot be combined into one graphic picture, it cannot be sent to those who do not have access to the SIPRNET. Only those in a center can view all the information on adjacent machines or applications.

Desert Storm

The air component in Desert Storm, led by the first-ever JFACC, General Horner, became responsible for accomplishing significant objectives. Warden's Instant Thunder had been such a powerful idea that it influenced Schwarzkopf to grant significant strategy-making authority to the air component. This prospect, in turn, influenced Horner to make the Black Hole an important part of the TACC, adding a longer-range planning capability to it. Before Desert Storm, there had been nothing like the AOC of today. The TACS was directed by the Combat Operations Division in the TACC, which was housed in a portable, "inflatable bubble" shelter, the AN/TSQ-92. As its name implies, it was concerned with "tactical air control." Then, on Christmas Eve of 1990, after Horner's reorganization of the air component, the Combat Operations Division, led by Lt Col William (Bill) Keenan, moved from the bubble to the basement of the Royal Saudi Air Force headquarters with the Black Hole and the rest of the TACC.[4] The authority that Schwarzkopf had delegated to the air component carried with it increased accountability that could only be maintained through a beefed-up organization.

Although the Black Hole was incorporated into the TACC, it was not well integrated. This is seen by looking at the process of creating the daily MAP and ATO. Lieutenant Colonel Deptula was the principal planner responsible for the master attack plan. He used markers, pens, and pencils to mark the target locations on charts, one of which still hangs in his office today. Because this graphic representation did not tell the whole story, as it could not show timing and weapons, Deptula consulted pilots from different aircraft. They helped him put together the types of "packages," or groups of aircraft, that would attack each target and which weapons they would use. He then adjusted the timing so each would occur in the right sequence. When the MAP was complete, Deptula handed it off as a hard-copy document to others who created target planning worksheets for each target on the MAP. This step added another level of detail and put the packages in a standard format that the ATO planners were used to dealing with. Finally, these target-planning worksheets went to officers, who set up the tankers and other support, and then gave them to technicians to put them into the ATO to be disseminated to the aircrews.[5]

This was the first point at which the information was input to a system that could distribute it electronically. It was the ATO planners' job to put the information from the target-planning sheets into a system called the computer-assisted force management system (CAFMS).[6] A CAFMS terminal was a desktop computer with a 12-inch monitor and dot matrix printer. The user manipulated data in templates: one for creating a new record, one for editing or purging an existing record, and one for listing the results of a query. When a technician entered data, the CAFMS stored it locally. One CAFMS system had up to 11 remote terminals that could share a database. The air component needed five of these systems, with 60–65 local workstations and 47 remotes, to reach all the wings and elements of the TACS. It was February before software engineers created patches to allow these five systems to use a common database.[7] Even then, the full ATO was visible only when all data was entered, and then only on the CAFMS terminals. To be useful, it had to be printed out in hard copy.

Consequently, there was no shared representation of the air strategy—no graphic picture of the way all the missions fit together to accomplish the objectives. The MAP and the corresponding brief to Schwarzkopf each night were Deptula and Glosson's representation, but those outside the Black Hole were not familiar enough with the planning to share that awareness. Thus, when combat started, Horner's new TACC found it difficult to accomplish the complete control loop. Deptula's effects-based method required a fine level of adjustment to ensure the attacks remained integrated. Ideally, the planners would have continually adjusted the attacks based on the effects that actually occurred. They would have taken Horner's and Schwarzkopf's guidance and used it to filter through target nominations and battle damage assessments from the intelligence shops to determine what to target each day. Then they could have looked at all the available assets and orchestrated a coherent plan where each attack fed off its relative timing with the others.[8] The MAP would have been the result of all this processing.

But the existing technology and processes did not support such an elegant plan. The intelligence organizations were accustomed to using imagery to determine damage, not effects. They were also reluctant to release preliminary estimates before final analysis. The intelligence product that Deptula needed to form a new plan, based on that day's results, arrived three days later. He needed it now.[9]

To offset this situation, Deptula and the planners started improvising. They spent a great deal of time on the combat operations floor trying to listen to what was going on so they would know what had gone as planned and what had changed. They had cockpit video from the attack aircraft carried in on C-21 aircraft and watched hours of film to determine whether the aircraft had struck their targets. As the war went on, they learned that the precision weapons were accurate enough to skip this step for some weapon systems. Just as importantly, they watched television news. If CNN showed the lights out in Baghdad, it did not matter how much damage had been done to the electrical targets. The effect was achieved.[10] Deptula's information did not come over data link in a systematic way, but rather from the informal links he was able to assemble from the sources within his reach.

Turning the assessments into operations was not an easy process either. Prior to the beginning of combat, the Black Hole had produced the MAPs and the ATOs for the first two days of the war. Horner did not want them to go beyond day two because he knew that things would change and the TACC would have to react. He wanted the TACC to "learn to do chaos war."[11] However, since the Black Hole worked in a top secret area, many in the rest of the TACC had never seen a MAP before day two of the war. When the time came to assemble the third day's

ATO on day two of the war, the rest of the TACC got baptized by fire when they were unable to translate the MAP into a working ATO in time. Maj Gen John Corder, whom Horner had charged with running the TACC after the reorganization, recalls telling them to send it out when it was four hours late and only 30–40 percent complete. He relied on the TACC change process to handle the rest.[12]

Handling the changes was Keenan's job. He had 124 people, only a handful of whom were regular Ninth Air Force staff. Most of the rest had not been formally trained in their jobs. He was most concerned that they be current in their weapon system, so he rotated people in for weeks at a time. A notebook on the combat operations floor kept records of the standard operating procedures they used, but their experience from Desert Shield constituted the biggest source of expertise. They knew how to make changes: there was a change form that needed to be filled out and signed by Keenan, Col James Crigger, Jr. (the director of operations), or Col Al Doman (the director of combat operations).[13] But there were many changes; if a target had been hit a day early because of increased priority, the next day's ATO would need to change. If a tanker or other support asset had maintenance problems, a whole chain reaction of changes would result. There were so many changes that, unless it was an unusual request, Keenan's people knew he would sign the change form after the change was already made—combat operations people did what they needed to do to make things work smoothly.[14]

Keenan's staff was hard-pressed to affect ongoing missions, however. Its members could not tell where all the aircraft were at any given time. The AWACS had a data link called the tactical digital information link (TADIL) B that allowed them to link to each other. TADIL B could only handle 100 targets at a time—too few for the TACC to show the whole picture. No software was available that could tie multiple TADIL B units together, so technicians slowed the update rate instead. Because of the slow update rate (in minutes), there was rarely a current picture.[15] Those in combat operations knew and accepted it.[16] It was so unusual to have an up-to-date picture from all the AWACS that when this did occur, on 20 February, there was a special entry in the current operations log: "An amazing event has just occurred: we were able to talk secure, direct to all four AWACS, simultaneously. . . . We also had an air picture from coast to coast at the same time. Unheard of."[17]

Yet, as will be seen, the TACC was drawn into the business of directing ongoing missions, especially during the Scud Hunt. There was no way for the aircraft to find the elusive targets on their own. They needed someone with sensor-communication loops to find the targets and direct them there.

To answer this call, the TACC developed a "change cell." Lt Col Phil Tritschler had been an F-4G EWO until his unit was closed down one year before Iraq invaded Kuwait. So when he received a call at Nellis AFB to be the chief of combat operations (CCO), he gladly accepted the chance to get close to the action. Upon his arrival ten days before the war, Tritschler found that Keenan was the CCO and had requested an augmentee to "handle stuff" as it came up. In the front of the combat ops floor, immediately behind Horner's front row of seats, in the middle of a U-shaped section where Keenan sat, was a small group of tables. Tritschler co-opted these tables for the purpose of planning missions to hit emerging targets during the day.[18]

Most of Tritschler's job was to redirect aircraft that had not yet taken off. When a target of opportunity popped up (such as a sighting of a mobile SAM), Tritschler tried to identify which of the aircraft that had not yet taken off could accomplish the mission. But the CAFMS was "a nightmare." It was not possible to go into the CAFMS and determine which assets were available to retask. Tritschler therefore gathered the fighter duty officers, support duty officers (for tankers and jammers), and intelligence officers around the change table. They laid a chart on the change table and plotted the location of the target and the specific targets within that area that potential aircraft were scheduled to attack (along with the type of weapons they would carry), and then set up support aircraft and attempted to plan the mission.[19] The team translated various information from several sources into a single analog, graphic illustration on a chart.

In Desert Storm, Horner's air component was given the opportunity to play a large part in the complete control loop, from developing strategy to assessing and changing it. Horner reorganized the air component around this capability, but the logistics involved in getting and using the information to perform the entire loop were lacking. The Black Hole was unable to share its representation of the strategy, the MAP. Black Hole planners also found it difficult to obtain the information it needed to assess and adjust the strategy. In the meantime, those in the rest of the TACC had to adjust the day's operations without a good handle on the overall strategy. While called on to obtain and use information to directly alter the ongoing missions during the Scud Hunt, they were unable to get real-time information and turn it into actions.

Allied Force

Between 1991 and 1999, IT and telecommunications technology both experienced huge innovations. It was during this period that the Web took off—in October of 1994, the World Wide Web Consortium was established to develop Web standards. The same year, the DOD established its SIPRNET. As previously noted, the first Predator flew in Bosnia in 1995, and then in 1996 Secretary Widnall and General Fogleman wrote their "Air Force Vision 2010," incorporating ideas about information and space. In 1997 the Air Force founded its Aerospace Command and Control Agency, began the expeditionary force exercise, and acknowledged the importance of ISR by incorporating it with C2 into command, control, communications, computers, intelligence, surveillance, and reconnaissance (C4ISR). By the time NATO decided to intervene in Kosovo, the world was a different place than it had been in 1991.

Technology available to the air component was also evolving. The Contingency Theater Automated Planning System (CTAPS) was a UNIX-based bundle of applications that was developed to try to create a "system of systems" that would allow the air planners to share data among themselves. The Air Force hoped this would eliminate the problem that occurred in Desert Storm where the Black Hole "dumped" the MAP on the ATO planners, forcing them to scramble to catch up.

Throughout this period, the organization of the air and space operations center changed as well. The earliest construct for the AOC's organization was a model adopted in joint doctrine in 1994.[20] Despite the Desert Storm experience, this model only specified a plans division and an operations division. There was no mention of a strategy or campaign plans division, and intelligence was a "horizontal" division that was split between plans and operations.[21] By 1998 Air Force doctrine included its own concept of the organization of an AOC. This concept did include a strategy division to plan for future operations and assess current and past operations—closely resembling Horner's TACC after the reorganization.[22]

As has been seen, the air component was not prepared or directed to exercise any such long-range strategy function at the beginning of OAF. The planners have related that high-level decision makers' expectations of a short war affected all levels of preparation.[23] The organization was not even set up to prosecute a sustained campaign. General Short had a CAOC at Vicenza, Italy, but it was not arranged along doctrinal lines. Because this was a NATO theater, Short's organization used a staff-type structure with C-X designations—C-2 for intelligence, C-3 for operations, C-5 for plans, and so forth. Unlike the USAF doctrinal version of the AOC at the time, the NATO version did not include a capability to do long-range strategy development. It instead concentrated more on the day-to-day planning and the staff functions of getting forces to the theater and supporting them. In the USAF doctrinal AOC at the time, the CFACC was to have a separate staff to perform these types of functions, while the AOC focused on running the combat operations.[24]

The air component did not have a mature process in place to plan, assess the plans, and turn the assessments into future plans. This can be seen through the eyes of those who had to try and put together an assessment of the actions of the air component. At first, there were only three people, who remained in Germany, designated to assess the results of the strikes. It was not until 17 April that three analysts from Germany deployed to Vicenza under Col Allen Peck, Short's C-5 (deputy for plans).[25]

According to these assessors, by that time the tools and processes had developed along divergent lines. NATO and US planners used different, incompatible information systems. US planners used the CTAPS to put together the air tasking order, while other NATO nations used a system called Integrated Command and Control. But the United States used only a portion of the CTAPS's capabilities because they were used to develop processes for low level-of-effort wars such as Deliberate Force and Deny Flight. At the beginning of Allied Force, the expectation was for much the same type of war. Many of the planners, unfamiliar or uncomfortable with all of the UNIX-based applications and products in the CTAPS, were unable to make the transition to a full use of the CTAPS in the high-intensity war that developed. Even the ATO was (and still is) produced in a message format that was readable only by special parsers.[26] As the war dragged on, planners developed their own Microsoft Excel spreadsheets, Word documents, and other tools to perform their own functions. Many were incompatible.

These electronic incompatibilities were amplified by physical access problems. The assessors were located in a separate building that did not even have SIPRNET access until the end of the war. They were able to put together the products that guided the planning effort of the air component only by establishing personal relationships with the other cells in the CAOC. With these relationships, assessors gained an understanding of the processes and inside access to the important products from each cell. They then took the information, converted much of it to Access format for manipulation, and created PowerPoint briefings for Short. The briefings showed him how many missions had been flown and aborted and why, what objectives the missions had been trying to accomplish, and the battle damage assessment (BDA) status for each target.[27] This enormous task was the digital equivalent of collecting everyone's yellow stickies to create napkin-sketches of the progress of the entire air campaign.

The assessors had better sources of intelligence than in Desert Storm. Mission reports and, later, edited clips of gun-camera video were available over the SIPRNET. However, the JAC was responsible for performing all BDA assessment and was required to confirm every kill with two sources. In the end, BDA still was not timely enough to be useful in the time-constrained planning cycle.[28]

As previously discussed, much of the attention in Kosovo turned to attacking fleeting targets. General Short brought in Col Edward Boyle, the commander of the air operations group in Germany at the time, and a tiger team to figure out how to do the job. They came up with a "cell" that actually had three parts: an ISR Cell, an Integrated Air Defense System team located with the ISR Cell in a sensitive compartmented information facility (SCIF), and a fielded forces team on the combat operations floor.[29] Their duties were, in fact, rather different.

The IADS team worked in a secret fusion center. The team used signals intelligence when it was available and then attempted to send other platforms like the U-2 or Predator to verify the position of the threats with electro-optics, infrared, or synthetic aperture radar. That the Serbs would park the threat vehicles in an area where a strike against them could cause collateral damage was always a possibility. It was a cat-and-mouse game to find and attack the threats before the Serbs could move them.[30] Because the very nature of the mission dictated it was not appropriate to have the strike aircraft loiter in the area to find the threats, this left the job to the scarce ISR aircraft. The IADS team found it difficult to cover the entire Kosovo and Serbia area with two slow-moving Predators and one U-2. Both U-2 and Predator imagery was sent back to RAF Molesworth to the JAC and then via transoceanic cable to the United States. At Beale AFB, California, analysts examined the data to cull useful information from it.[31] Much trial and error was required before the IADS team was able to get the analysts to give them the information they needed in the format they needed, and getting the information sometimes took hours.[32]

The fielded forces team did not have nearly the information processing capability of the Integrated Air Defense System team. Collocated with C-3 operations, the IADS team had the advantage of being able to use the same information that operations was getting—the common operational picture (COP) to show updated positions of the aircraft and a graphic version of Deptula's MAP (now called the MAAP).[33] The mere fact that it was able to see data-link information on the COP was a huge difference from Desert Storm. The flex targeters were often responsible for ensuring the ROEs were followed properly, including whether a target was valid. This ultimately entailed getting the information over the radio through several relays.

The picture in Allied Force is therefore one of only modest improvement. The technology to allow people from remote locations to view information existed in the form of the Web, so many different organizations were involved in the targeting process. This gave high-level decision makers visibility into the details of the operations, forcing them to start choosing whether they should exercise this ability or not. Although there were information systems like CTAPS, they were not tailored for this type of war and were, therefore, not used as designed. The CAOC had to devise its own procedures and information tools, making it difficult to assemble a picture of what was going on in the aggregate. The air component got deeper into the business of directing real-time operations, a function which now included the ability to get real-time information that many of the aircrews did not have. Since the resources that made this possible were scarce, most of the time the only way for the Fielded Forces Cell to become involved in these ongoing operations was to receive the information over the radio from the aircrews. This was a function that would take on even more significance in the next conflict.

Enduring Freedom

It was pointed out previously that General Franks and his CENTCOM staff were involved in the operational details of the war in Afghanistan. Strict ROEs and complex command relationships led General Franks's staff at Headquarters CENTCOM in Tampa Bay to exercise its authority in some of the operational details. It developed the targets that the air component was to attack and then held approval authority for many of the emerging targets.

Franks's staff exercised this approval authority by monitoring ongoing missions from a fusion cell in a secure facility at his headquarters. This fusion cell, basically CENTCOM's own "TST Cell," was manned by intelligence and operations experts, including Air Force lieutenant colonel Knaub. He had been involved in the initial setup of this cell, which was CENTCOM's link to sensor information like Predator video. Knaub's job was to monitor the intelligence analysis during missions and determine when there was a valid target, based on guidance from his boss, General Renuart (the J-3, or operations chief). Knaub then had to notify the appropriate decision maker, usually Renuart, although earlier on it could have been Franks.[34] The employment of this cell to direct ongoing operations contributed to the lack of empowerment at the air component.

The air component operated out of the new facility at PSAB. During JEFX 00, Gen John Jumper, USAF, retired, the ACC commander at the time, had pushed to develop an AOC with a network that allowed coalition forces to work on the computers side-by-side with US forces. When CENTAF staff members saw the plans, they wanted the same for the facility they were to build at PSAB. As a result, they met with Andy MacBrien, the MITRE lead engineer for the JEFX AOC, and gave a PowerPoint presentation showing 150 systems—the system design for the new CAOC. MacBrien pulled out his JEFX designs and tried to make the new facility similar. Although General Ryan had declared the AOC a weapon system at the end of JEFX 00, there still was no configuration control, so this became the de facto standard.[35]

Between these two facilities, workers at Knaub's level kept up a steady stream of communications, while Knaub maintained daily contact with officers at the air component. Maj (now Col) Mark Altobelli and Maj (now Lt Col) Mark Cline were in charge of developing the MAAP. One of the two talked to Knaub for hours each day ironing out the details of how to translate the guidance into plans for the air attacks.[36] They then developed a brief for the JFACC, General Wald, graphically showing what the air strikes would attempt to achieve for the next day. The MAAP still represented the link between the operational strategy and the tactical missions, but now the planners could portray it in a much more understandable, concrete way—and in a format that could be distributed to others more easily.

Cline and Altobelli had much improved technology to aid them in their tasks. In fact, the information technology involved had cut some formerly human tasks out of the process. The CAFMS, and even the CTAPS, had been so difficult to use that technicians had been specially trained to enter the information into the machines. But in EFXs 1998, 1999, and 2000, the Air Force had certified the theater battle management core system (TBMCS), and planners were using the new technology to develop strategy.[37] The TBMCS was a group of applications designed to be interoperable and to fulfill the functions in the AOC. These applications retrieved information from databases that updated and were updated by the GCCS. One of the applications was a MAAP Toolkit, a Windows-based program that allowed the planners to enter the information in familiar dialogue boxes. When they entered the information, it automatically produced the MAAP brief and then transferred the information to the ATO.[38]

Planners said that these briefing slides represented their view of the world. Because it was a graphic picture of the ongoing operations, the MAAP brief was a favorite tool to show even combat operations personnel what was occurring on a given day. It was also a way to learn how the operations applied to the objectives to be accomplished because it tied all the missions to those objectives.[39] In fact, this brief was so popular that a version of it got faxed out even to the air wings. It was much easier to understand than the ATO, which was sent out in a confusing message format.

The MAAP was only a "map" of ongoing operations—but combat operations staff also had improved capability to see what was actually happening. At the time, Air Force doctrine showed ISR was the job of a "specialty team" that was to coordinate with all the divisions. However, the doctrine was being rewritten to create a separate division for ISR, in recognition of the fact that the JFACC needs information but also has the job of providing information to the JFC and the other components.[40] Wald chose to organize a separate division for ISR, although it was housed in a separate building.[41] The Defense Department had arranged to buy up all the satellite-communications bandwidth available for the region on 12 September and deployed the Global Broadcast System to move high-bandwidth traffic around—even to the United States.[42] This was to prove especially useful in sharing sensor video.

Relative to the scope of the operations, the CAOS had a large number of sensors to bring back information from the battlefield. The use of Predator was much more prevalent in Enduring Freedom than it had been in OAF. Both the CIA and USAF had Predators flying in Afghanistan, and they were often used to find targets and direct aircraft to them. And the Predator video was available right on the Combat Operations floor, instead of only in the SCIF.[43] In fact, with JSTARS and RC-135 Rivet Joint aircraft working 24 hours a day, the CAOC had direct access to even better multispectral ISR than in Kosovo.[44] Most importantly, there were SOF on the ground with the Afghanistan opposition troops, so many times the air component would have direct access through radio to these "sensors" as well.

Information from these sensors became the driving force for air operations. For the first time, the air component had a "TCT Cell" at the outset of the conflict. Col Jeffrey Hodgdon deployed to PSAB with CENTAF from his job at Langley. He was to be the chief of the TCT Cell for the air component, and his team consisted of four others: the Predator liaison officer, an ISR collection manager, and two targeteers. None of the team members had been trained on any of the equipment, including the TBMCS. They looked at the ATO or the MAAP briefing to see the planned flow of aircraft and an application called Falcon View to see where the aircraft were in real time. There were no written procedures for their task. Yet after the first week, they coordinated on almost every attack mission, as the ATO became merely a scheduling tool to get aircraft in the right area to wait for updated information from sensors or special operations forces.[45]

Most of the attacks still had to be coordinated at the same levels as the preplanned missions—but faster. There was no doubt in Hodgdon's mind that CENTCOM was the decision maker on most of the strikes. Only when the strike occurred within a predefined geographical area, known as an engagement zone, or when the aircraft was talking to a ground controller in the area, could the mission proceed without CENTCOM's permission. Obtaining this permission was usually the long pole in the tent, sometimes taking hours. Those in the TCT Cell coordinated with others in the CAOC by walking around to get signatures on a routing spreadsheet, e-mailing, or telephoning. Since the Judge Advocate General was in another part of the building and the point mensurators were in another building with the ISR division, they walked around a lot.[46]

Because of the ad hoc nature of the operations, the air component was hard-pressed to translate the information from the directed telescope into an assessment of how things were going in the aggregate. Major Hathaway and his chief of assessment, Maj Stephen Murray, tried to link the missions accomplished to progress toward the objectives. They conducted what they called "operational assessment" each day for Wald, the JFACC, and later General Moseley. Unlike in Kosovo, the assessors were located in the CAOC with the rest of the workers and had access to the TBMCS functions. But this did not make their job much easier.[47]

Their directed telescope was still far from automatic. The TBMCS's functions still did not do everything the AOC staffers wanted, so they reverted to producing customized documents. For example, they developed a separate Microsoft Excel spreadsheet to track targets and results. CENTCOM and CENTAF were using two different databases to develop targets, and the two were incompatible.[48] Deptula had brought in Col Gary Crowder to handle "operations stuff," and he went to work on this problem. To track all the targets, he and Hodgdon developed a spreadsheet to combine all the targets from both databases, retrieve information from the ATO to determine what missions were sent against specific targets, and then attempt to incorporate BDA where it was available from mission reports or intelligence.[49] Once again, the only way for the assessors to find out what was happening was to gain personal access to the people in various divisions of the CAOC.

Overall, it does appear that the CAOS was able to achieve a much improved ability to move and process information. The CAOC was able to develop and share the MAAP much more easily than in the past. However, long-range planning became futile as both commands seemed to be more focused on the ongoing missions—the area in which they were seeing success. Headquarters CENTCOM and the CAOC both became centers of calculation, trying to control the periphery. These two centers were able to get an unprecedented amount of information from the sensors relative to the number of aircraft over the battlefield. Some of the information was fed over the radio, but much was digital information that could be combined. The fusion cell and the CAOC saw a display of the real-time position of the aircraft right next to video from the sensors. Nevertheless, the time-sensitive nature of most of the operations made it more difficult to assess the aggregate results. The centers could change plans in real time more easily than they could change the long-term plans.

Iraqi Freedom

As described in chapter 5, the process of developing plans evolved between OEF and OIF. The air component was now in charge of gathering the different components' targeting requests and making an apportionment recommendation to

Franks. CENTCOM still held a targeting board, but now its purpose was guidance and approval of the air component's targeting recommendations—not stipulation of the targeting. Similarly, as depicted later, General Renuart worked to get CENTCOM to move its TST Cell from the SCIF out to the operations floor. Here it acted more as an overseer of the TSTs rather than the decision maker. Authority for most of the important emerging targets was pushed down to the air component.[50] In fact, Franks developed a formal matrix that defined who had the authority to execute the different categories of TSTs. For many of these, it was the CFACC.[51]

Moseley had forcefully argued for this change, so he had to organize and plan to handle it. But the innovations were already in progress. JEFX 02, also known as Millennium Challenge, had experimented with tools and procedures for performing time-sensitive targeting. Among the tools was a system called the Joint Time-Sensitive Targets Manager (JTSTM), an application in an information system called the Automated Deep Operations Coordination System (ADOCS). ADOCS had been in use in a limited form in Korea for CAS and search and rescue. Then in the late 1990s, the Defense Advanced Research Projects Agency sponsored the ADOCS as an advanced concept technology demonstration—a modified pathway through the normally cumbersome military acquisition system. The ADOCS was programmed to tap into the GCCS and TBMCS, among other databases.[52]

This was to be the first use of the full-up AOC weapon system that General Ryan had started in 2000. The Block 10.1 Falconer at PSAB had achieved its full configuration, including the TBMCS, various planning and reconnaissance management tools, and the time-sensitive targeting tools mentioned above.[53] Moseley increased the manning in the PSAB CAOC from 672 to 1,966, 43 percent of which had received formal training through the Air Force Command and Control Training and Innovation Group at Hurlburt Field.

The ATO process and information-sharing tools had now reached a level of maturity, but there were still flaws. They had been tested during Millenium Challenge and accepted as the first block cycle of the AOC. The Air Force's emphasis on training had also increased knowledge of these procedures. In addition, the revised CENTCOM process meant that the MAAP was a more relevant product—the air component now actually had a hand in planning the air strikes. Still, after the first week of implementation most of the strike sorties took off without targets. The decision making inside the 72-hour ATO cycle increased the number of changes that had to be made. As a result, the ATOs usually got out late.[54] The good news was that they were now easily transmitted to almost all participants.

The air component was also able to better coordinate the space support it needed. As previously identified, Moseley was designated the space coordination authority just prior to OIF. This allowed the air component to synchronize the ATO with a space tasking order (STO). The ATO told the space operators in the CAOC when the critical times were for GPS accuracy, and the STO specified how to tweak the constellation to achieve greater accuracy. For critical periods, the 28-satellite GPS constellation was configured to reduce the normal 3.08-meter accuracy to 2.2 meters.[55]

Other parts of ISR were beefed up as well. The air component was able to fly a record number of ISR sorties and obtain multispectral feedback using electronic, infrared, electro-optical, moving-target-indicator and synthetic aperture radar. The "records" come from the fact that there were four Predators flying simultaneously and six U-2 flights on a single ATO.[56] Those in the ISR Division could view imagery and reports from these sensors and chat online with analysts about their interpretation in near real time, even though the analysts may have been in the United States. In May 2002 the Air Force had approved "remote split operations" by Predator units, which allowed about half of the 15 Predators in-theater to be operated from the United States.[57] The aircraft took off and landed in-theater, but the Predators were flown by operators in Nevada. U-2 sensors were directed by analysts at Langley AFB, where both Predator and U-2 analysts could evaluate the results.[58] The CAOC and CENTCOM could see the imagery in-theater, but this way only a fraction of the 1,500 support people at Langley had to be deployed to the theater. In two dozen dimly lit trailers inside an old B-52 hangar, this group supported six U-2 flights per day and three or four Predators at any given time.[59]

Despite the huge numbers of sorties, the CAOC did not have a complete picture of this immense area from its ISR coverage.

Although only one Global Hawk UAV was equipped with infrared and synthetic aperture radar sensors, it put out so much data that the analysts were overwhelmed.[60] Although Global Hawk and U-2s fly high enough to see a good portion of the country, the four Predators flying at speeds around 80 knots and looking at a soda-straw picture could not provide coverage for anything too far from their planned flight path. It is important to note that although the CAOC got unprecedented amounts of ISR information, it still could not see everything.

The process of putting this information together was much more developed in OIF than ever before. Several Millennium Challenge participants were present at the Scud-hunting practices at Nellis during late 2001 and early 2002. Lt Col Gary Backes (USAF) was one, and he brought with him his experience with JTSTM. Backes taught the rest of Hodgdon's handpicked team members about the tools they would use.[61] The JTSTM became a way to share all of the information about the emerging targets with anyone who had access to the SIPRNET—and to perform virtual coordination with all those involved. In fact, the Air Force thought so highly of it that it developed a companion tool in ADOCS to handle coordination within the air component for targets of interest.[62] Moseley called these "dynamic targets," whereas those designated by Franks as important were called TSTs.

Moseley put great care into the development of his TCT Cell for OIF. For one particular type of TST, the Scud, he took the authority that Franks had delegated to him and entrusted it to the TCT Cell chief on the combat operations floor.[63] His strategy division, led again by now Lieutenant Colonel Hathaway, wrote Moseley's daily guidance (the air operations directive [AOD]). Over time, Hathaway modified this AOD to guide the TCT Cell in choosing which emerging targets (other than TSTs) were important enough to warrant diverting aircraft and which preplanned targets could be sacrificed to hit emerging ones without disrupting the overall plan.[64]

The result was a section of the Combat Operations Division with a lot of authority to accomplish things in real time. Interviews with TCT Cell team members after the war indicate they were justifiably proud of their accomplishments. A total of 19 surface-to-surface missiles were launched (none on Israel) in the 21-day campaign to reach Baghdad compared to 88 Scud launches in a 43-day campaign in Desert Storm.[65]

The performance of the TCT Cell depended on a mixture of technology and teamwork. The cell divided the country of Iraq into three sectors: North, South, and West. The process was essentially the same for each—the division separated responsibility among attack coordinators and targeteers.[66] Participants at JEFX 04 in July 2004 set up a similar TCT Cell. The cell chief was Wing Commander Bryan Trace, who had also been a deputy cell chief during OIF. His observations were that, although there were "experiment-isms," and the team was not as well trained for JEFX as the one for OIF had been, the processes worked similarly. At JEFX 04, all team members had dual computer monitors at their stations, on which they each had at least four to six chat rooms open and some type of digital map in the background. Trace routinely watched at least 10 to 11 chat rooms.[67] These chat rooms linked people in the air component with others in the CAOC, at the other components, and at CENTCOM, including various intelligence channels. It was here that he caught bits of information from intelligence that tipped him off to the existence of an emerging target. The determination that something was an emerging target was made seemingly instinctively. In actuality, it was based on Trace's constant study of the CFC and CFACC guidance, such as the AOD that Hathaway put out daily. This guidance also told the chief whether the target was a CFC-designated TST or a CFACC-designated dynamic target.[68]

Guidance also determined who would have to coordinate on different types of targets. Trace used this information to enter the target into the JTSTM or the intra-AOC version in ADOCS. Figure 9 shows the front-end view of JTSTM, used to display a list of all TSTs along with essential information about each. To get more detailed information, any player had only to double-click any target and view a set of tab-driven dialog boxes. This application was the vehicle for coordinating among the components for all TSTs. It was so important, the TCT Cell chief's view was projected on one of the big wall screens in the CAOC—Backes described that it made you "think out loud."[69] Through a mixture of chats and phone-call prompts, the TCT Cell focused on getting all coordination blocks green before proceeding to attack a target.

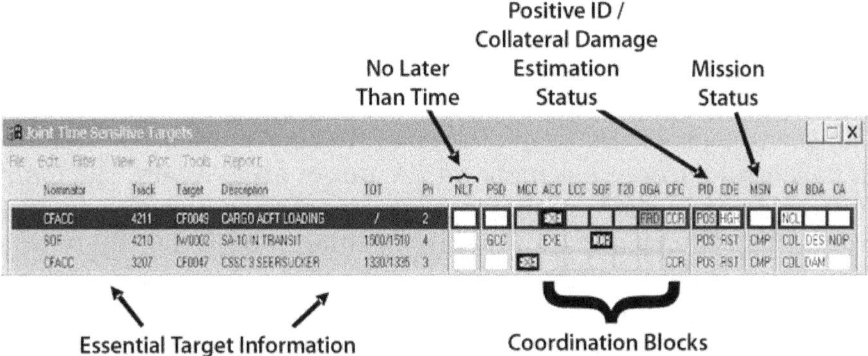

Fig. 9. ADOCS joint TST manager coordination view. (Adapted from Lt Col Gary Backes, USAF, "Joint Time Sensitive Target Manager," briefing, updated 27 June 2003. Received by e-mail from briefer. Author's personal collection.)

Of course, the TCT Cell team had to get all of the information into the JTSTM before anyone would sign off on the target. As soon as Trace had entered the initial information, he alerted the other affected team members by chat or in person to take a look at it (although many times they needed no prompting because they had been following the chats as well). At this point, two attack coordinators took over to determine how to prosecute the target. Using a graphic TBMCS application—much like a Gantt chart—they searched the ATO for aircraft that were available in the vicinity and armed with the appropriate munitions to attack the target. In doing this, they also had to consider the priorities of any other missions they wished to divert. They examined other options as well, such as the Navy's TLAM or the Army Tactical Missile System. The Navy and Army liaisons were key to informing them about these options. Upon making the choice of weapons and platforms, the attack coordinators started events in motion to get the weapons to the target while performing the rest of the coordination.[70]

The choice of weapon systems combined with the type of information the attack coordinators already had drove many of their remaining coordination actions. Some weapons required accurate, mensurated coordinates while others did not. Likewise, some sensors could readily be used to identify and supply accurate information while others could not. Furthermore, some scenarios required a positive visual identification by the CFC or CFACC, while others did not. Thus, the attack coordinators often had to set others on the TCT Cell team in motion to get another sensor to look at the target, mensurate coordinates, or perform a collateral damage estimate on the target area. Again, the team used a combination of chat and face-to-face, depending on the urgency or the richness of the information required. If there was some misunderstanding, team members always got up, walked over to the other person, and talked face-to-face. Finally, when the target was approved, they chatted the information to an individual who was talking to AWACS to pass the approval to the attackers (in the case of aircraft—otherwise to the Army or Navy liaisons for ATACMS or TLAMs).[71]

This is just a quick description of the team's functions. A MITRE study of TCT Cell interactions in OIF, JEFX, and several other experiments found its interactions to be much more complex than merely getting information and following business rules. It was managing a complex, fluid environment—detecting the cues on which it should act—while trying to keep in mind that other services and countries were involved, with all of the inherent security and political implications. The cell was interpreting and sharing information—often resolving ambiguous messages and determining who should see what and in what channel. Moreover, it was managing team dynamics—cueing others, teaching and learning roles, figuring out where they were in the process, and establishing trust.[72]

Elsewhere in the CAOS, other organizations were gaining the ability to combine real-time information from sensors to affect ongoing missions, too. The Army's V Corps, under General Wallace, deployed a headquarters to Kuwait that had similar capabilities on a smaller scale. He had an Analysis and Control Element to determine where the enemy was and direct Hunter UAVs, JSTARS, and even strike aircraft to look for targets. Then, when they found the targets, the collocated ASOC directed the aircraft or pushed them to a TACP to give terminal control. Wallace ascribed two functions to the ASOC: to directly support the divisions with CAS and to shape the deep battlefield for V Corps operations.[73] The latter seems to create a conflict with the air component's mission. Indeed, the Marine Corps chose to handle the deep missions differently, opening killboxes short of the established FSCL.

The inability of the air component to track the effects of its operations somewhat justified Wallace's desire to hold this control over deep operations. Army officers who worked for the BCD in the CAOC during OIF pointed out that the inability of the air component to determine and communicate the effects of airpower was the biggest source of friction between the air and land components. As the ground troops made their way through the sandstorms, they needed to know how big an effect the attacks were having on the Iraqi Republican Guard units. When the storms were finished, even General McKiernan, the CFLCC, was unable to pinpoint weaknesses in the enemy toward which he could have directed offensive actions to fracture them. Instead, he had to command a general maneuver called *movement to contact*, "a form of the offense designed to develop the situation and to establish or regain contact."[74] This was a formation suboptimal for the offense.[75]

The air component's practice of satisfying many of the land component's air support requests (ASR) with killbox interdiction did not give land commanders visibility into the results. These were missions sent to a patch of airspace, not a target, so the land component was unable to tell whether its requests were being serviced by the air component. The BCD had to get the air planners to add the ASR numbers into the remarks section and then build a spreadsheet from the ATO to show McKiernan and his staff how many support missions they were getting.[76] This did not guarantee the target would be the one that the aircrew chose to hit, and the mission reports by the aircrew did not always specify exactly what had been hit. Consequently, there was often no way to tell what killbox interdiction had accomplished.[77]

Part of this problematic situation can be attributed to the unwieldiness of the entire targeting process from a technical standpoint. The components had good relationships at the top, and they had worked out a joint strategy. Nonetheless, they had different and somewhat incompatible local systems for developing and tracking target data. For starters, CENTCOM and the air component were using different target databases. CENTCOM was using a system called the JTT, developed to take advantage of national intelligence databases. However, it did not hold enough records for the air component, which preferred the Interim Targeting Solution (ITS). The Army's main information system, the Advanced Field Artillery Tactical Data System (AFATDS), was technically capable of linking with the Air Force's TBMCS.[78] Prior to the beginning of OIF, the air and land components worked out a targeting architecture that used intermediate databases to update and receive updates from the various component systems. It was complicated but seemed workable.[79]

When the operation started, though, the people involved discovered many glitches that they had to work around. The AFATDS-TBMCS interface was only designed for certain specific actions. For example, AFATDS was designed to send targeting information to a targeting program called the Target Weaponeering Module (TWM) in TBMCS. As noted above, the air component used the ITS, which took information from TWM but had slightly different fields, so not all the information was passed. Those in the BCD had to manually enter the rest. When the land component sent a request for air support (the ASR), the TBMCS only took the information if it was designated an interdiction mission—CAS or any other support remained in a message format. Through the BCD, the Army worked out a way to send all ASRs as interdiction requests and then send code in the remarks section that would indicate the mission was other than interdiction.[80]

This was only part of the air component's frustrations with assessing the effects of airpower. Hathaway was again the deputy chief of strategy, and Major Murray was again Hathaway's chief of assessment. Together, these two were responsible for putting together the picture that would tell Moseley what was happening and how it was going. There were well over 100 colonels in the CAOC, and each seemed to have another problem like the BCD's problems to solve. The result was a lot of customized information formats.[81] To collect and process the information, Murray had to gain personal contact with the operations. He had seven to nine contractor analysts working for him, but instead of turning them loose to analyze the information, he had to send them to gather the data. He sent them to the different cells within the CAOC, including two or three on the combat operations floor at any given time, to figure out how the various cells turned data into information and which of it could be useful for their assessments.[82] It is no wonder when Moseley asked Hathaway for results on day two of the war, Hathaway could not even tell him *what* the air component had done, not to mention *how* it had gone.[83]

At a lessons-learned conference after the war, Moseley stated it flatly: "Two wars without [a real assessment process] are enough. . . . I never received adequate, timely feedback. I basically had to wait for CENTCOM to produce the official BDA to have any idea of what happened."[84] In this war as before, "official BDA" was not timely enough to adjust the ongoing operations. When Moseley told Hathaway to close the loop, Hathaway and Murray worked with their assessors to figure out what targets had been attacked, based on the mission reports. Then they made some assumptions based on the type of weapons used—precision munitions were given a high probability of hitting the target. It was a "Band-Aid" on a broken process, but it was the best they could do.[85]

Iraqi Freedom provides the best example of the increased ability of the AOC to act as a center of calculation. In this case, the AOC workers were able to put together and share a representation of the strategy in the form of a MAAP and meaningful guidance that even helped the TCT Cell pick targets. The technology for this function was not much advanced over that available in OEF, so this probably had much to do with the command relationships we have already covered. It was in the area of ongoing missions that the CAOC really excelled, however. TCT Cell members had the tools to see the real-time positions of the aircraft, chat logs full of information, and graphic TBMCS information all on their own computer screens. They could see sensor video on other screens close by. From this data, they could assemble the salient information in ADOCS and coordinate virtually with other components. Through a mixture of this electronic collaboration and good, old-fashioned face-to-face, they significantly advanced the art of changing plans based on real-time information. Others in the CAOC were also able to create innovative solutions to several problems they had passing data internally and among organizations in the CAOC. This autonomy had a price—it made it more difficult for the Strategy Division to determine the results in the aggregate.

Conclusions

Efforts to automate the process of integrating data from all the organizations continue. In 1998 the World Wide Web Consortium defined the specification for extensible markup language (XML), a different way to think about coding data for exchange over the Web. Conceptually, XML is a meta-language, a language about languages. Like its predecessor, hypertext markup language (HTML), XML consists of tags and content. But unlike HTML, the tags in XML describe and organize the content. The user can define new tags as desired—the tags are not needed to define how the browser displays the data. Users define the structure elsewhere in schemas or use existing schemas. Most importantly, XML is easily transported via simple Web protocols that make it possible for machines to exchange data. This property has enabled users to supply software known as Web services that other users can access over the Web.[86]

Engineers working on command and control equipment have seized the advantages of XML. It seems to provide a way around a nagging problem of C2 systems: different services design their systems to different specifications. In the past, systems could not transfer data unless there was a compatible hardware interface. Now they can pass data using Web protocols. With XML and Web Services technology, MITRE Corporation's Mike Butler has begun building translators to pass information from machine to machine. In 2002 Butler was working on a project to pass mensurated coordinates from the Raindrop mensuration system to F-15E aircrews patrolling the northern no-fly zone in Iraq. While looking at XML schemas, it occurred to him that he could really boil his problem down to four bits of information: what, where, when, and how accurate. Thirty days and $25,000 later, he had built the infrastructure to translate that information from Raindrop into a Link-16 format, and the problem was solved. He calls the program "cursor-on-target," borrowing a phrase from former CSAF, General Jumper, who had challenged the community to find a way to transfer information with the click of a mouse. When Butler showed up for the first spiral of JEFX 04, he was planning to try the same thing with three other systems. By the time the experiment concluded, there were 54 systems with translators.[87]

This is the reason the officers giving the tour of the Nellis CAOC were so intent on telling the machine-to-machine story. They were also careful to narrow the scope of their use of the technology. The CFACC for JEFX 04, Lt Gen Bruce Carlson, put it most succinctly when he said that "none of the machines are making decisions. Humans are still making decisions. All [they're] trying to do is give you more intuitive data to help make those decisions."[88]

Indeed, there are still many places where the people in the system simply need a better way to pass the information from one place to another. The transfer of ASR data from the land component to the air component is one example. In ADOCS, the TCT Cell still needs to manually cut and paste information from one tab to another, adding minutes to a process that is trying to shed them. The difficulties involved in integrating data from diverse organizations are well known and acknowledged in the corporate, as well as the government, world. Even if cursor-on-target can provide a way to read information from machine to machine, there are difficulties to be tackled. People still need the freedom to handle situations as they occur. When the information systems do not exactly fit the situation in which the people find themselves, they will have to invent work-arounds. Unless the people are able to use the same schema for the work-arounds that the other systems are using, the XML tags will be confusing. One person may develop a database with a field called "coordinates," whereas another calls it "position" or "location." There will be a need for some type of context mediation.

Digital information is the ultimate in "immutable mobile." The military has come a long way in creating a physical representation of the world, using sensors to send back the location of aircraft, vehicles, and people. In Desert Storm, it was a noteworthy event to be able to communicate with all of the AWACS planes simultaneously and combine their information into an air picture. In Afghanistan and Iraq, officers in the AOC said it was normal to have a good real-time picture. Furthermore, they got this assessment from the COP, available to anyone with access to the GCCS. Transforming the information to digital format and sending it over an increasingly high-bandwidth, low error-rate medium made the problem of transporting immutable mobiles seem trivial.

It was not so trivial for commanders to use the information to create knowledge of the aggregate results and assess whether the strategy is working. In fact, the better the centers get at intervening in real-time missions, the harder it is for them to determine what is going on in the aggregate. There may never be a common perception of this aggregate knowledge as long as human perspectives differ—no common operational picture of the strategic assessments. The clarity with which the highest levels define the goals, objectives, and command relationships can aid in this quest. Analyzing progress toward these goals will probably always put competing centers at odds with each other.

In addition, it should be obvious to the reader that this ability to act as a center is present only at the headquarters right now. Wallace's headquarters was the lowest level examined. While the Air Force's portion of his headquarters, the ASOC, is an echelon lower than the AOC, it is still not a very big step toward pushing information out. AWACS was not examined because its operators claimed they did not have the ability to get the information they needed. Of course, they had data-link capability and could see the relative positions of the aircraft in the air. But this was only part of the representation available to the headquarters—it lacked the positions of the ground participants and the other sensor pictures. AWACS operators also lacked the ability to communicate with other decision makers. The AWACS in OIF had only the ability to pass free-text messages at 28.2 kilobits per second—and even then, the formatting was all wrong, so it took three operators to sort out the messages and distribute them to the crew. Planned upgrades will not be complete until 2010.[89]

If these lower levels are to be a command presence with situational awareness, they will have to either bring the information in or get it from the centers. However, there is currently no single representation that combines all the information from these assets. It is not yet possible to combine the positions of all of the people, vehicles, and aircraft with the video and pictures from sensors like JSTARS and Predator in a way that can be sent to anyone in the system. In the headquarters like the AOC, all these different views can be located so close to each other that people in a minicenter like the TCT Cell can use them almost as a single representation. But there are space and bandwidth limitations on aircraft and combat vehicles that preclude their ability to display the same information.

The result is that, to react to the information in the sensor-communications loops, the centers must be involved. This is the current state of TST. But to what extent must the centers be involved, and how do they decide where to become involved?

Notes

1. Latour, *Science in Action*, 232.
2. Ibid.
3. Leonhard, *Principles of War*, 36.
4. Keenan, interview. Lieutenant Colonel Keenan, USAF, retired, was chief, Combat Operations Division, in Desert Storm.
5. Deptula, briefing.
6. Deptula, interview, 22–23 May 1991.
7. Hyde, Pfeiffer, and Logan, "CAFMS Goes to War," 38–46.
8. Deptula, briefing; and Deptula, interview by the author.
9. Ibid.
10. Ibid.
11. Horner, interview.
12. Corder, interview, 5–8, 14.
13. Keenan, interview; and Barton, notes, 5. Technical Sergeant Barton was an observer in the TACC during Desert Storm.
14. Keenan, interview.
15. Tom Ruimerman (Link 16 System Program Office), interview by the author, Hanscom AFB, MA, 5 May 2004. (Notes in author's personal collection.)
16. Keenan, interview.
17. CENTAF TACC/CC/DO, "Current Ops Log," vol. 2 of 2.
18. Tritschler, interview. Lt Col Phil Tritschler, USAF, retired, was the deputy CCO in Desert Storm. See also Keenan, interview.
19. Tritschler, interview.
20. JP 3-56.1, *Command and Control*, C-3.
21. Northrup, "Air Operations Center," 36.
22. Ibid., 37–39.
23. Crowder, interview (see chap. 5, n. 41). See also Lt Col Michael Rollison, USAF (Guidance, Apportionment and Targeting Cell chief, Strategy Division, OAF), interview by the author, Nellis AFB, NV, 28 July 2004. (Notes in author's personal collection.) Rollison was the MAAP chief for OAF. Both recalled that there was the expectation from very high up that the war would only last three days. This agrees with Ellis, "View from the Top."
24. "Analysis of the Effectiveness," vol. 2, sec. 2, Focus Area 4, 10.
25. Bird, "CAOC Mission Assessment," vol. 2, sec. 2, Focus Area 4, 3.
26. "Analysis of the Effectiveness," vol. 2, sec. 2, Focus Area 4, 26. See also Bradshaw, interview.

27. Bird, "CAOC Mission Assessment Trip Report," vol. 2, sec. 2, Focus Area 4, 4–6.

28. Schneider, Hura, and McLeod, "Command and Control," 39.

29. Caldera, interview. Lt Cdr Andrew L. Caldera, assistant intelligence officer for Battle Group Staff, CAOC, Vicenza, Italy; and an operations officer, Flex-Targeting Cell, OAF. See also Schneider, Hura, and McLeod, "Command and Control," 36; and "Seamless Integration," vol. 2, sec. 2, Focus Area 4, 417.

30. Caldera, interview.

31. Monroe, "Seamless Integration," vol. 2, sec. 2, 413; and Monroe, "New Age of Armed Reconnaissance," 8.

32. Caldera, interview.

33. Ibid.

34. Knaub to the author, e-mail, 22 Sept. 2004.

35. Andy MacBrien (MITRE Corporation, AOC lead engineer), telephonic interview by the author, 1 Feb. 2005. (Notes in author's personal collection.)

36. Knaub to the author, e-mail, 22 Sept. 2004; and Cline, interview (see chap. 5, n. 69).

37. "EFX 98 Assessment Report," executive 1-2.

38. Cline, interview.

39. Deptula, interview by the author; and Crowder, interview.

40. Northrup, "Air Operations Center," 39–40, explains the transition that occurred to the new construct of five divisions.

41. Hodgdon to the author, e-mail, 28 Dec. 2004. Col Jeffrey Hodgdon, 753d Electronic Systems Group deputy commander at the time of this writing, was the TCT Cell chief during OEF and OIF.

42. Ackerman, "Technology Empowers Information," 18–19. See also Ackerman, "Operation Enduring Freedom," 4.

43. Hodgdon to the author, e-mail, 28 Dec. 2004.

44. Deptula, "Operation Enduring Freedom."

45. Hodgdon to the author, e-mail, 28 Dec. 2004.

46. Ibid.

47. Hathaway, interview (see chap. 5, n. 54); and Maj Stephen Murray, USAF (609 CPS/DOXP at the time of this writing; chief of assessment, Ninth Air Force, USCENTAF, during OEF and OIF), interview by the author, Shaw AFB, SC, 24 Mar. 2004. (Notes in author's personal collection.)

48. Knaub to the author, e-mail, 22 Sept. 2004.

49. Crowder to the author, e-mail.

50. Knaub to the author, e-mail, 22 Sept. 2004.

51. Backes, interview.

52. Erwin, "Experimental Battle-Planning."

53. Butler, "Iraq War Underscores Need," 3.

54. "Operation Iraqi Freedom Observations," slides 3 and 4.

55. Scott and Covault, "High Ground over Iraq," 44.

56. Moseley, *Operation Iraqi Freedom*, 7.

57. Newman, "Joystick War."

58. Fabey, "Technology Amplifies War Games."

59. Schmitt, "6,300 Miles from Iraq."

60. Glenn to the author, e-mail; and Hodgdon to the author, e-mail, 4 Feb. 2005.

61. Hodgdon to the author, e-mail, 28 Dec. 2004.

62. Backes, "Joint Time Sensitive Target Manager."

63. Wg Cmdr Bryan Trace, RAF (assistant TCT Cell chief during OIF), interview by the author, Nellis AFB, NV, 30 July 2004. (Notes in author's personal collection.)

64. Hathaway to the author, e-mail, 21 Oct. 2004.

65. Keaney and Cohen, *Gulf War Air Power Survey*, 87–88. See also Moseley, *Operation Iraqi Freedom*, 3.

66. Hodgdon to the author, e-mail, 28 Dec. 2004.

67. Author's personal observations from JEFX 04 (notes in author's personal collection). With all these chats open, it was difficult to determine when a new message appeared. Wing Commander Trace had discovered a technical capability to solve this problem, involving highlighting all chats and using a function key that unhighlighted only the room that acquired a new message. There were lots of little quirks like this that were acquired only through experience.

68. Trace, interview.

69. Backes, interview.

70. Author's personal observations from JEFX 04.

71. Ibid. Surprisingly, passing the information through a single individual was a potential bottleneck at JEFX. It often took several minutes and, in one case, 20 minutes to pass this command.

72. Boiney and Drury et al., "Time-Sensitive Team Decision-Making."

73. Wallace, "Joint Fires in OIF"; and Hollis, "Trained, Adaptable, Flexible Forces."

74. JP 1-02, *Department of Defense Dictionary*.

75. Kelly and Andreasen, "Joint Fires," 21; and Wingenbach and Andreasen, interview (see chap. 5, note 80).

76. Kelly and Andreasen, "Joint Fires," 23.

77. "Task Force Enduring Look Lessons Learned," slide 49.

78. In Afghanistan, the Tenth Mountain Division had not deployed with the system since it had not brought organic artillery. Erwin, "Air Wars Demand More," 22.

79. CENTAF-PSAB Targeting Tiger Team, "CFACC Targeting Architecture."

80. Kelly and Andreasen, "Joint Fires," 22–23.

81. Murray, interview.

82. Ibid.

83. Hathaway, interview.

84. "Task Force Enduring Look Lessons Learned," slide 17.

85. Hathaway to the author, e-mail, 12 Apr. 2005.

86. Coyle, *XML, Web Services*, 5–12.

87. General Carlson speaking informally to a group of VIPs who were receiving a tour of the CAOC during JEFX 04.

88. Michael Butler (contractor for MITRE Corporation), interview by the author, Nellis AFB, NV, 29 July 2005. Butler is a MITRE engineer who showed

the author how to write XML translators prior to JEFX 04. (Notes in author's personal collection.)

89. Maj Samantha Helwig, USAF (AWACS senior director during OIF), interview by the author, Nellis AFB, NV, 2 Aug. 2004. (Notes in author's personal collection.)

Chapter 7

Decision Making Inside the Loop

War, however, is not the action of a living force upon a lifeless mass (total nonresistance would be no war at all) but always the collision of two living forces.

—Carl von Clausewitz

In the CAOC . . . we knew more about where the Iraqi forces were than the Iraqis did.

—Lt Gen T. Michael Moseley
Air Force Magazine, August 2004

"I went through this same thing in OIF—guys wouldn't tell you what was going on with their missions, so you didn't know what had happened."[1]

It was 2 August 2004, and JEFX 04 was in its final week. The group known as the TCT Cell in the Nellis combined air operations center had coordinated an attack on some mobile Scuds that had popped up in the experiment script. It had sent some (live) aircraft to strike the Scuds out on the Nellis Range, but now the cell was unable to determine whether the aircraft had found and attacked them. The attack coordinator had worked as the interdiction duty officer during Iraqi Freedom, where he had encountered the same problem.

As this scenario shows, now more than ever command centers such as the AOC come into contact with the aircrew during missions. Van Creveld advocated his directed telescope, a mechanism that enables a commander to ascertain what is happening and thus make good command decisions without burdening the troops on the battlefield. On occasion, however, the direction is reversed—those troops need information to which the commander's staff has access because of its ability to perform as a center. Possessing this information helps them react more quickly than the enemy. War is, after all, a competition—a duel, according to Clausewitz—between thinking, reacting opponents. Better information on one side can give that side an advantage.

The way living organisms compete is described well by John Boyd's theories. Boyd was an Air Force fighter pilot who combined his experience with flying fighters in combat with his reading of military history and his understanding of scientific laws. Integrating this knowledge, he developed a general theory documented in his briefing, "A Discourse on Winning and Losing." At the heart of his ideas is the observe, orient, decide, and act loop—a system that basically illustrates how organisms survive by continually accepting input from their environment and using that input to resolve uncertainty and succeed.[2] The essence of Boyd's war-fighting strategy is to get inside the opponent's OODA loop by executing your OODA cycle so quickly that the opponent cannot react effectively. In other words, the idea is to disrupt the opponent's frame of reference in that the expected results from certain actions or tactics have become null and void. Now the situation has become unpredictable, forcing the opponent to react to unexpected data and to go off course. This confusion of the opponents would then, ultimately, lead to their defeat. Boyd's ideas were instrumental in shaping much of current US Army and Marine Corps war-fighting doctrine.

Analysts have claimed that Boyd's ideas are equally well suited to all levels of war.[3] However, as has been illustrated, the US military has been much better at improving the OODA loop for ongoing missions than for long-term strategy. The air component's efforts to attack fleeting targets have been an attempt to get inside the OODA loop of the enemy on a tactical level. The sensor-communication loops, electronic collaboration, and information distribution have improved the way the AOC executes this short loop. For the longer-range operational strategy loop, the dynamics we saw in the previous chapter keep it from executing quickly.

The following analyzes where the sensor-communication loops are taking this business of shortening the OODA loop. At the beginning of the time period covered in this study, the only provisions for attacking emerging targets were armed reconnaissance (of which KI is a subset) and CAS missions. Throughout this span, airpower was called on to affect enemy ground operations in areas outside the reach of friendly ground troops. Someone had to put the information together in order to attack these emerging targets, so air commanders tried to develop the technology and procedures to do this in the AOC. At times, the AOC's job was to ensure compliance with the ROEs—in these cases, this enforcement actually lengthened the OODA loop. Because military and civilian leaders were wary of the consequences of military action in these particular instances, they accepted the loss of response capability. The TCT Cell gradually developed formal procedures and new technology to handle these situations as rapidly as possible, while still allowing close scrutiny. These strides also enabled it to help in other situations, including KI and CAS.

Through this evolution, the JFACC has developed the ability to shorten the OODA loop by delegating authority. Right now, the authority rests with the TCT Cell in the AOC and does not appear to be decentralized. This is partly because, as seen in the previous chapter, the AOC is where information for situational awareness is assembled. However, the TCT Cell suffers from its inability to communicate directly with the strike aircraft. The next step in technological development is the ability to either move the TCT Cell to an airborne platform or communicate with strike aircraft from the AOC. The former would be more in line with the proposed concept of deepening command relationships.

Desert Storm

In Desert Storm, the TACC had a very limited ability to direct real-time operations. Previous chapters revealed that the Desert Storm TACC had recently been transformed from its doctrinal organization and given a new strategy-development function. Subsequently, the TACC had been unable to develop smooth procedures for getting information to assess how strategy was going at an aggregate level. The Black Hole had to spend extra time gathering the results and compiling the MAP. The TACC also found it difficult to share a representation of the strategy; that is, to create a graphical depiction that would convey the concept of the strategy to others. Everything was passed in bits and pieces on target planning worksheets, change sheets, and the user-unfriendly CAFMS, so it was difficult for others to grasp the overall idea. Furthermore, the TACC did not have sufficient real-time information coming from the TACS to assemble a picture of the ongoing operations. Data links were unreliable, so it could not even see an up-to-date AWACS picture.

The TACC could not communicate well with the rest of the TACS, either. It was difficult to even get the ATO out daily. Even for those in the TACC with remote CAFMS terminals, it took over 12 hours to download and print the entire ATO. The ATO was over 800 pages long, and the lines supported only really slow speeds. Most turned to receiving the document either via a data port in a secure telephone unit III or via a message transmission system known as the Automatic Digital Network. Because the Navy had resisted the JFACC concept before the war and had not acquired compatible equipment, it had to resort to flying the document out on helicopters.[4] When it came to real-time communication, the TACC had to use the telephone to communicate with a ground-to-air transmitter at King Khalid Military City, through which it could then reach AWACS or ABCCC aircraft. This was a precursor to today's search for bandwidth.

The inability to direct real-time operations was not seen as a handicap since Horner did not want the TACC involved in the execution of the missions. He knew there would have to be adjustments made—the "enemy" gets a vote, so any plan would need changes when subjected to combat. Horner planned to let the TACS handle emerging situations. Tactical air control parties assigned to ground troops could find and direct aircraft to targets in the vicinity of the front lines. A steady stream of aircraft sent into the killboxes could find and destroy targets in the other areas occupied by the Iraqi army. In fact, after the war, Corder, who had performed the role that would later be called the CAOC director, was asked about the inability of intelligence to supply photos of targets in the killboxes. He did not think that had been a problem. The important thing, in his mind, had been keeping the stream of aircraft into the areas—a new flight of aircraft every seven minutes. Any delay to look for specific targets would have disrupted this flow and been counterproductive.[5]

Despite Horner's predilection, when the Iraqis surprised the coalition at Khafji, the TACC had to get involved to help adjust. Here, the importance of sensor-aided target location proved vital. Although Khafji was in an area close to friendly forces, the Marines responsible for control of CAS in the area became trapped in the town of Khafji when the Iraqis captured it. The Marines had Pioneer remotely piloted vehicles, but any target the Pioneers discovered had to be validated by an A-10 or OV-10 acting as FAC(A) because the RPV's position was very inaccurate.[6] The JSTARS became paramount in this battle.

The first two nights of the incursion, the TACC tried not to overreact to the Iraqi attack. On 28 January 1991, at 2224 local time, TACC officers realized a Saudi observation post was under attack. The AC-130 liaison officer diverted a Spectre gunship to assist but gave instructions to only hit targets that were clearly on the Kuwait side of the border. An attack so close to friendly forces needed to be controlled by troops in contact with the ground forces, and no such liaisons were available.[7] The next night, Horner learned through the JSTARS that this was a large invasion, probably an attempt to start the ground war. US Marine forces reported multiple convoys of enemy vehicles heading toward the Saudi border. Horner, still reluctant to fire in the vicinity of friendlies without control, ordered a Marine FAC to the area and directed JSTARS to look at the columns. Upon receiving verification from JSTARS that there were three columns of armor, Horner knew that the Iraqis were trying to get the ground war started.[8] With the Marines and A-10s attacking one of the columns; A-10s, F-16s, A-6s, and AV-8s working on another; and an AC-130 on the third, there was no need to significantly revise the attack plans. In the TACC, an observer noted the tempo was mainly unchanged as the air component attempted to react to the diversions without getting detracted from its main objectives.[9]

On the night of 30–31 January, the tempo increased. JSTARS imagery now showed an intersection in Kuwait through which the bulk of the Iraqi forces were deploying to divert to the three columns. Some F-15Es and F-16s had a low-altitude navigation and targeting infrared for night (LANTIRN) system to help them fly low-level routes at night, but it could also act as a sensor to help find targets. Planners had siphoned some of the LANTIRN-equipped F-15Es and F-16s from their Republican Guard missions to help strike the road to the southwest.[10] However, Marine general Boomer and Saudi lieutenant general Prince Khalid bin Sultan bin Abd al-Azziz both called Horner looking specifically for B-52 support. Without ground control, Horner thought it best to use the "Buffs" a little farther from the friendlies, so after repeated requests from Boomer, he finally allowed the TACC to retarget a four-ship of Buffs for the prominent intersection.[11] Just the A-10s and AC-130s were able to work with ground controllers, as an air and naval gunfire liaison company team had reached the coastal area to help defend the Saudis.[12]

As the only real-time picture of the ground battle, JSTARS imagery was seductive to commanders. It gave them a picture of the ground situation rather than a stream of words over the radio, which then had to be deciphered. On 29 January at 0800 local time, Maj Gen Burt Moore, Schwarzkopf's J-3 (director of operations), called the TACC to alert it that Schwarzkopf had pictures of a convoy of 75 tanks. The picture was already hours old, but Schwarzkopf wanted something done about them. Horner got a similar call from Schwarzkopf soon after, and he put Corder on it. While Combat Operations tried to send planes to the area, Corder confronted the Army JSTARS operators in the TACC. They were unable to tell him where the targets had gone, and Corder was livid. The next day, Colonels Mike Reavey and Charles Haar came up with procedures for passing targets from JSTARS to ABCCC to the fighters to "get headquarters out of the targeting business." The ABCCC talked directly to JSTARS. The fighters checked in with ABCCC to get target information.[13]

There were really not many provisions for directing attacks on emerging targets from the TACC. Black Hole planners indicated they kept F-111s on ground alert for the possibility of attacking leadership targets if the intelligence was available.[14] This would require a significant lead time, ruling out any targets that required immediate attack. In several cases, intelligence indicated the potential to attack Saddam Hussein directly. On 22 February 1991, intelligence located one of his famous "Command Winnebagos"—recreational vehicles that Saddam used for off-site or mobile conferences. Two F-111s returning from another mission struck this target, a serendipitous event.[15]

The Scud Hunt was therefore a significant strain on the system. The plans to neutralize the Scuds had included strikes against missile storage areas, strikes against fixed launchers, and alert aircraft to attack mobile launchers. When the Iraqis started launching Scuds at both Israel and Saudi Arabia even after the fixed sites had been destroyed, it was apparent the ground alerts would not work. At first, the reaction was to launch the alert aircraft. However, available assets did not support this response. Comments in a historian observer's log indicate that there actually was a shortage of available aircraft to engage the Scud sites—all other aircraft were scheduled.[16] Thus, planners started devoting resources to searching for these mobile threats. Lieutenant Colonel Tritschler was put in charge of the Scud effort.

Most of the time, Tritschler tried to redirect aircraft that had not yet taken off. To find and destroy mobile Scud launchers, though, the response needed to be faster. Since most of the Scud launches were at night, Colonel Haar brought in a group of Fighter Weapons School instructors to do nothing but work these changes at night.[17] They worked hard to get aircraft to the launch sites as quickly as possible. In one instance Tritschler, himself, had to do this. On 14 February 1991 at 1146 local time, one of Keenan's air defense troops yelled out, "Scud alert!" She was on the phone with Air Force Space Command officers at Falcon (now Schriever) AFB, Colorado, and three minutes later she wrote the coordinates down on a yellow sticky and passed it to Tritschler. He walked over to the senior air defense officer, who notified the AWACS to divert some aircraft to the launch area to try to get the launchers. At 1204 local, the AWACS replied that it would divert a four-ship of F-16s scheduled to hit a target about 20 minutes from the launch site.[18]

Ultimately, the coalition was unsuccessful at finding and destroying the mobile Scud launchers. Most of the necessary information was available somewhere, but the air component was unable to turn that information into successful attacks. Strategic Air Command had developed a way to use its strategic warning systems to give CENTCOM a launch warning and missile trajectory, which helped the Patriots determine where to look for the inbound missiles.[19] However, unless the aircraft were right over the site, they were unable to find the launchers. In fact, on 9 February, two F-15Es witnessed a launch but were still unable to find and attack the launchers.[20]

In Desert Storm, the TACC tried to stay out of the business of directing ongoing missions. This was the philosophy of its leadership and also a reflection of its capabilities. The plans were to use push CAS and killbox interdiction to react to the enemy—the enemy did not cooperate. TACC personnel found themselves in the position of having to piece together information in order to make the attacks on fleeting targets successful. This happened to some extent during Khafji, although even there the TACC resisted. The Great Scud Hunt represents an attempt at what we now call time-sensitive targeting. The CAOS was not mature enough to get and distribute the information among the various actors to find and destroy emerging targets employed by a thinking, reacting (hiding) enemy.

However, it was apparent this was the direction in which air war was headed. The *Gulf War Air Power Survey* analysts presciently said that certain incidents in the air war were "glimpses of a future, perhaps not very distant, when a theater air commander will be able to follow the course of an air campaign in real time, intervening selectively to take advantage of the flexibility of air power."[21]

Allied Force

It was in Allied Force that efforts to direct ongoing operations became controversial. Discussion thus far has shown that the job of the CAOC during Allied Force became one of attacking whatever targets had been cleared by the higher-level decision makers. This included many fleeting targets.

The air component was not initially set up to pursue these targets. The original plan included suppression of air defenses and bombing of a limited set of targets until Milosevic capitulated. When he did not, Short's CAOC staff looked for some way to increase the pressure. However, it was not allowed to expand the bombing of fixed targets beyond what was approved. Besides, General Clark wanted the CAOC to concentrate on Milosevic's fielded forces in Kosovo. These forces had dramatically increased the intensity of their ethnic cleansing campaign, and this presented an opportunity and a mandate for action for NATO. Lieutenant Colonel Crowder, the deputy director of operations and battle staff director (similar to Keenan's CCO position in Desert Storm), recalls they were just "looking for something to do in the daytime."[22]

The Serbs were winning a cat-and-mouse game with their air defenses. They rarely allowed their threat radars to radiate, so many of the Air Force's traditional methods of suppressing air defenses, such as shooting high-speed antiradiation missiles (HARM), were ineffective. Instead, the air component had to start handling the threats as emerging targets, similar to the Scud Hunt in Desert Storm.[23]

The Serbs were also winning a cat-and-mouse game in the Kosovo villages. Something also had to be done about the ethnic cleansing. Short knew that by itself, airpower was not very effective against ground troops, especially in an environment where they could hide or mingle with civilians. The lack of friendly ground troops meant this was not technically a CAS situation. But there were "friendlies" in the form of Kosovar civilians, so the aircrew had similar constraints against hitting anything but the enemy. Yet the lack of friendly ground troops also meant there were no "sensors" on the ground to identify the enemy and separate it from the civilians. Further, the enemy had no need to mass in order to defend itself against an invasion. Consequently, even finding the Serb troops from the air was a major task and, once found, engaging them without hitting civilians and before they made it back to hiding was even more difficult.

In response to both of these problems, Short set up a Flex-Targeting Cell in his CAOC. As described previously, it was actually composed of three elements: an ISR Cell, an IADS team, and a Fielded Forces team. The IADS team, collocated with the ISR Cell, had access to much real-time information but had a difficult time fusing it in time to strike the fleeting air defense targets before they were moved.

Once the IADS team had the target located, it had to get the information to the strike aircraft. For the most part, the team did this the same way the TACC in Desert Storm had done it: it passed coordinates by radio through either AWACS or JSTARS. A JSTARS representative was on hand in the IADS Cell to facilitate the transfer of information. However, other avenues were available in Kosovo. Late in the conflict, the air component acquired a real-time targeting system (RTS) that transmitted imagery to F-15Es from a van in Brindisi, Italy. When the IADS team got imagery off the server, an RTS operator transmitted it to the aircraft, where the aircrew could use it to find the target so they could guide a precision weapon (usually an

AGM-130). The F-15E was the only aircraft that was successfully retargeted this way.[24]

However, GPS provided another solution. The JDAM was a dumb bomb with an inexpensive tail kit that provided GPS-derived guidance. If the IADS team could provide accurate coordinates, the aircrew of a B-2 bomber could program a JDAM, which would then hit the target with incredible accuracy. To get these coordinates, the IADS team had to rely on agencies in the United States to mensurate the coordinates. Because these agencies were not always aware of the priorities, coordinating with them added time.[25] Mensuration is a process that translates coordinates from a flat chart to take into consideration the elevation of the target. If a weapon could fly to a target directly perpendicular to the earth, mensuration would not be necessary. Since it approaches at an angle, however, a weapon could be long or short if the target is at a low or high elevation.

The IADS team's successes were few. A briefing by Colonel Boyle after the war showed only three examples.[26] On one occasion, a U-2 reprogrammed its sensors in flight to take an image of an SA-6. It then sent the image back to Beale AFB for an assessment of its coordinates, which were then transmitted to the cockpit of an F-15E whose aircrew was just turning inbound toward the target with precision weapons. More typically, those in the CAOC had a hard time getting the information to the strike aircraft in time to allow them to attack before the targets moved.[27]

Basically, the Fielded Forces team had the same mission: find and attack elusive targets. However, the parameters of the job were different. As noted above, although this assignment was technically not CAS, it was just as demanding in terms of avoiding collateral damage. Yet there were neither ground troops nor representatives of the civilian population capable of directing the attacks and taking responsibility for ensuring Fielded Forces avoided this collateral damage. As a result, the CAOC became intimately involved in making decisions about which targets were approved for strikes.

Rarely did Fielded Forces team members have the information necessary to carry out this responsibility. By virtue of being collocated with the C-3 Operations staff, they were able to access the same data—including the COP and the MAAP slides. Unfortunately, this was not sufficient to answer the questions in which the flex targeteers were interested. Operations did not consider the COP a complete air picture over Kosovo or Serbia; thus, it left the tracking of the aircraft to the ABCCC, AWACS, E-2C Hawkeyes, JSTARS, and FAC(A)s. The Fielded Forces team's main job with respect to the operations in southern Kosovo was to approve targets in accordance with the ROEs.[28] This tasking became somewhat inconsequential since most of the time the targets were visually identified by FAC(A)s, and all the CAOC got was a verbal description over the radio, usually passed through the ABCCC. From the standpoint of our question about centralized and decentralized control, the approval of targets in southern Kosovo is one of the most crucial issues.

However, there were times when the Fielded Forces team in the CAOC was able to get information that was not available to others. In a book written by A-10 pilots after the war, these few situations stand out because the pilots have pointed words about the CAOC's actions in many other circumstances. On 11 May 1999, Lt Col Mark Koechle and Capt Slobee O'Brien were shocked at the directions they were given through "Moonbeam," the ABCCC. Moonbeam directed them to attack a permanent building, an act that was at that time against the ROEs for fear of collateral damage. Then, after the two pilots had completed the attack and moved on, Moonbeam directed them back to reattack because there were soldiers in and around the building. Finally, Moonbeam directed them to attack a nearby barn in which there were armored vehicles. The A-10 pilots complied, but warily, because they did not find out until later that the directions were being relayed from a Predator through the CAOC and the ABCCC to them.[29] In his written account, Koechle did not seem to mind getting the direction, especially since the mission was an extremely successful one.[30] This was clearly a case where the Flex Cell had more information than the FAC(A)s.

There were other times when the Flex Cell had information from electronic sources. It was difficult to fuse all these sources because they were not integrated. Predator and JSTARS video, U-2 imagery, and RC-135 electronic data were available only in the ISR Cell where the IADS team worked, so they were not available to people in the Battle Staff Division.[31]

In the beginning, the Flex Cell only intervened whenever it had such additional information. Short's guidance to the A-10 and F-16 FAC(A)s was that they had the "hammer" on identifying and approving the targets that would be attacked in the KEZ.[32] Along the way, several incidents caused the CAOC to withdraw the authority to approve targets back from the FAC(A)s. On 14 April, an F-16 FAC(A) mistakenly directed an attack on a column of civilian vehicles near Djakovica, thinking they were military. In response, planners tightened the ROEs to limit attacks to strictly military vehicles—ruling out attacks on civilian vehicles used by the military.[33] There were similar changes to the ROEs based on geography that further restricted the discretion allowed the FAC(A)s.

Later it will be seen that this caused pilots to become overly cautious about attacking any targets without permission. Gradually, the pilots became so tentative that they felt it was necessary to check with the CAOC for approval on most targets.[34] It seems this, in turn, drove the CAOC to become conservative, since it was now directly responsible for the decisions. The result was a situation where the Fielded Forces team was being asked to make judgment calls on nearly every target based only on information fed over the radio.

This changed during the last two weeks of the war. During this period, the KLA launched an attack near Mount Pastrik. The Serbs were eventually able to repulse the attack, but to do this they had to come out of hiding and mass for the defense. This made them vulnerable to airpower to an extent not seen before in the war. The ROEs were relaxed to allow the FAC(A)s to direct aircraft to targets without checking with the CAOC first, provided the targets were within a specified circle.[35] JSTARS aircraft were sometimes able to detect the Serb troops as they moved in their vehicles, even though the Serbs still tried to move as stealthily as possible. The JSTARS then radioed the coordinates to FAC(A)s, who took a closer look and directed strikes.[36] In fact, on one occasion, the JSTARS battle managers directed B-1s to attack a target without a FAC(A) involved.[37]

The shift to more decentralized authority near the end of the battle seems to indicate that the nature of the war had a great deal to do with the way control was handled. The objective was to outlast Milosevic—to show and maintain NATO's determination while causing Milosevic's resolve to crumble. This was a game of calculations. How much could the alliance take? How much could Milosevic? The attacks on the Serb Army in Kosovo were vital in that they were the right thing to do and, therefore, showed NATO was in the right. Regardless, the risk of a crack in the alliance due to careless bombing of civilians was far greater than the potential gain from succeeding in any one attack, or even the attacks in the aggregate. Consequently, when the mistaken attack of a civilian convoy near Djakovica proved the risk of collateral damage was high, Short's CAOC levied tight ROEs on the aircrews (although it also loosened the altitude restrictions). The ROEs were so restrictive that aircrews found themselves calling for permission in most cases, and probably more than was required. Although the Flex-Targeting Cell was developed to aid aircrews in putting together information to find the fleeting targets, it inadvertently became an inhibitor because of its focus on ensuring aircrews scrupulously followed the ROEs.

The KLA offensive that occurred near the end of May of 1991 changed the calculations. Now there was a potential to actually defeat the Serb Army and in the process cause Milosevic to crumble. With the potential gains outweighing the potential risk—especially since the offensive caused some amount of massing of Serb troops—the CAOC delegated more authority. This was still the best way to shorten the OODA loop.

Enduring Freedom

As it was with Kosovo, it is impossible to talk about the air operations in Afghanistan purely from the perspective of the CAOC at PSAB. As noted earlier, there was a great deal of uncertainty as to the strategy in Afghanistan. General Franks had a TST Cell at CENTCOM headquarters in Tampa Bay, Florida, that allowed him to monitor and even direct ongoing missions. But it was difficult to understand at the beginning how the operations would actually lead to victory—the mechanism for success.

One thing was certain, however. When, on the second night of the war, Mullah Mohammed Omar's convoy was discovered near Khandahar, it was a lucrative target. The strategic consequences of killing the Taliban spiritual leader so quickly could have been enormous. As the convoy moved toward the city, US military leadership that was separated by thousands of miles suddenly became united in its attention to this unfolding event.

In Tampa Bay, General Franks was watching. He'd been alerted by his aide that the CIA's Predator had a target. He went to the TST/fusion Cell described in the previous chapter, where he could watch and direct the action.[38] On this first instance of that process, Franks was the decision maker for the TST, although later in the war he would delegate the authority to Major General Renuart. In his book, Franks recalls asking Renuart to have the CAOC "set up a kill box" so aircraft could destroy the moving convoy before it reached the city. In this account, the CAOC was unable to do that fast enough, and the convoy made two stops in the middle of Khandahar, the second at a mosque. Here, Franks directed the Predator, armed with Hellfire missiles, to fire at a vehicle that he suspected was Omar's. The missile destroyed the vehicle, and the people scrambled into the remaining vehicles and sped away to another building. This time, Franks called and asked Secretary Rumsfeld for permission to have aircraft destroy the compound, a target he considered would produce high collateral damage. Franks insists his legal representative, Capt Shelly Young, US Navy, concurred with each target.[39]

At the CAOC in Saudi Arabia, Brigadier General Deptula was also carefully monitoring the situation, along with Lieutenant General Wald. They had positioned F-18s just 20 miles south. However, the compound from which the convoy started was a target that had been kept on the no-strike list, waiting for a special operations assault that occurred later in October. As the convoy moved toward Khandahar, Deptula remembers calling one of his contacts at CENTCOM while Wald tried unsuccessfully to reach Franks to ask permission to attack. While they were on the phone, Deptula was surprised to see a vehicle blow up with no apparent warning. He was frustrated by the inability to get permission to use the 500-pound (lb.) laser-guided bombs (LGB) on the aircraft to destroy the entire convoy, rather than merely scattering the people.[40]

At Langley AFB, CIA analysts were surveilling the unfolding events, as well. Franks recalls getting the unwanted input from them that the final target was a mosque—input with which he disagreed and which he ultimately ignored, as was his prerogative.[41] In an article that appeared a week later in *The New Yorker* magazine, insiders told investigative journalist Seymour Hersh that CENTCOM's legal advisors had balked at attacking the second building—the one Franks described as a mosque.[42]

It is difficult to reconcile the differences in the accounts. The CIA controlled the Predator that was used, and the command relationships had been set up so CENTCOM, instead of the air component, had operational control.[43] Since this was the first incident, it is predictable that Franks would want to make the decisions. It is also unsurprising that those in the air component would be upset at the direction of such details by a combatant commander, whose responsibilities seemed to them to lie on a higher level than this. The CAOC did not need to set up a killbox to attack the target, but could have done so easily had it gotten the word. What it needed was permission to engage the target.[44] Franks eventually delegated these decisions to Renuart, his Operations chief (J-3), but that still meant the decisions were made in Tampa by a staff officer instead of by the functional component.[45] As noted, Rumsfeld and the NSC had set up strict ROEs about hitting targets with high potential for collateral damage, so this tightly-held authority was probably a natural result of the strict accountability placed on CENTCOM.

One thing is certain, however: despite the technology that linked all of these decision makers, not one of them knew the whole picture. Franks apparently tried to get the air component to act while the convoy was out in the desert, but it appears the air component never got the word. It wanted to act, but did not have the authority. There were competing centers of calculation, as described in the previous chapter. The higher-level center, CENTCOM, did not have direct control over the aircraft but retained the authority to give permission for them to strike. This made it impossible for the lower-level center, CENTAF's CAOC, to execute even though it had the same information. According to Colonel Hodgdon, the TCT Cell chief at the CAOC, this occurred frequently—the biggest hurdle the team had was obtaining permission from CENTCOM.[46] This is another illustration of the fact that holding decision authority at a high level can sometimes dilute, rather than facilitate, centralized control.

The CAOC had new ways to get the information from the Predator to the weapons on the aircraft. Some, like the Predator's laser designator and a modification to AC-130s to accept the Predator feed, depended on the ability of the Predator to work with other aircraft. Others depended on the CAOC or even higher levels to intervene. As depicted above, some Predators carried Hellfire missiles, and these were directed at a very high level. Alternatively, Predator video could be translated into a still picture and used to find mensurated coordinates for a GPS-guided JDAM. The CAOC had a mensuration system, called Rainbow, right there at PSAB, although it was in another building.[47] If all else failed, the Combat Operations officers could talk the aircraft onto the target and let the aircrew perform its own delivery with laser-guided or dumb munitions. Although there was eventually a FAC-qualified individual working in the CAOC, at first staffers just did what they had to, often relaying instructions through AWACS to get to the aircrew. Eventually, the Predator operators received training to allow them to talk the aircrew onto the target directly, bypassing the CAOC.[48]

The UAVs had given the CAOC a way to find targets, but they were scarce resources. In addition, they could not help coordinate with the ground forces. There was a battle on the ground, and to be effective, airpower had to be coordinated with that battle. Those who were part of the system in Khandahar found, just as had those involved in Iraq and Kosovo, that eyes on the ground were a necessary part of coordinating efforts.

On 19 October, the first military special operations teams landed in Afghanistan. The CIA already had a team in country to lay the groundwork for their arrival, so the SOF were ready to go to work.[49] However, the two SOF teams evidently had different expectations about their priorities. One team, Tiger 1 (Team 555), went in on the Shamali Plains near Bagram. Tiger 1 had elected to take a special operations terminal attack controller (SOTAC), trained to control aircraft and equipped to provide precise target coordinates. The other, Tiger 2, went in south of Mazar-i-Sharif and did not bring a SOTAC or the associated equipment. Many key people on the Combat Operations floor of the CAOC did not even know the teams had been inserted. So when, on 22 October, the CAOC received a call for air support, Colonel Crowder—performing a role that was essentially the CCO—had to do some improvising.

The call came from Tiger 2 over ultrahigh frequency satellite radio. Crowder described the team's calls as "cryptic" because it did not follow doctrinal procedures. The CAOC was able to decipher the fact that Tiger 2 was on the south side of a gorge, receiving fire from the north side. Using rough directions like, "The enemy is located one mile north of my position," Crowder's people plotted an enemy position and directed the nearest aircraft, a B-52, to drop "spotting rounds" with precision, wind-corrected cluster bombs—CBU-103s. After the drop, Tiger 2 called to say the drop had been "one mile" east of the target. The CAOC directed the B-52 to drop the same precision weapons on a point 6,000 feet due west of the first point, after which Tiger 2 reported the strike had been "two miles east" of the target.[50] The officers in the CAOC were frustrated.

Tiger 1 had success immediately, whereas it was to take over a week to get the people and supplies to Tiger 2 to allow it to have similar success getting the support of airpower. From that time forward, all teams to enter Afghanistan took trained controllers and equipment to provide coordinates to the aircraft.[51] From three 12-man teams in mid-October, the United States built up to 17 teams by 8 December. These teams helped target all types of airpower, including supply airdrops for coalition forces as well as bombs on enemy targets.[52]

Aircrews that flew in Enduring Freedom were dependent on information from outside their own cockpits. The United States did not have a large conventional force on the ground, and the enemy was in pockets throughout the country. The push CAS and KI used in Desert Storm were not possible because the command structure was not there. Airpower's role was to deliver precision firepower on targets. For the fighter aircrew, ROEs were so strict that they were basically unable to find and attack targets on their own.[53] The CAOC did some preplanning to facilitate rapid retargeting. It made templates of mensurated coordinates for entire towns so it could direct aircrews to attack certain areas merely by referring to a number in the template.[54] Besides these efforts, the aircrews were reliant on either the CAOC or the teams to get them targets while they were airborne. They followed direction from the CAOC for almost all mission details until they were directed to contact a ground team. After that, they were under the team's control.[55]

While the CAOC was learning to prosecute this new type of war, lessons about the old type seem to have been lost. The fact remains that there were some largely conventional battles between the Northern Alliance and the Taliban forces. In classic land battle, there are some preparations that need to be made in order to smoothly integrate CAS. In Desert Storm, it was seen that the FSCL had a vital role in this planning. In the first part of the Afghanistan war, it was not possible to use this kind of control measure across the theater because there was no well-defined boundary between the "friendlies," with whom the SOF were working, and the enemy. But there are other preparations, such as designating IPs so controllers can flow many aircraft efficiently through an area without causing collisions. For OEF, planners divided the entire country into 30-nautical-mile killboxes and designated the corners as IPs—a quick fix that turned out to be inadequate for several of the battles, including Anaconda.[56] Normally, the link to ensure this happens is the Army's BCD in the CAOC. But in Enduring Freedom, the CAOC's link to the ground forces was through the special forces teams. Most of the time, the special forces requested GPS-guided munitions. Because of the small number of aircraft in a single area, detailed coordination was not necessary. The job of the CAOC was to get aircraft out to the teams and help them hit fleeting targets. The results were seen in chapter 5—poor or no coordination between the air component and ground forces during conventional assaults like Mazar-i-Sharif and Operation Anaconda.

Enduring Freedom appears to have been a transition point for the CAOS. The factors covered in the previous chapters combined to produce what has been seen in this chapter. There was significant uncertainty as to the military objectives for the war, and complex relationships took the air component out of the business of developing strategy. Consequently, those at the CAOC and CENTCOM turned to doing whatever it took to succeed. They had an increased ability to get and use information from their directed telescope. The air component's attention subsequently turned to directing ongoing operations in a sort of "TST war"—a revolutionary type of operation that turned the tide of the war against the Taliban and al-Qaeda. Unfortunately, when the time came to prosecute larger, more complex operations coordinated with other conventional forces, the air component did not have sufficient depth in its command relationships to do so effectively. Were it not for the relationship-building that occurred between Enduring Freedom and Iraqi Freedom, the latter may have been much more problematic than it was.

Iraqi Freedom

The practices at Nellis and Shaw AFBs in late 2002 and early 2003 were an essential part of that relationship-building process. By the time combat operations began for OIF, the air component had run three exercises dealing with Scud-hunting and dynamic targeting. Personnel at the 505th Command and Control Wing at Hurlburt had developed and written formal tactics, techniques, and procedures based on the lessons of these exercises and of Enduring Freedom, and all had been trained on the tools they would use. Some had worked together in Enduring Freedom, and others were handpicked from among the instructors at the Air Warfare Center at Nellis and the Naval Strike and Air Warfare Center at Fallon Naval Air Station in Nevada.[57]

The TCT Cell described in the last chapter was, essentially, the center of attention in the CAOC. The official air component report for the first phase of the war says the cell prosecuted 156 TSTs and 686 dynamic targets, including 50 strikes against "leadership" targets and 102 against WMDs, encompassing surface-to-surface missiles like the Scud. Only a fraction of the almost 20,000 strikes in the first month of the war, these are the only missions that Franks or Moseley strictly classified as time-sensitive or dynamic targets.[58] As in Enduring Freedom, the TCT Cell was involved in many other missions that did not have a target listed in the ATO. In all, the cell worked on over 3,500 targets, out of which it directed over 2,100 attacks in the first 21 days.[59] Each of these took a larger amount of attention than the normal mission. For these operations, the CAOC was required to validate the target, get more information from ISR assets if necessary, find the assets to attack the target, and coordinate with all the components. In OIF, coordinating a single mission took anywhere from minutes to hours.

Leadership targets, which required the highest level of approval, took the longest to organize. When CIA director George

Tenet got a tip from his agents in the field about Saddam's whereabouts prior to the planned start of the war on 19 March 2003, it took six and a half hours to get the players together, make the decision, and drop the bombs. In this case, the decision makers were President Bush and the NSC, the decision involved totally revamping the war plan, and the aircraft were not even airborne at the time of the tip.[60] On 7 April, it took only 45 minutes from a tip on the ground in Baghdad until a B-1, already aloft awaiting instructions, dropped four 2,000-lb. bombs on a residence in the exclusive neighborhood of Mansur.[61] In this case, the TCT Cell had to clear no higher than Franks, and the strike aircraft was airborne awaiting the task. Each of these missions was essentially a complete ATO cycle condensed into as little time as possible.

The good news was that the processes had improved since Enduring Freedom. Franks realized that his air component had a solid process in place to rapidly prosecute emerging targets. He developed a matrix that specified the decision maker and the level of verification needed for certain classes of targets. For Scud-hunting in the western deserts of Iraq, the permission went even below the CFACC's level—according to the procedures developed in mission rehearsals at Nellis, the AWACS could often direct these missions.[62]

The TCT Cell worked many other missions as well. As in Enduring Freedom, the war became one of reaction after the first week for the air component. Most missions after that took off without a preplanned target. Of the 2,100 missions the cell directed, only 842 were classified as either TSTs or dynamic targets. For all of the others, the focus was on KI or CAS.

Still, the TCT Cell's contribution was felt in only a fraction of these missions. There were over 15,000 missions dedicated to killbox interdiction and close air support.[63] Moseley's CAOC had a cell dedicated to these missions: it was called the KI/CAS (proudly pronounced "kick- . . ." by its members) Cell. Some members of the cell were dedicated to attending all the planning meetings, getting interdiction targets from the approved target list (JIPTL), and planning CAS so it complemented the maneuvers of the land component. But the authority to attack a target was generally delegated lower than the CAOC.[64]

The CAOC usually set the aircrew up to make the final decisions about which targets to attack on KI missions. Based on the requests from the land component, the CAOC tasked an aircraft in the ATO to perform interdiction in a specific killbox. If possible, the ATO listed a specific target in the remarks—normally, there was a list of priorities (armor, artillery, etc.). But the CAOC also did something else that the aircrew really found helpful. In the remarks, planners also briefly described the intent of the mission, so the aircrew knew how to apply its judgment in unforeseen situations.[65]

Still, by virtue of its ability to gather the information, the CAOC at times played a role in some ongoing KI missions. The ISR Division had the ability to find targets and then pass them to the aircrews. In most of these cases, as seen in the next chapter, the CAOC was facilitating the process of getting information to the aircrew. When the CAOC was able to get updated target information via sensors, especially Global Hawk UAVs, it passed the information onto the aircrews to aid them in finding the targets. Based on the numbers, it appears the CAOC got involved in as many KI missions as it could and was limited by resources—either the ability of sensors to find targets or the ability of the TCT Cell to handle the coordination for all of those targets. The CAOC was not necessarily making the decision not to get involved in KI missions—it just did not have the ability to get involved in any more.

CAS missions also saw more intervention from commanders than in Desert Storm. The CAOC was generally not involved in finding targets for CAS missions. This task was left to others in remote positions who were able to use sensor-communication loops to assist the aircraft in finding the targets. These individuals were able to accomplish this out to a fairly long range, lowering the risk of hitting friendly troops. The result was that there were fewer instances of Type 1 controlling—the controller can see both the aircraft and the target. Instead, there were an increasing number of Type 2 cases, where the controller can see either the target or the aircraft but not both, or Type 3 cases, where the controller can see neither and calls "cleared to engage" rather than "cleared hot."[66]

This is an indication that others down the line faced the same decisions about whether to direct missions or to delegate the authority. Chapter 5 describes how the Army tried to closely synchronize fires—including airpower—and maneuvers in its area. One reason Wallace gave for preferring "corps shaping" to KI is that he saw it as much more effective. His data showed that enemy strength did not decrease appreciably after KI, but did after his corps shaping.[67] The problem with this claim is that there was no good way to keep track of the damage done by KI. We saw that the tasking process between the land and air components left the commanders unable to track the location or results of attacks in killboxes. Consequently, ground commanders had to order general "movements to contact" rather than pinpoint attacks. This was partly due to the nature of the war. Even Wallace admitted in an interview later that every move at the platoon through the brigade level had been a movement to contact because it was impossible to define the enemy.[68] This seems to be the real reason Wallace preferred "corps shaping" to killbox interdiction. He said the 30-nautical-mile square killbox was too big and wanted to be able to open smaller, more precise areas.[69] Killbox interdiction did not give Wallace the ability to decide where the attacks should occur, or even the visibility into where they *had* occurred.

The Marines and the Army made quite different decisions with respect to CAS. The Marines' DASC concentrated on maximizing the flow of aircraft into and out of their sector. Aircrews related that there was seldom any delay when they were handed off to the DASC—they were almost immediately handed to a controller for CAS or sent to a killbox. In addition, as we showed, the Marines opened killboxes short of the FSCL. In the Army's sector, every mission short of the FSCL followed strict CAS procedures. Some of them were controlled by the ASOC as if they were mini-TSTs.[70]

In Iraqi Freedom, the TCT Cell at the air component came into its prime. Refined procedures and equipment combined with a conscious delegation of authority from Franks and Moseley to make it a very productive team. The cell was able to run the TSTs and dynamic targets, getting the execution times down to minutes in some cases. It was also able to contribute to some of the KI/CAS missions when it had ISR information that could aid the aircrew in finding targets. The push CAS and KI system still handled most of the real-time reactions. But now, the CAOC got involved whenever it could. Due to the limited resources (compared with the scale of the war), this was not very much. The ASOC also had the ability (noted in the previous chapter) to get involved in a similar manner. This kind of intervention was not the universal choice of control method. The Marines' DASC chose to maximize the flow of aircraft into open killboxes and delegated the targeting authority to the aircrews, rather than trying to pick the targets themselves.

Conclusions

Warfare has always contained an element of time-sensitive targeting. The competition to outmaneuver your opponents, and thus cut off all their options while maintaining yours, leads to a race. Boyd calls it the OODA loop. His ideas were developed from dogfighting concepts, where the observe, orient, and decide phases were done by a single individual. The complex organizational actions of the center of calculation from the previous chapter are so cumbersome that they inhibit tactical actions. The potential upshot of this convoluted process led van Creveld to write that commanders had to train their organizations to be able to act independently in periods of uncertainty. It is the same reason that in Desert Storm, Horner wanted to let push CAS and KI handle all the emerging targets. The pilots' eyes and those of the TACPs would find and direct the attacks.

There was no conscious decision to get into the business of directing real-time operations. Rather, as discussed earlier, it was an evolution. The air component was called on to accomplish some missions it did not count on. The Scud Hunt in Desert Storm was considered necessary to hold the coalition together. In Allied Force, airpower had to attack enemy fielded forces without the aid of ground troops because the strategic level determined the interests involved did not warrant the use of friendly ground troops. Short had to come up with something, so he and his CAOC developed a Flex-Targeting Cell. In Enduring Freedom, the job of developing strategy was again held above the air component's level, though for different reasons this time. The CAOC's workers became focused on doing whatever they could to contribute. The rapidly moving ground battle in Iraqi Freedom created a fluid environment where aircrews did not know where the targets would be when they took off. In these last three conflicts, air operations enabled by air superiority became increasingly geared toward taking off without a target and finding the target while airborne. Thus, the TCT Cell became a fixture in the AOC. From the ad hoc change cell in Desert Storm, it became a formal, 25-person team in Iraqi Freedom.

The Air Force put significant effort into developing the procedures and tools to handle emerging targets. Time-critical or time-sensitive targeting played big parts in the JEFX experiments in 1998, 1999, 2000, 2002, and 2004. The TCT Cell faced the problem of shrinking the targeting cycle from days to minutes. It had to get information about a target, determine how to attack it, coordinate permission to do so, enable the strikers to attack, and assess the results (find, fix, target, track, engage, and assess—the kill chain). The ISR enhancements above helped in finding the targets. Chats and the ADOCS helped them coordinate. The tools are improving, so it seems we have not hit a physical barrier to reducing the time it takes to hit a target.

In some cases, the AOC played this role because someone had to tie all the players together in order to accomplish the mission. When the opportunity or necessity to react to the enemy is detected by a sensor without the ability to act, someone has to find an actor who can respond and get that actor to the scene. This was the case in the Scud Hunt, Khafji, and many of the incidents in Allied Force, Enduring Freedom, and Iraqi Freedom. It appears that now the ability to do this is limited mainly by scarce resources.

There were other cases where the AOC played a real-time role because it was imperative to ensure compliance with a strategy. In Allied Force and Enduring Freedom, the inability to tolerate tactical mistakes led to tight ROEs that brought the CAOC (and, sometimes, higher headquarters as well) in on many of the tactical decisions. This happened when there was some type of judgment involved in the ROEs. For example, in Allied Force A-10 pilots gradually began checking with the CAOC before attacking targets. In Enduring Freedom, the CAOC had to clear targets with CENTCOM unless it was in specially designated areas. In the beginning, CENTCOM had to clear targets with moderate or high potential for collateral damage with Secretary Rumsfeld. These are the cases where the intervention of the commander inhibits the execution of the tactical mission. It may be that the negative strategic goals outweigh the positive tactical goals. This is the decision the commanders must make.

It is clear that military commanders still agree the way to shorten the OODA loop is to delegate authority to those able to affect the actions most directly. Both the fusion cell at CENTCOM headquarters in Tampa Bay and the TCT Cell in the CAOC in Saudi Arabia had the ability to direct ongoing missions in Afghanistan. The discussion that led to a change between Enduring Freedom and Iraqi Freedom happened because the air and land components had not been empowered to work to the full extent of their capabilities during Enduring Freedom. CENTCOM had taken over some part of each component's responsibilities, so that each thought the coordination was above its level. CENTCOM had to make conscious efforts to empower its subordinates through the definition of the command relationships.

The AOC has learned a similar lesson, although it escapes many observers. It can be confusing that the AOC plays two different roles in the CAOS. It is simultaneously the air component's portion of the plans subsystem and the lead agent in the adjustment subsystem. In the last three conflicts, its plans role was to allocate resources and give guidance to the adjustment subsystem as to how those resources should be used. The AOC specified fewer and fewer of the details prior to the missions. The TCT Cell and others in Combat Operations then used those resources, the guidance, and the sensor-communications information to prosecute the war as it occurred—with a shorter OODA loop than the full ATO cycle.

This confuses many observers because, as shown in the previous chapter, it is not currently possible to delegate the role of information gathering and distribution much lower than the AOC. There is no single representation that includes the digital position data and the sensor video; therefore, even if the bandwidth and network existed, it cannot be passed to lower echelons. The TCT Cell can be looked at as an entity that could be moved an echelon down from the AOC if it were possible to either distribute the information to them or gather the information somewhere else. The ASOC has a limited ability to gather information because it is collocated with corps headquarters. It would be more convenient to put the TCT Cell in an aircraft with instant communications to both the AOC and the strike aircraft to skip the radio relays. This would be a big step toward the kind of depth of command relationships for which we are searching.

Prophets of network-centric warfare envision a time when all in the system will have the ability to access the same information. If this occurs, there will then be a necessity to make conscious decisions about who should make determinations. General Franks made a move in this direction when he established the matrix for TSTs in Iraqi Freedom. This will have to be done in a way that affirms and emphasizes command relationships, or there will be more problems of the sort that we studied in chapter 5.

The next chapter explains how the move toward getting more people involved in making decisions and providing information has other side effects. Officers in the CAOC did not like CENTCOM being involved in ongoing missions. What is the effect of the CAOC's intervention into ongoing missions on the aircrews—is there a similar effect at this level?

Notes

1. Author's personal observations from JEFX 06.
2. Hammond, *Mind of War*, 13–16.
3. Gray, *Modern Strategy*, 91.
4. Hyde, Pfeiffer, and Logan, "CAFMS Goes to War," 43–44.
5. Corder, interview.
6. 8th Air Support Operations Group, *Operations Desert Shield/Storm*, 2.
7. Hosterman, notes, 105, 2224Z. Sergeant Hosterman was an observer in the TACC during Desert Storm.
8. Ibid., 107, 2005Z, 2048Z.
9. Jamieson, *Lucrative Targets*, 100–101; and Barton, Notes, 40, 0915 hours.
10. Hosterman, notes, 109; and Jamieson, *Lucrative Targets*, 103.
11. Hosterman, notes, 108–10, 2253L/1956Z.
12. Ibid., 110, 2346L/2046Z.
13. Horner, interview by the author; Corder, interview, 48; and Hosterman, notes, 109, 2053L/1753Z.
14. Deptula, interview, 10 Dec. 1991.
15. Cohen and Keaney, *Gulf War Air Power Survey*, vol. 2, p. 1, *Operations*, 241–42.
16. Technical Sergeant Barton noted on 31 Jan. 1991, "With all of the aircraft in theater, I found it difficult to believe that we were actually 'short' [of aircraft to engage in the Scud Hunt]. We do, however, have that problem.

With the number of packages and individual missions scheduled in the ATO, there are, in fact, very few unscheduled aircraft available!"

17. Corder, interview.

18. Tritschler, interview. Barton, notes, 14 Feb. 1991, 66–67.

19. Cohen and Keaney, *Gulf War Air Power Survey*, vol. 1, pt. 2, *Command and Control*, 249–52.

20. CENTAF TACC/CC/DO, "Current Ops Log," vol. 1 of 2, 9 Feb, 0036Z.

21. Cohen and Keaney, *Gulf War Air Power Survey*, vol. 1, pt. 2, *Command and Control*, 74.

22. Crowder, interview (see chap. 5, n. 41).

23. Ibid.

24. Caldera, interview.

25. "Seamless Integration," vol. 2, sec. 2, Focus Area 4. The B-2 was also capable of using its radar to further reduce the error of the mensurated coordinates. See Sweetman, "B-2 is Maturing," 53.

26. "Flex Targeting Success Stories."

27. Lambeth, *NATO's Air War for Kosovo*, 159–60.

28. Crowder, interview.

29. Haave and Haun, *A-10s over Kosovo*, 245–47.

30. This was verified by another of the authors. See Haun to the author, e-mail, 11 Mar. 2004.

31. "Command and Control/Intelligence," X-2. See also Haave and Haun, *A-10s over Kosovo*, 146.

32. "KEZ Mission," X-14; and Haun to the author, e-mail.

33. Haun to the author, e-mail.

34. Ibid.

35. Ibid. See also Lt Col Mustafa Koprucu, USAF (552 OSS/DO at the time of this writing; JSTARS senior director during OAF), telephone interview with author, 6 Apr. 2004. (Notes in author's personal collection.)

36. Cappacio, "JSTARS Led Most Lethal Attacks," 13.

37. Koprucu, interview.

38. Franks, *American Soldier*, 289.

39. Ibid., 290–94.

40. Deptula, interview by the author; and Grant, "War Nobody Expected," 39.

41. Franks, *American Soldier*, 294.

42. Hersh, "King's Ransom," 38.

43. Franks, *American Soldier*, 290; and Woodward, *Bush at War*, 166, 193–94, 247.

44. Comments on an earlier draft of this book from Deptula to the author, e-mail.

45. Knaub to the author, e-mail, 22 Sept. 2004.

46. Hodgdon to the author, e-mail, 28 Dec. 2004. Colonel Hodgdon was the TCT Cell chief in OEF and OIF.

47. Ibid.

48. Deptula, interview by the author; Hathaway, interview (see chap. 5, n. 54); and Crowder to the author, e-mail.

49. Woodward, *Bush at War*, 249.
50. Crowder to the author, e-mail.
51. Ibid.
52. O'Hanlon, "Flawed Masterpiece," 51.
53. Coe, interview.
54. Crowder to the author, e-mail.
55. Coe, interview.
56. Jansen, "JCAS in Afghanistan," 25–26, 29.
57. Hodgdon to the author, e-mail, 28 Dec. 2004.
58. Moseley, *Operation Iraqi Freedom*, 9. Actually, the comparison between TST/dynamic targets and almost 20,000 total may not be accurate. The report claims a total of 19,898 desired mean points of impact (DMPI), while it reports the number of TSTs and dynamic targets as *missions* (some of which could have had multiple DMPIs). The point is still valid—the number was a small fraction.
59. Hodgdon to the author, e-mail, 28 Dec. 2004.
60. Thomas and Klaidman, "War Room."
61. Sanger and Schmitt, "U.S. Blasts Compound," 1.
62. Hodgdon to the author, e-mail, 4 Feb. 2005.
63. Moseley, *Operation Iraqi Freedom*, 7.
64. Defore, "Killbox Interdiction," S Annex, 9–13, describes the KI/CAS planning process; 18 defines the execution authority.
65. Coe, interview.
66. Defore, "Killbox Interdiction," S Annex, 3. See also Wallace, "Joint Fires in OIF," slide 7, "Type 1/2/3 employed, mostly Type 2/3."
67. Wallace, "Joint Fires in OIF," slide 12.
68. Hollis, "Trained, Adaptable, Flexible Forces."
69. Ibid.
70. Coe, interview.

Chapter 8

Distributed Cognition in the CAOS

The computational power of the system composed of person and technology is not determined primarily by the information-processing capacity that is internal to the technological device, but by the role the technology plays in the composition of a cognitive functional system.

—Edwin Hutchins
Cognition in the Wild

Some futurists seem continuously anxious to replace humans . . . in certain tasks without quite appreciating how people accomplish those tasks. In general, it will be better to pursue not substitution but complementarity. . . . But complementarity requires seeing the differences between information-processing agents and human agency.

—John Seely Brown and Paul Duguid
Social Life of Information

On Saturday, 31 July 2004, the JEFX 04 took a break from flying missions. The missions that week had gone well enough that they were on schedule and did not need the extra day. Instead, JEFX workers staged an "AOC 101" class in which CAOC workers taught the flyers what goes on in an AOC. At one point during the lecture, a lieutenant colonel who had been acting as the chief of Combat Operations implored his audience to "bear with us" when the instructions the pilots received from the CAOC over the radio seemed a bit odd. Unusual instructions could result from "experiment-isms," or from any situation where the CAOC simply had more information than the aircrew. After all, he reminded them, "We in Combat Operations represent the 'decentralized execution' part of command and control."[1] The stone-cold reception this declaration received from the aircrew in the audience was unmistakable. A moment later, it gave way to murmurs of disbelief.

We have seen that the AOC has become more involved in ongoing missions. Sensor-communication loops have provided the AOC with the "immutable mobiles" it needed to become the most knowledgeable entity in the CAOS. The need to attack some emerging targets with a high level of accountability provided the impetus for the AOC to do this quickly and during the operations, rather than during the planning. The end result is a certain amount of confusion about who is really executing. In fact, the operations required to accomplish a strike mission are now sometimes performed by a distributed group of people.

In his book *Cognition in the Wild*, Hutchins describes the actions of a Navy ship's crew in navigating their vessel. He examines the way different crew members performed specific parts of the task of navigating by using specially made instruments and following predetermined procedures. Crew members used a variety of tools to gather information, translate it from analog to digital or vice versa, store it, transport it, and eventually bring it together on a chart in a way that made the solution to the question "Where am I?" obvious. Hutchins observes that no single person was performing the entire, complex task of navigating. Each was performing only a small task requiring much different cognitive abilities than that complex task would require.[2] Furthermore, he remarks that the tools these crew members used did not amplify their abilities; they transformed the nature of the task that the human performed.

In this chapter, we examine the actions of the people in the CAOS in a similar manner. We will take a fifth look at the period from Desert Storm to Iraqi Freedom, this time concentrating on the actions of the aircrew and ground controllers. We will look at the process of attacking a target as a sort of "fix cycle," where the entire process consists of deciding to hit a certain type of target, finding the target, getting a weapon system to the target, and getting the target information into a format that the weapon can use to strike the target. The kill chain of find, fix, track, target, engage, and assess is the way Air Force officials talk about this sequence. We will not be held tightly to these terms, but will look at the actions required to get and pass the information needed for an attack.

The role of the aircrew in this sequence is in the process of changing. In Desert Storm, those in the physical vicinity of the targets performed almost the entire sequence. While this was fine for performing CAS and KI, it was insufficient to solve the problem of the Scud Hunt. The consequences of using sensor-communication loops and precision weapons that can accept information passed via these means is that the entire sequence may now involve a distributed team. A single sequence can be performed by people distributed from the United States to the ground and air near the target. The successful attack of emerging targets depends on a "distributed cognition" rather than the cognition of the aircrew alone. Because those in the battlespace are being asked to perform different tasks now than they were in the past, depth of command relationships becomes more essential. Without this depth, the CAOS becomes more capable of conducting strikes and therefore more deadly, but the lack of clarity in the coordination of strikes makes it coincidentally more chaotic.

In other words, the distribution of kill-chain tasks makes the CAOS more capable of performing missions like Scud hunting. But it also causes people to perform different tasks depending on the scenario. If there is sufficient depth in the command relationships, there will be a C2 node able to coordinate the actions of these diverse actors and ensure their actions fit the situation. If not, there is a lot of uncertainty about the authority to take actions that are feasible but not necessarily prescribed. For example, the F-16 pilots who are sent out to await tasking from the CAOC discover that with their GPS-guided weapons, all they need are coordinates passed by a joint tactical air controller (JTAC) on the ground. While feasible, and maybe even desirable, the F-16 pilots had a hard time getting clearance to do that, and often did it on their own when the CAOC didn't have time to address the issue. If there was sufficient authority at the ASOC level to clear this, it would not have been so chaotic.

Desert Storm

In Desert Storm, as we have shown, the people in the TACC had very little real-time information to help them figure out what was going on. They assembled the change cell to respond to new information by trying to adjust the day's missions. But the real-time adjustment required by the Scud Hunt was beyond anyone's capabilities at the time.

In the Scud Hunt, the sequence often started when wide-area surveillance was able to detect a launch. The US Space Command alerted CENTCOM when Defense Support Program satellites detected a large infrared signature. CENTCOM then alerted the Army's Patriot batteries to give them enough notice to get the missiles pointed in the right direction.[3] In the example from the previous chapter, the TACC got word of a launch by phone. Space Command gave the center the time of launch and rough launch coordinates.

TACC staffers passed the information over the radio. In most cases, they had no way to get more information about the launcher. They could determine the best attack option by getting the experts together over the map table, but in most cases where a launch had already occurred, this was too slow. In our example, the TACC let the AWACS direct the nearest aircraft to the area. Thus, the same rough coordinates were passed to the aircrew by voice over the radio.

The aircrew then had to translate these coordinates into a visual picture of the launcher. The launch site coordinates were enough to get the aircraft to the general area of the site, with AWACS direction. At that point, the aircrew had to get updated or refined information to the weapons to get them to the target. The launcher may have moved in the time it took to arrive at the site. Even if it had not moved, the pilot had to visually find the target in order to engage. To do this, the aircrew needed sensors with the ability to pick the launchers out of the background, which usually included night conditions. The F-15E was the favorite platform because it had infrared and synthetic aperture radar (SAR) sensors, so it could search at night. F-16s with infrared LANTIRN sensors were devoted to this task as well. Even the lumbering AC-130 gunships were used because of their infrared and low-light-level television.[4]

People on the ground near the site would have made good sensors. One of the recommendations Tritschler proposed was to send special operations forces into western Iraq to hunt for Scud launchers. When they were finally sent, he was hopeful—the British Special Air Service (SAS) came to coordinate with him at the TACC. At the beginning of each day, Tritschler rolled out a piece of acetate on top of a chart, and a SAS representative showed him where their special forces were going to be that day. Tritschler then developed no-fire areas to protect them. For the American special forces, the process was reversed. They did not coordinate with the air component but, instead, called the western AWACS on guard to notify them they were establishing a no-fire area. The AWACS had to distribute this information to all affected aircraft, whose pilots had to try and mark their charts while flying. This was so difficult that the pilots gave the entire area significant latitude.[5] In the end, the SOF were no more successful than the air component at finding and destroying mobile Scuds, and the two were not able to link up as a sensor-weapon team.

The process was very similar for KI. The difference was that the targets—Iraqi armor and artillery—were much more plentiful and predictable. They were part of a large, regular army that was massed and dug in for the defense. Therefore, US intelligence was able to determine where in general the targets would be—wide-area surveillance was not necessary as it was in the Scud case. In addition, the desert battlefield environment afforded the targets little opportunity to hide. However, the Iraqis made good use of the five months' preparation time and their experience from the Iran-Iraq War to bury and camouflage their equipment. Combined with the extent of the theater and the dispersal of the Iraqi equipment, this made it difficult to determine the location of specific targets.[6]

So the aircrew knew what, but not exactly where, it should attack. The sequence started with the Army's intelligence determining what it wanted airpower to attack. Aircrews took off with their ATO tasking, which included an area in which to search and a prioritized list of targets for which to search. They were directed to the killboxes by AWACS. They then contacted the ABCCC or the Marine Direct Air Support Center, if the killbox was in the 1st MEF's area, which gave them updated targets to attack.[7]

But no one in the existing TACS knew where the targets would be when the aircraft arrived. Neither the AWACS nor the ABCCC could see what was on the ground, and therefore their role in assembling information was limited to relaying it by voice over radio. Only the JSTARS or the Army or Marine RPVs could pick up targets on the ground. In fact, in some instances, the JSTARS provided target cueing to aircraft in the killboxes.[8] In these cases, the JSTARS operators or the analysts at the ground stations had to find coordinates for the graphic picture on their screens and transfer these coordinates to the attack aircrew. Then, at least the aircrew knew there were potential targets in the area. They did not know what they were or how to find them visually. The RPVs, on the other hand, were not well integrated into the operation. Army and Marine commanders viewed them as a means to see the deep battlefield, not to direct real-time operations.[9]

By 3 February, the pilots of the interdiction aircraft could tell they were not accomplishing much in these killboxes. Weather kept them from picking out targets until they started an attack run. This did not give them time to discern the primary targets from others, which looked the same at their medium altitude. Early in the planning process Lieutenant Colonel Deptula, the chief Iraq Cell planner, had designed attack packages to remain at medium altitude to keep aircraft and aircrew losses low by staying above the reach of Iraqi antiaircraft artillery. Horner had concurred in that approach and endorsed it. At this altitude, the accuracy of nonprecision munitions from the F-16 or F-18 dropped substantially.[10] After a bomb drop, the smoke took so long to clear that the pilots could not assess the damage before they went back above the weather or evaded threats.[11] Both the pilots and those at CENTAF knew something had to be done.

They came up with identical plans. The group of Fighter Weapons School instructors that had formed the night-change cell, led by Lt Col Bob Phillips, resurrected a concept that was called "Fast FAC" in Vietnam. Shortly after, General Glosson got a message, sent by pilots in the 388th Fighter Wing (FW), telling of the pilots' frustrations and recommending a solution. The CENTAF and pilots came up with a plan to have specific, experienced pilots fly over the killboxes to validate targets, find new ones, direct other planes to the targets, and assess the damage. They chose F-16s and F-18s to do the job. These Killer Scouts stayed over the same areas day after day, logging missions averaging five and a half hours, and became so successful at directing and assessing strikes that Glosson and the air component wholeheartedly embraced the concept, increasing their numbers from eight to 32 after the first couple days. They had only binoculars and the moving target indicators on their radars, but they were able to piece together a picture of the battlefield that was far more useful than the ABCCC's and the DASC's outdated target lists.[12]

Now the aircrew had help finding the targets. Nevertheless, for the most part, the aircrew still had to acquire the target visually and then drop a dumb bomb on the target. The results suffered because of this awkward method of transferring the information to the weapon.

In early February, the air component figured out how to use precision munitions to perform some of these attacks. At that time, F-111 crews noticed that their infrared sensors could detect the buried armored vehicles at the end of the day, when the sand cooled more quickly than the metal.[13] Now pilots had a way to transfer the information to the weapons. Cueing from Killer Scouts or the JSTARS told them where to look. They found the target visually, using infrared sensors. Then they put a laser spot on the target, and the weapon followed it in. Aircraft with infrared sensors and the ability to drop laser-guided weapons, like the F-111, F-15E, and A-6E, were able to "engage" with a single, 500-lb. bomb per tank. In the desert environment, the only constraint this arrangement was unable to overcome was bad weather—it still required the pilots to "see" the target with their infrared sensors.

Precision munitions made up only about 10 percent of the munitions used in Desert Storm. For the most part, they were the same type that had been used in the Linebacker campaigns during Vietnam—LGBs.[14] These required the aircrew to keep a laser spot on the target throughout the missile's flight so the missile could guide to the reflected energy. Mavericks were new. The Maverick missile tracked infrared energy from a target and therefore needed the aircrew's help only to lock onto the target signature, after which the crew could "launch and leave." Only A-10s and F-16s were capable of employing Mavericks; F-16 pilots were not trained to employ them, and F-16 avionics were not optimal for Mavericks. Just 130 F-16 sorties employed Mavericks, while over 8,700 employed dumb bombs.[15]

The Killer Scouts added another level of depth to the command relationships the air component had already set up. Before the Killer Scouts, aircrews were on their own in the target area; with the Killer Scouts, they were given targets. The find, fix, and target portions of the chain were all performed by the Killer Scout.[16] The strike aircrew still had to find the target visually and then engage, but the scout even helped assess the attack. Because the Killer Scouts were guided by the ATO and ABCCC target lists, they extended the TACC's ability to align these attacks with the overall strategy to an area where this alignment had been absent.

With the CAS mission, the terminal control was more formal. Airmen had long been convinced of the need for terminal guidance in supporting ground troops. Back in WW II, Airmen had learned that someone in the vicinity of the ground troops had to identify targets and keep the attacking aircraft clear of the friendly forces. By Desert Storm, the concept of the tactical air control party was well established. The TACPs included an air liaison officer (ALO) and several enlisted controllers. They were Air Force people attached to Army battalions, brigades, or divisions. Then, at the corps level, an ASOC coordinated the efforts of all the TACPs under it.

As with KI, there was never much doubt about the general area of the targets. By definition, CAS is performed in the vicinity of friendly forces. But just as with KI, aircrews did not know where the targets would be until they got there. Unlike KI, there is another imperative besides engaging the target: staying clear of friendly forces.

Therefore, TACP controllers filled two roles—they were there to provide information on the location of the targets and to avoid fratricide. They were sensors and traffic directors. They had sensors, in the form of ground troops. The TACPs or their associated ground troops detected the targets, aiding the aircrews in finding targets that emerged and could not be put into an ATO because of their time latency. For this purpose, they had only binoculars and radios.[17] The corps level had RPVs, but as we said, these were viewed as assets for the corps commander to see the deep battle, not to aid the close battle.[18] Of course, unlike with the Killer Scouts, the TACP did not make the decisions about which targets to attack—the Army chain of command did.[19] Even more importantly, the TACPs were there to avoid fratricide. They were trained to follow strict procedures, transmitting a "9-line" brief to the fighters for each target. The TACPs also had suitcase-sized GPS receivers, making them popular with the Army commanders.[20]

TACPs directed the aircraft, while the ASOC coordinated to get the aircraft to the target area. The CAS sequence started when troops encountered the enemy and decided they needed air support. If the target was not urgent, Army channels sent it up the chain as an air support request to become part of the ATO. If it was urgent, they notified the TACP, which passed it up from battalion to brigade to division and finally to the ASOC at the corps level.[21] At each level, the ALO filtered the requests to determine which were priorities to receive the available push CAS sorties. The ASOC had the final say, allocating sorties, informing the ABCCC, and sending the information back down the chain to the originating TACP, who took over directing the aircraft.[22] Battalion TACP Airmen directed most of the aircraft, and those above that level served more as "traffic cops" to prioritize and allocate resources.[23]

Then the TACP member or a FAC(A) transferred his knowledge of the target to the strike aircrew. A ground controller or a FAC(A) who could see the target and the strike aircraft could try to perform a talk-on. This was done by voice, over radio, essentially translating the controller's view of the target into a verbal description that could be transmitted to the aircrew over the low-bandwidth medium of voice communication by radio. Aircrew members then had to assemble this information and relate it to what they were seeing on the ground to create their own knowledge of the target location. This talk-on was and is an essential skill for these controllers, and in Desert Storm they are the only ones who performed it. If the target and strike aircraft were visible, then the ground controller or FAC(A) could try to perform a talk-on.

The sequence worked well for the very few CAS sorties flown during Desert Storm. The TACPs found the targets, the chain of command up to the ASOC determined whether a target would be engaged, the AWACS and ABCCC got the aircraft to the area, and the TACPs or FAC(A)s helped them find the target visually. After action reports estimated that, with the push CAS system, it never took longer than 15 minutes for an aircraft to respond to a request.[24]

Still, aircrews were unable to overcome some of the constraints imposed by the demanding mission. Weather hampered their ability to find the targets they were being directed to attack. When 20-year-old Air Force sergeant Bryan Lanning headed into

Kuwait through the Rumaliyah oil fields with the 24th Infantry Division (ID), it was not long before he needed CAS. Although Lanning worked at the battalion level, getting clearance up the chain was easy—the brigade TACP was already screaming for help. They were given A-10s within minutes. In fact, aircraft stacked up, waiting to help. But the weather was bad—low clouds obscured the battlefield from the pilots. Having gotten guidance from Horner that all stops were to be pulled out, the pilots dipped low beneath the clouds, but were unable to visually sort out the friendlies from the targets before the Iraqis zeroed in on the perfectly-contrasted black aircraft against backlit clouds. It was more than three hours before the weather cleared enough to allow the aircraft to come in with laser-guided munitions and aid the 24th ID in destroying the RG forces.[25]

In Desert Storm, for missions where it was impossible to know the exact target or location beforehand, the aircrew had a great deal of freedom and responsibility in executing the kill chain sequence. Even when there was a specific target, aircrews were usually only given rough coordinates. C2 aircraft directed the strike aircraft to the general location, but then the aircrew had to find the target visually and transfer the information to a weapon. Killer Scouts, TACPs, or FAC(A)s could sometimes guide aircraft to a specific target by transferring their knowledge over the radio to the strike aircrew members, who then had to assemble that knowledge relative to their own view of the world. But in all cases, the aircrew had to find the target visually (although sometimes aided by infrared) in order to transfer the information to a weapon through an aimed delivery or a laser spot on the target.

Because of this awkward method of transferring information, the TACC was not involved in very much of the process. The ATO merely allocated sorties to Scud hunting, KI, or push CAS. Tritschler did his best to give guidance to the Scud hunters, and the change cell did get together to assemble information for some missions. But even in these cases, the aircrew still had to find the target on its own.

Allied Force

In Kosovo, the question of what to target was more complicated than it had been in Iraq. We have discussed the disagreement between Lieutenant General Short and General Clark over how to fight the war and the fact that at the outset, the air component was not equipped to fight a ground war without friendly ground troops. The establishment of the Kosovo Engagement Zone on 14 April seems, at first, similar to the establishment of killboxes in Iraq. Indeed, the purpose was to allow aircraft to engage ground targets without the help of friendly ground troops—just like in Iraq. Specially designated A-10s, F-16s, and F-14s flew over the KEZ, found targets, and directed other aircraft to strike them. But that is as far as the similarities went.

Target identification was 95 percent of the problem in the KEZ.[26] The Iraqi military had been deployed in defensive positions in flat terrain, so wide-area search to find the equipment was not difficult. In Kosovo, there was no invading army to force the Serbs to take up positions, move to reinforce each other, or even use heavy supply convoys. The Serbs were free to move in small numbers, at will, and in unorthodox vehicles if necessary. It was like the problem of finding the mobile Scud launchers, without the tell-tale launch. In addition, Kosovo afforded mountainous regions and vegetation that aided the Serbs' efforts at camouflage and concealment.

The FAC(A)s had little to aid them in the quest to find and fix targets. Before they took off, they were given a list of the most up-to-date targets the CAOC had to offer, but it was 12–24 hours old. Invariably, the targets were not there by the time the FAC(A)s showed up. The pilots were unable to get imagery from satellites or UAVs at their units, so they could not get previews of any targets identified earlier. Thus, they took off with very little information about where the targets were.[27]

These pilots coordinated with the other airborne elements of the TACS for help in solving this problem. In Kosovo, this was the ABCCC, the AWACS, and the JSTARS. For the majority of the missions in the KEZ, the FAC(A)s dealt with the ABCCC. By this time, the ABCCC had an updated electronics suite that included Link 16 data-link information, so the 12-person battle staff in the back of the EC-130 aircraft could view a computerized image of all friendly aircraft and known enemy positions superimposed on a map of Kosovo and Serbia. On a laptop, they could view a detailed map of the ground, provided by the National Imagery and Mapping Agency.[28] This did not help them locate the type of targets the FAC(A)s were looking for. Essentially, the ABCCC became an extension of the AWACS, handling part of the job of directing air traffic and passing information back and forth between the FAC(A) and the CAOC.

The JSTARS was more help, with its moving target indicator and SAR sensors, and FAC(A)s sometimes worked directly with them. However, the mountainous terrain of Kosovo made it difficult to keep track of moving vehicles, which were sometimes lost in the shadow of a hill. The crew searched in moving-target-indicator mode most of the time, but switched to SAR if a target disappeared to determine whether it was masked by the terrain or just stopped. The main problem with JSTARS was that it could not identify the targets. FAC(A)s had to fly to the area to visually identify the targets.[29] At first, they responded to every JSTARS prompt, but eventually the FAC(A)s found this a waste of time if they were already working on another target.[30]

Later in the war, the air component started to use JSTARS and Predator as a team. The wide surveillance of JSTARS and narrow, high-resolution picture of the Predator seem to be natural complements. But JSTARS crew members remarked it was not standard procedure. Airmen onboard the JSTARS or in the CAOC started to use Predator to refine JSTARS targets mainly when JSTARS had to leave an area for another target. The Predator was also too slow to fly over and check out all promising JSTARS targets.[31]

Most of the time, the FAC(A) was on his own. The A-10 pilots flew in the daytime and had only their own eyes and gyrostabilized binoculars. The F-16 and F-14 pilots flew most of the night missions because they had night vision goggles and a targeting pod, their most often used piece of equipment. The F-16's targeting pod was an infrared device that displayed video of the temperature differential on a four-inch square monitor near the pilot's knee. The pod had two settings: narrow, with a 1.7-degree field of view; and wide, with a six-degree field of view.[32] Neither was satisfactory for finding targets from 10,000 feet above ground. After the Djakovica incident, where an F-16 FAC(A) mistakenly directed a strike on a column of vehicles that contained civilian vehicles, Short allowed the FAC(A)s to descend to 5,000 feet to verify targets.

It was also the Djakovica incident that tightened the rules for targeting. We have already discussed the fact that the Fielded Forces part of the Flex-Targeting Cell started becoming more involved in approving targets, even though they often had only the information they were fed over the radio. This was frustrating for the FAC(A) pilots. In the A-10 pilots' account, the veterans claimed it "usually took 15 to 20 minutes to obtain approval." On one occasion, Lt Col Christopher Haave asked the CAOC—through the ABCCC—for permission to attack a target and waited 25 minutes, after which the answer was to "use the gun and not hit any houses!" During the wait, clouds moved in and foiled the opportunity. Haave cited the delay and tactical direction as "absurd" and a "clear violation of the principle of 'centralized control and decentralized execution.'" He argued that the pilot was the expert on the decisions that needed to be made, and had been "fully capable of making a real-time execution decision consistent with ROEs that centralized control had generated."[33]

The incident suggests that a lack of empowerment took away the aircrews' initiative. Why did Haave even ask for permission if there were ROEs to guide the decision? Coauthor and fellow A-10 pilot Lt Col Phil Haun explained that as the ROEs got tighter and started to change regularly, pilots got wary of making decisions. Once they found they had to ask permission to attack some targets, they started asking permission for almost all.[34]

On occasion, the CAOC had more information than the FAC(A)s. In those few instances when the CAOC had Predator video of a target, it truly did have a better picture than the FAC(A) did. In these situations, the visual representation of the battlefield (albeit a "soda straw" view of it) was digitized, sent back to the CAOC, and reconstructed exactly as the sensor saw it. This is what made possible the centers of calculation, as we saw in chapter 6. As was discussed, aircrews did not seem to mind being directed when they were receiving a new target—conflict occurred when the aircrew had to ask permission to strike a target only it could see.[35] Still, this put the CAOC people in a position that was formerly only occupied by a Killer Scout or a TACP.

In these cases, the CAOC had to transfer the target location to the FAC(A) by means of a talk-on. As we discussed, the talk-on was formerly an exclusive tool of the TACP and FAC(A), both trained and experienced in this method of knowledge transfer. It is a procedure so conceptually simple it seems to be common sense. Yet the book published by A-10 pilots after the Kosovo war pointed out that, in their view, it was frequently performed incompetently. In one case, Capt Joe Brosious remembers being so confused by a particular talk-on from Moonbeam that he wrote it out in grease pencil on his canopy. He then made sense of it by comparing it with various features he saw on the ground.[36] In another case, the pilots pointed out that the narrow field of view of a Predator made it difficult to translate the UAV's picture to the wide field of view the pilot had with only his eyes at his altitude.[37]

Even after this part of the sequence had been accomplished, the next problem was getting other aircraft to strike the targets. The FAC(A) could store the target location in his memory and direct other aircraft to it as they became available, so the Predator could be released to other areas. Transferring the information to a strike aircraft was still difficult. None of the strike aircraft were equipped with Link 16, although some of the F-16s had an Improved Data Modem that allowed them to send data to similarly equipped F-16s.[38] But most of the strike aircraft still dropped weapons that required the pilot to see the target himself—dumb bombs, LGBs, or Mavericks. The F-16 targeting pod could "buddy-lase" for another aircraft's weapons in certain situations.[39] Sometimes the FAC(A) could drop a bomb or smoke to mark the target. Much of the time, however, the FAC(A) had to perform a talk-on to get the other pilots' eyes on the target.

Even transferring the information using target coordinates was difficult for the A-10s. F-16 pilots with a targeting pod could merely center the pod on the target and read digital coordinates off the screen. But A-10s did not have this capability. Colonel Haave explained that the process of getting coordinates for a target entailed:

1. finding the general area on a large-scale map that could translate the area to a small-scale chart (from a 1:250,000 to a 1:50,000 ratio, for example);

2. finding the corresponding small-scale chart and determining the target coordinates by matching the terrain features to those the pilot could see on the ground, and then following the contour lines to determine the target's elevation;

3. storing the coordinates and elevation by writing them (often in grease pencil on the canopy of the aircraft);

4. using aircraft avionics as slide rules to convert the coordinates and elevation to units the other pilots could work with; and

5. passing the information over the radio to the other pilots.[40]

This is all very similar to the process we described in Desert Storm. The kill-chain sequence was performed by passing visual pictures over the radio to a receiver who then had to assemble another visual picture in his mind. There were improved sensors in that Predators were available and, when used, they made a big difference. However, not enough of these UAVs were on hand to make an appreciable impact. Most of the time, the FAC(A)s' eyes were the sensors. The engagement part of the sequence was also similar, except that there were more precision munitions. In Kosovo, 29 percent of the munitions expended were precision munitions.[41]

The interaction of a different kind of war and a different environment did cause several distinct differences. First of all, there was not as good an idea of where the enemy troops could be found. The Serbs did not have to fight from conventional, prepared positions and could use the terrain to hide. Second, there were no ground troops to aid in target identification and collateral damage avoidance. Third, the CAOC frequently got involved in the targeting part of the sequence. It often made the decisions about whether to execute a strike, to the frustration of the pilots.

However, although this may look like only a minor evolution from Desert Storm, it masks the important changes that were occurring. In 1997 and 1998, the B-2 underwent operational testing to allow it to drop a new munition: the 2,000-lb. JDAM, a GPS-guided bomb. The B-2 was the only aircraft to employ the weapon during Allied Force. Furthermore, because the JDAM was useful only against fixed or, at best, relocatable targets, it could not be used for KEZ missions.[42] Therefore, it had minimal effect on the operations of the fighter pilots who flew those missions.

Enduring Freedom

This was not the case in Enduring Freedom. By the time the United States went to war against the Taliban and al-Qaeda in Afghanistan, other aircraft had been certified to carry JDAMs.

Because the bombs were inexpensively made by attaching a tail kit to MK-84s and BLU-109s—older bombs stored in huge numbers around the world—many of the weapons were available as well. Their big advantage was that they were not reliant on visual acquisition of the target (by the aircrew or the weapon). They were guided by an inertial unit that could receive updates through a simple GPS receiver during the bomb's fall to the target. Therefore, they could be launched at night or through bad weather.[43]

Of course, this capability only solved problems in one part of the kill-chain sequence: the "engagement." The JDAM did not make it any easier to find targets. In fact, it required extremely accurate intelligence about the location of the target. And in this war, the decision about what was a valid target was most often made at a high level. The policy makers were very concerned about the possibility that collateral damage in Afghanistan could send the wrong message. The United States was not fighting against Muslims—only terrorists and those who would harbor and aid the terrorists. Without accurate, discriminating information about the locations of these targets, airpower would be subject to some of the same limitations that had frustrated aircrews over Kosovo. Concern in the CAOC was that the CENTCOM leadership was taking the approach of fighting Enduring Freedom using the approach of the last war—Allied Force—even though the conditions in Afghanistan were very much different than those in Serbia and the impetus for war was different—the United States had just lost over 3,000 innocent civilians.[44]

The solution was to deploy sensors that could get the required information. We have seen that the process of trial and error convinced the special forces troops that they must have the ability to get accurate coordinates and then direct aircraft to those coordinates. The technology to which these SOTACs turned was much improved over the equipment used in Desert Storm. They had the option of taking a laser designator or a range finder, both of which could provide precise coordinates for a target. Later, they started deploying with laptops that had digital maps that could provide accurate coordinates. These special operations terminal attack controllers were able to provide target coordinates and elevations. This was good enough information for the JDAMs, in most cases. The SOTACs did not have UAVs at their direction but could ask aircraft with sensor pods to perform reconnaissance for them. In fact, several of the controllers related they had broad permission from the CAOC to work directly with the aircraft. They also had clear guidance on what types of targets they could have the aircraft attack without coordinating, and what types required higher-level coordination. The mountainous terrain allowed them to see for miles and detect targets before they came into contact with them.[45]

Thus, the kill chain that involved these SOTACs was often significantly different than it had been for typical CAS in Desert Storm. Just as with typical CAS, the SOTACs were in areas where the enemy was—they traveled with the anti-Taliban troops—so wide-area surveillance was not a factor. The SOTACs could aim the laser designator at the target and read accurate coordinates in digital form. They could then pass these by voice-over radio—passing numbers over the radio is much easier than trying to talk someone's eyes onto a target when you do not even share the same vantage point. If the target was stationary, the target coordinates did not change, and there was no need to track it. There was also no need to talk the aircrew onto the target—"engage" meant drop the weapon within the envelope that allowed the bomb to guide to those coordinates. The aircrew could do this through the clouds or at night, as well. The fact that the weapon could use digital information meant the people involved could pass that information much more easily.

To find targets outside the areas where the SOTACs were deployed, the United States had airborne and space sensors. The workhorses were the Predators from the CIA or the Air Force, which sent streaming video back to anyplace that could link into SIPRNET.[46] To drop a JDAM on a target from this information, the CAOC had to mensurate the coordinates. The air component had a new tool called "Rainbow" right in the CAOC, so it could do this in less than an hour—a major reduction from Allied Force, where the CAOC had to rely on analysts in the United States to perform this service. Intelligence analysts had to take a still image from the Predator and use features to line it up with a special digital image map. Then the analyst used special "stereo" glasses to pick out the elevation of the target area. The end result was the same: digital information that was easily passed to the aircrew and, ultimately, to the weapon. The difference was that the CAOC and even analysts in the United States were inserted into the sequence. If the target required high-level approval, General Franks or even Secretary Rumsfeld was sometimes involved in the decision to engage. But as long as the weapon was a JDAM, engaging was easier.

Of course, not every weapon was a JDAM, although the JDAM became the most popular of weapons in Enduring Freedom. Weapons using GPS guidance were only appropriate for stationary targets, and not every platform could carry them. All other weapons required the aircrew to acquire the target visually before engaging. Since the CAOC and CENTCOM both had Predator pictures, they were often able to talk the aircrew onto the target from there. Again, telecommunications technology enabled the CAOC or CENTCOM to share the sensor's representation without having to corrupt it during the transmission process. And again, this allowed remote decision makers to play a part in the sequence that they had been unable to play before.

In cases where the command and control arrangements and the ROEs allowed, CENTCOM and the CAOC tried to push these actions down to lower levels. When the AC-130U gunship was involved, there was a technological aid to this delegation. The AC-130U model had a modification called "Rover," consisting of a receiver and monitor to display the Predator video to allow the crew to orient itself to the target.[47] Now the sensor and shooter could share the representation by passing it digitally, much the way the SOTACs and JDAM-shooters shared information by passing coordinates. The difference, of course, was that in the Rover case, the aircrew still had to translate the representation into information that the weapons could handle. The gunship crew had to relate the Predator's picture to what they were seeing, find the target with one of their sensors (either infrared, all-light-level television, or radar), and then aim the guns at the target by flying the plane in the correct geometry around it.

The air component also started to train the Predator operators to control aircraft in the absence of the Rover modification. On 8 December 2001, during the battle for Khandahar, an AC-130U aircrew got a call from a Predator operator to attack a target in the town of Mushkill. However, the crew's radio and Rover modification were not working, so it passed the mission to an AC-130H aircrew. Without the benefit of the Rover modification, the

Predator and gunship crews had to pass information that built a mental picture. The Predator was orbiting over the town, while the gunship was seven miles away, avoiding detection by the enemy. The Predator operator passed coordinates for the target, but at this distance, the AC-130's sensors could not show the crew enough detail for it to find the target—a walled compound with enemy soldiers in it. The Predator operator did not know the gunship crew could not discern the details near the target, so he spent almost half an hour trying to describe the buildings and empty fields nearby. The gunship crew did not realize the details it was being asked to discern were too small, so it was searching bigger areas farther from the target. Finally, the two crews verbally backed out of the city and found large landmarks, like a river and a road to lead them into the target area. This accomplished, the gunship crew went into the target area.[48]

In this case, the CAOC, and even CENTCOM, were aware of the mission—it was a TST. Moseley and Franks were both listening in but chose not to intervene.[49] To the AC-130 crew, the efforts to talk them onto the target were a bit cumbersome but within the normal C2 procedures. The crew's only complaints were that, after the talk-on, the Predator crew tried to direct the AC-130 crew's shots. In effect, the Predator operator was trying to control the "engage" part of the sequence as well.

Another sign of delegation to the lower levels was that the ground controllers were afforded a high degree of authority to clear attacks on targets. There was no ASOC at the time because, as we saw earlier, the conventional US forces with whom the ASOC usually works were not engaged in the fight. Aircrew members related that they were often sent off on a mission with nothing but the approximate location of a ground team and a frequency on which they could communicate with the team. The CAOC did not know the exact position of the teams in real time because there was no tracking system for this. The team's word was the clearance to fire. In one case, on 25 November 2001 during the fight for Konduz, an AC-130 gunship crew stumbled upon a single vehicle heading back into the city. The crew relayed that fact to the ground team, which recognized that this vehicle was part of a plan to launch a counterattack under the guise of surrender. The team cleared the gunship to fire on the vehicle instantly.[50] Essentially, this was equivalent to a TST, but executed in a matter of minutes. The rapid reaction was made possible by the fact that the team on the ground had authority to clear the attack. It had the authority because the ROEs allowed it, since the target was in an area where an attack would not cause collateral damage and the attacking aircraft was working with and for the ground team.

Because of this authority, their unique mission, and their ability to transfer digital information almost directly to the weapons, the controllers often did not follow standard procedures. In a conference in Kuwait after Operation Anaconda, aircrews recalled most of the calls for fire in the early parts of the Afghanistan conflict were abbreviated. The controllers usually neglected to use the standard nine-line request, but there was such a low volume of aircraft that this probably did not put anyone at risk, although it undoubtedly cost time and efficiency.[51] There were no ABCCC aircraft in-theater and no ASOC, and the overworked AWACS often used nonstandard language to communicate. Because the munitions were predominantly JDAMs, marking the target was often not needed because the aircrew did not have to visually acquire it.[52] The use of the SOTAC-airpower teams to create effects on the ground in the absence of conventional US ground troops was revolutionary, an occurrence which analysts are right to point out. Indeed, it was a capability sadly missing in Kosovo. But a joint group of participants in Anaconda pointed out that CAS "did not adhere to agreed upon fundamental mechanics." They cited that "the amount of self-induced friction experienced by all players during the Operation Anaconda was so significant that a Joint Close Air Support Conference was convened at Al Jaber Air Base in Kuwait immediately after the operation."[53] The authors pointed out that all the lessons from the conference were already addressed in the current joint doctrine, Joint Publication 3-09.3, *Joint Tactics, Techniques, and Procedures for Close Air Support.*[54]

It is important to realize that this shows a lack of depth, as we have defined it, in command relationships. While the troops at the lowest level had a great deal of freedom, this was not as a result of intentional decision making on the part of the C2 agencies that could monitor the troops and hold them accountable. On the contrary, this freedom resulted from the impossibility of attaining this level of control. The lack of fully empowered components created a gap in the C2 chain. In the fluid environment that existed during Anaconda, there was no way for the existing C2 agencies to become part of the kill chain. There was no way for them to get information except through the interpretation of the aircrew, so they had a low-fidelity and slightly delayed picture of the battlefield. When things went wrong, the decisions and actions needed to happen quickly.

Even after Anaconda, when troops came into contact in desperate circumstances, the digital equipment was often too cumbersome to be of use. Frequently, the only solution was to just put the aircrew in touch with the troops and let the two work things out. On 2 December 2002, Air Force staff sergeant Frank Lofton was working with an operational detachment-Alpha (ODA), or special operations A-team. The team was tasked to do reconnaissance of a possible al-Qaeda hiding location just west of Jalalabad. He and two others drove to an observation point and got grid coordinates off the hiding place, a cave complex near the crest of a ridge. When the three had finished getting the information, they noticed people coming from a town only 500 meters away, carrying lanterns. They were close enough for the three to see they were carrying AK-47 rifles. Lofton and his teammates waited until the unknown group got within 30 meters and turned on their lights, putting themselves at an advantage. They identified themselves as American in their best Pashtu, but the opposing group started to spread out, enveloping them. The Americans opened fire, but found they were outnumbered and outgunned—troops from a rooftop in the town had opened up on them with a 14.5 mm weapon as well. They got in their jeep and sped off in the only avenue of escape left. Because it was night and the terrain unfamiliar, they ended up racing down a boulder-strewn wadi at 45–50 miles per hour, launching themselves off a ledge and cracking the front axle of the jeep on the landing. The other two team members left the jeep to find higher ground; Lofton remained to try and radio for CAS.[55]

It was under these circumstances that Lofton had to try and direct aircraft to help him out. While receiving sporadic fire, he fumbled through his scattered and damaged equipment to find his night vision goggles. He flipped to a familiar frequency on the radio, relayed grid coordinates from his GPS to the Special

Operations Task Force commander, and got out of the jeep to try and find an escape route. Finding himself blocked by a ledge on one side and dangerous open space on the other, he got back into it to await the aircraft or the enemy, whichever came first. Seven minutes later, two A-10s caught him in mid-prayer as they checked in with him on the radio. Lofton directed the first to make a low pass and drop flares to try and direct the pilot to his position. Fortunately, although the pilot did not see Lofton, the pass was perfect, so Lofton cleared the pilot to shoot 2.75-inch rockets down the wadi, halting the enemy fire. The other two of Lofton's team members contacted the pilot of the aircraft on guard frequency, and the pilot helped direct them back to Lofton's position so ODA could come, an hour and a half later, and pick them up at the broken vehicle.[56]

How ironic that a mission to obtain the type of information that could be passed digitally, almost automatically, from ground controller to the weapon ended up relying on good old-fashioned CAS for a rescue. This did not erase the fact that in Afghanistan, the seeds of distributed cognition that had been sewn in Desert Storm and Allied Force came to fruition. In Enduring Freedom, we started to see how people in different parts of the system interfaced with technology to play their roles in a series of actions that, together, led to the resulting attack. It merely underlined the fact that the distributed way of war was not a substitute for developing depth in the command relationships—only an aid for getting information to the weapons. As Lofton was recovering from his near-fatal mission, the rest of CENTCOM was preparing for Iraqi Freedom, a war that would go even a step further toward making the job of attacking a target a distributed job where the pilots' tasks were a mere part of the entire sequence.

Iraqi Freedom

In Afghanistan, the missions seemed to be unorthodox. Everything seemed to be either a TST, characterized by the use of Predator or precise coordinates, or traditional CAS, where the aircraft and ground controllers worked together over the radio.

Iraqi Freedom was a much more conventional fight from the US standpoint. The US military had conventional forces on the ground. Franks had developed a command structure with a full complement of functional component commanders. The air component would be performing the standard missions: counterair, strategic attack, interdiction, and CAS, along with some other not-so-standard ones. The air component, under Moseley, was satisfied with the prominent role it would play in the targeting process. Underlying these comforting relationships, however, the roles played by the people involved were continuing to change. The "standard" missions were not always so standard when we examine how the parts of the kill chain were accomplished.

Killbox interdiction was based on the same concept that had served the air component in Desert Storm. There was still a provision for a Killer Scout of sorts; only now it was called a strike coordination and reconnaissance (SCAR) mission.[57] The SCAR aircrew took off with a briefing from intelligence about the current state of the ground war. Since the coalition forces were moving so rapidly this was old news, the SCAR could not use this information to determine targets. The pilots went to their ATO-assigned killbox, but if it was empty they had to find work elsewhere. The SCAR would often be an F-15E with LANTIRN or a Litening pod, a targeting pod similar to those the F-16s had used in Allied Force. The pod and even the F-15's radar only gave the aircrew members a limited view. They needed a surveillance mechanism to put them in the right place. So they tried to get an idea where to look by talking to the other pilots as they were leaving the killboxes to find out what they had seen.[58]

But once in a while, they became part of a distributed team. The ISR division of the CAOC programmed the Global Hawk UAV to fly over suspected enemy positions a few hours in advance of the missions to find targets. Global Hawk put out so much data that it was impossible for the CAOC to keep up with it. (Then) Maj Kevin Glenn worked as the ISR manager in Combat Operations, and he recalled that the data from Global Hawk was so overwhelming that they frequently had to ignore it, putting it in the "penalty box." Fortunately, analysts in Reno, Nevada, were devoted to scouring this information. When they found a target, they sent the imagery to the CAOC over SIPRNET and sent word by chat to Glenn. He, in turn, notified the interdiction duty officer or the TCT Cell on the Combat Operations floor, who sent a data-link message to the F-15E SCAR crew.[59]

For example, on 3 April Maj Richard Coe was the weapon systems officer on an F-15E performing SCAR in a killbox south of Baghdad. He and the pilot had taken off, gone to a tanker, and almost immediately been contacted by the AWACS to alert them of a data-linked message. In the cockpit, Coe could see a tank symbol on his Situation Display. The display was a view of his world from above, showing his aircraft and his wingman traveling over a map of the battle area. It showed any threats that Rivet Joint or other data collectors had identified in the area, and it now had a yellow tank. The yellow color alerted him that it was improperly identified—the tank was the best symbol the CAOC could find for the target. While the pilot flew the aircraft toward the area, Coe put a cursor on the symbol and slewed the aircraft's radar and Litening pod to the location to get a view of the actual target. This was a night mission, and the Litening's infrared showed him a large group of self-propelled artillery pieces. The two F-15E crews expended their laser-guided weapons and then called in F-16s and F-18s with GPS-guided munitions. Since the other aircraft did not have Link 16, the SCAR crews had to get coordinates with their pods and read them to the other crews, which typed them into their aircraft's computers.[60]

In this case, the CAOC had a digital means of transmitting information to the aircrew, which could then almost automatically translate that information into a form that the weapons could handle. The aircraft's computer translated the data-link message from the CAOC into a position on its digital map. By placing the cursor there and slewing the sensors to that position, the aircrew pointed the sensors to a location in the real world. By flying the aircraft close to the location and doing some fine adjustment of the sensors, it found the target in that location and pointed the laser designator at it. This gave the weapon, a 500-lb. GBU-12 LGB, the information needed to guide it to the target.

When the aircraft had JDAMS, they could even perform this work in bad weather. In late March, fierce sandstorms hit the area. With surface visibility of less than 30 feet at times, aircraft could not find targets on the ground using their optical or infrared sensors. Even ground troops could not find targets no matter how close they were. But during this period, the Republican Guard divisions began moving toward the south to surprise the US troops under what the Iraqis thought was the cover of impenetrable weather. The JSTARS moving-target-indicator radar picked up tracks of moving vehicles. JSTARS and Global Hawk SAR searched suspected areas for targets that could be attacked with JDAMs. The result was that, although aircraft were working in killboxes and were authorized to execute their missions without terminal control, they were given help through the CAOC at finding the targets to engage. With the JDAMs, the aircrew did not need to (and could not in many cases) find the targets visually, so engagements became a routine part of the sequence.

People in the ASOC were also part of the same type of distributed cognition. When members of the 3rd ID were heading north along the west bank of the Euphrates River, Iraqi troops and Fedayeen from the city of An Najaf fought them viciously. The 3rd Squadron, 7th Cavalry got the task of seizing a bridge south of Najaf to help isolate the city. After fighting its way across the bridge, the squadron came in contact again. While it was engaged in an extremely close-in fight, a JSTARS was monitoring. The crew saw returns on its MTI radar, moving south from Al Hillah toward the bridge fight. With night and weather hampering any optical deliveries, the ASOC in Kuwait chose to send in a B-1 bomber armed with JDAMs. The people in the ASOC used satellite imagery to pick targets along the road where the convoy was passing, with the intent to at least crater the road, if not destroy some of the vehicles. The B-1 dropped its full load of JDAMs and successfully stopped the reinforcements.[61]

Like the people in the CAOC, those in the ASOC had access to UAV and JSTARS video. In Desert Storm, RPVs had mainly been used to show the division and corps commanders what was happening in the deep battle, allowing them to adjust their operations. In Iraqi Freedom, the Hunter UAVs allowed the ASOC people to become part of the kill chain.

Sergeant Lofton had returned from Afghanistan in November of 2002 and was soon deployed to work in the V Corps ASOC. The main ASOC traveled with the 3rd ID, but was unable to set up permanent operations during the rapid move to Baghdad. So Lofton worked out of a rear ASOC in Kuwait. They had rigged an international maritime satellite telephone to relay information to a mobile communications vehicle that traveled with the 3rd ID, so the people in the ASOC could talk directly to the aircraft. During the 3rd ID's quest to cross the Euphrates River near Karbala, the Hunter UAV flew over an Iraqi multiple-launch rocket system (MLRS) at the exact instant it fired a volley across the river at the US troops. Suddenly, the ASOC in Kuwait was swamped by Army troops from the collocated tactical operations center (TOC), which had been watching the Hunter video as well. As the MLRS scooted away to a hiding place to reload, Lofton tried to talk two A-10s onto the target, using the Hunter video. When the talk-on became too time-consuming, the air boss in charge of the ASOC decided to bring in two F-15Es with LGBs. Lofton simply fed them the grid coordinates from the Hunter video and let them guide the bombs in the general vicinity of the hiding place. When the second bomb produced a huge explosion, the entire TOC erupted with elation.[62]

This was not a typical CAS mission. Obviously, it had an immediate impact on the close fight. But the request was generated at the corps headquarters in Kuwait—the troops at the front line could not have located the MLRS to direct CAS on it. The ability of the ASOC to use sensor-communication loops allowed Lofton to find, fix, track, and target the enemy instantly. Then he transformed the "engage" part by passing information that could be transferred to the weapon without the need for the aircrew to visually find the target. The pilots found the spot on the ground by looking through their heads-up display at a cursor that gave them a readout of the coordinates where the laser spot would go. Obviously, this is not quite the same as a JDAM because the LGB did not carry the information with it—it needed to follow the laser spot provided by the pilot. But it is another case where people in remote places contributed information about a fleeting target that the aircrew then had to verify and attack.

There were still plenty of opportunities to execute close-in CAS as well—it was an important part of the success of the land invasion. Whenever there was a troops-in-contact situation, that received everyone's attention right away. Although many aircraft performed CAS, the Air Force's workhorse for the under-the-clouds, eyes-on-target tasks was the A-10 Warthog.[63] The A-10s and the primary Marine CAS platform, the AV-8B Harrior, were in the midst of upgrades to their information capabilities. The

Harriers and one squadron of Warthogs had Litening pods. The Marines also had a downlink system to send the video from the targeting pod down to a FAC's vehicle.[64]

The ground controllers were more capable in OIF than ever before. Joint Forces Command had begun a program to train all controllers as JTACs and provide them with compatible equipment that could get, process, and distribute information digitally.[65] Bryan Lanning, the Air Force controller we introduced in the Desert Storm portion of this chapter, was now a technical sergeant deployed to Iraq with an Army battalion just as he had been 12 years before. Except, where he had worked with an armored division in Desert Storm, he now "hoofed it" with the infantry of the 101st Airborne Division (air assault). Up until 11 September 2001, the equipment with which he did his job had not changed much since Desert Storm, but since then it had improved immensely. He now had a night vision device and a laser designator that interfaced with GPS to give him fairly accurate coordinates. Although many TACP units now had laptop computers with the ability to download and filter the ATO, Lanning did not need it. When he needed CAS, he relayed his request up the chain. Lofton and the others at the ASOC sent the aircraft when they heard the call, so that by the time they received approval from the division and brigade levels, Lanning had his aircraft—usually within five minutes. Almost every time Lanning called for CAS, he was in contact with the enemy.[66]

This is the situation in which he found himself on 6 April 2004. After US troops seized the Baghdad airport, they moved in toward east Baghdad. The 3rd ID had gone quickly through the area on its way to a "thunder run" into Baghdad, leaving in its wake an empty palace under construction on the northern side of the airport. The Fedayeen had staked out the palace as their stronghold, and 101st troops were engaging them rifle-to-rifle. Lanning could see enemy troops in a tower of the palace with his thermal scope, but did not have the firepower to knock them out. He called for CAS and quickly got British Tornados with 1,000-lb. JDAMS—not his first choice because he did not want to take the time to get accurate coordinates. He would have preferred to talk the aircraft onto the target and let them drop laser-guided bombs. But he needed the firepower, so he pulled out his Mk-VII laser designator, got coordinates to the bottom of the tower, estimated its elevation, and fed the information to the aircrews by radio. Because of the inherent errors, the JDAMs missed, but the shock from the explosion knocked the people out of the tower. The fight lasted another eight or nine hours, during which time Lanning called in A-10s to strafe with their 30 mm guns and drop 500-lb. air-burst bombs.[67]

Such an engagement, reminiscent of the SOTAC airpower teams from Afghanistan, reinforced the fact that ground controllers and aircrew were now a very capable team. If the ground controller could obtain accurate coordinates and the aircrew had JDAMs, the kill-chain sequence was easy. During the push to Baghdad, the controllers never worried about obtaining mensurated coordinates—there was no time, and the weapons got close enough without them.[68] The flat terrain probably helped here.

This was the backdrop when the F-16s of the 77th Fighter Squadron (FS) from Shaw AFB, were tasked to perform airborne alert for attack missions. The squadron's mission is normally to perform suppression of enemy air defenses (SEAD). The fighters carry HARMs that lock onto enemy surface-to-air missile radars. But like the Serbs four years earlier, the Iraqis were not using their radars. As a result, although the Iraqis seemed afraid to use their air defenses, they were still present, and air operations were necessarily curtailed in the high-threat areas. So three days into the war, Moseley made the decision to turn from SEAD to destruction of enemy air defenses. Instead of waiting for the threat radars to radiate, the air component would seek and destroy them, whether they were in use or not. The ATO required the F-16s to be loaded with 25 percent HARMs and 75 percent precision munitions. The aircrews were to fly to a specified killbox and await instructions. They were to rapidly attack threats when directed by AWACS.[69]

It was a mission that openly called for aircrews to perform only the small portion of the kill chain that we have been describing. The pilots could not plan for anything because they did not know what the mission would entail. The only factors that affected their pre-mission planning were the type of weapons they would carry and where they would refuel. The aircraft in the 77th FS had no targeting pods or LANTIRN, so the pilots could not search for targets. They took off, went to an air-refueling tanker, and then sat in an orbit at their designated position. When they were out of fuel, they went back to the tanker. Each aircraft could stay for three orbit periods (called "vuls" for "vulnerability periods") interspersed with refueling before their time on station was over and they headed home with their bombs, without having (in their minds) contributed to the war effort that day—a point which was not lost on these fighter pilots.[70]

Their response was predictable. In the beginning, the pilots waited through the three vuls. But near the end of the third, they started "flipping through freqs," asking various C2 agencies whether anyone had a target that required their bombs. They found the ground parties receptive to these offers—the only requirement was a set of coordinates suitable for JDAMs or CBU-103s, and as we have shown, personnel on the ground could obtain coordinates that were good enough.[71] When the pilots found a target, they checked with the CAOC through the AWACS for permission. The usual response was "stand by," followed by a 15–20 minute wait while the people in the CAOC checked to see whether the target was suitable, including any collateral damage concerns. After a while, the pilots stopped waiting until the third vul to find targets because this increased their chances of finding a target to attack. The 77th FS squadron commander, Lt Col John Norman, encouraged them to "get out there and help Americans."[72]

The distribution of tasks also had the effect of making pilots information gatherers at times. The pilots from the 169th FW, a South Carolina Air National Guard F-16 wing, were directed to perform a mission similar to that of the 77th FS. They also started trying to find targets just as the 77th FS pilots did. But aircraft in the 169th FW were equipped with Litening pods, so the pilots could search for targets autonomously. They could also offer another service to the troops on the ground: performing reconnaissance. Many times, the ground troops sent them to locations where there were suspected targets. In fact, even after the F-16s were out of bombs, they were in demand. The pilots recorded the target coordinates in mission reports so the CAOC could task others to attack them.[73]

The tendency of pilots to become service providers increased after the 21-day push to Baghdad, when the nature of the Iraq war started to change. On 8 April three A-10s were hit by SAMs while providing support to troops near Baghdad. The CAOC decreed that no flights would go below 10,000 feet above ground without permission. On 9 April a statue of Saddam Hussein was toppled, providing a visual symbol that power had changed hands. The flow of CAS, which had been so abundant before, stopped like an abrupt end to a rain shower.[74] The urgency had decreased, and the need to limit damage and risk of losses became greater than the need to destroy—especially since the fighting had moved to the urban environment.

The role of airpower was then to do whatever was needed in support of the ground troops. Those in the CAOC had less ability to plan the missions that would be in the ATO. Most missions were flown to fill air-support requests from Army or Marine officers. The Army considered any ASRs submitted within 48 hours "immediate" requests, meaning they were forwarded directly to the ASOC and the CAOC never saw them.[75] In fact, the procedures were now flipped: the aircrews got the ASRs and told the CAOC which requests they would be supporting.[76] Much of the time, the ground troops were only interested in using the aircraft as ISR assets. The aircraft with Litening or LANTIRN were preferred. AC-130s with their multiple sensors were even more in demand. In chapter 5, we saw an example of the Marines using the AC-130s as an ISR asset—until the enemy shot at the Marines. In this type of war, with an enemy that looked like the civilians, there was no room for error. There was also no way to determine who had the best information at any given time.

Conclusions

Our short history of the engagement sequence gives us a basis to see that new technology has made the air component more capable of finding and engaging emerging targets. In Desert Storm, the TACC was not able to get involved in ongoing missions. TACC people rarely had an up-to-date air picture and had difficulty even talking to the aircraft. Their plan was to let the TACS handle the engagement of emerging targets. They therefore had significant difficulties finding and destroying mobile Scuds. Because the Iraqi army provided more predictable targets in an open environment, killbox interdiction was more effective. Still, aircrews had to develop ways to find and direct them to the targets. They turned to the Killer Scout concept. Precision laser-guided weapons allowed the aircrew to be effective while remaining at medium altitude, above the reach of many defenses. But this, like the visual delivery, only worked in good weather. Above all, the process of passing target information to the aircrews was a tedious job, involving breaking a visual description down into bits of information that could be passed via radio, to be reconstructed in the mind of the receiver. It was inefficient and inaccurate and could really only be done by those in the immediate vicinity of the target.

Several advances aided the evolution. The development of the JDAM provided a weapon that could be guided to a target based only on a piece of information that was easily passed via digital means: target coordinates. If the aircrew had accurate coordinates, there was no need for a visual acquisition of the target. The drawback was that more accurate target information was required. The ground troops got better sensors, and the CAOC obtained the ability to pull accurate information off of imagery with mensuration systems like Rainbow. These processes really came together in Enduring Freedom, although the pieces were available in Kosovo as well. The air component's capability continued to improve in Iraqi Freedom, where the CAOC was able to prosecute time-sensitive targets more quickly and also aid the SCAR teams in finding interdiction targets, even during bad weather.

Along with this evolution to greater capability came a subtle and possibly unacknowledged change in the aircrews' tasks. The process of engaging a target gradually came to include many people distributed in remote places. The aircrew's part in the attack sequence was in some cases just a small part of the chain, while the ground controller, the CAOC worker, and even the analyst back in the United States took over other parts of the sequence. The aircrews also started to take on other tasks as their aircraft became capable of gathering information because of new pods or more capable radars. They became service providers in someone else's attack sequence.

What this all means is unclear right now. The number of missions for which this distributed cognition applies is still low. Perhaps there will always be a mix of some missions where the aircrews have to perform the entire sequence and some where they will be a small part. This makes it difficult to train aircrews to perform in the cases where their role is limited. Training cannot ignore the other cases, because they are the ones that require the most competence from the aircrew. However, training must also address the limited-role case so aircrews will know how to play that role.

This distributed cognition also makes a demand on the leadership. When aircrew, ground controllers, CAOC workers, and even analysts can find themselves on a team in an instant, the command relationships can be confusing. Suddenly, as in the case we studied earlier where the Marines worked with an AC-130 in Fallujah, the commander in charge may not be the one with the best situational awareness. Commanders must determine a way to discern who is on the team at a given point and dynamically shift control to the one in the best position to exercise control. But this demand runs headlong into the organizational problems we studied earlier.

There is also another potential problem with the limiting of the aircrew's role. If it is not accompanied by a redefinition and training, there may be a latent potential in the aircrews—the ability and ambition to do more than they are allowed. The next chapter will show us that this could be highly effective in certain circumstances but dangerous in others.

Notes

1. The author was in the audience for a "CAOC 101" class that the CAOC people gave for aircrews during JEFX 04.

2. Hutchins, *Cognition in the Wild*, 173–74.

3. Cohen and Keaney, *Gulf War Air Power Survey*, vol. 1, pt. 2, *Command and Control*, 249; and Shaw, "Influence of Space Power."

4. Cohen and Keaney, *Gulf War Air Power Survey*, vol. 2, pt. 1, *Operations*, 183–88. The F-15 and F-16 infrared sensors were called LANTIRN for low-altitude navigation and targeting infrared for night. General Corder wrote up the tactics and procedures for the Scud Hunt in CENTAF TACC/CC/DO, "Current Ops Log," vol. 1 of 2, 27 Jan 2300Z.

5. Tritschler, interview.

6. Cohen and Keaney, *Gulf War Air Power Survey*, vol. 2, pt. 1, *Operations*, 267–68.

7. Cohen and Keaney, *Gulf War Air Power Survey*, vol. 1, pt. 2, *Command and Control*, 310–14. This posed another problem: without access to the current ground situation, the ABCCC had only its targeting lists to guide the

crew. The Army liaison officer on the ABCCC had the US Army Central Command's (ARCENT) prioritized list, which did not match the list in the ATO because the ATO reflected Schwarzkopf's guidance instead of ARCENT's. The ABCCC was caught in a conflict between two different constituencies, neither of which was necessarily reflective of the up-to-date ground situation, with no means to rectify the difference. Soboul, memorandum.

8. Jamieson, *Lucrative Targets*, 77; and 8th Air Support Operations Group, *Operations Desert Shield/Storm*, 2.

9. 8th Air Support Operations Group, *Operations Desert Shield/Storm*, 2; and Cronin, "C3I during the Air War," 36.

10. Cohen and Keaney, *Gulf War Air Power Survey*, vol. 2, pt. 1, *Operations*, 260.

11. Welsh, "Day of the Killer Scouts," 67. Lt Col Mark Welsh (a student at National Defense University at the time of this writing) was commander, 4th FS, and one of the first Killer Scouts in the war.

12. Ibid., 67–68.

13. Jamieson, *Lucrative Targets*, 81.

14. Mets, *Long Search for a Surgical Strike*, 35.

15. Cohen and Keaney, *Gulf War Air Power Survey*, vol. 2, pt. 1, *Operations*, 261.

16. Comments on an earlier draft of this paper from Haun to the author, e-mail, 11 Apr. 2005.

17. Lanning, interview. TSgt Bryan Lanning, USAF, a joint tactical air controller instructor, Air-Ground Operations School (at the time of this writing), was a battalion enlisted terminal attack controller in Desert Storm and OIF.

18. 8th Air Support Operations Group, *Operations Desert Shield/Storm*, 2.

19. Comments by Haun to the author, e-mail, 11 Apr. 2005.

20. One ALO recalled he traveled as the number three vehicle in his brigade's convoy so his brigade commander could keep track of its position. The commander instructed the ALO to call the ASOC every 30 minutes to update the brigade's position. Sams, interview. Lt Col Walter Sams, USAFR, 79th FS, assistant director of operations at the time of this writing, was the brigade ALO in Desert Storm. He was also an F-16 pilot and SEAD duty officer in the CAOC in OIF.

21. Lanning, interview.

22. The ASOC had CAFMS terminals and could look at the ATO to determine which aircraft should support a request. The TACPs did not look at the ATO very often. They noted the only way to get it from the ASOC to them was to hand deliver it by floppy disk or hard copy because there was no way to get it to the TACPs. Sometimes that meant an extra 150-mile trip per week to coordinate. 602d Tactical Air Control Wing (TAIRCW) Deputy Commander for Operations, *Desert Storm Conference, Lessons Learned*, "I. Operational Issues."

23. Sams, interview.

24. Desert Storm Conference, Lessons Learned. "4 ASOG Desert Shield/Storm," 6.

25. Lanning, interview.

26. "KEZ Mission," X-3; and Haun to the author, e-mail, 11 Mar. 2004.
27. Haave and Haun, *A-10s over Kosovo*, 138.
28. Gordon, "A War out of the Night Sky," 1.
29. Koprucu, interview (see chap. 7, n. 35).
30. Haave and Haun, *A-10s over Kosovo*, 138.
31. Koprucu, interview.
32. McDaniels, "Viper FAC-A."
33. Haave and Haun, *A-10s over Kosovo*, 147–48.
34. Haun to the author, e-mail, 11 Mar 2004.
35. This is backed up by the Haun e-mail as well (ibid.).
36. Haave and Haun, *A-10s over Kosovo*, 203–5.
37. Ibid., 211.
38. McDaniels, "Viper FAC-A."
39. Ibid.
40. Ibid.
41. United States Air Force, "Air War over Serbia," 6. Although precision-guided munitions were only 29 percent of the weapons dropped, they hit 64 percent of the desired mean points of impact.
42. Ball, "JDAM Weapon Effectiveness," slide 7.
43. Mets, *Long Search for a Surgical Strike*, 43.
44. Comments on an earlier draft of this paper in Deptula to the author, e-mail. He further notes the CAOC's concern that CENTCOM was more focused on collateral damage than on accomplishing the military objectives.
45. Unattributed interview by the author with technical sergeant from AFSOC/XP, 720th Special Tactics Squadron. See also Lofton to the author, e-mail, 6 May 2004. SSgt Frank Lofton, USAF, 12th Combat Training Squadron at the time of this writing, was an enlisted terminal attack controller with the 19th Special Forces Group (SFG), 2nd Battalion (Bn), Operational Detachment Alpha (ODA) 923d and 20th SFG, 1st Bn, ODA 2025, from 26 Aug. 2002–29 Jan. 2003. He also worked in the V Corps ASOC during OIF.
46. The first Global Hawk UAV was not quite ready for operational service, although it was redirected to look at Khandahar during the prison riot in Nov. 2001. Grant, "Eyes Wide Open," 38.
47. Ackerman, "Operation Enduring Freedom," 3. See also Maj Don Richardson, USAF (16th Special Operations Squadron/DOXT at the time of this writing; navigator on AC-130H gunships, OEF), interview by the author, Hurlburt Field, FL, 28 May 2003. (Notes in author's personal collection.)
48. Richardson, interview; and Benoit, Miller, and Gregg, interview.
49. Richardson to the author, e-mail. In fact, General Franks sent the aircrew a personal note congratulating them for a fine mission. The personal note was displayed in a glass showcase in the 16th SOS operations building, next to other war memorabilia. Richardson, interview.
50. Benoit, Miller, and Gregg, interview.
51. Haun to the author, e-mail, 11 Apr. 2005. He gave a personal example where imprecise communication had cost him 10 minutes of searching, where a nine-line request would have given him a hint that the directions were faulty.

52. Jansen, "JCAS in Afghanistan," 24–25.
53. Ibid., 24.
54. Ibid., 26.
55. Lofton to the author, e-mail, 5 May 2004. See also Lofton, interview, 28 July 2004.
56. Lofton, interview, 28 July 2004.
57. Defore, "Killbox Interdiction," 3.
58. Coe, interview.
59. Grant, "Eyes Wide Open," 38. See also Glenn to the author, e-mail, 20 May 2004; and Glenn, interview, 25 Mar 2004.
60. Coe, interview.
61. Lofton, interview, 29 July 2004; and History, 3rd Squadron, 7th Calvary Regiment, 3rd ID.
62. Lofton, interview, 29 July 2004.
63. Butler, "As A-10 Shines in Iraq," 1; Wallace, "Joint Fires in OIF"; and Hollis, "Trained, Adaptable, Flexible Forces."
64. Ripley, "Close Air Support."
65. Heidal, "USAF TACP Modernization."
66. Lanning, interview.
67. Ibid.
68. Ibid.
69. Manning, interview. Lt Col Scott Manning, USAF, 55th FS/DO at the time of this writing, was an F-16 pilot, 77th FS, OIF.
70. Manning interview; Stolley, interview; and Mahajan, interview (Capt Jay Mahajan, USAF, 77th FS at the time of this writing and F-16 pilot during Iraqi Freedom).
71. Stolley, interview; and Mahajan, interview.
72. Manning, interview.
73. Sams, interview.
74. Lofton, interview, 29 July 2004; and Lanning, interview.
75. Lt Col James Prior, USAF (worked in CAOC KI/CAS Cell during Iraqi Freedom), interview by the author, Shaw AFB, SC, 26 Mar. 2004. (Notes in author's personal collection.)
76. Lt Col Charles Stoner (4 SOS assistant director of operations at the time of this writing and AC-130U aircraft commander during Iraqi Freedom), interview by the author, Hurlburt Field, FL, 27 May 2004. (Notes in author's personal collection.)

THIS PAGE INTENTIONALLY LEFT BLANK

Chapter 9

System Accidents in the CAOS

We have now navigated four conflicts five times, each time telling a slightly different but related story. We have analyzed Desert Storm, Allied Force, Enduring Freedom, and Iraqi Freedom with a view to politico-military interactions, intercomponent command relationships, the quest to gather and distribute information at the air component, and the sometimes competing pursuit to execute the kill chain at the force-application level. Through it all, we have been most interested in identifying the role of information and tools in the behavior of the Combat Air Operations System. We have delved only shallowly into the implications of those interactions and whether they were appropriate or not. This is partly because the main point of this book is to define the tradeoffs commanders must consider—the variables involved and their potential consequences—as they wrestle with how much control to delegate and how much to retain. It is also due to the difficulty of establishing, in retrospect, how appropriate an action was. Even success is not always a good measuring stick—flawed decisions can be successful with forceful execution or overwhelming advantage in other areas.

How does the JFACC deal with F-16 pilots who are aggressively trying to contribute to the war effort rather than doing only what they are ordered to do? If they take taskings from the ASOC or DASC, the JFACC loses control of them—they become supporting assets for another commander's objectives. Worse, the air component, in all probability, also loses the ability to track the effects of its attacks. The targets it is after may never have reached the land component's awareness, and the results may be difficult to track, especially since the weapons may be JDAMs dropped at night. The JFACC knows he needs to support the JFLCC, but he also has objectives of his own. Those pilots are there in case the air component needs to use them to destroy threats to other aircraft or execute a TST.

Commanders must also be mindful of the potential for system accidents. Scholars of systems theory have proposed that assembling players together in networks creates a tremendous robustness against random failures. That is, one part of the system can serve as a backup for a malfunction somewhere else, enabling its continued functioning. Concurrently, however, the increased complexity of the system makes it more vulnerable to unpredictable and dramatic cascading failures.[1] For example, Perrow prophesies that "we have not had more serious accidents of the scope of Three Mile Island simply because we have not given them enough time to appear."[2] Others have claimed that big blackouts are a natural product of the electrical power grid. The forces to minimize cost put more power onto existing lines until they reach a critical point. After a power outage, angry feedback from the public drives improvements that make the system more stable. Then the forces to minimize cost take over again, starting another cycle.[3]

The CAOS may have similar propensities. Political pressures and technological development have combined to produce innovation in the form of sensor-communication loops that distribute the attack sequence tasks. This has produced a complicated web of possibilities that makes it more difficult to predict the outcomes of some military actions.

We will now look at several mechanisms by which this evolution could lead to accidents. The "friendly fire" shootdown of UH-60 Black Hawks in the NFZ over Iraq in 1994 illustrates the possibility that deviation from procedures (practical drift) combined with altered dynamics in the system can cause accidents. The change in aircrew roles that we saw in the last chapter has led to such drift several times in our study—the F-16 destruction of enemy air defense missions in Iraqi Freedom and the CAS procedures at the beginning of Enduring Freedom are two prominent examples. However, not all such chain of events lead to accidents. A system accident requires an incident of such magnitude that it affects the output of the system. The nature of the war determines the type of incident that will trigger this. While commanders try to avoid these situations by imposing constraints on the aircrews, the opposite effect of drift may instead occur if procedures are too constricting for a loosely coupled situation. Tight restrictions also risk the loss of human innovation where it is desirable. Technological development can also help by taking the human out of the loop, in some cases. Relegating humans to only supervisory roles, however, often takes away their ability to intervene when it is necessary or desirable.

In discussing military actions, it seems almost paradoxical to talk about accidents. In an endeavor so violent, chaotic, and full of risk, how can we even define what an accident is, much less be concerned about them? In his book *Normal Accidents*, Perrow defines an accident as "a failure in a subsystem, or the system as a whole, that damages more than one unit and in doing so disrupts the ongoing or future output of the system."[4] The transition from incident to accident generally involves engineers installing safety features like redundancy to try to avoid accidents. He also distinguishes between component failure accidents, due to malfunctions linked in a foreseeable sequence, and system accidents, resulting from the unanticipated interaction of multiple breakdowns.[5]

According to Perrow, two key characteristics predict whether a system is prone to system accidents. One of the keys is the type of interactions among components in a system, which Perrow labels either linear—meaning components interact in a predictable chain—or complex.[6] According to his reasoning, concurrent with complex interactions is the potential for failure sequences that are unanticipated. In a system with only linear interactions, failure sequences can be anticipated and, therefore, defended against. Another of Perrow's keys to whether failures will result in system accidents is the degree of coupling among components, whether loose or tight—this has been one of our running themes. Perrow claims that complex interactions combined with tight coupling causes unanticipated failure sequences. By now the reader should be convinced that the CAOS has complex interactions—people at any given place in the system are not completely aware of the effects of their actions on others in the system. In addition, our historical study has shown that as the technology evolves, those in the CAOS are creating new interactions among distributed players. Finally, we will borrow the idea that the principle-defining characteristic of a system-level accident is that it disrupts the ongoing or future output of the system.

The accidental shootdown of two UH-60 Black Hawks in northern Iraq in 1994 was a system accident—a series of unintended interactions caused an incident so tragic and so unpredictable that it sparked two years of investigation and major redesigns to the "system." On 14 April of that year, two US F-15C pilots were conducting a sweep of the area of operations for Operation Provide Comfort (OPC), the multinational humanitarian effort to ease the suffering of hundreds of thousands of Kurdish refugees who had fled to the hills during Operation Desert Storm. The F-15s detected radar contacts and, after trying to identify the helicopters electronically and visually, determined they were Soviet Mi-24 Hinds and shot them down. The entire engagement lasted only eight minutes, during which time the F-15 pilots were in contact with an AWACS crew that originally had radar contact with the helicopters and was in radio contact with the AOC-equivalent organization. Both helicopters were destroyed immediately, and all 26 people on board perished. Hours later, a team of over 30 technical experts assembled in Turkey to conduct an investigation. The review of this accident was followed over the next two years by separate military service investigations, congressional inquiries, and uniformed code of military justice hearings.[7] This scrutiny led to many lessons learned and procedural changes. It did not, however, lead to any "smoking gun."

Accidents like the Black Hawk shootdown are disasters—not just because of the lives lost, but because of the inevitable (and seemingly unanswerable) question: "Why?" There were multiple safeguards in place designed to avoid what happened. Military professionals had designed formal organizational relationships and a system of procedural constraints conveyed in an ATO and special instructions to the different organizations. The errors were avoidable. Yet, apparently, no one was held accountable.

In retrospect, there were many points in this catastrophe at which the constraints put in place did not function as designed. One individual in the organization who was responsible for coordinating procedures between the Army helicopter unit and the air component staff had been reassigned and not replaced, so the Black Hawk pilots had a different version of the ATO than the others. The Black Hawk pilots went about their business in a manner unfamiliar to the fighter pilots: their schedule was so flexible that it could not be published in the ATO. Furthermore, the UH-60s and the F-15s had incompatible radios—the F-15s had antijam radios for which the UH-60 radios were not keyed, and the F-15 pilots were not instructed to use another mode. The day of the shootdown, the AWACS crew did not switch the helicopters to a separate controller when it entered the area. Then, when the helicopter returns faded because the helicopters entered mountainous territory, the AWACS crew lost track of them. The crew then failed to inform the F-15 pilots that there were helicopters in the area and did not step in to take control of the situation. Also, the F-15 pilots used sloppy language and a hasty—and ultimately inaccurate—visual identification pass to confirm that they were cleared to fire on the helicopters. The identify-friend-or-foe equipment did not operate as expected.[8] These are just a few of the many ways that the checks that should have prevented the accident were violated.

But why were they violated? In Snook's book *Friendly Fire*, he looks at the accident through several different lenses to determine why the people involved did what they did. The fighter pilots, making sense of their world based on their training and preflight preparation, essentially did what came naturally to them. The commanders involved relied on the fact that each unit was trained to do its job and that procedural controls would harmonize them. But one of the teams involved (AWACS) was a new crew, untrained in the procedures and not accustomed to working with each other, not to mention the other teams. Another team (Black Hawks) was not considered an integral part of the overall organization. Since the Army crew members went about their business in a different way than the Air Force constituent, they were considered to be playing by their own rules and were treated as somebody else's business.

Every player involved had slowly drifted away from strict adherence to the global procedures over time. Because of this behavior, in an emergency the measures that were supposed to guarantee safety were nonexistent—a graphic illustration of Snook's practical drift concept. Over time, organizations go through different stages that determine how strictly they adhere to procedures. In OPC, when units were initially assigned to the command, they probably followed written procedures strictly. Then they found more convenient ways of doing things as the operation went on. When these deviations were not punished (and were, in fact, rewarded by the added convenience), they became the norm. For example, the Black Hawk crews did not change Mode 1 IFF codes when they entered the NFZ because they did not have the right air tasking order. The AWACS crews accepted this because they did not feel the need to get into the Black Hawk crews' business and because the Black Hawks were generally only in the NFZ for a short period of time. The AWACS crews responded by keeping the Black Hawks on a single radio frequency so they could stay with a single en route controller instead of switching, as they were supposed to. The OPC commander did not know anything was wrong because he was in tune with the F-16 procedures, which included a non-standard personal communication network with the Black Hawk crews (something the F-15 pilots did not have).[9]

According to Snook, these locally adapted procedures were all seemingly harmless because the different organizations were very loosely coupled. Not much happened on a day-to-day basis, so there was rarely any consequence to going outside of global procedures. In fact, there were perverse incentives—the locally adapted procedures were more convenient.

But when chance intervened and there was an emergency, the players needed tighter control. When the F-15 pilots got radar contact with the helicopters, the actions of the Black Hawk crews, the F-15 pilots, the AWACS crew, and all the staff were tightly coupled—actions taken and even words spoken by one significantly affected the others. By this time, however, global procedures had given way to local accommodations. What had taken over was culture-based action.[10] Worse, there was no one who could take charge and step in because there were so many who were supposed to be in charge that everyone thought someone else was in control.[11]

Snook's contribution to Perrow's theory is that the degree of coupling and the type of control are variables. Instead of centralization and decentralization, Snook focuses on the "logics of action" that drive the actors. People shift back and forth from focusing on the task at hand to following rules, depending on the context of the situation, and these shifts have a predictable effect on the smooth functioning of the organization.[12] In the end, a complex system is neither tightly coupled nor loosely coupled but dynamic. Perrow stipulates that a certain degree of centralization is desirable in a given situation. However, Snook shows that, in reality, those involved may at times shift behavior in ways that defy centralized control, whether by procedures or constraints.[13]

We have studied other examples where this kind of drift has occurred. In Afghanistan, the SOTACs worked out procedures to quickly and efficiently direct aircraft onto a target. Most of the time, these procedures involved skipping lines one through three of the standard nine-line briefing usually given to CAS aircraft. These three lines describe an initial point, a heading into the target, an offset left or right, and the distance from the initial point to the target.[14] As we discussed in previous chapters, several factors made this possible. The pilots did not need to see the target to launch the JDAM weapons they usually carried. There were rarely enough aircraft in the area to require traffic control. The targets were often not in close proximity to friendly troops—the SOTACs had equipment to allow them to find target coordinates from a distance. In fact, we saw that many analysts and military officers alike claimed the mission was so different than a normal CAS mission that it called for new procedures. Nevertheless, there never were any standard procedures developed, so the adaptations could be called drift. For the relatively loosely coupled situation that existed during the initial phase of Enduring Freedom these modifications were not only appropriate, they were beneficial. This drift enabled the revolutionary marriage of special operations and airpower that helped the Afghanistan opposition forces rapidly overthrow the Taliban.

Then, during Operation Anaconda, the situation transitioned to a tightly coupled situation. Now there were large numbers of friendly troops in close contact with the enemy, and the enemy was not retreating as had been expected. Many aircraft in close proximity were trying desperately to help the ground troops. In this situation, the actions of any of the participants could have significantly affected the others.

For example, during the battle for Takur Ghar peak, the crew of an AC-130H gunship observed evidence of unintended interactions and tight coupling. While the crew, under call sign "Grim 32," was heading to its mission area, it overheard a radio call from a helicopter, call sign "Razor 04," that was looking for a lost wingman. Two helicopters, Razor 04 and Razor 03, had attempted to insert special operations troops to take over the 10,000-foot Takur Ghar peak to observe and call in CAS for the unfolding Operation Anaconda below. Upon landing, Razor 03 had been met by heavy enemy fire. The crew had hastily taken off and maintained control of its damaged aircraft long enough to execute a controlled crash landing seven kilometers away. But in the escape, Petty Officer 1st Class Neil Roberts—one of the sea-air-land (SEAL) team members whom the helicopter had been trying to insert—had fallen out the back of the helicopter and been left behind.[15] Grim 32 asked if it could help, and with its infrared and low-light television, it was able to locate the crash site of the helicopter that had been shot down.[16]

While helping out was the right thing to do, this put Grim 32's crew at the crossroads of several groups of agencies that were evidently not prepared to interact with each other. The first group was the C2 agencies. The crew was under the command and control of one of the joint special operations task forces (JSOTF) and was therefore considered to be in a different category than the fighters and bombers. Although the AC-130H gunship's missions were represented in the ATO, crew members received their tasking directly from the JSOTF through one of the two joint special operations air components (JSOAC) that worked for the JSOTF.[17] Consequently, they were responsible to one JSOAC, while the mission they were flying was the responsibility of the other. A discussion ensued of who was in charge over satellite radio. The issue was muddled by the fact that there was also another JSOTF, with which the crew was unfamiliar. This JSOTF also claimed some responsibility for the mission and, at one point, cleared Grim 32's crew to fire on the landing zone. The crew could not identify the friendly and enemy troops at the time and did not know what authority this agency had, so it refused to fire.[18]

Crew members were also powerless to affect the action of the friendly ground troops. After Razor 04 had picked up Razor 03's crew and flown back to base, it made the decision to go back after Roberts. Razor 04 inserted the remaining SEAL team members at the same point where Roberts had fallen, but the SEALs quickly took three casualties and found themselves in a deadly cross fire. They disengaged under covering fire from the gunship. However, a quick reaction force (QRF) of Army Rangers and an Air Force pararescueman had already taken off and were unable to communicate with Grim 32. The gunship crew tried to tell the two MH-47E helicopters in the QRF to avoid the hot landing zone and use an "offset" area 2,000 feet down the mountain because the SEALs had vacated the area.[19] Oblivious, the helicopters attempted to land at the hot landing zone, but one of the two was shot down before the other decided to go to the offset zone.[20]

In the meantime, the conventional air component seemed to be unaware of the ongoing rescue. The copilot was talking to the AWACS, which kept trying to clear the gunship from the area so two B-52s could drop their ordnance on a preplanned target. The crew of Grim 32 felt the rescue efforts were higher priority and refused. Later, the crew was ordered by the JSOAC to return to base. Neither the ground C2 agencies nor the AWACS were able to help find a replacement to take over, so the crew had to find its own replacement. Finally, the pilot called on guard (the emergency channel) for "any daylight CAS aircraft," and found an F-15E whose crew agreed to take over.[21] Conventional CAS began dropping bombs on enemy positions, sometimes within 50 meters of the Rangers' position near the downed helicopter, to enable them to survive. After the other Ranger group made it up the steep mountain through three feet of snow, the two groups organized a heroic attack on the enemy positions to gain control of the top of the hill. Finally, that night, they were extracted by helicopter.[22]

In this example, practical drift led to some mistakes in a complex, tightly coupled situation that resulted in a near accident. The complicated command structure identified in chapter 5, combined with the nonstandard arrangements for providing CAS during the initial, loosely coupled period of Enduring Freedom, produced confusion during the tense moments of the tightly coupled Anaconda. It is impossible to determine whether things would have been different if there had been a classic component structure with a full ASOC, and if the controllers and aircraft had been following standard procedures the entire time. The types of confusion the crew of Grim 32 experienced are exactly what these measures are meant to avoid.

The above illustrates how distributed cognition comes with the associated risk for ambiguity, also described in the previous chapter. With the tasks to attack a target dispersed among several remote locations, the teams involved in any attack are less coherent. More potential avenues to accomplish the same tasks also become available. Even though the F-16 pilots had no preplanned targets and could not see at night (in the case of the 77th FW aircraft), they were able to find a way to get target coordinates that allowed them to drop precision weapons. Involving more players increases the likelihood of their devising ad hoc procedures and drifting from standard procedures when it is convenient.

On the other hand, the advantage is that there is more potential for innovation to solve problems. In Enduring Freedom, the use of SOF, with high technology sensors to call in support for foreign troops, was a highly innovative adaptation. It likely turned the tide of the war and made possible the rapid victory to wrest control from the Taliban. Although we have claimed that the preplanned targeting of airpower was done in a very centralized manner, it is also true that the command structure that General Franks put in place gave special forces significant freedom to develop these innovations for emerging targets. In Iraqi Freedom, the F-16 pilots' actions may have contributed to the ground troops' ability to march to Baghdad in 21 days.

It is also worth noting that the Battle of Takur Ghar was not an "accident" under our definition of the term. Though it could be argued that there were mistakes that led to more loss of life than necessary, the system was not halted. The troops performed heroically and continued the mission.

Whether a failure leads to an "incident" or an "accident" is determined by whether the system is required to halt its ongoing or future output. There is an issue of scope here: one system's incident is another system's accident. If a panel of experts examines the wreckage of a fighter aircraft and finds that the crash was caused by an unforeseeable interaction of components, the crash may be deemed a system accident. However, if it occurs during a war where numerous aircraft are involved, the air commander will probably treat it as an incident and continue the war. An aircraft and crew together constitute merely a "part" in our system, however tragic it may be to lose an aircraft and the human beings on board. Still, in certain cases the loss of an aircraft and crew in combat could be an accident, where in others it is merely an incident.

For example, there was a significant difference between the way commanders in Desert Storm approached losses compared with those in Provide Comfort. In his post-war autobiography, General Schwarzkopf put it this way:

> I detest the term "friendly fire." Once a bullet leaves a muzzle or a rocket leaves an airplane, it is not friendly to anyone. Unfortunately, fratricide has been around since the beginning of war. The very chaotic nature of the battlefield, where quick decisions make the difference between life and death, has resulted in numerous incidents of troops being killed by their own fires in every war that this nation has ever fought. . . . This does not make them acceptable. Not even one such avoidable death should ever be considered acceptable. And in a war where so few lives were lost on our side, the tragedy is magnified when a family loses a son or daughter in such a way.[23]

Similarly, General Horner also noted that, although he tried hard to avoid fratricide, it was "a battle we did not win." However, he also said, "Though all were great tragedies, when placed against the total of air-to-ground attacks, their numbers were quite small—especially compared with other wars. Moreover, we must also weigh in the lives of friendly ground forces saved because air attacks on the Iraqis were so devastating."[24]

The implication is clear. Military commanders want to keep the level of friendly losses as low as possible, but they have a larger purpose: to win the war. Losses to both friendly and enemy fire occurred during Desert Storm. In the Battle of Khafji alone, two such events involved losses of large numbers of US troops. On the evening of 29 January 1991, a malfunctioning Maverick missile from an A-10 killed 11 US Marines. Then on the morning of 31 January, an AC-130 was shot down by Iraqi fire, killing all 14 crew members on board. Neither of these incidents, tragic as they were, caused any break in the air component's efforts.[25]

The calculated risks to forces varied even among different periods of Desert Storm. Horner took great care to get aircraft to fly at medium altitudes where they would be above the reach of most antiaircraft artillery during the initial air campaign, despite the fact that it likely decreased the effectiveness of some of the weapon systems. Then at the beginning of the ground war, Horner made it clear that aircrews would significantly increase their risk tolerance in order to support the ground invasion. In his comments on 24 February, he stated, "Make sure that the air is there where they need it, when they need it—that's your job. No excuses. I don't want to have any weather abort or any of that crap. Get up there and do the job the best you can."[26]

Determinations of whether the system must halt its output are based on the strategic feedback loops we identified earlier. If the interests are great enough, decision makers will perceive that the public can accept a higher cost in money and lives to achieve the goals of the war. The loss of 18 Rangers was significant relative to the US goals of trying to stop Mohammed Farah Aideed from interfering with humanitarian aid efforts in Somalia in 1993. The loss of 26 UN civilians and troops during a relatively peaceful period was significant relative to the US goals of trying to contain Saddam Hussein and give humanitarian aid to his people in 1994. The loss of 25 troops in 1991 while conducting a major war to eject his entire army out of a nation he had invaded was not nearly as significant. In addition, in the latter case, the troops died defending US troops on the ground.

Similar mechanisms seem to operate in other types of accidents. Friendly fire is not the only type of failure that can halt the output of air operations. When F-117s struck the Al Firdos bunker in Baghdad in 1991, television media showed pictures of dead civilians. When bombs from a B-2 hit what later turned out to be the Chinese Embassy in Belgrade, Serbia, in 1999, the incident triggered a diplomatic crisis between Washington and Beijing, disrupting negotiations to end the Kosovo conflict.

Policy makers and commanders alike have become extremely sensitive to these feedback loops throughout the 1990s. When the results of military action could have undesirable effects on the public's perception of policy, policy makers act quickly to show that the actions were a mistake and that they will not happen again. After the Al Firdos incident, Schwarzkopf effectively halted strategic bombing in Baghdad. The Chinese Embassy strike prompted a halt to bombing of targets in Belgrade for two weeks thereafter. Ever since the media made it possible to speed up these feedback loops, this type of information warfare has occurred.

This is why, in Iraqi Freedom, the CAOC handled situations differently. During the initial push to Baghdad, the CAOC did not deny many requests to attack the targets that the F-16 pilots got over the radio. In fact, when Lt Col Walter Sams performed reconnaissance with his targeting pod and found new targets, he provided the coordinates to the CAOC through his mission report. The CAOC planners then typed them into the remarks section for interdiction missions on the next day's ATO.[27] Pilots accepted coordinates directly from ground troops even though they had not been mensurated. In fact, the JTACs admitted they never worried about mensurating the coordinates during this period.[28] The accuracy of their equipment was considered good enough for their purposes. The pilots' immediate concern was getting ordnance on the target quickly. As we saw in Sergeant Lanning's case, sometimes almost any weapon would do. However, after the statue of Saddam Hussein fell, the flow of CAS stopped. The goal of toppling the regime was in sight, and the fight progressed to the streets of Baghdad, where a mistake could mean significant unnecessary deaths and unwanted media attention.

In this environment, the CAOC came up with a plan to provide calibrated firepower when necessary. In the airspace around Baghdad, it stacked aircraft with different weapons loads, from 5,000-lb. bunker-busters to 500-lb. bombs with seekers but no explosives, each tailored to a different situation. The CAOC knew the specific weapons on each aircraft and could therefore pick the correct weapon for each situation.[29]

Since this solution reduces the role of the aircrew in the attack sequence, it carries with it the potential to cause the drift we discussed earlier. The aircrew's diminished role, together with its latent excess capability (as noted in the previous chapter), caused some tension for the F-16 pilots in Iraq in our earlier example. These highly trained pilots, capable of more complex tasks and wanting to contribute, went in search of ways to advance the war effort. The Black Hawk shootdown also shows how this drive to contribute, when combined with other factors, can produce disastrous consequences. The F-15 pilots in this case did not have to respond as quickly as they did—they were in no danger and could have watched the helicopters while working through any confusion that was present. But the pilots were conditioned to respond aggressively; in addition, they also had a rivalry with the F-16 pilots who had made all the kills after Desert Storm (as well as over Bosnia to this point) and would be entering the NFZ in 10 to 15 minutes.[30]

What will determine whether the situation over Iraq during the insurgency becomes like that over Iraq in Provide Comfort is the depth of command relationships. In 1994 the command relationships, although stipulated in procedures, were deteriorated. There was no agreement about who was in charge at any particular time. The players performed their missions by following procedures, which they then modified to better fit their missions. When all the players came together unexpectedly, there was no one with the situational awareness to step in and make command decisions. The CAOC does not yet have the ability to perform this task because it does not have capacity to communicate with all the aircraft during missions. None of the other TACS nodes have the ability to combine the air picture and sensor videos. Only when these two capabilities come together will there be an on-scene command presence with the ability to handle the shift from loose to tight coupling.

The problem with changing the roles of the aircrew is not just in the fact that crew members may drift from procedures but that their role may become inappropriate. The precision, information, sensor, and telecommunications technologies we have been discussing are making the CAOS much more capable, to the point where it may be overreaching the system's ability to keep up. At the same time, the people are being moved to more supervisory and less hands-on types of tasks. In her book *Safeware,* Nancy Leveson argues against the myth that machines make a system more reliable. Automation does not remove people from systems—it merely moves them to maintenance, repair, and higher-level supervisory control and decision making. It removes them from the immediate control of the energies of the system and locates them in central control rooms with only indirect information. This can make those involved less familiar with what is actually happening in the system and less able to intervene when necessary.[31]

That more advanced technology can dangerously lower the situational awareness of people in the CAOS was evidenced in the Black Hawk shootdown. The AWACS was tracking the helicopters until they entered mountainous terrain. At this point, the IFF return faded, and the air surveillance officer's display dropped the "H" symbol used to identify the helicopters, but the AWACS computer continued to move their symbol at the last known speed and direction. The air surveillance officer placed an "attention arrow" on the senior director's display to indicate an area of interest where the helicopters had been. But the senior director failed to acknowledge the arrow, and the computer dropped it after 60 seconds. Later, one minute before the F-15 pilots detected the helicopters on their radars, the AWACS crew dropped the helicopters' symbols from the scopes, and all reminders were gone.[32] The AWACS crew did not know exactly what was happening with the helicopters or why they had dropped from the scope. The same thing had happened earlier when the helicopters had landed, so they may have assumed that is what happened again. The crew was reduced to monitoring the automatic actions of the sophisticated radar and computer system. When the F-15 pilots checked in on the radio, the AWACS crew was unable to tell them there were helicopters in the area.[33]

With the change in the aircrew's role in the kill chain, the aircrew at times undertakes a similar supervisory role, with the potential for decreased situational awareness that entails. As we said before, when an aircrew drops a GPS-guided weapon on a target at night or in the weather, it is often unable to verify that the weapon is aimed at the correct target. The aircrew's job is to type in the coordinates and then drop the weapon when the symbols in their heads-up display line up. Humans are notoriously bad at transferring data by hand.

The same thing could happen in the AOC. We saw previously that there has been a move toward machine-to-machine interfaces, demonstrated by MITRE engineer Mike Butler's success at developing XML translators for machines for JEFX 04. The "cursor on target" program holds the potential to drastically improve the ability of the CAOS to share data and reduce the transference of data by hand. Concurrently, it also has the potential to change the jobs of those people working in the AOC to a much more supervisory role.

During JEFX 04, the officers in the TCT Cell were confronted by questions from contractors who were looking at ways to automate the functions of dynamic targeting. The officers were skeptical, and perhaps a bit defensive, about the feasibility of replacing their positions with a machine. For one thing, they were unable to specify a set of "business rules" that could be used to automate the decisions they were making and the actions they were taking.[34] As we saw in chapter 6, their actions and decisions are based on pieces of information from many different sources, including contextual information about the validity of other information or about the status of the team.

Even if the functions were automated, someone would still have to be accountable. This person would most likely lose visibility into the actions that the machines take and be less capable of intervening to stop potentially undesirable actions. The person would also be less capable of developing innovative work-arounds in situations that did not fit the business rules.

Of course, developing the ability to distribute actions and decisions can also avoid many hazardous situations. Scholars of network theory have shown that networks are incredibly resistant to failure from random attacks. They fail only after a critical number of nodes have been destroyed. However, in most networks all nodes are not equal. Most networks have stronger nodes, called *hubs*, which are connected to numerous nodes. If an attack is not random, but instead targeted against these hubs, the network can fail rather easily.[35] The AOC would definitely be considered a hub in the CAOS. If information processing can be distributed throughout the system rather than at the hubs, the network can be made more robust against failure.

Additionally, the distribution of roles has made the system more capable. We must keep in mind that changes in the aircrew's role have resulted from efforts to improve the quality of sensors that gather the information, processors that make sense of it, and weapons that make use of it. Precision weapons were developed during Vietnam to more effectively destroy hardened structures such as bridges.[36] In Desert Storm, these weapons were married with stealth technology to allow the air component to attack the enemy as a system versus concentrating on key targets as it had in WWII. During the conflicts of the 1990s, air commanders also found that these same weapons, paired with better sensors, allowed them to more precisely target within areas where there was danger of collateral damage, taking away the enemy's ability to use the city as a sanctuary. GPS guidance allowed them to deny the opponent the cover of night and bad weather. Time-sensitive targeting is aimed at negating the advantages of rapid movement and concealment. For TST to be successful, these technologies require many different players to work together to devise a solution for each attack. Thus, the pieces of the kill chain are more distributed. If the air component can solve the problem of allowing all the pieces to communicate and share information rapidly, network-centric warfare means the CAOS will become more effective and more resistant to attacks.

To this end, the Air Force is working on many solutions. Cursor-on-target and an alternative, gateways that tie systems together, will help solve the infrastructure problems. In addition, a major project of Carmen Corsetti, one of MITRE's JEFX managers, is to experiment with airborne Internet protocol (IP). This involves tying airborne platforms together so they could pass data and voice to anyone in a linked communications network governed by established conventions. Voice-over-Internet protocol could provide a way to ensure communications with all players in the system—voice communications could be sent to any player in the network, regardless of whether the communicating parties are within line-of-sight. With this capability, the air component might even have the ability to perform many of the AOC's command and control functions in the E-10A multisensor command and control aircraft (MC2A) when it comes online later. Clearly, this would also make it more difficult to secure the communications.

The purpose of this chapter has been to alert decision makers to the hidden consequences that may stem from the systemic changes described. Netting people together increases the number of unintended interactions that are possible. While this can be a great facilitator of innovation, it is also a potential cause of failure sequences. For military commanders, this causes the tension we have been studying. They have to be sensitive to the strategic-level feedback loops that may occur and impose constraints to ensure these are not activated—this would be one way the CAOS could have an accident. In imposing these constraints, commanders must keep in mind that they may be creating situations where individuals in the CAOS will drift from the established procedures during slow times, only to foil the effectiveness of the constraints and procedures when they are really needed.

Any attempts by leadership to treat pilots like cogs in a machine must acknowledge that there may be side effects to this latent capability and aggression. While it may be possible to address this situation through training, this mind-set would not be without a price—the loss of the very warrior qualities that have always been desirable in military leaders. As long as these traits are present in the aircrew, there will always be the chance that these human beings will act in innovative ways to increase their contribution to the war effort, potentially in ways that are contrary to the commanders' desires. Like the nuclear reactors or the electrical power grid, it may be a problem just waiting to happen.

Notes

1. Barabasi, *Linked*, 121–22.
2. Perrow, *Normal Accidents*, 60.
3. Fairley, "Unruly Power Grid," 25.
4. Perrow, *Normal Accidents*, 66.
5. Ibid., 70.
6. Ibid., 78. Perrow notes that these terms are not opposites, although his usage seems to denote such a relationship. His purpose is to describe the degree to which a sequence of events can be understood and predicted based on the perceived interactions in the system. Nonlinear and simple did not seem to apply to these characteristics.
7. Snook, *Friendly Fire*, 4–10.
8. Leveson, *New Approach*, 87–128.
9. Snook, *Friendly Fire*, 199–200.
10. Ibid., 182–200.
11. Ibid., 124–30.
12. Ibid., 188.
13. The idea that organizations do not implement policy as it was intended is not new; in fact, we have introduced the idea already in this work. One of the classic works on this subject is Allison's *Essence of Decision*. However, Snook introduces a new mechanism for this phenomenon: practical drift.
14. JP 3-09.3, *Joint Tactics*, V-23.
15. Department of Defense, "Executive Summary," 1–4.
16. Marr, interview. Maj Ian Marr, USAF, 19 SOS/DOI at the time of this writing, was a fire control officer on AC-130H gunships in OEF.
17. This may seem confusing to some readers. A theater combatant commander can set up a JSOTF alongside the conventional JTF if there is a significant job for the SOF to perform. The JSOTF would then have its own air component, the JSOAC, just like the JTF has its own air component, the joint force air component (commanded by the JFACC). In this case, there were multiple JSOTFs and multiple JSOACs in one of the JSOTFs.
18. Marr, interview.
19. Ibid; see also Department of Defense, "Executive Summary," 5–9.
20. Department of Defense, "Executive Summary," 7–8.
21. Marr, interview.
22. Department of Defense, "Executive Summary," 10.
23. Schwarzkopf with Petre, *It Doesn't Take a Hero*, 500.
24. Clancy with Horner, *Every Man a Tiger*, 497.

25. Jamieson, *Lucrative Targets*, 99–100, 104. The AC-130 incident, however, was to have significant impact down the road, as it sparked a revision of gunship C2 procedures.

26. Daily comments of General Horner, quoted in Cohen and Keaney, *Gulf War Air Power Survey*, vol. 2, pt. 1, *Operations*, 296.

27. Sams, interview; and Prior, interview (see chap. 8, n. 75).

28. Lanning, interview.

29. Tirpak, "Air Boss's Plan," 9.

30. Snook, *Friendly Fire*, 95–96; and Leveson, *New Approach*, 98.

31. Leveson, *Safeware*, 10–11.

32. Leveson, *New Approach*, 88–89.

33. There were other factors involved here as well. Snook points out this was a new crew and therefore not up to speed on the procedures used in this area.

34. Lt Col Larry Haskells, USAFR (TCT Cell attack coordinator for JEFX 04 and interdiction DO for OIF), interview by the author, Nellis AFB, NV, 28 July 2004. (Notes in author's personal collection.)

35. Barabasi, *Linked*, 111–22.

36. Mets, *Long Search for a Surgical Strike*, 9.

THIS PAGE INTENTIONALLY LEFT BLANK

Chapter 10

Conclusions and Implications

What a commander wants to take with him into war is a set of organizations that can learn while they execute their missions. What those organizations can learn in peacetime is not so much precisely what to do in war but how to learn, and learn quickly, what to do. . . .

However, there always will be a tension between organizational adaptability and organizational procedures in military command and control. . . .

Command and control personnel must, therefore, balance the need to respond to the situation against the equally important need to maintain a structure within which information can be organized and analyzed and decisions made and quickly communicated.

—*Gulf War Air Power Survey*

The incredible pace of technological development throughout the last decade and a half has not altered the fundamental truths about C2 of airpower, which are similar to the fundamental truths about the C2 of other military power. This CAOS we have studied is an intensely human system, as war is an intensely human experience, facilitated by technology. The information, telecommunications, sensor, and weapons technologies have altered the methods by which these humans perform their jobs. They have even changed to some extent the jobs that are performed. But they have not changed the fact that the commander's job is to get these humans to work together with others of different cultural backgrounds to accomplish an ill-defined mission in an environment of uncertainty. In our five different walks through the last four major US wars, we have seen an important pattern. At every level, the more a decision maker tried to use the near-complete information to manage the details of subordinates' actions, the less they were able to handle the inevitable uncertainty that accompanied war—the less they were able to act like a "learning organization." The system diagrams in chapter 3 are pared down to one simpler diagram that shows this pattern in figure 10, described later in this chapter.

This concept of a learning organization is the major point of the story. When decision makers were afforded time to adjust, they realized that ensuring their subordinates were empowered as well as constrained was the key to command and control. Most vividly, between Enduring Freedom and Iraqi Freedom, both policy makers and theater-level military commanders worked hard on developing command relationships that would allow them to remain out of the details of the ongoing military actions. More subtly but just as surely, the air component has evolved a method of pushing authority down as well. Sending aircraft up without targets and then having the TCT Cell work the targets in real time may appear to be an overcentralized process now because the TCT Cell works in the CAOC. But it is a way for the JFACC to avoid specifying the details of the missions in advance and relying instead on the lower levels to work together. The balance between learning and accountability requires depth in the command relationships.

This chapter lays out these conclusions in answer to the four questions we asked in the first chapter: (1) How has the information age affected the C2 of combat airpower? (2) Have these changes impacted the military's adherence to the doctrinal tenet of centralized control and decentralized execution? (3) Is there a general formula that better characterizes C2 of the system? and (4) Where are these changes heading?

How Has the Information Age Affected C2 of Combat Airpower?

A combination of political, organizational, and technological developments has brought the US military to a point where it is more vital than ever for commanders to intentionally balance empowerment and accountability. In the 1990s a change in the international security environment combined with stealth and precision technology advancements made airpower a favorite instrument of policy makers. Without a superpower peer, the United States could get involved in conflicts where there were less than vital interests at stake. The interests in these conflicts did not support high costs in terms of friendly or innocent lives lost; thus, airpower seemed to be the answer. Policy makers chose strategies that depended on their ability to control military action by ROEs and target approval because the results of air strikes could have been disastrous to their strategies.

Constraints from the strategic level affected the way the JFCs defined command relationships. In Kosovo, the stipulation that there would be no ground troops combined with the high-level target approval process drew General Clark into many of the details of the air strikes. In Afghanistan, the uniqueness of the CIA-military relationship and the ROEs about collateral damage had the same effect on General Franks. The more the constraints from the strategic level, the less the JFC empowered component commanders under him. The less these components were empowered, the less they coordinated with each other, regardless of their technological capability to communicate.

Within the air component, the JFACCs initially tried to stay out of ongoing missions. However, two parallel trends led to the development of the TCT Cell in the AOC. First, sensor-communication loops that the Air Force developed to help accomplish the complete control cycle also made it possible to direct the missions. In fact, the air component gained much more success at intervening in these missions than at assessing the aggregate results of operations. At the same time, it was called on to accomplish some politically sensitive missions, as noted above. This required someone to pull information together quickly and feed it to the strike aircraft. The same processes used for these missions were useful in others that required quick reaction, such as KI/CAS. The result is a very active cell on the Combat Operations floor that handles numerous real-time decisions about targeting airpower.

The use of sensor-communication loops and precision munitions led to a distribution of the tasks in the attack sequence, sometimes known as the kill chain. In the last three conflicts, most of the missions were accomplished by sending up aircrews without preplanned targets so they could respond to the fleeting targets that emerged during the battle. On some of these missions, the job of finding targets and compiling information to attack them was done by people distributed all over the globe. With a GPS-guided munition (or, in the future, sensor-aided weapons), the aircrew's job became one of delivering the munitions based on information provided by someone else. With new sensors on the aircraft, the job of the aircrew was sometimes to collect information for someone else's attack sequence. However, in many cases, the aircrew still needs to perform the whole sequence, so it cannot be simply reprogrammed to perform a different role. The result is an increase in the number and complexity of ways to accomplish the emerging target mission.

The fact that this distribution increases the potential for people to find alternative ways to exploit opportunities makes it a blessing or a curse. Depending on the type of war, a commander may want the aircrew to use this "latent potential" to go find new opportunities and exploit them, or the commander may want the aircrew to follow strict orders. The trouble with the second situation is that it depends too much on the ability of humans to monitor compliance. Evidence shows that, when the orders have not been strictly enforced because deviations did not make much difference, people drifted from established procedures. Then, when the system transitioned from loose coupling to tight coupling (where deviations can be fatal), global procedures meant to avoid accidents were nonexistent. There is also reason to believe this gets worse when humans are relegated to roles where they supervise machines—they become less able to intervene when needed. Somehow, the CAOS has to be given the capability to intentionally shift between being responsive to directives and adapting to opportunities.

Have Technological Changes Impacted the Military's Adherence to the Doctrinal Tenet of Centralized Control and Decentralized Execution?

Commanders must realize that the way to cope with the uncertainty involved in military operations is to build depth in the command relationships. Focusing on specific details rather than these relationships has the unintended consequence of making lower levels unresponsive to directives and unable to adapt to opportunities. Our system diagrams from chapter 3 illustrated this, but it was buried in the complexity of the CAOS.

We can now use them to construct a simpler model to show this tension. Because the diagrams noted areas where there were common components in different subsystems, we can follow the links to show the major feedback pattern that causes the tension between centralized and decentralized control.

Figure 10 shows that the tension is between the need to accomplish specific actions precisely and the need to create a learning organization. There is an obvious inner loop, called the *direct control loop*, which policy makers have to manage. But there is also a not-so-obvious balancing loop, called the *learning loop*, that they must also manage.

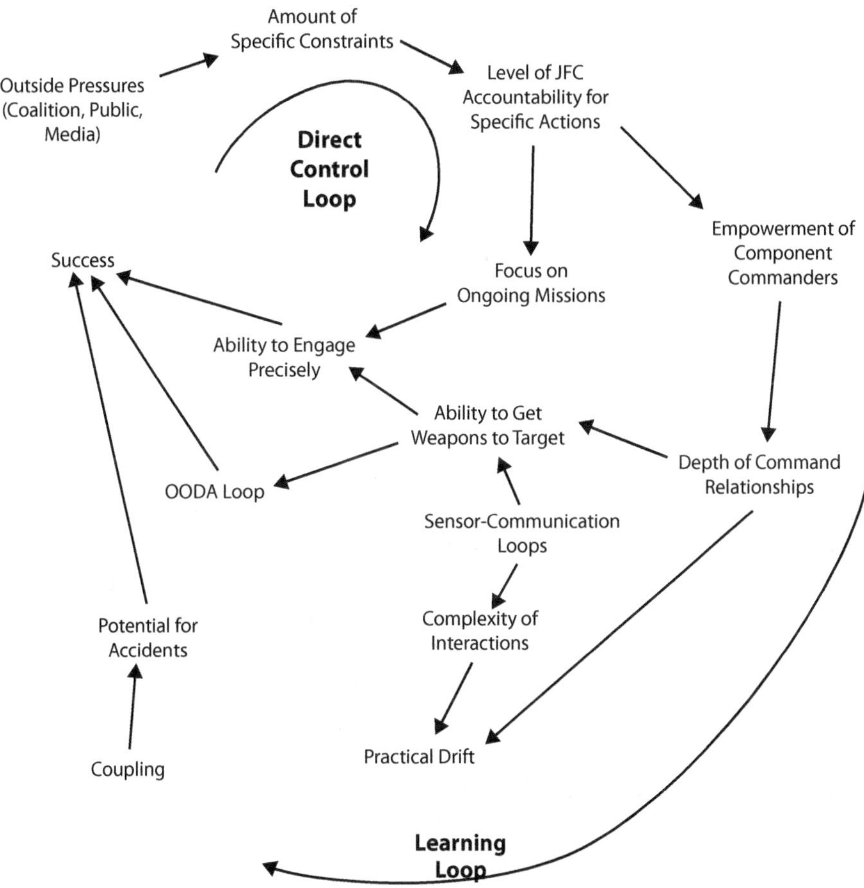

Figure 10. Overall command and control feedback pattern in the CAOS

Policy makers begin the cycle by determining the extent to which their strategy will depend on controlling the military through the use of specific constraints, as opposed to objectives and guidance (while leaving the specifics to the military). This is usually an unconscious decision that is tied to the—also usually unconscious—determination of the nature of the war. There are, of course, some of each of these methods embedded in each situation. But each war can be characterized by a predominance of one or the other method. We would say Desert Storm predominantly used objectives and guidance, whereas Allied Force tended to use specific constraints (a target-approval process at the strategic level, a prohibition against the use of ground forces, and strict ROEs about targeting). Policy makers use specific constraints when there are outside pressures to make the military action conform to some desirable outcome (or avoid some undesirable outcomes). Leaving the details to the military could jeopardize this, as we saw in the cases of the Al Firdos bunker and the Chinese Embassy.

The desired outcome from these constraints is that they should raise the accountability level for the undesirable actions, so the military actions produce politically desirable results. Indeed, we saw that targets and ROEs set at the strategic level became very high priority in the consciousness of the commanders in both Allied Force and Enduring Freedom. This raised the level of accountability of the JFC for the details of tactical actions; the JFC, in turn, had a high incentive to hold the authority for these actions. In these cases, this translated to a high level of target approval and the JFC's decision to hold the target development process at his level, with his staff instead of the war-fighting components. In theory, with the use of sensor-communication loops, the ability to target precisely would increase, leading to the politically desirable outcome.

We also saw unintended consequences from the use of specific constraints. Component commanders were afforded less authority than their doctrinal procedures recommended and were not empowered to the full extent of their capabilities. Consequently, they lost the ability to coordinate well with other components and did not set up the mechanisms that assure deep command relationships down to the tactical level. In an ironic twist, the ROEs and command relationships in Enduring

Freedom kept the targeting authority at General Franks's level, but this left him without the ability to ensure the actions of the SOTACs conformed to his strategy. There were no C2 nodes like the ASOC at the lower levels to allocate resources and enforce procedures, so when they were needed in Anaconda the controllers and aircrew had to fend for themselves. By contrast, between Enduring Freedom and Iraqi Freedom Franks and his component commanders worked hard on both command and personal relationships. Franks gave his component commanders more authority and also delegated authority over the targeting process and some TSTs to the air component.

In fact, this lack of depth of command relationships can potentially affect the achievement of the desired political outcome. The same sensor-communication loops that allow the JFC to intervene in ongoing operations also redistribute the tasks involved in the kill chain. As the interactions have become more complex, the paths to accomplishing a given mission have diversified. These variances could make it more difficult to hold people to global procedures, allowing them to engage in practical drift. Depending on the amount of coupling involved, this could lead to accidents or innovation, both of which could have a dramatic impact on the results.

With depth in the command relationships, this drift can be held to a minimum while the opportunities afforded by the sensor-communication loops are still exploited. The aircrews in Iraqi Freedom still felt the CAOC was involved in their decisions; however, the relationships that were set up allowed them to use their own discretion at times. While the crews were directed to the killboxes, they were left to find their own targets once there. When the CAOC contributed information that led to new targets, it was welcome.

Depth of command relationships facilitates the deliberate choice of the time and place to exploit opportunities while also avoiding drift. If command relationships are of sufficient depth, the aircrew will be aided in their tasks by the ASOC, ground controllers, AWACS, JSTARS, and others according to the procedures. However, if some of these relationships are not present or not strong, then there may be ambiguity about who is in charge. This was the case during Anaconda, when the AC-130 crew members found themselves being directed by three different C2 agencies, not one of which knew the entire story. No one was able to prioritize and direct aircraft to the fight. The Black Hawk shootdown is another instance where command relationships broke down. As was discussed, the Army helicopters were left out of the loop, and the AWACS crew was not really in command of the mission.

Is There a General Formula That Better Characterizes the System's C2?

The theoretical solution to these problems is a synthesis of the maxims that we have been exploring. The Air Force's tenet of centralized control and decentralized execution aims to give a single air commander the ability to make air operations conform to a strategy while leaving room for those closest to the battle to show initiative to overcome unforeseen obstacles emerging during the battle. This tenet suffers because it can imply a laissez-faire attitude toward execution—we have seen that it is important for the commander to be able to pull information together for his subordinates and to ensure they conform to the orders. Similarly, Huntington's "objective control" has been misconstrued to mean civilians should stay out of military matters. Cohen clarifies this misconception by suggesting that civilian leaders maintain a "bruising dialog" with the military to ensure it adheres to their overall strategy. Neither of these theorists says much about how to get and assess the results. Van Creveld helps to fill in this gap by advocating that commanders use technology to its fullest extent, institute a directed telescope to find out what is happening and make command decisions, but organize and train subordinates to operate in uncertainty.

Together these theories describe an optimum way to approach the cycle of control to avoid the pitfalls we have uncovered. To follow the general formula for control, a commander at any level should:

1. set the goals for the organizations that are to be unified under his or her command;
2. empower subordinates to come up with plans for their respective parts;

3. enter a bruising, running dialog to critique and correct subordinates' plans, essentially making them his or her own and ensuring the different parts are coordinated;
4. create depth in the command relationships by defining authority and providing situational awareness in the places where diverse organizations will need to coordinate;
5. use people and technology to create a directed telescope to track the actions and hold subordinates accountable; and
6. assess the effectiveness of the actions and the need for a change in plans.

In doctrinal terms, as a bumper sticker, "centralized control and decentralized execution" is still an excellent philosophy. As guidance, it suffers from imprecision, and it does not portray the complete control cycle as accurately as the above series of statements. However, the evidence from this study gives weight to even more specific recommendations. We should give commanders a better idea of the specific trade-offs. Let us be more specific in pointing out where current practices agree and disagree with our general formula and the trade-offs.

At the strategic level, the theater (JFC) level, and the component (JFACC) level, the exercise of control depends on answering questions about effects, coupling, and depth of command relationships.

Trade-offs at the Strategic Level

At the strategic level, policy makers have the difficult task of trying to define the nature of the war, setting goals and strategy for the war, and then ensuring the military action is coherent with these goals and strategy. The decision makers at this level include the president, secretary of defense, the Joint Chiefs of Staff, and the rest of the NSC. Congress and coalition governments are heavy players as well. The media, although not a strategic decision maker per se, also plays a big role by determining what the public sees and thereby helping to shape their perception. According to our general theory of control, the central decision makers should develop a broad, grand strategy, give the military goals and guidance for the war, force the military to come up with military plans, and then enter a bruising debate to shape those plans in accordance with the strategy. They should then develop a directed telescope to ensure the military follows those plans and to assess the results.

However, at the strategic level, strategy is very nebulous, depending as it does on the shifting perceptions of what is friendly and enemy or the public and government. Decision makers at this level cannot foresee everything that may affect the success of the strategy. They are forced to get information through a very slow and methodical military C2 channel but to be wary of feedback through relatively rapid, and sometimes not so methodical, media channels.

Decision makers at this level are therefore predisposed to use more direct methods of control. They can impose ROEs that limit the possible actions the military can take. They can force the military to clear actions through them—like the target-approval processes. They can develop the courses of action for the military, as the Johnson administration appears to have done with the Rolling Thunder operation. As we have shown, these actions carry unintended consequences.

Therefore, the policy makers need to consider two questions regarding the nature of the war: (1) whether they can determine the precise effects that will obtain the strategic goals, and (2) whether these effects require military actions that tightly couple the different organizations.

If there is a clear mechanism for success and it is possible to plan military actions in detail, then it may be possible to put constraints on the actions without adversely affecting them. These would normally be small, precise efforts like special operations actions, rescues, or limited strikes. The achievement of the military mission will normally be either secondary to or vitally dependent on achieving some other negative goal. For example, if it was more important to avoid an incident that would fracture NATO than to stop the ethnic cleansing in Kosovo, then the administration was correct to rule out ground troops and approve targets. But the decision makers should also realize that it will be difficult to shift gears from this mode of operation to a more conventional mode. In Afghanistan, the complex, but shallow, command relationships that resulted from tight controls in the beginning were unable to adjust to a more intense mode of operations in Anaconda.

If the mechanism for success is uncertain or depends on adjustment among the military organizations (e.g. heavy cooperation between air and ground forces), then it will be better to follow the general formula we have laid out. In these circumstances the strategic level needs the military to accomplish military goals and adapt to the changing battle. Policy makers should give the military goals and guidance, force it to come up with details it will perform, and then debate those details until they are satisfactory. They should then use sensor-communication loops to verify that the operations are going according to plan. In Desert Storm, when Secretary of Defense Cheney perceived the military was not taking the Scud Hunt seriously enough, he asked to see the ATO. When this was unsatisfactory, he demanded it be fixed—and it was, despite grumblings from the commanders. Abraham Lincoln had to fire four commanding generals until he found one that followed his strategy.

There is a subtle difference between this type of back-and-forth struggle and the outright stipulation of details. The former admits the difficulty of translating policy into action; the latter attempts to engineer the details of this translation. The former method forces the military to take ownership of the strategy; the latter invites it to lay blame elsewhere.

Trade-offs at the Theater Level

At the theater level, the JFC has the task of turning policy into military strategy. The JFC falls beneath the secretary of defense in the chain of command, but often receives the orders through the chairman of the Joint Chiefs of Staff. The joint chiefs, though not as influential today as they were prior to the Goldwater-Nichols Defense Reorganization Act, still wield some influence since they are the ones who train and equip the services to do their jobs. The JFC has a staff but also organizes component commanders to direct the forces in battle. According to our general formula, the JFC should organize the components, set up command relationships among them, give them objectives and guidance, force them to come up with plans to achieve these objectives, and grill them on the details until they are satisfactory. This should include ensuring the components develop depth in their command relationships by setting up C2 nodes to provide authority and information at all the places where forces will come into contact with each other. Then, the JFC should use sensor-communication loops as a directed telescope to ensure the operations proceed as planned and to assess the results.

In reality, the JFC is subject to the constraints levied by the strategic level. The joint commander can use the arguments laid out above to lobby for the preferred method of control. But the military is and should be subject to civilian control and must, in the end, salute smartly. Under such circumstances, as in Kosovo and Afghanistan, it is understandable that the JFC may want to keep a tight authority for those aspects for which accountability is required at the strategic level. This calls for the JFC to keep a close eye on the targeting process and even the operations. But in doing so, the JFC risks ending up with component commanders who are uncertain of or even frustrated with their role in the command structure. These are components that will not be able to transition easily to more complex operations in the future. Uncertain of their authority, they will be unable to structure command relationships below them so that, at the pilot and troop level, the confusion will be great if this transition occurs.

The JFC needs to consider two similar questions about the military strategy: (1) whether it is possible to plan the precise actions that will achieve the objectives, and (2) whether these plans will require tight coupling of the different components under the JFC's command. It is important to note that it is probably easier to have different strategies for different phases or objectives in the war than it is to change the nature of the war; therefore, the JFC may be able to adopt different methods of control in different phases of the war. The only caveat would be that this must be intentional so that the change is properly conveyed to the subordinates.

If it is possible to plan the actions in advance, and the different components are loosely coupled, then it may be possible for the JFC to maintain control of these actions at his level. In these cases, there may be no need to have fully empowered components because the JFC knows exactly what needs to happen—or not happen—and does not need to coordinate much at the tactical level. These instances would again be narrow in scope, such as a missile strike without the potential for follow-on operations. Even in these cases, it may be wise for the JFC to empower components but place them in the same building as the staff—in a sort of joint operations center. Then, in the case of a transition, the component commanders could relocate to their own headquarters, clearly marking a new phase.

If it is unclear how the operations will unfold after first contact, or if the plans require lots of adjustment among different components, then the JFC would be better served by the general formula. One of the most important trends we have seen in this book is bringing diverse players into contact with each other: airpower working indirectly with foreign troops with whom it has no contact; airpower working directly with special operations troops; remotely-located analysts contributing to the kill chain; and pilots becoming information suppliers using their sensor capabilities. All of this is made more urgent by the realization that these interactions must occur as rapidly as possible. The result has been that many of the contacts that occur in the course of an attack may be among people who are not familiar with each other and who may not have practiced working together. In these cases, it is important to develop depth in the command relationships so changes can be made on the scene without violating control procedures.

The JFC has the important job of ensuring these interactions occur in a way that strengthens command relationships. One way to look at this is that the JFC takes on the role of the designer of the organization that is the joint team. As designer, the JFC should figure out how all the players will be interacting and structure the relationships so these exchanges happen in the right ways.[1] This appears to be what happened between Enduring Freedom and Iraqi Freedom, when Franks worked with his component commanders to smooth out the processes. He redesigned the targeting process so that the air component was the lead, although Franks was still the approval authority. Furthermore, he designated supported and supporting commanders for each objective. Franks also came up with a matrix that delegated decision authority for certain types of time-sensitive targets. It appears these moves had the effect of empowering the component commanders to work together better than they had in Afghanistan—although the fact that it was a different war makes this hard to say for certain.

This function of the JFC becomes even more important as the war becomes less conventional. In the unconventional warfare that continues in both Afghanistan and Iraq to this day, the job of airpower is less the delivery of firepower than the delivery of troops, supplies, humanitarian aid, and information. Many nongovernmental organizations are often involved, and although they do not fall within the typical military command structure, they play an important part in the effort to make and keep the peace. Airpower should often be put in a supporting role to the things that are happening on the ground. But there are times, like the night the AC-130s worked with the Marines in Fallujah, when the aircrew may be in a position to provide more. The JFC may not be able to foresee these types of interactions. Just as with developing strategy, it is not necessary that the JFC be able to see exactly what will happen. The job of the designer is to set up an environment where the lower commanders anticipate these situations and prepare for them—and then to prod them until the JFC is confident the commanders have thought the relationships through. Focusing on specific actions stunts this process; focusing on the command relationships that handle the actions fosters it.

With respect to airpower, the biggest indicator this book pointed to was the target-approval process, both preplanned and real time. Managing the joint guidance, apportionment, and targeting process at the JFC level, as CENTCOM did in Enduring Freedom, was viewed by the air component as micromanagement. The arrangement Franks set up in Iraqi Freedom was more like our general formula—the air component led the process, but CENTCOM approved the results and reserved the right to interject a special category of targets. The story was similar with respect to approval of real-time targets. Holding approval for all time-sensitive targeting at the JFC level stifled the initiative of the air component in Enduring Freedom. In Iraqi Freedom, Franks delegated some of this authority to the air component. But at the same time, ADOCS made the air component's TCT Cell "think out loud" so CENTCOM could see what was happening.

Trade-offs at the Component Level

The component commanders have to take this process a step further. At this level, the decision makers are the combined/

joint force air, land, special operations, maritime (etc.) component commanders. These are the functional component commanders under the JFC. There are also service component commanders for the Army, Air Force, Navy, and Marines who provide the forces and logistics for the functional component commanders. Often the service component commanders are also the functional component commanders—the Air Force service component commander becomes the JFACC, the Army or Marine service component commander becomes the JFLCC, etc. Underneath these component commanders are the smaller units, to whom the component commanders should theoretically pass authority to plan specific attacks.

The JFACC must consider two questions. Is it possible to define the precise effects needed for specific missions? Will these effects require tight coupling of the different players? At this level, it is definitely possible for the JFACC to use different types of control for different missions.

When the mission can be planned in advance and requires little coupling, the details of the mission can be controlled by the AOC. Attacks on preplanned targets using only assets of one service (or at least only air component assets) may fall into this category. The ATO can specify precise parameters for the desired mean point of impact and munitions for these missions. Many air mobility missions, like resupply and humanitarian relief, may also apply.

However, when the mission is uncertain, or will require the close interaction of different organizations, the JFACC should use the general formula. In these cases, it is most important to develop enough depth in the command relationships that there is a command presence with situational awareness able to mediate among the different players and adjust the mission. Most examples of dynamic targeting, such as CAS and some types of air defense, should apply. Ideally, the JFACC would want to provide the resources—push CAS and TST missions—and give guidance, then provide the authority for subordinate commanders to plan and execute the missions. In many of these cases, "planning" may be very short, since the missions deal with emerging targets.

Subordinate commanders in the air component are not in a position to do this type of planning. In conventional ground combat, the component commanders can often break down their guidance by geographical area. In these cases, it may be appropriate to empower the subordinate units to develop their own strategy for their particular areas. This was the case in Iraqi Freedom, where V Corps worked the western attack axis and I MEF worked the eastern attack axis. Then the individual commanders just have to coordinate for the flanks and seams. Not so with airpower. Almost every air asset must be considered a theater-level asset, able to coordinate with almost any other air asset in a strike package depending on the situation. Each new sortie is a new battle fought with different teammates and in a new area. Wing and squadron commanders are not developers of operational strategy because they are called upon to execute different parts of that strategy on a day-to-day basis, as needed.

The way for the JFACC to develop the depth of command relationships we have called for is to invest in the TACS nodes a degree of command authority for portions of the air effort. In Iraqi Freedom, Moseley delegated some of this authority to the TCT Cell, which was located in the AOC. Right now it is not feasible to have these nodes anywhere other than in the AOC because that is the only place where a digitized picture of the assets in the battlespace comes together with video from the sensors and the ability to coordinate collaboratively with other players. It is not possible to put the digitized picture and the videos together in a multimedia format and send them to an aircraft. However, the ASOC made steps toward getting a smaller version of this capability. The ASOC in Iraqi Freedom did not have a working TBMCS, but did have the ADOCS, Hunter and JSTARS video, and all of the Army's digitized battlespace pictures.

The move to give the TACS nodes command authority would not be unprecedented. In Desert Storm, the AWACS had an Air Command Element on board to make real-time decisions about changes to the ATO. This was usually someone who worked in the Plans Division and was familiar with the details of the planning process.[2] But AWACS crew members related the person was not usually seen as a command presence—more of an aid to understanding the ATO. It was a difficult position to fill, and the program ended in the late 1990s. In Desert Storm and Iraqi

Freedom, the AWACS was sometimes put in the position to run TST-like missions because that was the quickest way.[3]

Whether consciously or not, the air component has already started to make the move toward giving guidance and resources and letting the lower levels work the details. Air component planners still put as much detail as they can into the ATO, when possible, because this ensures the strikes go more smoothly. The opening days of Desert Storm and Iraqi Freedom were acclaimed by flyers and planners alike for their efficiency.[4] Aircrews are much happier to have details to use in route planning, threat avoidance, and fuel consumption before the mission so they can prepare for all the things that might go wrong. But in the last three wars, the percentage of missions with target details in the ATO after the first couple of days has dropped significantly. After that, most missions became KI/CAS, TST, or other types of dynamic targeting missions. In Iraqi Freedom, the planners even put the mission intent in the ATO to guide the aircrews in using their discretion. The TCT Cell still handled the targeting for many of these missions, so it appeared as if the AOC was still involved. However, if the TCT Cell were moved away from the AOC with the authority it had in Iraqi Freedom, this would be a significant step in delegation to a lower level. This would also help the cell communicate with the strike aircraft more directly and rapidly.

If the technology were available, the next step would be to move mini-TCT Cells (or miniteams) to airborne platforms, each of which has responsibility for missions with specific ground or special operations units or in specific areas. If the E-10A MC2A were to attain the ability to give its crew the same digital picture, sensor pictures, and collaborative communications as the AOC, this would be an ideal place for these miniteams. This would leave overall control in the hands of a single air commander but give the ground commanders the comfort of a command presence dedicated to their geographic area. It would be smart for them to even have a liaison aboard, as they did in the ABCCC. The JFACC's AOC would still have the ability to see what these miniteams saw and did but could push the authority to them where appropriate. In turn, these commanders could delegate control to the aircrew where suitable.

Of course, airborne platforms are not the only answer. The same technology that would allow these platforms access to the information—airborne IP—would allow all information to be fed to the AOC beyond line-of-sight. Some would argue this eliminates the necessity to move a battle command cell out to an airborne platform. Indeed, all control nodes could theoretically be remoted some day.

The point here is that there is a reason to have separate nodes to which commanders have to delegate authority. Whether the platform is airborne or not, a commander needs to develop an organization where authority and responsibility are intentionally infused into lower nodes because each place where players interact needs a command authority.

Where Are These Changes Heading?

Let us extend the analysis into the future a bit. The trends we have seen in our brief period of airpower history can give us an idea of what will happen as technological development continues. When set against the backdrop of airpower history, none of our trends were unpredictable. The development of the JFACC, ISR sensors, increased digital transfer of information (and the means to process it), and GPS-guided weapons have added to the ability of commanders to direct the details of ongoing operations. Yet, commanders are learning to make decisions that push down the authority for these details. The technological capability for this decentralization will follow. We can expect the same pattern with other new information-related developments: use of the new technology first to enhance the ability of the commander; then, when the benefits become apparent, to enhance the ability to push down authority.

There is one area, however, where commanders cannot push the responsibility down. Even in our idealized model of C2, the commander at each level has the responsibility to determine how the chosen strategy will lead to success—the "mechanism" for success. We have proposed that the link from tactical actions to strategic success is so nebulous that the commanders should not undertake to specify this mechanism in too much detail. This would overly constrain the actions so they cannot adjust to reality if the mechanism is slightly off.

This difficulty in finding the mechanism for success has not gotten any easier during our period of study—airpower has not uncovered any "silver bullets." Indeed, if we were to say there has been any development in this area, it has been the realization that airpower must become more effective at denying enemy ground forces sanctuary—the sanctuaries of night, weather, hiding places, and time. Because airpower is not as limited geographically as land forces, it can be used to affect the enemy throughout the theater of conflict, instead of merely at the point where friendly ground forces can physically make contact with the enemy. But this realization came about through experimentation. It occurred while commanders were trying to figure out some way to accomplish their objectives amid constraints from the policy makers. It was the Scud Hunt in Desert Storm, the hunt for Serb troops in southern Kosovo, and the link between SOTACs and airpower in Enduring Freedom that showed this reality. None of these was the primary mechanism for victory in the mind of the air commanders at the time.

The difficulty is increased by the fact that concentrating on emerging targets makes it harder to assess whether the strategy is working. In fact, it becomes challenging to even assess the effectiveness of the attacks at hitting their targets. Preplanned attacks lend themselves well to assessment because there is a list of places to look for effects. When the primary method becomes adjustment in real time, it becomes difficult to even determine what happened, much less its success.

Therefore, we can say that the information age has not brought the US military any closer to the ability to determine how to affect the enemy. Strategy development and assessment are still the primary problems with which commanders must wrestle. So we would have to disagree when the Air Force Transformation Plan predicts that "before long, Joint Force Commanders will be able to select the precise targets necessary to achieve desired effects and they will focus on the quality, not the quantity, of targets attacked. They will be able to identify an adversary's key centers of gravity and relay that information to combat forces in near real time to attack the centers of gravity in the particular sequence that will be most devastating to the adversary."[5] The Air Force still has not found—and likely will not ever find—a way to win wars by finding the magic targets that produce disabling effects on the enemy. This will hold even as military forces move into an even more ubiquitous medium than air—that of information.

Thankfully, Air Force leaders have not acted as if that is all they are after. While they have always put forth a plan to win the war with airpower alone, they have striven to find and use whatever works, even though in most cases it is not what the air component was prepared to do. In Desert Storm, the opening air campaign arguably brought Iraq to the point where its army was impotent. In Allied Force, the increase in attacks on Milosevic's sources of individual wealth and power in Belgrade arguably had a great effect on his decision to capitulate. But in both of these cases, airpower also took part in other efforts that contributed to the final outcome. The planning for Iraqi Freedom was a decidedly joint venture, where the components learned how they would support each other rather than searching for the magic plan that would negate the need for each other. Although it probably would have helped to catch Saddam Hussein in one of the over 50 leadership attacks, and the effort arguably made him less effective at commanding his forces, it is now obvious that his absence did not spell the end of the war.[6] Though airpower was a major contributor to the rapid success in the conventional part of the war, the enemy was able to turn the war into an insurgency in which airpower's strengths are not as advantageous. Airpower must now play a largely supporting role in helping the troops on the ground by gathering information; providing platforms for command, control, and communications; and moving and resupplying the ground troops.

So in the end, nothing has changed or will change about the fundamental challenge of command and control of airpower. Airpower must still be flexible and responsive enough to adapt to what is happening in the battlespace, but precise and obedient enough to avoid creating undesirable incidents that foil the whole strategy. Let us take a look at some ways that technological development could aid in this quest for balance, based on the lessons we have discovered.

The increased use of unmanned aerial vehicles expands the amount of airpower that is automated and controllable from a central location. The generally accepted strengths of UAVs are endurance, persistence, and expendability. Endurance stems from their capacity to be made much lighter without consideration of human inhabitants; therefore, they can remain aloft longer. Persistence and expendability are related: UAVs can remain in an area longer without risking a human life. Thus, every experienced commander sees in them the ability to penetrate and soften enemy defenses prior to sending in the more risky and expensive manned aircraft.

There is another important characteristic to consider: UAVs do nothing but follow orders (right now, at least). They are not subject to morale issues and need for empowerment that we have addressed previously. In fact, unmanned systems would be a good choice where the object is to avoid mistakes rather than react quickly. When UAVs are involved, the decision makers can view the video rather than having to assemble information from a radio conversation. There is no human being in the vehicle loitering over hostile territory and getting frustrated while awaiting the decision. If the unmanned systems were armed, the decision makers would not waste time trying to talk an aircrew onto the target. Manned aircraft could be concentrated in those areas where discretion can be allowed. Of course, those are usually the more dangerous areas, since they are the ones where the enemy is most concentrated.

UAVs will always need to be supervised by humans for accountability and to make them more flexible. While the supervision can be done at the centers, this puts an extra burden on the AOC staff just when the Air Force is trying to reduce the size of this critical node. It also concentrates all control and execution in a single place, making any hierarchical distinctions fuzzy. The air component had been working on allowing the Predator controllers to work directly with the strike aircraft, beginning with the modification to the AC-130s, and then training the Predator operators to control fighters. If some of the dynamic targeting duties are moved out to lower TACS nodes, as we have discussed, those nodes could also be logical places to control the UAVs. The key will be getting the information from multiple sensors to the airborne or ground-based node. The commander at the control node would still have the option of allowing the individual Predator operators to work directly with the strike aircraft. This could eventually include manned strike aircraft escorting unmanned platforms.

Munitions development may blur the line between manned and unmanned systems. There are new developments in weapons that can loiter in an area, detect targets, and selectively attack the targets after launch. The CBU-105 sensor-fused weapon is an example. Right now, these weapons do not take inputs from off-board sensors after launch, so they are dependent on prelaunch positioning and postlaunch sensor performance to find targets. As the munitions become smarter, they will need increasingly sophisticated fail-safe modes, probably including data link of the information the sensor is using for discrimination. This would indeed make them similar to UAVs, except for the inability to control their flight path.

Space sensors are another area where automation will increase. The capability of these systems did not seem to increase appreciably during the writing of this book. However, the use of the information from them did. In the last two conflicts, space was a consideration in the earliest stages of planning, when policy makers bought all the available bandwidth over the theaters of war. It will increasingly become an operational consideration, now that the precedent has been set to give the JFACC the ability to control tasking of the assets in-theater. This was a command relationship similar to putting Marine aircraft on the ATO, only in a much bigger way.

The future may, of course, hold more of a role for space. There is the potential for force applied from space—to deny an enemy's ability to use its space systems or even to create effects on the earth. This would be full remote control warfare and would, therefore, be controllable at very high levels. In the beginning, it would no doubt receive attention from policy makers because of the lack of precedent. Force from space to create effects on the surface would be especially subject to this scrutiny.[7] But as far as C2 is concerned, weapons deployed from space are little different than weapons launched from a CIA Predator. There are organizational barriers to setting up the command relationships, but these should be overcome just as they were with the Predator. The use of both sensors and weapons from space should eventually be delegated to the same levels we are recommending for the Predator—the AOC or an even lower-level control node.

This, of course, requires much better information-sharing capability than is possible today. Relying heavily on the ability to build machine-to-machine interfaces using XML and Web services technology as we discussed, the Air Force is moving toward the ability to send information among airborne platforms using IP. An airborne IP network would enable beyond-line-of-sight communication of information. The Air Force is also developing gateways that forward the current data links beyond line of sight. In the AOC, the Air Force is trying to make its information systems Web-based so they are more easily shared with and updated by multiple remote locations.

As we have already pointed out, even network and information-sharing success will not guarantee data integration. Undoubtedly, the AOC will still have trouble getting the correct information to assess results. In fact, if the dynamic targeting cell is broken off, out of sight of the AOC, those in the AOC may be even more likely to develop their own local work-arounds that cause the assessors headaches when they try to reconstruct the battlespace actions.

Increased communication avenues will, however, allow deeper command relationships. It will provide C2 nodes closer to the battlespace with direct access to all of the information and players. The ability to fuse the information will be one level closer to the strike aircraft, in physical proximity and direct communications with the aircrew engaged in combat missions. For aircrews, which regularly converge from geographically remote locations to perform a mission together, an MC2A would be a command presence, as opposed to a communications relay. If ground commanders were to have representatives on board, the command authority of the node would be strengthened.

Creating a command presence with AOC-like information one level removed from the AOC will accentuate the importance of making decisions about delegating authority to strengthen command relationships. The AOC will have to use our control principles to give the MC2A or ground control node crew guidance, maintain awareness of their actions, and assess the results. The control node crew will have to make similar decisions about releasing authority to the strike aircraft and allowing strike aircraft to work directly with the other sensors.

Finally, many analysts propose that the future of C2 is nodeless. The goal, they say, is to achieve "self-synchronization" of forces, where two or more networked entities with a shared awareness and a rule set can execute a value-adding interaction without the need to waste time with formal requests for support and communication of position information.[8] It is true that such a capability would be helpful, particularly in those areas, like CAS, where different entities are performing mutually supportive roles.

This overlooks some of the lessons we have learned in the information age. Even if it is possible to develop common physical representations of the battlespace, "shared awareness" is a long shot. The technology that was developed and employed during the period we have reviewed brought information to more people—it did not help that these people think the same way about the information. When different players bring different solutions to the same situation, there is the potential for system accidents. This is only growing more likely as the number of participants increases. The development and employment of technology are increasingly breaking the overall task of conducting military action into smaller, more focused tasks that must be combined. Many of the people whose work is combined in a single engagement do not even know what others are involved. Fewer of the humans working in the system have a complete grasp of the overall sequence of events that leads to the accomplishment of an engagement. This combination of tasks does not happen automatically—and it would be dangerous to make it so. If humans will always be accountable for the actions, then humans must be given better visibility into why the actions are occurring.

War is an ugly thing. It is started, commanded, and fought by humans, with all of their passions and shortcomings. During war, humans have to motivate other humans to do things that are against their nature. In one case, this means getting them to put aside the natural survival urge and risk death for some distant cause. In another, this means keeping them from being too violent where this violence contradicts moral or practical considerations. Command and control must handle both of these, while also realizing its own shortcomings. Even if the technology becomes available to make the CAOS nodeless, it cannot be. Likewise, should future innovation enable commanders to access virtually comprehensive and flawless information, they cannot always act on it. C2 must balance the need to empower people to adapt and overcome new situations with the need to hold them accountable. The way to do this is by developing depth in the command relationships that tie people together. Technology has enhanced the visibility of this imperative, making it increasingly important to determine who can make decisions.

Notes

1. Senge, *Fifth Discipline*, 298–300.
2. Feinstein, interview.
3. Hodgdon to the author, e-mail, 28 Dec. 2004.
4. Feinstein, interview; and Cline, interview (see chap. 5, n. 69).
5. HQ USAF/XPXC, *U.S. Air Force Transformation*, xii.
6. One cannot dismiss the idea that if Saddam Hussein had been caught or killed early in the war, the insurgency would not have gotten started, but neither can one reliably count on it.
7. In WWII, both Great Britain and Germany had doctrine and capability that allowed them to bomb each other's cities, based on WWI and the Spanish Civil War. But neither did during the initial period of the Battle of Britain because neither wanted to set off the chain reaction. Then, when errant German bombs missed their seaport targets and hit a British city, the British retaliated by bombing Berlin. The Germans, in turn, retaliated by bombing London, and the strategic bombing campaign was in full force.
8. Alberts, Garstka, and Stein, *Network Centric Warfare*, 175–77.

THIS PAGE INTENTIONALLY LEFT BLANK

Abbreviations

AAF	Army Air Forces
ABCCC	airborne battlefield command and control center
AC2A	Aerospace Command and Control Agency
ACO	airspace control order
ACP	airspace control plan
ADOCS	Automated Deep Operations Coordination System
AFATDS	Advanced Field Artillery Tactical Data System
AFC2ISRC	Air Force Command and Control, Intelligence, Surveillance, and Reconnaissance Center
AFDD	Air Force doctrine document
AFI	Air Force instruction
AFM	Air Force manual
ALO	air liaison officer
AOC	air and space operations center
AOD	air operations directive
ARCENT	United States Army Central Command
ASC2A	Air and Space Command and Control Agency
ASOC	air support operations center
ASR	air support request
ATACMS	Army Tactical Missile System
ATO	air tasking order
AU	Air University
AWACS	Airborne Warning and Control System
BCD	battlefield coordination detachment
BCL	battlefield coordination line
BDA	battle damage assessment
C2	command and control
C4ISR	command, control, communications, computers, intelligence, surveillance, and reconnaissance
CAFMS	computer-assisted force management system

CAOC	combined air operations center
CAOS	Combat Air Operations System
CAS	close air support
CCO	chief of combat operations
CENTAF	Central Command Air Forces
CENTCOM	Central Command
CFACC	combined force air component commander
CFC	combined force commander
CFLCC	combined forces land component commander
CIA	Central Intelligence Agency
CINC	commander in chief
CJCS	Chairman of the Joint Chiefs of Staff
CJTF	combined joint task force
CLIOS	complex, large-scale, integrated, open system
COCOM	combatant command authority
COP	common operational picture
CSAF	chief of staff, US Air force
CTAPS	Contingency Theater Automated Planning System
DASC	direct air support center
DOD	Department of Defense
EFX	Expeditionary Force Experiment
EWO	electronic warfare officer
FAC(A)	forward air controller (airborne)
FM	field manual
FOFA	follow-on forces attack
FS	fighter squadron
FSCL	fire support coordination line
FW	fighter wing
GCCS	Global Command and Control System
GPS	global positioning system
HTML	hypertext markup language

IADS	Integrated Air Defense System
ID	infantry division
IFF	identification, friend or foe
IP	Internet protocol
ISR	intelligence, surveillance, and reconnaissance
IT	information technology
ITS	Interim Targeting Solution
JAC	Joint Analysis Center
JCS	Joint Chiefs of Staff
JDAM	Joint Direct Attack Munition
JEFX	Joint Expeditionary Force Experiment
JFACC	joint force air component commander
JFC	joint force commander
JFLCC	joint force land component commander
JGAT	joint guidance, apportionment, and targeting
JIPTL	joint integrated prioritized target list
JP	joint publication
JSOAC	joint special operations air component
JSOTF	joint special operations task force
JSTARS	Joint Surveillance Target Attack Radar System
JTAC	joint tactical air controller
JTCB	joint targeting coordination board
JTF	joint task force
JTSTM	Joint Time-Sensitive Targets Manager
JTT	Joint Targeting Toolkit
KEZ	Kosovo Engagement Zone
KI	killbox interdiction
KLA	Kosovo Liberation Army
LANTIRN	low-altitude navigation and targeting infrared for night
LGB	laser-guided bomb
MAAP	master air attack plan

MAP	master attack plan
MC2A	multisensor command and control aircraft
MEF	Marine expeditionary force
MIT	Massachusetts Institute of Technology
MITRE	Massachusetts Institute of Technology Research
MLRS	multiple-launch rocket system
NAC	North Atlantic Council
NATO	North Atlantic Treaty Organization
NCW	network-centric warfare
NFZ	no-fly zone
NSC	National Security Council
OAF	Operation Allied Force
ODA	operational detachment-Alpha
OEF	Operation Enduring Freedom
OIF	Operation Iraqi Freedom
OODA	observe, orient, decide, act
OPC	Operation Provide Comfort
OPCON	operational control
PSAB	Prince Sultan Air Base (Saudi Arabia)
QRF	quick reaction force
RAF	Royal Air Force
ROE	rules of engagement
RTS	real-time targeting system
SAC	Strategic Air Command
SAF	secretary of the Air Force
SAM	surface-to-air missile
SAR	synthetic aperture radar
SAS	Special Air Service
SCAR	strike coordination and reconnaissance
SCIF	sensitive compartmented information facility
SEAD	suppression of enemy air defenses

SEAL	sea-air-land
SEATO	Southeast Asia Treaty Organization
SecDef	Secretary of Defense
SIPRNET	SECRET Internet Protocol Router Network
SO	special operations
SOF	special operations forces
SOP	standard operating procedure
STO	space tasking order
SWC	Space Warfare Center
TACC	tactical air control center
TACON	tactical control
TACP	tactical air control party
TACS	theater air control system
TADIL	tactical digital information link
TBMCS	theater battle management core system
TCT	time-critical targeting
TLAM	Tomahawk land attack missile
TOC	tactical operations center
TST	time-sensitive target/targeting
TWM	Target Weaponeering Module
UAV	unmanned aerial vehicle
UN	United Nations
USA	United States Army
VTC	video teleconference
WMD	weapons of mass destruction
WOC	wing operations center
WWI	World War I
WWII	World War II
WWMCCS	Worldwide Military Command and Control System
XML	extensible markup language

THIS PAGE INTENTIONALLY LEFT BLANK

Bibliography

Books

Alberts, David S., John J. Garstka, and Frederick P. Stein. *Network Centric Warfare: Developing and Leveraging Information Superiority*, 2nd ed. (revised). Washington, DC: DOD C4ISR Cooperative Research Program, 1999.

Allard, Lt Col Kenneth C., USA. *Command, Control, and the Common Defense*. New Haven, CT: Yale University Press, 1990.

Allison, Graham T. *Essence of Decision: Explaining the Cuban Missile Crisis*. New York: Harper Collins, 1971.

Arquilla, John, and David Ronfeldt. "The Advent of Netwar (Revisited)." In Arquilla and Ronfeldt, eds., *Networks and Netwars*, 1–25.

———. "Looking Ahead: Preparing for Information-Age Conflict." In *In Athena's Camp: Preparing for Conflict in the Information Age*. Edited by John Arquilla and David Ronfeldt. Santa Monica, CA: RAND, 1997.

———, eds. *Networks and Netwars: The Future of Terror, Crime, and Militancy*. Santa Monica, CA: RAND, 2001.

Barabasi, Alberto-Laszlo. *Linked: The New Science of Networks*. Cambridge, MA: Perseus Publishing, 2002.

Bertalanffy, Ludwig von. *General System Theory: Foundations, Development, Applications*. Revised ed. New York: George Braziller, 1969.

Biddle, Stephen. *Afghanistan and the Future of Warfare: Implications for Army and Defense Policy*. Monograph, ISBN 1-58487-107-5. Carlisle, PA: Strategic Studies Institute, US Army War College, Nov. 2002. http://www.carlisle.army.mil/usassi/welcome.htm.

Bowden, Mark. *Black Hawk Down: A Story of Modern War*. New York: Penguin Books, 2000.

Builder, Carl H. *The Masks of War: American Military Styles in Strategy and Analysis*. Baltimore: Johns Hopkins University Press, 1989.

Byman, Daniel L., Matthew C. Waxman, and Eric Larson, *Air Power as a Coercive Instrument.* Santa Monica, CA: RAND, 1999.

Campen, Alan D., ed. *The First Information War: The Story of Communications, Computers, and Intelligence Systems in the Persian Gulf War.* Fairfax, VA: AFCEA International Press, 1992.

Castells, Manuel. *The Rise of the Network Society.* 2nd ed. Malden, MA: Blackwell, 2000.

Chandler, Alfred T., Jr. *The Visible Hand: The Managerial Revolution in American Business.* Cambridge, MA: Harvard University Press, 1977.

Clancy, Tom, with Gen Chuck Horner, USAF, retired. *Every Man a Tiger.* New York: Berkley Books, 2000.

Clark, Gen Wesley K., USA, retired. *Waging Modern War: Bosnia, Kosovo, and the Future Combat.* New York: Public Affairs, 2001.

Clausewitz, Carl von. *On War.* Edited and translated by Michael Howard and Peter Paret. Princeton, NJ: Princeton University Press, 1989.

Clodfelter, Mark. *The Limits of Air Power: The American Bombing of North Vietnam.* New York: Free Press, 1989.

Cohen, Eliot A. *Supreme Command: Soldiers, Statesmen, and Leadership in Wartime.* New York: Free Press, 2002.

Cooling, Benjamin Franklin, ed. *Case Studies in the Achievement of Air Superiority.* Washington, DC: Air Force History and Museums Program, 1994.

———. *Case Studies in the Development of Close Air Support.* Washington, DC: Office of Air Force History, 1990.

Conetta, Carl. *Strange Victory: A Critical Appraisal of Operation Enduring Freedom and the Afghanistan War.* Cambridge, MA: Commonwealth Institute Project on Defense Alternatives Research Monograph no. 6, 30 Jan. 2002. http://www.comw.org/pda/0201strangevic.pdf.

Coyle, Frank P. *XML, Web Services, and the Data Revolution.* Boston: Addison-Wesley, 2002.

Daalder, Ivo H. *Getting to Dayton: The Making of America's Bosnia Policy.* Washington, DC: Brookings Institution Press, 2000.

Douhet, Giulio. *The Command of the Air*. Translated by Dino Ferrari. Washington, DC: Air Force History and Museums Program, 1998.

Franks, Gen Tommy, USA, retired, with Malcom McConnell. *American Soldier*. New York: HarperCollins, 2004.

Futrell, Robert. *The United States Air Force in Korea, 1950–1953*. Washington, DC: Office of Air Force History, 1983.

Gaddis, John Lewis. *The Strategies of Containment: A Critical Appraisal of Postwar American National Security Policy*. New York: Oxford University Press, 1982.

George, Alexander, and William Simons. *The Limits of Coercive Diplomacy*. 2nd ed. San Francisco: Westview Press, 1994.

Gordon, Michael R., and Gen Bernard E. Trainor, USMC. *The Generals' War: The Inside Story of the Conflict in the Gulf*. New York: Little, Brown and Company, 1995.

Gray, Colin S. *Modern Strategy*. New York: Oxford University Press, 1999.

Haave, Col Christopher E., USAF, and Lt Col Phil M. Haun, USAF, eds. *A-10s over Kosovo: The Victory of Airpower over a Fielded Army as Told by the Airmen Who Fought in Operation Allied Force*. Maxwell AFB, AL: Air University Press, 2003.

Hammond, Grant T. *The Mind of War: John Boyd and American Security*. Washington, DC: Smithsonian Institution Press, 2001.

Herring, George C. *America's Longest War: The United States and Vietnam, 1950–1975*. 2nd ed. New York: Alfred A. Knopf, 1986.

Hughes, Daniel J. and Harry Bell, eds. *Moltke on the Art of War: Selected Writings*. Translated by Hughes and Bell. Novato, CA: Presidio Press, 1993.

Huntington, Samuel P. *The Soldier and the State: The Theory and Politics of Civil-Military Relations*. New York: Vintage Books, 1964.

Hutchins, Edwin. *Cognition in the Wild*. Cambridge, MA: MIT Press, 1995.

Jamieson, Perry D. *Lucrative Targets: The U.S. Air Force in the Kuwaiti Theater of Operations*. Washington, DC: Air Force History and Museums Program, 2001.

Jervis, Robert. *Perception and Misperception in International Politics*. Princeton, NJ: Princeton University Press, 1976.

Keaney, Thomas A., and Eliot A. Cohen. *Revolution in Warfare? Air Power in the Persian Gulf*. Annapolis, MD: Naval Institute Press, 1995.

Kennett, Lee. *The First Air War, 1914–1918*. New York: Free Press, 1991.

Lambeth, Benjamin S. *NATO's Air War for Kosovo: A Strategic and Operational Assessment*. Santa Monica, CA: RAND, 2001.

———. *The Transformation of American Air Power*. Ithaca, NY: Cornell University Press, 2000.

Latour, Bruno. *Science in Action: How to Follow Scientists and Engineers through Society*. Cambridge, MA: Harvard University Press, 1987.

Leonhard, Robert R. *The Principles of War for the Information Age*. Novato, CA: Presidio Press, 2000.

Leveson, Nancy G. *Safeware: System Safety and Computers*. Reading, MA: Addison-Wesley, 1995.

March, James G. *A Primer on Decision Making: How Decisions Happen*. New York: Free Press, 1994.

Mark, Eduard. *Aerial Interdiction in Three Wars*. Washington, DC: Center for Air Force History, 1994.

McMaster, Maj H. R., USA. *Dereliction of Duty: Lyndon Johnson, Robert McNamara, the Joint Chiefs of Staff, and the Lies That Led to Vietnam*. New York: HarperPerennial, 1997.

McNamara, Lt Col Stephen J., USAF. *Airpower's Gordian Knot: Centralized vs. Organic Control*. Maxwell AFB, AL: Air University Press, 1994.

McNeill, William H. *The Pursuit of Power: Technology, Armed Force, and Society since A.D. 1000*. Chicago: Chicago Press, 1982.

Mets, Col David R., USAF, retired. *The Long Search for a Surgical Strike: Precision Munitions and the Revolution in Military Affairs*. CADRE Paper no. 12. Maxwell AFB, AL: Air University Press, 2001.

Michel, Col Marshall L., III, USAF, retired. *The Eleven Days of Christmas: America's Last Vietnam Battle*. San Francisco: Encounter Books, 2002.

Mierzejewski, Alfred C. *The Collapse of the German War Economy, 1944–1945: Allied Air Power and the German National Rail-*

way. Chapel Hill, NC: University of North Carolina Press, 1988.

Mindell, David A. *Between Human and Machine: Feedback, Control, and Computing before Cybernetics*. Baltimore: Johns Hopkins University Press, 2002.

Mitchell, Brig Gen William, USA. *Winged Defense: The Development and Possibilities of Modern Air Power—Economic and Military*. New York: Dover Publications, 1988.

Momyer, Gen William W., USAF, retired. *Airpower in Three Wars*. Washington, DC: Department of the Air Force, 1978.

Pape, Robert A. *Bombing to Win: Airpower and Coercion in War*. Ithaca, NY: Cornell University Press, 1996.

Pearson, David E. *The World Wide Military Command and Control System: Evolution and Effectiveness*. Maxwell AFB, AL: Air University Press, 2000.

Perrow, Charles. *Normal Accidents: Living with High-Risk Technologies*. Princeton, NJ: Princeton University Press, 1999.

Reynolds, Col Richard T., USAF. *Heart of The Storm: The Genesis of the Air Campaign against Iraq*. Vol. 1. Maxwell AFB, AL: Air University Press, 1995.

Schelling, Thomas C. *Arms and Influence*. New Haven, CT: Yale University Press, 1966.

Schwarzkopf, Gen H. Norman, with Peter Petre. *It Doesn't Take a Hero: The Autobiography of General H. Norman Schwarzkopf*. New York: Bantam Books, 1992.

Senge, Peter M. *The Fifth Discipline: The Art and Practice of the Learning Organization*. New York: Currency Doubleday, 1994.

Sharp, Adm Ulysses S. G., USN, retired. *Strategy for Defeat: Vietnam in Retrospect*. Novato, CA: Presidio Press, 1998.

Sherry, Michael. *The Rise of American Air Power: The Creation of Armageddon*. New Haven, CT: Yale University Press, 1987.

Showalter, Dennis. *Railroads and Rifles: Soldiers, Technology and the Unification of Germany*. Hamden, CT: Archon Books, 1975.

Simpkin, Richard, in association with John Erickson. *Deep Battle: The Brainchild of Marshal Tukhachevskii*. New York: Brassey's, 1987.

Smith, Edward A., Jr. *Effects Based Operations: Applying Network Centric Warfare in Peace, Crisis, and War*. Washington, DC:

Department of Defense Command and Control Research Program, Nov. 2002. http://www.dodccrp.org/publications/pdf/Smith_EBO.PDF.

Snook, Scott A. *Friendly Fire: The Accidental Shootdown of U.S. Black Hawks over Northern Iraq.* Princeton, NJ: Princeton University Press, 2000.

Sterman, John D. *Business Dynamics: Systems Thinking and Modeling for a Complex World.* Boston: McGraw-Hill, 2000.

Stueck, William. *The Korean War: An International History.* Princeton, NJ: Princeton University Press, 1995.

Thies, Wallace J. *When Governments Collide: Coercion and Diplomacy in the Vietnam Conflict, 1964–1968.* Berkeley, CA: University of California Press, 1980.

Thompson, James D. *Organizations in Action.* New York: McGraw-Hill, 1967.

van Creveld, Martin. *Command in War.* Cambridge, MA: Harvard University Press, 1985.

Weick, Karl E. *Sensemaking in Organizations.* Thousand Oaks, CA: Sage, 1995.

Werrell, Kenneth P. *Blankets of Fire: U.S. Bombers over Japan during World War II.* Washington, DC: Smithsonian Institution Press, 1996.

———. *Chasing the Silver Bullet: U.S. Air Force Weapons Development from Vietnam to Desert Storm.* Washington, DC: Smithsonian Books, 2003.

Williams, Phil. "Transnational Criminal Networks." In Arquilla and Ronfeldt, eds., *Networks and Netwars,* 61–97.

Wilson, James Q. *Bureaucracy.* New York: Basic Books, 1989.

Winnefeld, James A., and Dana J. Johnson. *Joint Air Operations: Pursuit of Unity in Command and Control, 1942–1991.* Annapolis, MD: Naval Institute Press, 1993.

Wood, Derek, and Derek Dempster. *The Narrow Margin: The Battle of Britain and the Rise of Air Power, 1930–1940.* Revised ed. Washington, DC: Smithsonian Institution Press, 1990.

Woodward, Bob. *Bush at War.* New York: Simon and Schuster, 2002.

———. *Plan of Attack.* New York: Simon and Schuster, 2004.

Worden, Col Michael, USAF. *Rise of the Fighter Generals: The Problem of Air Force Leadership, 1945–1982.* Maxwell AFB, AL: Air University Press, 1998.

Periodicals

Ackerman, Robert K. "Operation Enduring Freedom Redefines Warfare." *Signal* 57: no. 1 (Sept. 2002): 3–5.

———. "Technology Empowers Information Operations in Afghanistan." *Signal* 56: no. 7 (Mar. 2002): 17–20.

Arkin, William M. "The Rules of Engagement." *Los Angeles Times*, 21 Apr. 2002. http://www.latimes.com (accessed 21 Apr. 2002).

Butler, Amy. "As A-10 Shines in Iraq War, Officials Look to JSF for Future CAS Role." *Inside the Air Force*, 23 May 2003, 1.

———. "Iraq War Underscores Need for Improved and Standardized AOCs." *Inside the Air Force*, 16 May 2003, 3.

Cappacio, Tony. "JSTARS Led Most Lethal Attacks on Serbs." *Defense Week* 20 (6 July 1999): 13.

———. "U.S. Launched More Than 50 'Time Sensitive' Strikes in Iraq." DOD's *Current News Early Bird*. http://ebird.dtic.mil (accessed 14 Apr. 2003).

Carter, Phillip. "The Road to Abu Ghraib." *Washington Monthly*, Nov. 2004. http://www.washingtonmonthly.com/features/2004/0411.carter.html#byline (accessed 18 Feb. 2005).

Crocker, Chester A. "The Lessons of Somalia: Not Everything Went Wrong." *Foreign Affairs* 74, no. 3 (May/June 1995): 2–8.

Cronin, Maj William R., USMC. "C3I during the Air War in South Kuwait." *Marine Corps Gazette* 76, no. 3 (Mar. 1992): 34.

Davis, Anthony. "How the Afghan War Was Won." *Jane's Intelligence Review* 14, no. 2 (Feb. 2002): 6–7.

Department of Defense. "Executive Summary of the Battle of Takur Ghar." *Defenselink News*, 24 May 2002. http://www.defenselink.mil/news/May2002/d20020524takurghar.pdf (accessed 6 Jan. 2005).

Deptula, Maj Gen David A., USAF. "Air Force Transformation: Past, Present and Future." *Aerospace Power Journal* 15, no. 3 (Fall 2001): 85–91. http://www.airpower.au.af.mil/aichronicles/apj/apj01/fal01/phifal01.html (accessed 10 Oct. 2002).

Deptula, Maj Gen David A., USAF, and Lt Col Sigfred J. Dahl, USAF. "Transforming Joint Air-Ground Operations for 21st Century Battlespace." *Field Artillery*, no. 4 (July–Aug. 2003): 21–25.

Erwin, Sandra I. "Air Wars Demand More Inter-Service Coordination." *National Defense* 88, no. 598 (Sept. 2003): 22.

———. "Experimental Battle-Planning Software Rushed to Iraq." *National Defense* 88, no. 599 (Oct. 2003): 22. Accessed via the DOD's *Current News Early Bird,* http://www.ebird.afis .osd.mil.

Fabey, Michael. "Technology Amplifies War Games at Langley." *Newport News Daily Press*, 12 Dec. 2003. Accessed via the DOD's *Current News Early Bird,* http://ebird.afis.osd.mil.

Fairley, Peter. "The Unruly Power Grid." *IEEE Spectrum* 41, no. 8 (Aug. 2004): 22–27.

Federation of American Scientists. "Secret Internet Protocol Router Network." http://www.fas.org/irp/program/disseminate/ siprnet.htm (accessed 20 Sept. 2004).

Gellman, Barton, and Dana Priest. "CIA Had Fix on Hussein; Intelligence Revealed 'Target of Opportunity.'" *Washington Post,* 20 Mar. 2003.

Gordon, Michael R. "A War out of the Night Sky: 10 Hours with a Battle Team." *New York Times*, 3 June 1999, A1.

Grant, Rebecca. "Eyes Wide Open." *Air Force Magazine* 86, no. 11 (Nov. 2003): 38–42.

———. "Reach-Forward." *Air Force Magazine* 85, no. 10 (Oct. 2002): 43–47.

———. "The War Nobody Expected." *Air Force Magazine* 85, no. 4 (Apr. 2002): 34–40.

Grossman, Elaine. "Was Operation Anaconda Ill-Fated from the Start? Army Analyst Blames Afghan Battle Failings on Bad Command Set-Up." *Inside the Pentagon,* 29 July 2004, 1.

Haag, SSgt Jason L., USAF. "OIF Veterans Discuss Lessons." *Air Force Print News*, Air Warfare Center Public Affairs, 31 July 2003. http://www.af.mil/news/story.asp?storyID=123005 347 (accessed 1 Oct. 2004).

Hersh, Seymour M. "King's Ransom." *New Yorker* 77, no. 32 (22 Oct. 2001): 35–39.

Holley, Maj Gen Irving B., Jr., USAFR. "Command, Control, and Technology." *Defense Analysis* 4, no. 3 (Sept. 1988): 267–86.

Hollis, Patrecia Slayden. "Trained, Adaptable, Flexible Forces = Victory in Iraq" (Interview of Lt Gen W. Scott Wallace, CG of V Corps in Iraq during OIF [Operation Iraqi Freedom]). *Field Artillery*, no. 5 (Sep/Oct 2003): 5–9. http://www

.highbeam.com/library/doc3.asp?DOCID=1G1:11073225 1&num=6&ctrlInfo=Round6%3AProd%3ASR%3AResult&ao=24 Aug 04.

Jacobs, W. A. "The Battle for France, 1944." In Cooling, *Case Studies in the Development of Close Air Support*, 237–93.

Jansen, LtCol John M., USMC; LCDR Nicholas Dienna, USN; Maj Wm Todd Bufkin II, USMC; MAJ David I. Oclander, USA; MAJ Thomas Di Tomasso, USA; and Maj James B. Sisler, USAF. "JCAS in Afghanistan: Fixing the Tower of Babel." *Field Artillery*, no. 2 (Mar/Apr 2003): 24–29.

Kelly, Lt Col Thomas L., USA, and Lt Col John P. Andreasen, USA, retired. "Joint Fires: A BCD Perspective in Operation Iraqi Freedom." *Field Artillery*, no. 6 (Nov/Dec 2003): 20–25.

Kohn, Col Richard H., USAF, retired. "The Erosion of Civilian Control of the Military in the United States Today." *Naval War College Review* 55, no. 3 (Summer 2002): 9–59.

Leibstone, Marvin. "War against Terrorism and the Art of Restraint." *Military Technology* 25, no. 11 (Nov. 2001): 18–21.

Moorman, Lt Gen Thomas S., Jr., USAF. "Space: A New Strategic Frontier." *Airpower Journal* 6, no. 1 (Spring 1992): 14–23.

Neuenswander, Col Patrick, USAF. "JCAS in Operation Anaconda: It's Not All Bad News." Letters to the editor. *Field Artillery*, no. 3 (May/Jun 2003): 2. http://www.findarticles.com/p/articles/mi_m0IAU/is_3_8/ai_10319 4043.

Newman, Richard J. "The Joystick War." *U.S. News & World Report*, 19 May 2003. Accessed via the DOD's *Current News Early Bird*, http://ebird.afis.osd.mil.

O'Hanlon, Michael E. "A Flawed Masterpiece." *Foreign Affairs* 81, no. 3 (May/June 2002): 47–63.

Owen, Col Robert C., USAF. "The Balkans Air Campaign Study: Part 1." *Airpower Journal* 11, no. 2 (Summer 1997): 4–24.

———. "The Balkans Air Campaign Study: Part 2." *Airpower Journal* 11, no. 3: (Fall 1997): 6–26.

Palmeri, Christopher. "A Predator That Preys on Hawks." *Business Week Online*, 17 Feb. 2003. www.businessweek.com/magazine/content/03_07/b3820093_mz017.htm (accessed 9 June 2004).

Porter, Michael, and Victor Millar. "How Information Gives You Competitive Advantage: The Information Revolution Is

Transforming the Nature of Competition." *Harvard Business Review* 63, no. 4 (July–Aug. 1985): 149–60.

Priest, Dana, and Peter Finn. "NATO Gives Air Support to Kosovo Guerrillas; But Yugoslavs Repel Attack From Albania." *Washington Post*, 2 June 1999.

Rees, Elizabeth. "Naming CFACC the Space Coordination Authority in Iraq Proved Vital." *Inside the Air Force*, 5 Sept. 2003, 1.

Ricks, Thomas E. "A War That's Commanded at a Distance; Some Criticize Keeping Headquarters at Tampa." *Washington Post*, 27 Dec. 2001.

Ripley, Tim. "Close Air Support: Closing the Gap." *Jane's Defence Weekly*, 2 July 2003. Accessed via the DOD's *Current News Early Bird*, http://ebird.afis.osd.mil.

Roberts, Adam. "NATO's 'Humanitarian War' over Kosovo." *Survival* 41, no. 3 (Autumn 1999): 102–23.

Sanger, David E., and Eric Schmitt, "U.S. Blasts Compound in Effort to Kill Hussein." *New York Times*, 8 Apr. 2003, A1.

Sbrega, John S. "Southeast Asia." In Cooling, *Case Studies in the Development of Close Air Support*, 411–90.

Schmitt, Eric. "6,300 Miles from Iraq, Experts Guide Raids." *New York Times*, 24 June 2003, A13. Accessed via the DOD's *Current News Early Bird*, http://ebird.afis.osd.mil.

Scott, William B., and Craig Covault. "High Ground over Iraq." *Aviation Week & Space Technology* 158, no. 23 (9 June 2003): 44.

Shaw, John E. "The Influence of Space Power upon History 1944–1998." *Air Power History* 46, no. 4 (Winter 1999): 20–29.

Stigler, Andrew L. "A Clear Victory for Air Power: NATO's Empty Threat to Invade Kosovo." *International Security* 27, no. 3 (Winter 2002/03): 124–57.

Sweetman, Bill. "B-2 is Maturing into a Fine Spirit." *Janes International Defense Review* 33 (May 2000): 53.

Syrett, David. "Northwest Africa, 1942–1943." In Cooling, *Case Studies in the Achievement of Air Superiority*, 223–63.

———. "The Tunisian Campaign, 1942–43." In Cooling, *Case Studies in the Development of Close Air Support*, 153–92.

Talbot, David. "The Ascent of the Robotic Attack Jet." *Technology Review.com*, 2 Feb. 2005. *U.S. Air Force AIM Points*, http://aimpoints.hq.af.mil/display.cfm?id=667.

Taylor, Joe Gray. "American Experience in the Southwest Pacific." In Cooling, *Case Studies in the Development of Close Air Support*, 297.

Thomas, Evan, and Daniel Klaidman. "The War Room." *Newsweek* 141, no. 13 (31 Mar. 2003): 23. Accessed via the DOD's *Current News Early Bird*, http://ebird.afis.osd.mil.

Thomas, Evan, and Martha Brant. "The Education of Tommy Franks." *Newsweek* 141, no. 20 (19 May 2003): 24–29. Accessed via the DOD's *Current News Early Bird*, http://ebird.afis.osd.mil (10 Mar. 2004).

Thompson, Wayne W. "After Al Firdos: The Last Two Weeks of Strategic Bombing in Desert Storm." *Air Power History* 43, no. 2 (Summer 1996): 48–65.

Tirpak, John A. "The Air Boss's Plan; Moseley's Handshake Deal; The Bomb Catalog; BDA Fades Away. . . ." Washington Watch, *Air Force Magazine* 87, no. 8 (Aug. 2004): 8–10.

_______. "Short's View of the Air Campaign," Washington Watch, *Air Force Magazine* 82, no. 9 (Sept. 1999): 43–45. http://www.afa.org/magazine/watch/0999watch.html (accessed 10 Dec. 2003).

"U.S. Troops Topple Saddam Statue." CNN.com, 9 Apr. 2003. http://www.cnn.com/2003/WORLD/meast/04/09/sprj.irq.int.war.main1400 (accessed 18 Feb. 2005).

Vego, Milan. "Network-Centric Is Not Decisive." *Proceedings* 129, no. 1 (Jan. 2003): 52–57. http://www.usni.org/Proceedings/Articles03/PROvego01.htm.

Venkatraman, N. "IT-Enabled Business Transformation: From Automation to Business Scope Redefinition." *Sloan Management Review* 35, no. 2 (Winter 1994): 73–87.

Weick, Karl E. "Educational Organizations as Loosely Coupled Systems." *Administrative Science Quarterly* 21, no. 1 (Mar. 1976): 1–19.

Welsh, Lt Col Mark A., USAF. "Day of the Killer Scouts." *Air Force Magazine* 76, no. 4 (Apr. 1993): 66–70.

Unpublished Documents

Crawley, Lt Col Charles G., USA. "How Did the Evolution of Communications Affect Command and Control of Airpower: 1900–1945?" Master's thesis, Air University, Maxwell AFB, AL, 1996.

Dodder, Rebecca S., Joseph M. Sussman, and Joshua B. McConnell. "The Concept of the 'CLIOS Process': Integrating the Study of Physical and Policy Systems Using Mexico City as an Example." Paper presented to the Massachusetts Institute of Technology Engineering Systems Symposium, Cambridge, MA, 31 Mar. 2004.

Ehrhard, Lt Col Thomas P., USAF. "The Armed Services and Innovation: Function, Structure, Culture," adapted from "Unmanned Aerial Vehicles in the United States Armed Services: A Comparative Study of Weapon System Innovation." Dissertation, Johns Hopkins University School of Advanced International Studies, June 2000.

Gerber, Maj David K., USAF. "Adaptive Command and Control of Theater Airpower." Master's thesis, School of Advanced Air and Space Studies, Air University, Maxwell AFB, AL, 1997.

Harmer, Todd P. "Enhancing the Operational Art: The Influence of the Information Environment on the Command and Control of Airpower." Master's thesis, School of Advanced Air and Space Studies, Air University, Maxwell AFB, AL, 2000.

Koprucu, Maj Mustafa R., USAF. "The Limits of Decentralized Execution: The Effects of Technology on a Central Airpower Tenet." Master's thesis, School of Advanced Air Power Studies, Air University, Maxwell AFB, AL, 2001.

Leveson, Nancy G. "A New Approach to System Safety Engineering." Manuscript in preparation, 2004. Draft at http://sunnyday.mit.edubook2.pdf.

McDaniels, Maj Jeffrey R., USAF. "Viper FAC-A: Effectiveness of the F-16 Block-40 (U)." Master's thesis, Air Command and Staff College, Air University, Maxwell AFB, AL, Apr. 2000.

Monroe, Maj Robert E., USAF. "A New Age of Armed Reconnaissance: A New Role for Predator (U)." Master's thesis, Air Command and Staff College, Air University, Maxwell AFB, AL, Apr. 2000.

Northrup, Lt Col Parker W., III, USAF. "The Air Operations Center as a Weapons System: Thinking at the Operational Level of War." Master's thesis, School of Advanced Air and Space Studies, Air University, Maxwell AFB, AL, June 2003.

O'Mara, Maj Raymond, USAF. "Stealth, Precision, and the Making of American Foreign Policy." Master's thesis, Air Command and Staff College, Air University, June 2002.

Official Documents

Air Force Doctrine Document 1. *Air Force Basic Doctrine*, Sept. 1997.

Air Force Doctrine Document 2. *Organization and Employment of Aerospace Power*, 17 Feb. 2000.

Air Force Instruction 13-1AOC, *Operational Procedures–Aerospace Operations Center*, 1 July 2002.

Air Force Manual 1-1. *Basic Aerospace Doctrine of the United States Air Force*. Vol. 2, Mar. 1992.

———. *Functions and Basic Doctrine of the United States Air Force*, 14 Feb. 1979.

———. *United States Air Force Basic Doctrine*, 15 Jan. 1975.

———. *United States Air Force Basic Doctrine*, 28 Sept. 1971.

Air Force Operational Tactics, Techniques, and Procedures 2-3.2. *Air and Space Operations Center*, 25 Oct. 2002.

Air Force Policy Directive 13-1. *Theater Air Control System*, 11 May 1995.

"Analysis of the Effectiveness/Efficiency of the Combined Air Operations Center." Vol. 2, sec. 2, Focus Area 4: Command and Control, *Air War over Serbia: Aerospace Power in Operation Allied Force*. 12 July 2000. (Secret/NOFORN) Information extracted is unclassified.

Cohen, Eliot A., and Thomas A. Keaney. *Gulf War Air Power Survey*. Vol. 1, pt. 1, *Planning*, by Alexander S. Cochran. Washington, DC: Government Printing Office, 1993.

———. *Gulf War Air Power Survey*. Vol. 1, pt. 2, *Command and Control*, by Thomas C. Hone, Mark D. Mandeles, and Sanford S. Terry. Washington, DC: Government Printing Office, 1993.

———. *Gulf War Air Power Survey*. Vol. 2, pt. 1, *Operations*, by Barry D. Watts and Williamson Murray. Washington, DC: Government Printing Office, 1993.

Department of Defense. *Kosovo/Operation Allied Force After-Action Report*." Report to Congress. 31 Jan. 2000.

Department of the Air Force, Chief of Staff. "Global Vigilance, Reach, and Power: America's Air Force Vision 2020." Washington, DC: HQ USAF, 2000.

"EFX 98 Assessment Report." Executive Summary, executive 1–2. https://jefxlink.langley.af.mil/index.asp (accessed 11 Dec. 2003). The report is unclassified, but in order to view it you must get permission from the Air Force Experimentation Office.

General Accounting Office. *Kosovo Air Operations: Need to Maintain Alliance Cohesion Resulted in Doctrinal Departures*. Report to Congressional Requesters. Report number GAO-01-784. Washington, DC: General Accounting Office, July 2001.

Headquarters Air Combat Command. "Combat Air Forces Concept of Operations for Time-Critical Targeting." Draft, Oct. 2000 update.

Headquarters US Air Force. *The Air War over Serbia: Aerospace Power in Operation Allied Force*. Initial Report. Washington, DC: Department of the Air Force, 2000.

HQ USAF/XPXC, Future Concepts and Transformation Division. *The U.S. Air Force Transformation Flight Plan 2004*. Nov. 2003. http://www.af.mil/library/posture/AF_TRANS_FLIGHT_PLAN-2004.pdf (accessed 16 Feb. 2005).

Joint Publication (JP) 0-2. *Unified Action Armed Forces (UNAAF)*, 10 July 2001.

Joint Vision 2010. Washington, DC: Joint Chiefs of Staff, 1996.

JP 1-02. *Department of Defense Dictionary of Military and Associated Terms*, 12 Apr. 2001 (as amended through 22 Mar. 2007).

JP 3-0. *Doctrine for Joint Operations*, 10 Sept. 2001.

JP 3-09.3. *Joint Tactics, Techniques, and Procedures for Close Air Support (CAS)*, 3 Sept. 2003.

JP 3-30. *Command and Control for Joint Air Operations*, 5 June 2003.

JP 3-52. *Doctrine for Joint Airspace Control in the Combat Zone*, 22 July 1995.

JP 3-56.1. *Command and Control for Joint Air Operations*, 14 Nov. 1994.

JP 5-0. *Doctrine for Planning Joint Operations*, 13 Apr. 1995.

JP 5-00.2. *Joint Task Force Planning Guidance and Procedures*, 13 Jan. 1999.

Keaney, Thomas A., and Eliot A. Cohen. *Gulf War Air Power Survey Summary Report.* Washington, DC: HQ USAF, 1993.

Magee, C. L., and O. L. de Weck. "An Attempt at Complex System Classification." In *Proceedings of the ESD Internal Symposium.* Working Paper Series. ESD-WP-2003-01.02-ESD Internal Symposium. Cambridge, MA: Institute of Technology Engineering Systems Division, 2002. http://esd.mit.edu/WPS/ESD%20Internal%20Symposium%20Docs/ESD-WP-2003-01.02-ESD%20Internal%20Symposium.pdf.

Moseley, Lt Gen T. Michael. *Operation Iraqi Freedom—By the Numbers.* Shaw AFB, SC: CENTAF, Assessment and Analysis Division, 30 Apr. 2003.

"Seamless Integration of Intelligence, Surveillance, and Reconnaissance is Critical to Rapid Target Destruction (U)." Vol. 2, sec. 2, Focus Area 4: Command and Control, *Air War over Serbia: Aerospace Power in Operation Allied Force.* 12 July 2000. (Secret/NOFORN) Information extracted is unclassified.

United States Air Force. *Global Engagement: A Vision for the 21st Century Air Force.* Washington, DC: Headquarters USAF, 1996. http://www.au.af.mil/au/awc/awcgate/global/nuvis.htm (accessed 9 Dec. 2003).

United States Strategic Bombing Surveys: European War, Pacific War. 1987. Reprint, Maxwell AFB, AL: Air University Press, Mar. 2001.

US Joint Forces Command. *Commander's Handbook for Joint Time-Sensitive Targeting.* Norfolk, VA: Joint Warfighting Center, 22 Mar. 2002.

White House. A *National Strategy of Engagement and Enlargement.* Washington, DC: US Government Printing Office, Feb. 1996. http://www.fas.org/spp/military/docops/national/1996stra.htm#II (accessed 6 Dec. 2003).

Sources from Official Archives

"Air Component Coordination Element (ACCE) Concept of Operations (CONOPS)." USCENTAF, 13 Nov. 2002. File "030329 _CFSOCC-ACCE CONOPS_Mar 03 final.doc" in Task Force Enduring Look (TFEL) database, Air Force Historical Research Agency (AFHRA), Maxwell AFB, AL.

Ball, Jeffrey R. "JDAM Weapon Effectiveness and Accuracy over Serbia (U)." Briefing. *Air War over Serbia*, Force Applications Operations Focus Area, Interim Report, 14 Mar. 2000. (Secret) Information extracted is unclassified.

Barton, Technical Sergeant, USAF, USAF/HO (observer in the tactical air control center [TACC] during Desert Storm). Notes. In TACC Noncommissioned Officer Log. Call no. TF6-46-482, IRIS no. 872960, *Gulf War Air Power Survey* (*GWAPS*) Task Force VI Collection, AFHRA, Maxwell AFB, AL.

Bird, Richard F. "CAOC Mission Assessment Trip Report." Vol. 2, sec. 2, Focus Area 4: Command and Control, *Air War over Serbia: Aerospace Power in Operation Allied Force*. 12 July 2000.

Caldera, Lt Cdr Andrew L., USN (assistant intelligence officer for Battle Group Staff, combined air operations center (CAOC), Vicenza, Italy; and an operations officer, Flex-Targeting Cell, OAF). Oral history interview summary sheet. Air War over Serbia (AWOS) stand-alone database, AFHRA, Maxwell AFB, AL. (Secret) Information extracted is unclassified.

CENTAF reply to "CFC ORDER 002, PHASE II CONTINUED OPERATIONS. File "CENTAF Edits." TFEL database, AFHRA, Maxwell AFB, AL. (Secret/Rel GCTF [Global Counterterrorism Task Force]) Information extracted is unclassified.

CENTAF TACC/CC/DO, "Current Ops Log." Vol. 1 of 2, 17 Jan.–14 Feb. 1991. Call no. NA-215, IRIS no. 873486. Entry dated 27 Jan. 1991 2300Z. *GWAPS* Collection, AFHRA, Maxwell AFB, AL. (Secret) Information extracted is unclassified.

———. Vol. 2 of 2, 14 Feb.–11 Apr. 1991. Entry dated 20 Feb. 1991 1030Z. Call no. NA-215, IRIS no. 873487. *GWAPS* Collection, AFHRA, Maxwell AFB, AL. (Secret) Information extracted is unclassified.

"Command and Control/Intelligence, Surveillance and Reconnaissance (C2/ISR)." Draft *Tactical Analysis Bulletin* 99-1. Nellis AFB, NV, Aug. 1999. (Secret) Information extracted is unclassified.

"Concept of Operations for Command and Control of TACAIR in Support of Land Forces." 22 Feb. 1991, attach. 2. Call no. K239.0472-51, Desert Story Collection, AFHRA, Maxwell AFB, AL. (Secret) Information extracted is unclassified.

"CTBM CONOPS and Execution Development, July 2002–29 Jan. 2003." Briefing. Received from Lt Col Kevin Glenn, USAF (30th Intelligence Squadron/CC; chief, Combat Operations ISR Cell, OIF). (Secret/ORCON//Rel USA GBR AUS) Information extracted is unclassified.

Corder, Maj Gen John, USAF (TACC director during Desert Storm). Transcript of interview by Kurt Guthe et al., 18 May 1992. Call no. TF5-7-124 v. 30, *GWAPS* Collection, AFHRA, Maxwell AFB, AL.

Defore, Gregory. "Killbox Interdiction-Close Air Support Concept of Operations Annex." File "030209 Killbox Interdiction-Close Air Support CONOPS.doc: KI/CAS Annex," 9 Feb. 2003. TFEL database, AFHRA, Maxwell AFB, AL.

Deptula, Lt Col David, USAF (SAF/OSX Chief of Iraq/MAP Cell in Campaign Plans during Desert Storm). Memorandum for record. Subject: "Feedback from SECDEF/CJCS Meeting with CINC and Component Commanders," 9 Feb. 1991. CHP-5A in Desert Story Collection, AFHRA, Maxwell AFB, AL.

———. Transcript of briefing to Richard Davis, 20 Nov. 1991. Call no. TF-5-1-53, Desert Story Collection, AFHRA, Maxwell AFB, AL.

———. Transcript of interview by Lt Col Richard Reynolds, USAF, and Lt Col Edward Mann, USAF, 10 Dec. 1991, 53–58. Call no. K239.0477-83, Desert Story Collection, AFHRA, Maxwell AFB, AL.

———. Transcript of interview by Lt Col Suzanne B. Gehri, USAF; Lt Col Edward C. Mann, USAF; and Lt Col Richard T. Reynolds, USAF, 22–23 May 1991. Call no. K239.0472-82, Desert Story Collection, AFHRA, Maxwell AFB, AL.

8th Air Support Operations Group. *Operations Desert Shield/ Storm.* After Action Report. Call no. TF4-12-230, *GWAPS* Task Force IV Collection, AFHRA, Maxwell AFB, AL.

Ellis, Adm James O., USN (Commander, Joint Task Force Noble Anvil during Allied Force). "A View from the Top." Briefing, 15 Oct. 1999. AWOS stand-alone database, AFHRA, Maxwell AFB, AL.

"Flex Targeting Success Stories." Briefing, no name or date, file (S) FlexTargetSuccess.pdf. AWOS stand-alone database, AFHRA, Maxwell AFB, AL. (Secret/Rel NATO) Information extracted is unclassified.

Harvey, Lt Col Ben, USAF. Memos for record, 10 Aug. and 11 Aug. 1990. CHP-7, Desert Story Collection, AFHRA, Maxwell AFB, AL.

Headquarters United States Air Force. "Task Force Enduring Look, Operation Anaconda: An Air Power Perspective." Washington, DC: HQ USAF, 15 Jan. 2004. (Secret) Information extracted is unclassified.

History. 3rd Squadron, 7th Calvary Regiment, 3rd Infantry Division. http://www.stewart.army.mil/Display.asp?Page=6D468FDF-4A90-4B87-9FE5-EA681A1C9369 (accessed 8 Nov. 2004).

History. Aerospace Command and Control Agency. Vol. 1, 1 Oct. 1997–30 Sept. 1998. Call no. K401.07-2 v. 1, Maxwell AFB, AL: AFHRA.

Horner, Gen Charles, USAF, retired (joint force air component commander [JFACC] in Desert Storm). Transcript of interview by Perry Jamieson, Richard Davis, and Barry Barlow, 4 Mar. 1992, HQ 9th Air Force, Shaw AFB, SC. Call no. K239.0472-94, Desert Story Collection, AFHRA, Maxwell AFB, AL. (Secret) Information extracted is unclassified.

Hosterman, TSgt Ted, USAF (USAF/HO, observer in the TACC during Desert Storm). Notes. Call no. TF6-46-482, *GWAPS* Task Force VI Collection, AFHRA, Maxwell AFB, AL.

"KEZ Mission." Draft Tactical Analysis Bulletin 99-1. "Operation Allied Force Lessons Learned." Nellis AFB, NV, Aug. 1999. (Secret) Information extracted is unclassified. AWOS stand-alone database, AFHRA, Maxwell AFB, AL. (Secret) Information extracted is unclassified.

Message. 011241Z NOV 01. USCINCCENT. To COMUSARCENT et al. TFEL database, AFHRA, Maxwell AFB, AL.

———. 011330Z FEB 91. Gen Norman Schwarzkopf, USA. Personal letter for Lt Gen Boomer, info Lt Gen Horner. Subject: "Marine Aviation (U)." Current Operations Log entry. Call no. TF4-11-199, IRIS no. 874664, *GWAPS* Collection, AFHRA, Maxwell AFB, AL.

Moseley, Lt Gen T. Michael, USAF (combined force air component commander [CFACC] in Operation Enduring Freedom [OEF] and OIF). Transcript of interview with Rebecca Grant, 1 May 2003, Prince Sultan Air Base, Saudi Arabia. TFEL database,

AFHRA, Maxwell AFB, AL. (Secret) Information extracted is unclassified.

"Offensive Campaign: Desert Storm." Briefing. HQ Central Command, 24 Aug. 1990. Call no. NA-208, *GWAPS* Collection, AFHRA, Maxwell AFB, AL.

"OIF Targeting CONOPS Update." Briefing. 11 Apr. 2003. File "030411_OIF_Targeting_CONOPS.pdf." TFEL database, AFHRA, Maxwell AFB, AL. (Secret/Rel MCFI) Information extracted is unclassified.

"Operation Iraqi Freedom Observations: Air Warfare." Briefing. File "TFEL Lessons Learned Air Warfare_jts.ppt," TFEL database, AFHRA, Maxwell AFB, AL. Information extracted is unclassified.

Rice, Donald B. (secretary of the Air Force). Transcript of interview by Lt Col Richard Reynolds, USAF; Lt Col Suzanne Gehri, USAF; and Lt Col Edward Mann, USAF, 11 Dec. 1991. Call no. TF5-1-52, Desert Story Collection, AFHRA, Maxwell AFB, AL.

Schneider, James, Myron Hura, and Gary McLeod. "Command and Control and Battle Management: Experiences from the Air War over Serbia (U)." Progress report briefing, RAND AB-404-1-AF, 9 June 2000. (Secret) Information extracted is unclassified.

Soboul, Capt Randall, USA. Memorandum. Subject: "Desert Storm After Action Review." Call no. NA-287, *GWAPS* Collection, AFHRA, Maxwell AFB, AL.

"Task Force Enduring Look Lessons Learned." Briefing. File LLConf.pdf," TFEL database, AFHRA, Maxwell AFB, AL. (Secret/NOFORN) Information extracted is unclassified.

United States Air Force. "Air War over Serbia Fact Sheet." 31 Jan. 2000. AWOS stand-alone database, AFHRA, Maxwell AFB, AL.

0602 TAIRCW Dep Cmdr for Ops (602d Tactical Air Control Wing Deputy Commander for Operations). *Desert Storm Conference, Lessons Learned.* "4 ASOG (4th Air Operations Support Group) Desert Shield/Storm Lessons Learned." 26 Apr. 1991–11 Feb. 1992, Call no. TF4-12-228, IRIS no. 872637. *GWAPS* Task Force IV Collection, AFHRA, Maxwell AFB, AL.

———. *Desert Storm Conference, Lessons Learned.* "I. Operational Issues." 26 Apr. 1991–11 Feb. 1992. Call no. TF4-

12-228, IRIS no. 872637, *GWAPS* Task Force IV Collection, AFHRA, Maxwell AFB, AL.

Other Briefings, E-mails, Speeches, and Interviews

(Job descriptions given are those held by the individuals at the time of this writing. For interviews by the author for which there is no formal documentation, the full citations are given in the endnotes and are not included in the bibliography. For interviews by the author with transcripts or recordings, the shortened note form is given in the endnotes and the full citation is included in the bibliography.)

Backes, Lt Col Gary, USAF, retired (Time-critical Targeting [TCT] Cell trainer during OIF). Interview by the author, Hurlburt Field, FL, 27 May 2004. Recording in author's personal collection.

———. "Joint Time Sensitive Target Manager." Briefing, updated 27 June 2003. Received by e-mail from briefer. Author's personal collection.

Benoit, Capt Marcel, USAF; Maj Jason Miller, USAF; and Maj Steve Gregg, USAF (19th Special Operations Squadron. During OEF-Afghanistan, Benoit was an electronic warfare officer (EWO) on AC-130H gunships; Miller was a pilot on AC-130H gunships; and Gregg was a pilot on MH-53J Pave Low helicopters. During OIF, Miller and Gregg were also planners). Interview by the author, Hurlburt Field, FL, 28 May 2004. Recording in author's personal collection.

Boiney, Lindsley, JoAnn Brooks, Jill Drury, Priscilla Glasow, Laura Kurland, and Lewis Loren. "Time-Sensitive Team Decision-Making." Internal briefing to MITRE Corporation personnel, Bedford, MA, 25 Aug. 2004. Author's personal collection.

Bradshaw, Lt Col Jim, USAF, retired. Interview by the author, Ninth Air Force, Shaw AFB, SC, 25 Mar. 2004. Recording in author's personal collection.

Bush, George W. "Address to a Joint Session of Congress and the American People." Speech. United States Capitol, Washington, DC, 20 Sept. 2001. http://www.whitehouse.gov/news/releases/2001/09/20010920-8.html (accessed 21 June 2004).

Coe, Maj Richard, USAF (AF/XORC; F-15E weapon systems officer during OEF and OIF). Telephone interview by the author, 24 Jan. 2005. Recording in author's personal collection.

Crowder, Col Gary, USAF (505 CCW/CV; deputy C-3, OAF; and senior offensive duty officer, OEF, 7 Oct.–28 Nov. 2001). To the author. E-mail, 22 Sept. 2004. Author's personal collection.

"Daily Refugee Flow" and "Total Refugee Flow." Briefings, 13 May 1999, NATO. http://www.nato.int/pictures/1999/990513/b990513d.gif and e.gif.

Deptula, Maj Gen David, USAF (director of Air and Space Operations, HQ PACAF; chief of Iraq Cell, TACC, Desert Storm; CAOC director, OEF). Interview by the author, Hickam AFB, HI, 22 Apr. 2004. Recording in author's personal collection.

———. "Operation Enduring Freedom—Highlights, Challenges, and Potential Implications: Some Observations from the First 60 Days." Deptula briefing received by e-mail from Maj Stephen Murray, Ninth Air Force, 24 Mar. 2004. (Secret) Information extracted is unclassified. Author's personal collection.

———. "Reflections on Desert Storm: The Air Campaign Planning Process." Briefing, version 8, 20 Oct. 1998. Provided to author by General Deptula. Author's personal collection.

———. To the author. E-mail, 3 Apr. 2005. Author's personal collection.

Feinstein, Lt Col Jeffrey, USAF, retired (ace in Vietnam and TACC plans officer during Desert Storm). Interview by the author, Shaw AFB, SC, 25 Mar. 2004. Recording in author's personal collection.

Fogleman, Gen Ronald, USAF, retired. "Air Power and National Security." Transcript of speech to the Defense Forum Foundation, Washington, DC, 24 Jan. 1997. http://www.af.mil/news/speech/readroom2.shtml (accessed 5 Dec. 2003).

Glenn, Lt Col Kevin, USAF. To the author. E-mails, 19 and 20 May 2004. Author's personal collection.

Goldberg, Capt Jason, USAF (AC-130U copilot, OIF); 2d Lt Joseph Valentino, USAF (AC-130U EWO, OIF); and MSgt Don Frazee, USAF (AC-130U sensor operator, OIF). Interview by the author, Hurlburt Field, FL, 1 June 2004. Recording in author's personal collection.

Hathaway, Lt Col David, USAF (20th Fighter Wing chief of safety; chief of air campaign strategy for USCENTAF, June 2001–Sept. 2003; and deputy chief of strategy, OIF). To the author. E-mails, 29 Sept. 2004, 21 Oct. 2004, 21 Mar. 2005, and 12 Apr. 2005. Author's personal collection.

Haun, Lt Col Phil, USAF (355th Fighter Squadron [FS]/CC; A-10 pilot during OAF and OIF; and A-10 foward air controller [airborne] in Kosovo). To the author. E-mails, 11 Mar. 2004 and 11 Apr. 2005. Author's personal collection.

Heidal, MSgt Charles, USAF (AFC2ISRC). "USAF TACP Modernization Program Capabilities." Briefing. Received from MITRE Corp. personnel. Author's personal collection.

Hodgdon, Col Jeffrey, USAF (753d Electronic Systems Group deputy commander; TCT Cell chief, OEF and OIF). To the author. E-mails, 28 Dec. 2004 and 4 Feb. 2005. Author's personal collection.

Horner, Gen Charles A., USAF, retired (wing planner and pilot in Vietnam; JFACC in Desert Storm). Interview by the author, Shalimar, FL, 29 May 2004. Recording in author's personal collection.

Jones, Lt Col William, USAF. "505th Command and Control Wing Mission Brief." Briefing to author, Hurlburt Field, FL, 1 June 2004. Author's personal collection.

Keenan, Lt Col William "Bill," USAF, retired (chief, Combat Operations Division, Desert Storm). Interview by the author, Shaw AFB, SC, 26 Mar. 2004. Recording in author's personal collection.

Knaub, Lt Col Brett, USAF (20 EBS/DO). To the author. E-mail, 5 Nov. 2004. Author's personal collection.

———. To the author. E-mail, 22 Sept. 2004. Author's personal collection.

Lanning, TSgt Bryan, USAF (joint tactical air controller instructor, Air-Ground Operations School; battalion enlisted terminal attack controller in Desert Storm and OIF). Interview by the author, Nellis AFB, NV, 31 July 2004. Recording in author's personal collection.

Lofton, SSgt Frank, USAF (12th Combat Training Squadron; enlisted terminal attack controller, 19th Special Forces

Group [SFG], 2nd Battalion [Bn], Operational Detachment Alpha [ODA]; and 923d and 20th SFG, 1st Bn, ODA 2025, 26 Aug. 2002–29 Jan. 2003. He also worked in the V Corps air support operations center during OIF.). Interview by the author, Nellis AFB, NV, 28 and 29 July 2004. Recording in author's personal collection.

———. To the author. E-mails, 5 and 6 May 2004. Author's personal collection.

Mahajan, Capt Jay, USAF (F-16 pilot, 77th FS, OIF). Interview by the author, 25 Mar. 2004, Shaw AFB, SC. Recording in author's personal collection.

Manning, Lt Col Scott, USAF (55th FS/DO; F-16 pilot, 77th FS, OIF). Interview by the author, 26 Mar. 2004, Shaw AFB, SC. Recording in author's personal collection.

Marr, Maj Ian, USAF (19 SOS/DOI; fire control officer on AC-130H gunships, OEF). Interview by the author, Hurlburt Field, FL, 2 June 2004. Recording in author's personal collection.

Message. R 230952Z AUG 00. HQ USAF, Washington, DC/CVA. To MAJCOMs. Subject: "Air Force Senior Mentor Program and Operational Command." Author's personal collection.

Moseley, Gen T. Michael, USAF (CFACC, OEF and OIF). Interview by Air University students, 4 Feb. 2004, Maxwell AFB, AL. Approved notes with executive officer's comments. Notes in author's personal collection.

Pritchard, Lt Col James, USAF, retired (tanker coordination officer in TACC during Desert Storm). To the author. E-mail, 21 Nov. 2003. Author's personal collection.

Richardson, Maj Don, USAF (16th Special Operations Squadron/DOXT; navigator on AC-130H gunships, OEF). To the author. E-mail, 1 Nov. 2004. Author's personal collection.

Sams, Lt Col Walter, USAFR (79th FS, assistant director of Operations; brigade air liaison officer in Desert Storm; and F-16 pilot and suppression of enemy air defenses duty officer in the CAOC, OIF). Interview by the author, Shaw AFB, SC, 26 Mar. 2004. Recording in author's personal collection.

Smyth, Col Joseph, USAF. "MC2A: Multi-sensor Command and Control Aircraft." Briefing, 5 Dec. 2002. http://esc.hanscom.af.mil/esc-mc2a/1 (accessed 16 Feb. 2005).

Stolley, Lt Michael, USAF (77th FS; F-16 wingman, OIF). Interview by the author, Shaw AFB, SC, 25 Mar. 2004. Recording in author's personal collection.

Tritschler, Lt Col Phil, USAF, retired (deputy chief of combat operations, Desert Storm). Telephone interview by the author, 24 Sept. 2004. Recording in author's personal collection.

Unattributed interview by the author with technical sergeant from the 720th Special Tactics Squadron during OEF-Afghanistan, Oct.–Dec. 2001. Recording in author's personal collection.

Wallace, Lt Gen William S., USA (commander, Combined Arms Center). "Joint Fires in OIF: What Worked for the Vth (US) Corps." Briefing, 12 Mar. 2004. Received in digital format from USAF Air to Ground Operations School. Author's personal collection.

Wilkinson, Lt Col Dave, USMC (P-3 pilot). To the author. E-mail, 29 Oct. 2005. Author's personal collection.

Index

Command in Air War

Centralized versus Decentralized
Control of Combat Airpower

Air University Press Team

Chief Editor
Jeanne Shamburger

Copy Editor
Tammi Long

Cover Art and Book Design
Steven C. Garst

Composition and
Prepress Production
Mary P. Ferguson

Quality Review
Mary J. Moore

Print Preparation
Joan Hickey

Distribution
Diane Clark

www.ingramcontent.com/pod-product-compliance
Lightning Source LLC
LaVergne TN
LVHW080309110826
845155LV00023B/95

* 9 7 8 1 9 0 7 5 2 1 0 3 4 *